PUNISHMENT	Date of Punishment	REMARKS
	1845	
12 lashes with Cats	Aug't 26	
12 " " "	" "	
9 " " "	" "	
12 " " "	" "	
Disrated to Seaman	Sept 2	
9 lashes with Cats	" "	
6 " " "	" "	
6 " " "	" "	
8 " " "	" "	
4 " " "	" "	
6 " " "	" "	
6 " " "	" 3	
9 " " a colt	" "	Punished by Executive Officer
9 " " "	" 5	" " " "
6 " " Cats	" 9	
4 " " "	" "	
4 " " "	" "	
6 " " "	" "	
6 " " "	" 11	
6 " " "	" "	
6 " " "	" "	
6 " " "	" 15	
6 " " "	" "	
6 " " "	" 17	
6 " " "	" "	
12 " " Boys Cats	" "	Punished as usual in such cases
12 " " Cats	" 30	
12 " " "	" "	
6 " " Boys Cats	" 22	Punished as usual in such cases
12 " " " "	" 25	" " " " " "
9 " " Cats	" "	
4 " " "	" "	
6 " " "	" "	

Rocks&Shoals

Rocks & Shoals

ORDER AND DISCIPLINE
IN THE OLD NAVY 1800–1861

—————————————*James E. Valle*——

NAVAL INSTITUTE PRESS · ANNAPOLIS, MARYLAND

Copyright © 1980
United States Naval Institute
Annapolis, Maryland

Library of Congress Catalog No. 79-91914
ISBN: 0-87021-538-8

Printed in the United States of America

End papers: Excerpt from the records of the USS *Columbus*. Courtesy of Special
Collections, Nimitz Library, U.S. Naval Academy.

Uncharted the rocks that surround thee,
    Take heed that the channels thou learn,
Lest thy name serve to buoy for another,
    That shoal, the Courts-Martial Return.

Though armor, the belt that protects her,
    The ship bears the scar on her side;
It is well if the court acquit thee;
    It were best hadst thou never been tried.

"The Laws of the Navy"
Captain Ronald Hopwood, Royal Navy

Contents

Acknowledgments

In compiling a book of this complexity, an author becomes indebted to many people. It is safe to say that without the interest and assistance of fellow scholars, librarians, and typists, and the cheerful cooperation of spouses, few manuscripts would ever see the light of day. Over a period of four years, I have been accorded a full measure of kindness.

My earliest benefactor was Dr. James E. Merrill, Sea Grant Professor of Maritime History at the University of Delaware. It was Dr. Merrill who first alerted me to the potential of naval discipline as a subject for serious historical inquiry and put into my hands the incomparable source material that furnished the basis of *Rocks and Shoals*. Thanks are also due to John Munroe, Raymond Callahan, and Frank Dilley of the University of Delaware faculty who read and commented on the manuscript and encouraged me to seek a publisher for it.

The task of reading reels and reels of microfilm would have certainly defeated my efforts as a researcher had it not been for the generosity of Daniel Coons, Director of the William C. Jason Library-Learning Center at Delaware State College, who lent me a microfilm reader to use at home. When the beast suddenly developed an inordinate appetite for unobtainable replacement bulbs, Arthur Foster of the Morris Library of the University of Delaware kept me supplied with them.

As the pile of rough manuscript grew, still others made their contribution. James R. Hartnett, my departmental chairman at Delaware State relieved me of many time consuming obligations and cheerfully adjusted my teaching schedule to accomodate my hunger for working time. My wife Vicki encouraged me at every step of the way. Struggling with the demands of her first full time job in many years, she cheerfully contributed from her earnings the necessary funds to hire a competent typist. This was Oleta Bordeaux who contributed a beautifully executed and meticulously correct manuscript, which went a long way towards "selling" the work to the editorial staff at the Naval Institute Press.

Once committed to the project, the personnel at the Institute moved forward with a degree of speed and competence that I had never before witnessed on the part of a publisher. Every promise was kept, every pledge fulfilled. Lost time, wasted motion, and general frustration were reduced to an absolute minimum. I imagine that few authors ever have such a pleasant experience and I am indeed grateful for it.

James E. Valle
Dover, Delaware,
November 7, 1979

Introduction

The general subject of early American naval history is one that has long been popular with maritime historians. The battles, leaders, voyages of exploration, and diplomatic activities which the small but potent U.S. Navy engaged in from 1800 to 1865 have been discussed and studied in tremendous detail both for the instruction of the student of military science and for the pleasure and edification of a large following of interested laymen.

Much less well known and understood are the studies and research done in the area of the routine operation of the Navy Department and of the individual ships, squadrons, and shore stations that made up the navy during the early years of the Republic. Only recently have there appeared a few monographs and books that probe personnel practices, the management of the Navy Department, and the general character of the Old Navy.*

This lack led to a marked distortion of the actual significance of much of our naval history, a history that forms the core of the traditions of our sea service. A survey of naval historical and inspirational lore contained in *The Book of the Navy*, a compilation edited by W. Adolphe Roberts and Lowell Brentano for the midshipmen of the Naval Academy, contains accounts of forty-three combats taking place between 1776 and 1944, nine scientific or exploratory expeditions, and one notable feat of small-boat navigation.[1] These selections give the future officers of the navy an excellent orientation as to what is expected of them in battle and in other circumstances of extraordinary peril. Little or nothing in this body of lore prepares the prospective naval officer for long periods of routine peacetime service. The virtues of teamwork, judicious treatment of subordinates, graceful subordination to higher authority, patience, and selflessness are neglected.

This is something of a tragedy, because an officer can normally expect to spend most of his service life in routine peacetime activities. The navy was on a peacetime footing for fifty-two of the years between

*In general, the navy of 1800–1861 will be referred to as the "Old Navy," that of 1862–1865 as the "Civil War Navy," and the twentieth-century fleet as the "Modern Navy."

1800 and 1865, yet the vast bulk of naval history deals with the events of the thirteen years of warfare rather than the peaceful interludes that lasted for decades at a stretch.

We need to know much more about these periods of peaceful routine activity. Much of what occurred then is relevant to the affairs of the Modern Navy, which is also a service that spends long periods of time on a peacetime footing. One area that is of great import, although it has been largely neglected, is that of discipline.

Naval disciplinary problems, policies, and crises are more than just "dirty linen" to be aired for the satisfaction of morbid curiosity. The state of discipline within a service is the key to much more. The morale of naval personnel, both officers and enlisted men, the levels of stress within the organization, the equity and effectiveness of personnel practices, the degree of professionalism exhibited by naval officers, and their willingness and ability to reform their procedures and purge their ranks of undesirables are all intimately bound up in the workings of the naval system of discipline. For these reasons it should prove as useful to study the disciplinary methods and traditions of the Old Navy as it is to study its battles, leaders, and scientific activities. Indeed, the more one probes the disciplinary problems and policies in the Old Navy, the more one is struck by their similarity to problems within the modern service.

Today's drug addiction among young seamen and officers might well have had its counterpart in the widespread alcoholism of the officers and men of yesteryear. The abolition of flogging in 1850 touched off a crisis much more severe than that created by the introduction of the Uniform Code of Military Justice in 1950. Problems of uncooperativeness and insubordination among the high-ranking officers of today's navy, as evidenced by those Admiral Elmo R. Zumwalt faced in overcoming the opposition of other flag officers (notably Hyman G. Rickover and George W. Anderson)[2] while he was chief of naval operations, also had their counterparts in the defiant behavior and disregard of regulations of Commodores Isaac Hull, Stephen Decatur, and Thomas ap Catesby Jones.

In dealing with the subject of discipline in the Old Navy, one can tap a rich body of manuscript material. Evidence concerning the routine chastisement of enlisted men is to be found in old logbooks and accounts of voyages and expeditions. For serious offenders who were investigated or tried formally, the verbatim transcripts of general courts-martial and courts of inquiry from 1800 to the mid-1920s have survived and are available on microfilm.[3] The general state of discipline in the nineteenth-century navy was discussed in letters, diaries, books, pamphlets, and even novels. Congressional committees made inquiries and conducted investigations; and various secretaries of the navy wrote reports and made recommendations, as each one in his turn wrestled with the tightly ingrained naval establishment of the early Republic.

The picture that emerges from these sources is engrossing and highly instructive. The Old Navy was, like most military organizations of that day, an authoritarian system based on the principle of dominance and domination. It was characterized by organizational rigidity and sought solutions for disciplinary problems through the mechanical application of traditional practices and routine policies. As were many other institutions of the time, it was noteworthy for its strong reliance on ceremonialism, conventional gestures, and formal observances that were built into its structure out of veneration for tradition and nostalgia. Its officers were, in conformity with the conventional culture from which they sprang, susceptible to an exaggerated sense of professionalism where concern with the forms and symbols of status outweighed regard for practical results and functional performance.[4]

Out of this atmosphere there developed a curious quality of inconsistency characterized by a code of iron discipline which imposed the strictest possible control over the enlisted men. Because they were seen as the lowest class of humanity, reliance was placed mainly on flogging, confinement in irons, and the threat of capital punishment, on the grounds that that was all they could be expected to comprehend. Junior officers were under somewhat looser control. They could usually evade being punished for offenses that would send an enlisted man to the gratings; but let them incur the wrath of a senior officer, and they might find themselves summarily dismissed from the service or living under a regimen of petty harassment designed to elicit a resignation. Senior officers were somehow immune to most disciplinary restraints. They could feud, split the service with their factionalism, bend or break regulations, and indulge in highly autocratic behavior with little threat of serious reprisal. There was a great deal of favoritism about the way the navy administered justice, and the general public occasionally detected this and criticized the service for these habits.

Public concern about disciplinary methods in the federal navy first manifested itself in 1799 when Seaman Neal Harvey was executed for cowardice on board the frigate *Constellation* under Captain Thomas Truxtun. Harvey had deserted his post, apparently in panic, during the engagement with the French frigate *L'Insurgente* and was killed by his division officer, Lieutenant Andrew Sterett. The incident became known after the arrival of Truxtun with his prize in Philadelphia, and

3

a certain amount of indignation arose in the anti-federalist press, which was hostile to the navy generally and opposed to the Quasi-War policy of John Adams's administration. Seizing on Sterett's boast, "We put men to death for even looking pale on this ship," the *Aurora* editorialized that such remarks were perfect illustrations of "the arrogance that always accompanies military command."[5] Sterett's actions were not condemned by naval authorities, however; and the summary execution of men who fled their posts in action became one of the traditions of the sailing navy.

From time to time, other naval disciplinary cases came to the attention of the public. Two courts-martial, that of Commodore James Barron and his officers for the surrender of the *Chesapeake* to the British in 1807 and that of Alexander Slidell Mackenzie for the hanging of three members of his crew for attempted mutiny on board the brig *Somers* in 1842, became so controversial that the proceedings of the tribunals were published by the government. Other officers who underwent courts-martial or courts of inquiry received permission to publish privately the records of their trials.

Naval courts had a significance in the sailing navy that went beyond mere matters of discipline. There was considerable internal friction in the service based on grudges and factionalism. Dueling among the officers, especially the junior officers, was fairly common. After 1840, efforts to suppress it began to make headway, and officers sometimes resorted to bringing charges and countercharges against one another as a substitute for a passage at arms. Many of these proceedings were rooted in personal enmity, and dragged on out of all proportion to the offense being tried.[6]

Morale in the Old Navy was often poor, but the most pervasive crisis in leadership and discipline occurred during the 1850s, which began with the abolition of flogging, continued with a clumsy attempt to purge the officer corps, and ended with the entire nation drifting towards disunion and civil war. This last event split the naval establishment badly, engendering a period of great suspicion and distrust between brother officers that lasted from 1859 to 1861. These traumas and crises were far more severe than anything experienced by the Modern Navy. It is interesting to note that during this crisis-ridden decade the number of courts-martial and courts of inquiry increased to triple and quadruple the normal average. This was because of the great number of serious offenses committed by enlisted men, the introduction of the summary court-martial as a disciplinary tribunal for moderately serious cases, and the necessity of hearing the appeals of officers retired by the Naval Efficiency Board of 1855.[7]

4

In addition to being indicators of stress within the naval officer corps, courts-martial and courts of inquiry have another use. In an article written for the journal *Armed Forces and Society*, Paul L. Savage and Richard A. Gabriel, two former career army officers now employed as college professors, identified an unusual level of certain crimes—mutiny, desertion, assaults upon superior officers, attempted assassination of leaders, and large-scale drug addiction—as indicators of disintegration within a military organization.[8] Although Savage and Gabriel were mainly concerned with the experience of the French and American armies in Vietnam, some of what they said is relevant to the problems of the Old Navy. Mutiny, mutinous conduct, and mutinous language represented about 8 percent of all charges brought in naval tribunals between 1800 and 1861. Offenses related to drunkenness and illicit trading in liquor represented a similar percentage of judicial charges and constituted the largest single cause for the awarding of nonjudicial punishments.[9] Desertion was rife in the navy throughout the nineteenth century. It was the most common court-martial offense, accounting for 18 percent of all charges. Assault on a superior officer and related charges were also prominent and accounted for 4 percent of all charges lodged.[10]

The burden of Savage's and Gabriel's article is that a high incidence of these particular offenses is a result of poor personnel practices, low officer quality, and bad relationships between officers and enlisted men which breed contempt on the part of the men for their officers. That such conditions were present in the Old Navy can be deduced from many sources but perhaps nowhere so clearly and graphically as in *White Jacket*, Herman Melville's fictionalized account of a cruise in the USS *United States* on the Pacific Station in 1843.[11] The Old Navy never did disintegrate, of course, and came close to it only during the years immediately after the abolition of flogging, when the crews of a few ships apparently became uncontrollable for short periods of time.[12]

Since the end of the Civil War, the general trend within the navy has been one of slow but steady improvement in virtually every phase of personnel administration and living conditions. The status of enlisted men has steadily grown, and a new awareness of the importance of good leadership and high morale has emerged to replace the old iron-discipline methods imposed on polyglot crews. The officer corps has also become more settled and orderly. The last really rancorous public feud occurred in the wake of the Spanish-American War, when Admiral William T. Sampson and Commodore Winfield Scott Schley engaged in a lengthy and acrimonious debate over command responsibility, insubordination, and disregard of orders that had its roots in the latter's conduct during the Battle of Santiago. Charges and countercharges proliferated, and a court of inquiry collected enough testimony and documents to fill two thick volumes, which were subsequently published at public expense.[13] No conclusion was ever reached in this affair, and no court-martial resulted from the inquiry. As was the case in so many naval controversies where the real issue was a personality clash, neither party was able to gain much satisfaction from the naval justice system.

In the Modern Navy, the officer corps, strongly influenced by the ethos of the Naval Academy, has different methods of handling internal disputes. It implants within its midshipmen a sense of separateness, a loyalty to naval traditions and codes, and a spirit of brotherhood. Modern naval officers rarely seek publicity for themselves. Instead, they seek it for their service. In internal matters, they function like a men's club, keeping those members who prove unfit or incompetent out of sight until they can be quietly retired. Courts-martial and courts of inquiry are a last resort, rarely publicized, and care is taken to see that they do not become a platform for the airing of personal grudges.[14]

Occasionally, however, this veneer of silence cracks and a case does come before the public. The capture of the electronic-surveillance ship *Pueblo* in 1968 under circumstances somewhat analogous to those of the *Chesapeake* affair created a controversy that split the service and resulted in the publication of more books on naval justice than has any other case in history. As with the Barron trial, the court of inquiry that investigated the actions of Lieutenant Commander Lloyd M. Bucher's crew produced 3,392 typed, single-spaced pages of testimony and a verdict that left all sides dissatisfied.[15] Only the *Somers* affair can be said to have generated a similar quantity of written commentary and polemics.

Another controversy in the sixties surrounded the relief of Lieutenant Commander Marcus A. Arnheiter from the command of the destroyer escort *Vance*. Arnheiter was a highly individualistic skipper who apparently engaged in certain irregular and illegal practices while serving in the *Vance*. His real crime was that he completely destroyed the morale and effectiveness of his officers and men through excessive zeal and extremely poor leadership. The Arnheiter affair also split the service emotionally. Arnheiter tried the tactic, well known to the officers of the Old Navy, of bringing his case before Congress in an effort to have the disposition the navy had made of the affair set aside. A friend of Arnheiter, Captain Richard G. Alexander, published an open letter in an attempt to go public with the controversy and rally a faction in support of Arnheiter. In the Old Navy, such flamboyant tactics would not have been unusual and could well have resulted in Arnheiter's reinstatement. The Modern Navy defused the issue by refusing to convene a court-martial or court of inquiry, and both Arnheiter and Alexander faded from the navy, their careers ruined.[16]

These and other examples of contemporary naval justice reveal an interesting anomaly. In the slow evolution of naval law since 1800, the relatively privileged officer corps of the Old Navy has seen its options and advantages decline significantly to the point where few officers today can successfully challenge the navy in legal controversy. Conversely, the position of the enlisted men has greatly improved, at least theoretically, since the Uniform Code of Military Justice gives them more and more of the constitutional rights and safeguards enjoyed by civilians.

That naval law has undergone profound changes is regretted in some quarters, but it was inevitable given the rudimentary nature of the original ordinances and structures provided. As conceived in 1800, under the Articles of War approved by Congress in April of that year, the navy's legal system was extremely sketchy. Moreover, it was a system that would be operated almost entirely by laymen untrained in the philosophy or technicalities of the law. The duties of judges, prosecutors, defense counselors, recorders, and bailiffs would be discharged by regular officers whose only preparation was repeated reading of the Articles of War and their own study of privately published manuals of court-martial procedure. No official reference work analogous to Naval Courts and Boards existed in those days and the *Naval Regulations* of 1802 confined itself to five brief sentences for the guidance of the perplexed.

1. All courts-martial are to be held, offences tried, sentences pronounced, and execution of such sentences done, agreeably to the articles and orders contained in an act of Congress made on the 23d of April, in the year 1800, entitled "an act for the better government of the navy of the United States."

2. Courts-martial may be convened as often as the President of the United States, the secretary of the navy, or commander in chief of a fleet, or commander of a squadron, while acting out of the United States shall deem it necessary.

3. All complaints are to be made in writing, in which are to be set forth the facts, time, place, and the manner how they were committed.

4. The judge advocate is to examine witnesses upon oath, and by order of the commander in chief, or in his absence, of the president of the court, to send an attested copy of the charge to the party accused, in time to admit his preparing his defence.

5. In all cases, the youngest member must vote first, and so proceed up to the president.[17]

The justice dispensed by this system was often irregular and clearly incompatible with the system of civilian law in force throughout the United States. Coupled with this problem were other difficulties which arose out of the smallness and ingrained nature of the Old Navy. Modern commentators who deplore the vast, impersonal, and highly bureaucratic nature of the Modern Navy often lose sight of the fact that a small and familiar service can have just as many disadvantages as a large one. The naval justice system shows this clearly. It had to deal with problems arising from cronyism, factionalism, grudges, and feuds that festered deeply because the participants could not escape one another in the enforced intimacy imposed by a small fleet with a limited number of berths. It was also hard to organize impartial courts and render disinterested justice in an environment where everyone was well known to everyone else.[18]

In spite of these problems, the evolution of naval law took place slowly. This was primarily because, until the twentieth century, the navy grew slowly. Awareness and understanding of the *need* for revising naval law had been even more retarded. The navy is a service bound by tradition, and its legal system is intimately bound up with certain of its most cherished articles of faith. Its officers and administrators are usually compelled to make changes against their will. This is, to some extent, because the navy has never developed a really deep *factual* understanding of its past methods and procedures.

Indeed, the Navy has been remiss in undertaking any significant studies of its disciplinary codes and system. There have been no significant reformers or writers in the field of naval justice to compare with such army scholars as William Winthrop and Samuel T. Ansell, both of whom served as army judge advocates general during the nineteenth and early twentieth centuries.[19] The only institutional inquiry into the quality and competence of naval justice ever undertaken was a study of courts-martial and nonjudicial punishments awarded during World War II, and its results indicated that there were then serious deficiencies in the administration of naval law under the Articles of War.[20]

So little is known about naval jurisprudence that there is not even an accurate count of the number of men who have been sentenced to death by naval courts and subsequently executed. Even such authorities on military law as William T. Generous, author of a pioneer study of the origins of the Uniform Code of Military Justice, erroneously

8

states that the navy has executed only three men, the famed *Somers* mutineers, in its entire history.[21] Robert E. Johnson, a highly qualified naval historian, adds the names of two men who were hanged in San Francisco in 1849 as a result of the *Ewing* mutiny.[22] In the course of compiling his biography of Commodore Matthew C. Perry, Samuel Eliot Morison turned up one more, a young seaman named Samuel Jackson, who was hanged after being convicted of mutiny during the war with Mexico.[23] These six men are the only ones known by contemporary naval historians to have been executed at the hands of the navy. A careful examination of the judge advocate general's index of naval courts-martial for the years 1800 to 1861 actually indicates that naval courts sentenced twenty-six men to death, of whom seventeen were either certainly or probably executed, and that forty-nine more were given punishments of more than one hundred lashes, which was considered tantamount to a death sentence.[24]

Considerable lack of accurate information was also displayed during the trial of Lieutenant Commander Bucher when many naval officers and newspaper men asserted that no American ship of war had surrendered without resistance to enemy forces since the *Chesapeake* did so in 1807. The judge advocate general's records actually show that, between 1798 and 1823, no less than eight naval vessels, not counting the *Chesapeake*, surrendered to enemy forces under circumstances similar to those attending the capture of the *Pueblo*. Few of the commanding officers involved were found guilty of any wrongdoing by the naval courts that heard their cases.[25]

To uncover new knowledge and provide a better perspective on early American naval history, and the naval justice system in particular, a close and systematic study of the file of court-martial and court of inquiry transcripts compiled by the judge advocate general's office is vitally important. It is hoped that this study, based on hitherto neglected material, will alert naval historians to the wealth of information that can be mined from the thousands of pages of testimony and scores of reels of microfilm that make up the collection.

Chapter I

Ships & Men of the Old Navy

No discussion of discipline in the navy during the early and middle years of the nineteenth century would be intelligible without some preliminary examination of the general form and character of the service. In many ways the Old Navy was a singular military organization characterized by smallness, scattered deployment, and peculiar values and ethos. The Civil War Navy, while representing a dramatic departure from these basic characteristics, was still firmly rooted in the past, especially with respect to its most prominent and influential leaders. It is noteworthy that after the Civil War the navy soon reverted to prewar practice, so that general conditions first established in the early-nineteenth century lasted until the age of Alfred Thayer Mahan and Theodore Roosevelt.

The Federal Navy had its origins in the old Continental Navy, which was organized by the Continental Congress to fight the Revolutionary War and completely disbanded when the Treaty of Paris was concluded in 1783. After the Constitution had been ratified and put into operation, the new Republic waited six years before authorizing the construction of a small fleet of frigates which would form the basis of the first national naval squadron. By 1798 the ships and men of the Federal Navy were in action against the French in the Caribbean, and since that time there has always been a fleet in being under the Stars and Stripes.

The Federal Navy fluctuated greatly in size and prestige. After proving its usefulness in protecting trade and commerce under President John Adams, it was employed by Thomas Jefferson against the Barbary pirates, and shortly thereafter greatly contracted for economic and ideological reasons. During the War of 1812, it expanded and won its first real fame in a series of single-ship duels and squadron actions on the northern Lakes. Indeed, Congress and the public were so pleased with its performance that in 1816 the first comprehensive building program designed to create a "balanced" fleet was undertaken. By 1819 the euphoria had worn off, and the navy entered a cycle of atrophy and neglect that lasted until a modest program of naval expansion was undertaken in the 1850s. Thus, between 1820 and the advent of the Civil War, it passed through a long, desolate era during which there was little significant technological development or combat action. The tedium was barely broken by various exploratory voyages and by the war with Mexico, 1846–1848, which was predominantly an army operation.[1]

This state of affairs was temporarily set aside by the Civil War, which caused the navy to expand dramatically and to branch out into the unaccustomed role of pioneering new technology in the fields of steam propulsion, armor, and ordnance. These developments gave the U.S. Navy the largest and perhaps the most modern fleet in the world for a short period in the middle 1860s; but, when peace came, the old pattern of decay and decline repeated itself, and by the end of the 1870s it had reached its absolute nadir in size and technology relative to the fleets of the other naval powers.[2]

Smallness and neglect, which were the normal conditions of the Old Navy, were further aggravated by the role and mission assigned to it. No real attempt was made to create a battle fleet or maintain a concentration of forces. Instead, the ships were sent out to "show the flag" and protect American seaborne trade and property on a variety of foreign stations.

First organized during the Barbary Wars, the Mediterranean Squadron was put on a permanent footing in 1815. It was usually the largest U.S. naval detachment abroad and the choicest duty station. Increasing concern with hemispheric affairs resulted in the formation of two more squadrons in 1821: the West India Squadron, which grew out of a force organized in 1816 to hunt pirates, and the Pacific Squadron, which upheld American interests from Chile to Oregon and among the islands of the western Pacific. In 1826 the formation of the Brazil Squadron completed American efforts to encircle Latin America and assure its shipping some protection along the vital Cape Horn route.

These four squadrons sufficed to meet American naval requirements until 1835, when increasing trade and commerce with the Orient stimulated the organization of the East India Squadron, which was eventually designated the Asiatic Fleet. The deployment of the African Squadron in 1843 completed the roster of foreign stations covered by the Old Navy.[3] In addition to these regular assignments, the navy detailed individual ships or small squadrons to undertake specific tasks, such as the transporting of diplomats to posts abroad and the exploration of unknown or uncharted areas. Occasionally, a punitive expedition was sent out against such diverse and exotic foes as the pepper pirates of Quallah Battoo and the Kru people of Little Bereby in the Bight of Benin. Interestingly, little thought was given to the

11

defense of the eastern seaboard of the United States, although a Home Squadron was constituted on paper in 1841. This squadron carried the principal responsibility for blockading the east coast of Mexico during the war of 1846.[4]

This widely dispersed, piecemeal deployment of the Old Navy, especially after 1815, created something of an image and identity crisis in the service. Since a large part of it was always away on distant stations, it did not have much visibility at home and consequently attracted few recruits and very little economic support. The war service of the navy prior to 1816 had created a combat tradition that overemphasized single-ship actions, with the result that there was little sense of strategic mission and virtually no concept of fleet action to be found among the navy's senior officers. Squadron evolutions were rarely held, squadron efficiency was low, and individual cruising was the rule, much time being taken up merely in going to or departing from foreign stations.[5] Duty under these conditions was stultifying, lackluster, and boring. It consisted mainly of assisting merchant vessels in trouble and helping to expand American commerce.[6]

Throughout the nineteenth century, this scattered and uncoordinated collection of squadrons was administered by a singularly rudimentary Navy Department. In 1820, for example, the civilian personnel of the Department consisted of less than ten people, including the messenger boy whose salary was one dollar per day. The secretary of the navy was on a somewhat more exalted level, since he drew about six thousand dollars per year, in return for which he administered a total budget for all naval expenditures that amounted to less than six million dollars annually.[7] By 1846 the staff of the department had grown to a strength of twenty-five men, including messengers and copy clerks, and there were six bureau chiefs, of whom Gideon Welles, chief of the Bureau of Provisions and Clothing, was the only civilian.[8] There was no assistant secretary and no legal officer of any kind.

Although small, the Navy Department defied the principles of Parkinson's Law. It was a byword for inefficiency. Commander Samuel Francis Du Pont called it "the most rickety and stupid of all the Federal Departments."[9] Its main weakness lay in the senior bureau chiefs, most of whom were superannuated commodores clinging like barnacles to their departmental posts because there were few other positions ashore for men too enfeebled to go to sea, and there was no provision to retire officers on anything like an adequate pension. Thus, the bureau chiefs were men long past their prime, totally unfitted by temperament or inclination to work with the secretaries or the Congress, and positively reactionary in their attitude towards all professional matters.[10] Under their dead hands, the navy languished, unable to break the cycle of conservatism and decay that old age and lack of vigor imposed on it.

Technological and intellectual stagnation took its toll of the officer corps as well as of the Department. Life afloat was physically exhausting, drab, claustrophobic, and offered little opportunity for personal development or initiative. Added to these stresses and strains were the vicissitudes of truly chaotic systems of allotments, appointments, and promotions.

The exact personnel strength of the navy was never precisely fixed by Congress, although in practical terms manpower was limited by the amount of money appropriated to meet the payroll. Appointments and promotions were determined entirely by the president and his secretary of the navy, and the political needs of the administration in power were the primary consideration. In 1829, the lame-duck administration of John Quincy Adams paid off some political debts by appointing fifty midshipmen, a move that the incoming Jacksonians saw as an attempt to cheat them of "spoils."[11] Consequently, the following year saw the appointment of only ten midshipmen. Nor had President Adams neglected the higher ranks. From 1818 to 1824, under President Monroe, only one captain was added to the navy; but in 1825, Adams created nine new captaincies in much the same manner as a medieval pope might expand the college of cardinals. Lieutenancies were dispensed with similar lack of consistency. In 1836, crusty old Andrew Jackson signed commissions for only five new lieutenants; but in 1837, his successor, Martin Van Buren, promoted forty-nine men to that coveted post.

Needless to say, scant attention was ever paid to the actual requirements of the navy or to the numerical ratios that should have existed between the various grades of officers. The system was rife with absurdities and unfairness. In 1842 Congress stepped in after John Tyler's administration had treated itself to a particularly wild binge of appointments that increased the size of the officer corps by 20 percent in a single year. Maximum strengths were established for all grades of officers, and this effectively "froze" the size of the navy. The cycle of stagnation alternating with periods of intense movement became instead unrelieved stagnation.[12] After 1842 the only avenue to advancement and promotion was attrition; and, since few naval officers retired, that meant waiting for the oldest men to die and create vacancies so that everyone could move slowly and painfully up the navy list, one notch at a time.

Two other factors worked to slow the pace of promotions. These were the relatively small number of officers in the senior grades and the few steps that existed on the ladder of promotion. In 1824 the navy

13

had only 24 captains, 29 masters commandant, 172 lieutenants, 69 passed midshipmen, and 310 midshipmen, for a total of 225 commissioned line officers, and 379 warrant officers, exclusive of staff personnel.[13] The transition from warrant rank to commissioned status was a slow process symbolized by the existence of the rather nebulous grade of "passed midshipman." A passed midshipman was a midshipman who had passed his lieutenant's examination but could not assume that rank because no vacancy existed. In fact, six or seven years might elapse before a berth became available. Both John Rodgers and David Dixon Porter spent seven years in this grade.

Problems arising from the smallness of the navy were further complicated by the inbred nature of the officer corps. Although most appointments were by virtue of political influence and patronage, naval careers tended to run in families, and intermarriage between naval families created a tight web of social and kinship ties that often transcended professional considerations in shaping the lives of naval officers. A brief summation of the career of David Dixon Porter serves as an excellent example. His first sea duty as a midshipman in 1829 was in the *Constellation*, the same ship that his father, David Porter, had served in as one of Truxtun's midshipmen thirty years earlier. David Dixon's first captain, Alexander Wadsworth, and his first commodore, James Biddle, had both sat on the court-martial that tried his father on charges of disobedience of orders and insubordination in the Fajardo Affair.[14] In 1834, Passed Midshipman Porter found himself serving under the command of another enemy of his father, Commodore James Barron, commandant of the Philadelphia Navy Yard, who was president of the court that tried old Commodore Porter.

David Dixon Porter seems to have handled these awkward situations well. At any rate, he moved up the ladder of promotion at a pace that could be considered normal in the Old Navy. He was commissioned a lieutenant in 1841 and spent the next twenty years in this grade. In 1861 he was still a lieutenant, but by 1865 he had become a vice admiral.[15] As a naval hero of the Civil War, he was never called upon to retire and he dominated the post-Civil War Navy until his death. His style in his later years was dictatorial and autocratic, and he was a relentless foe of technological progress.

Clearly, service in the officer corps of the navy was dismaying and frustrating. Thirty-year-old midshipmen, gray-haired lieutenants, and elderly commodores stuck to it out of a grim and uncompromising sense of duty and patriotism. Their feelings of resentment and abuse festered deep within them, however; and they were too often vented in jealousy and rancorous feuds that gave rise to a good deal of indiscipline and many courts-martial.

If the officer corps was poorly organized and contained many structural defects, at least it had the satisfaction of knowing that it constituted the permanent, hard-core cadre of the regular navy. Enlisted men had no such assurance. The average seaman of the Old Navy entered the service by signing on in a warship for the duration of a commission, normally a three-year cruise on a foreign station. This meant that in reality he belonged to the ship rather than to the navy. At the end of a typical cruise, the whole crew was "paid off" and left the ship and the service entirely, even if less than three years had elapsed. The relationship of a naval seaman to his ship resembled that of a merchant seaman to *his* ship, except that the naval man was ruled by the Articles of War rather than by shipping articles and he signed on for a commission rather than for a voyage.

Under these circumstances there could be no such thing as a corps of career enlisted men, although a few petty officers signed up for commission after commission, and some seamen alternated between merchant and naval service. A typical warship's crew, such as that of the frigate *Congress* on the Brazil Station in 1844, consisted of five hundred men averaging twenty-five years of age. According to Chaplain Charles S. Stewart, one-tenth of the crew were criminals or fugitives from the law and the rest "honest hearted" sailors or inexperienced landsmen. There were twenty-four boys aged between ten and fifteen years and fourteen officers.[16] From other sources we can surmise that there were probably around fifty blacks or other "colored" seamen and that at least one-third of the crew was not of American citizenship.

Once enlisted on board an American naval vessel, the typical recruit found himself confronting a singularly harsh and forbidding environment. He faced a collection of aristocratic officers whose ideas of leadership revolved almost exclusively around the code of iron discipline embodied in the Articles of War, an equally narrow-minded group of petty officers sporting short, thick rope "colts," or "starters," and a devious, hard-bitten band of veteran "topmen" or "sheet anchormen" who formed a society that excluded or ridiculed the newcomer.[17] It was the special delight of these grizzled, old hardcases to lure the younger men into self-destructive vices while withholding from them whatever knowledge and skills they possessed.[18] It took a determined landsman to surmount such a crushing environment and become a useful sailor.

Morale among the enlisted men in most naval ships was poor, but the conditions of service life in the nineteenth century rendered this state of affairs unimportant in practical terms. A warship's crew was extremely large in relation to her tonnage because of the tremendous amount of manpower required to work the guns. Half a thousand men typically manned a forty-four-gun frigate that could be sailed by one-tenth of that number. The men who did sail the ship, the artisan petty officers, topmen, and prime seamen, were the only members of the crew who had really significant jobs to perform under normal conditions. The others—ordinary seamen, landsmen, "waisters," "holders," and marines—were kept occupied with unskilled and trivial work, endlessly holystoning decks and polishing brightwork or, in the case of marines, drilling, while liberal use of the cat-o'-nine-tails and the bosun's starter enforced outward conformity to the rules and customs of the service.

A rough equilibrium between sullen defiance and conformity seems to have been the norm in naval ships. The men performed their tasks with an outward show of willingness. Slackness and inefficiency were scarcely detectable with so many hands to do the work. Fear of swift corporal punishment ensured deference to authority, while rebellion took passive rather than active forms. The men got drunk whenever possible, made shambles of their meager liberties on shore, and deserted in droves. By modern standards, deserters were hunted only half-heartedly and quickly replaced, often by foreigners who spoke little English and were themselves deserters from some other navy or from some merchant vessel.

Nineteenth-century naval ships could be manned this way because of their relatively low order of technological complexity, but American naval officers often worried about how such crews would stand the test of battle. It was beyond the mental horizons of anybody in the naval establishment of that day to engage in systematic or rational thinking concerning questions of morale; indeed, it would hardly have occurred to them to even attempt to do so. Still, a modest effort was made to keep up the spirits of the prime seamen, the "topmen" who formed the elite of a sailing man-of-war's crew. They were much less closely supervised and often exempted from the more galling pinpricks of regulation and discipline that were imposed on their less fortunate shipmates of the spar and gun decks.[19]

Although few efforts were made by the officers of an American man-of-war to sponsor activities that might improve crew morale, the men themselves occasionally provided their own diversions, usually in the form of amateur theatricals. These consisted of skits, playlets, songs, and other amusements put on by the crew subject to the approval of the commanding officer. Many officers looked upon these events with disapproval. Captain John A. Dahlgren, for example, condemned the Seaman's Amateur Theatre organized at Port Mahon in 1845 in terms that most discipline-conscious officers could readily subscribe to:

These three vignettes of sailor life in the Old Navy depict something of the spartan existence that most man-of-warsmen led in the first half of the nineteenth century. Normally, only the topmen worked aloft. The rest of the crew, landsmen, holders, waisters, and the like, were kept occupied with an endless round of gun drills and spit and polish work about the decks. (*The Kedge Anchor*, collection of the Nimitz Library)

> My belief is that any association in a military body is likely to mar discipline. Therefore, I object to [seaman's theatricals]. It matters little whether the object be good or bad. The law is sufficient to insure order, religion, and morality, each being provided for in separate clauses. . . .[20]

In point of fact, Dahlgren may have had good reason to take this attitude. Any theatrical production that the crews did put on was likely to lampoon the officers, not excluding the lordly commodore himself, either mercilessly or subtly; and the resulting hilarity completely overwhelmed the normal spirit of iron discipline, if only for a few hours.[21] Seen in the context of the distrust the officers harbored for the enlisted men, theatricals were the only opportunity the sailors had to return the compliment.

For the enlisted men *did* hold many of their officers in contempt. Equally despised were the midshipmen, especially those not yet "passed," who covered up their lack of knowledge and general unsuitability as leaders by indulging in petty tyranny and callous disregard for the feelings and comfort of their men. Such officers were labeled "rose water sailors" and cordially detested.[22] Mutual distrust bred an atmosphere aboard many American men-of-war that was more appropriate to a penal institution, with the seamen treated as convicts and the officers cast in the role of guards. Indeed, the navy's greatest disciplinary problems were, on the subjudicial level, alcoholism, and on the judicial level, desertion. Both offenses can be interpreted as a form of escape. The desertion rate was particularly significant. It averaged around 10 percent per year throughout the nineteenth century. In the year 1880, there were 1,000 desertions out of a total strength of 8,500 men.[23]

Rarely was the pressure eased. A theatrical might be held once or twice during a three-year cruise, at the captain's discretion, and some ships had a tradition of allowing the crews to "skylark" and indulge in rough horseplay during the dogwatches on uneventful passages. When this occurred, the rules governing conduct on deck were not enforced, the captain and commodore retired decorously to their cabins, and some of the more vigorous junior officers even joined in the fun. When the watch ended, so did the skylarking, and the officers signaled the end by resuming their habitual stiff and formal demeanor. "Shipping their quarterdeck faces again" the old seamen called it.[24] Another source of relief available to the men until 1862 was the serving out of a ration of rum or whiskey twice daily.

The regimen of duty and discipline imposed on the enlisted men has been described by one authority on the history of the Old Navy as the strictest and most oppressive in force in any nineteenth-century fleet.[25] This state of affairs, coupled with the fact that promotions into the officer corps from the enlisted ranks were practically unknown in the American service, made it difficult for the navy to attract and hold native-born American seamen. The Old Navy thus became the repository of so many foreign-born sailors that both officers and congressmen were alarmed. David Dixon Porter once summed up the situation thus:

> As fine a body of Germans, Huns, Norsemen, Gauls, Chinese, and other outside barbarians as one could wish to see, softened down by time and civilization. . . .[26]

Crews turned over at a rate of almost 60 percent per year; and as late as 1888, less than half the men were native-born. Few even of those men whom the navy had taken special pains to train and indoctrinate in the apprenticeship programs set up in 1875 stayed in the service for long.[27] The normal distrust of enlisted men as a class was magnified considerably when foreign recruits were considered. In his annual report to Congress in 1828, Secretary of the Navy John Branch complained that the foreign seamen were:

> a distinct class of people from those useful citizens who have sought protection under our institutions, and made our country their home. Very few of them have their interest located here, or are bound to us by one of all the ties which connect a man with his country. They produce a large proportion of the offences and insubordination of which we have to complain. . . .[28]

It was primarily these men whom the officers had in mind when they worried about the fighting qualities of their crews.

Unfortunately, the fears of the officers and the charges of Secretary Branch are hard to substantiate. Although laws were passed from time to time limiting the number of foreigners who could be shipped on board naval vessels, they were often evaded through the use of fraudulent certificates of citizenship which could be purchased for as little as fifty cents.[29] Because of this practice and also because American officers followed the old British practice of assigning "purser's names," often Anglicized versions of their proper names, to foreign seamen, it is impossible to estimate the proportion of foreigners in the navy.[30] It is also impossible, by combing court-martial records and punishment lists, to arrive at an accurate percentage of foreigners subjected to disciplinary sanctions. Certainly almost no obviously foreign names can be seen in the Judge Advocate Generals' Records for the years 1800–1868.

The role and status of Negro enlisted men in the Old Navy presents a similar problem. The shipping of black crewmen was just as unpopular with the Navy Department as the enlisting of foreigners. Orders issued by the Navy Department during the Quasi-War with France flatly forbade the enlisting of Negroes,[31] but there seems never to have been a time when there were not at least a few on board.[32] The War of 1812 caused the blanket restriction to be lifted, and by 1816 one out of every seven sailors on board the frigate *Java* was black. In 1818 regulations were adopted forbidding the use of slaves in navy yards, and in 1839 it was provided that "free blacks and other colored persons were to be [enlisted] only with the consent of the station commander." Still later, Commodore Isaac Chauncey, acting in his capacity as a naval commissioner, issued a circular limiting black enlistments to 5 percent of the total because of frequent complaints about the number of blacks and other colored persons in the navy.[33] Chauncey's quota could not be maintained, however; and in 1842 the complement of the frigate *Brandywine* contained forty blacks, or about 10 percent of the total. The highest percentage of blacks to be found in U.S. naval vessels was encountered towards the end of the Civil War, when approximately one-quarter of all enlisted men were of that race.[34]

A few of the blacks in the navy were slaves. William McNally, a naval critic of the 1830s, charged that slaves were serving as crewmen in the *Java* and in various Southern navy yards and that their masters were drawing their pay.[35] On the African Station the navy frequently hired Kroomen, a tribe of seafaring West Africans, to replace men who died or deserted on that coast, but they were usually discharged before their ships returned to the United States to pay off.[36] Presumably other blacks who were not of American origin were also recruited on the West India and Brazil stations.

Once the blacks were aboard ship, the Old Navy treated them and everybody else with a fine impartiality that was dictated by extremely close and crowded conditions and the monotonous unison labor that was required to run a sailing man-of-war. Pay, privileges, and promotions were scanty at best, but what existed was shared out equally among all hands.[37] This policy of equal treatment lasted until 1862, when large numbers of "contrabands" entered the navy, and all attempts to enforce some sort of racial quota were abandoned. Secretary of the Navy Gideon Welles issued new regulations restricting blacks to the rating of "boys" and instituting segregation in living quarters. Later he amended his restrictions so that blacks could hold a variety of ratings, including ordinary seaman, fireman, and coal-heaver; but he stipulated that a black who transferred from one ship to another would lose any rating he held above that of a landsman.[38] By the end of the Civil War, a few ships were manned entirely by blacks, many

ships were experiencing racial tensions, and a few race riots had occurred.

The behavior and treatment of blacks in the Old Navy is hard to
determine. Naval logs and records of courts-martial do not note the
race of persons tried and punished, except incidentally, in the transcripts of the proceedings. Therefore, there is no way to compile statistics as to whether or not blacks were court-martialed, flogged, or confined more frequently than whites. An 1843 memorandum to Congress
does call attention to the fact that black seamen were automatically
confined to jail when their ships visited Southern ports.[39] In *White
Jacket,* Herman Melville describes how one black crewman, the slave
of the purser, was exempted from nearly all disciplinary action and
was even excused from witnessing punishments meted out to the rest
of the crew.[40] Apparently, the rationale for this was that since he was
a slave, disciplining him was exclusively the prerogative of his master.
In 1855 Secretary of the Navy James C. Dobbin ruled that when a
slave deserted his ship or station, his wages would not be paid to his
master but forfeited to the navy. This was in line with the regulation
that held that the wages of free men who deserted were not to be paid
to relatives or dependents.[41]

In his studies of Negro military personnel during the Civil War,
Benjamin Quarles states that the navy's treatment of black enlisted
men was, in general, better than that of the army, with segregation
and discrimination at a minimum.[42] It appears that he was unable to
find any significant examples of undue harshness towards blacks on the
part of the naval justice system. He also notes that four black seamen
received the navy's Medal of Honor for conspicuous bravery in action.
If institutional racism was minimal in the navy, the transcripts of some
courts-martial and courts of inquiry indicate that individual naval
officers did display the prejudicial attitudes typical of the nineteenth
century. Some blacks and mulattoes were employed in such menial
jobs as sick-berth attendants and wardroom servants, and there seems
to have been a feeling among a certain class of officer that they could
be slapped, kicked, or otherwise cuffed around in a manner not sanctioned by the Articles of War for the punishment of seamen and
marines.[43]

Besides foreigners and blacks, there was one other group of men
who represented a special class within the Old Navy—the marines.
Marines were present aboard American warships from the earliest days
of the Continental Navy. During the era of the sailing navy, the complement of marines on board a given ship was roughly in the ratio of
one to a gun, so that a forty-four-gun frigate would carry approxi-

mately fifty marines. They did guard duty, furnished landing parties, stood watches, and lent a hand with hoisting and trimming sails. In battle they manned the tops as snipers. In recognition of the fact that the marines constituted something of a police force and were frequently posted as sentries over naval enlisted men under confinement and awaiting courts-martial, they were the only noncommissioned personnel permitted to go armed on board ship at all times.[44]

Relations between the marines and naval men varied from ship to ship, and in some they were tense and strained. Marines were subjected to a discipline fully as harsh and uncompromising as naval discipline, but they had the added burden of having to maintain a dress uniform and to participate in close-order drill. In fact, man for man, the marines were probably more prone to cause disciplinary problems than were the navy's enlisted men because they were all riflemen and other ranks whose function was purely military. They had none of the artisan petty officers and strikers who constituted a significant percentage of the navy's enlisted strength. It is a well-recognized fact that skilled men cause less trouble than unskilled ones. Indeed, even among the contemporary services, the Marine Corps has a much higher rate of disciplinary offenses than the navy on a man-for-man basis, precisely because so much of its manpower is made up of unskilled combatants.[45]

Enforcement of marine discipline was in the hands of the officer corps of the navy and its justice system when marines stationed aboard ship were accused of offenses. For this reason, the trials and punishments of marine officers and enlisted men are an integral part of the navy's records and statistics on courts-martial and courts of inquiry. Marines sailed and fought under the same Articles of War as naval men, committed essentially the same misdeeds, and were punished in the same ways.

When Richard Rush sailed for England in 1817 in the ship of the line *Franklin* to take up his post as minister to the Court of St. James, he was impressed by the excellent discipline and quiet efficiency of the crew. The marines presented a complete contrast. In conversation with Commodore Charles Stewart, the *Franklin*'s commanding officer, Rush learned that it was customary to keep well-trained and disciplined marines at home for ceremonial purposes and to send the raw recruits to sea. It took a great deal of effort, Stewart declared, within the confines of a ship to instill discipline in and teach close-order drill to men who had been only a few days in service before reporting aboard and who were, at best, the dregs of society.[46] However much this generalization may or may not have applied to the marines afloat, the corps is certainly well represented on the punishment rolls and in the records of courts-martial. Nineteen percent of all cases in the judge advocate general's records index for the years 1800 to 1861 involve marines. They also account for 30 percent of all death sentences handed down by naval courts. (See Table III, Chapter V.)

Commodore Stewart questioned the usefulness of the contingent of raw and untrained marines on board the *Franklin*, but the general feeling in the navy was that they were essential to the good order and safety of any major warship. Many of the officers of the Old Navy were extremely conscious of the danger of mutiny and, according to Melville, put much reliance on the antipathy that usually existed between the sailors and the "leathernecks." These officers assumed that a mutiny or insurrection among the sailors would be put down by the marines, who would have few scruples about treating the sailors with complete ruthlessness. By the same token, any disturbance among the marines could be quickly dealt with by arming the sailors. To Melville, this represented a classic case of divide and rule.[47] Needless to say, such calculations indicate a very jaundiced view of the enlisted men of both services.

The navy, burdened as it was with its aura of suspicion and mistrust, was deeply in need of reforms of all sorts during the early-nineteenth century. In keeping with the spirit of institutional reform movements that characterized nineteenth-century America, the navy sought to put its house in order in a variety of ways. The most compelling and dramatic stimulus to naval reform was the publication in 1850 of Herman Melville's semidocumentary novel, *White Jacket*, a work that did for the navy what Richard H. Dana's *Two Years Before the Mast*, published ten years earlier, did for the merchant marine.[48]

Prodded by Congress and an unfavorable climate of public opinion, the navy concentrated its reform efforts in four major areas: the inculcation of Christian religiosity, the creation of a career enlisted corps through indoctrination and an apprenticeship program, the establishment of a more humane disciplinary system, and the abolition of the rum ration.[49] These efforts were all pushed forward in an intermittent and haphazard way; and, with the exception of the abolition of flogging in 1850 and the discontinuance of the spirit ration in 1862, none of them made much of a difference in the lives of the seamen. The teetotalist, prayerful navy of the post-Civil War era, even with its "colts" and cats-o'-nine-tails permanently laid aside, was still a hard and remote service that could never attract enough free-born, native Americans to man its tiny squadrons of far-flung ships.

The officer corps needed reforming fully as much as the enlisted men did, but efforts to procure improvements were even more futile on the quarterdeck than on the berth deck. Being a more articulate body of men and more permanently engrafted onto the navy, the officers had to be consulted before any changes relevant to their condition could be made. Naturally, the most influential of all the officers were those highest on the seniority list, the powerful, conservative, and often elderly commodores, who threw their not inconsiderable weight into the balance against any reforms or changes suggested from outside the service or by the lower ranks. As is often the case in military organizations, it was the junior officers who were most interested in promoting equitable and progressive personnel practices. Denied a hearing within the navy itself, they occasionally went outside channels and published anonymous exposés, formed semisecret cliques of like-minded individuals, and conspired with sympathetic politicians to bypass their stubbornly conservative superiors.

And the senior officers *were* stubborn. A healthy sense of professionalism and a decent spirit of subordination to the Navy Department were characteristics conspicuously lacking in the Old Navy. The Quasi-War with France and the War of 1812 had yielded a crop of overwhelmingly proud and egotistical young commodores pathologically preoccupied with personal "honor" and incapable of sacrificing private considerations for the good of the service.[50] In 1815 they were youthful and energetic, at the apex of their careers, and subsequently became more and more embedded in the generally declining peacetime navy, unable to advance in rank and unwilling to retire. Isaac Hull, Charles Stewart, Thomas ap Catesby Jones, Jesse Duncan Elliott, and others like them were still to be found on the navy list twenty, thirty, even forty years after the great age of fighting sail that had made their fortunes. Indeed, Charles Stewart was a force to be reckoned with as late as 1862, when he was retired in his dotage so that younger men could become the navy's first admirals.

It was against these crusty old curmudgeons, who had themselves been molded by the imperious commodores of the early Federal Navy, Thomas Truxtun, Edward Preble, and John Rodgers, that the reform-minded juniors struggled, many of them growing old themselves in the process. A good example of their efforts was the campaign waged by Lieutenant Matthew Fontaine Maury in the *Southern Literary Messenger* under the pseudonym "Harry Bluff." Maury's articles, entitled "Scraps from the Lucky Bag," touched on many aspects of naval life, but his main concern was the lack of educational opportunities for young officers and the stubborn resistance to technological progress that pervaded the navy. One article was devoted to graft, inefficiency, and incompetence in the navy yards and the antiquated methods em-

As a typically long-lived and well-travelled frigate of the Old Navy, the *United States* figures prominently in the annals of disciplinary records and lore. In the years immediately following the War of 1812, she was the reputed "hell ship" of the Fleet. Decades later she wore the broad pennant of Commodore Thomas ap Catesby Jones during one of his most notorious escapades. Finally, she was immortalized by Herman Melville as his fictional frigate *Neversink* in the documentary novel *White Jacket*. (*The Kedge Anchor*, collection of the Nimitz Library)

ployed by the Board of Naval Commissioners in procuring ships and materiel for the Navy.[51] Maury was protected from the wrath of his superiors by sympathetic friends in Congress and continued to write articles under the name of "Union Jack" after his identity as Harry Bluff was uncovered.[52]

Another reform-minded officer was Samuel F. Du Pont. He became active in the movement for naval reform as the result of a controversy he entered into with old Commodore Isaac Hull during a cruise in the Mediterranean in 1838 and 1839. Hull was commander in chief of the Mediterranean Squadron, flying his broad pennant in the ship of the line *Ohio*. Du Pont sailed as a lieutenant in the *Ohio*, joining her in Boston and remaining with her while she cruised about on the commodore's various errands. Hull had permission to take his wife and sister-in-law to Europe in his flagship. On station, the ladies remained on board in permanent residence against regulations and in defiance of the secretary of the navy's request that they be lodged ashore. To make room for them, Commodore Hull arranged through his flag captain to have all the ship's lieutenants removed from their quarters on the gun deck and berthed on the orlop deck, which was below the waterline and thus exceedingly unhealthy as well as uncomfortable and inconvenient.[53]

Du Pont and several of the other lieutenants, who protested vigorously against this state of affairs, were dismissed from the flagship and sent home by Hull on the pretext that they had shown him disrespect by refusing to make a social call on him and his wife. Once home, the lieutenants told their story and escaped official censure. They were returned to the squadron to resume their duties armed with another directive from the secretary that Mrs. Hull and her sister should be put ashore. Hull ignored these instructions and distributed the unwelcome lieutenants among the smaller ships of his squadron, refusing to bring any of them back to the flagship.[54]

After this drawn battle, Du Pont became a member of the clique of reform-minded officers that included Matthew Calbraith Perry, Alexander Slidell Mackenzie, and others. Their efforts to curb the power of dictatorial superiors and retire the more obviously unfit culminated in the convening of the Naval Efficiency Board of 1855, but the practical effect of their activities was slight. Some of Du Pont's frustration with the higher echelons of the navy's command was expressed in his letters. Once he described four successive secretaries of the navy in the most unflattering terms, citing the "gross ignorance of old Branch; the contemptible meanness of old Woodbury; the honest imbecility of Dickerson; and the dog-in-office bearing of Paulding."[55]

Rent by factionalism between junior and senior officers, the Old Navy was further bedeviled by a bitter, damaging feud between staff and line officers. One of the main causes of this quarrel was that the civilian community accorded higher social status to the staff officers, possessed as they were of valuable skills in medicine, accounting, engineering, and construction, than it did to ordinary line officers. Within the navy, however, staff men were looked upon as socially inferior to the "fighting" officers of the line. They were denied access to the rank structure that gave the line officers their place within the military hierarchy and had their own seniority lists separate from those of line. Even more importantly, line officers resented the fact that staff men were paid out of the funds that Congress allocated for officer pay. Thus, every staff officer on the payroll meant that less money was available to compensate line officers, give them raises, or increase their numbers.[56]

Perhaps most damaging to good relations was the regrettable propensity of staff officers to criticize the service in public. For every line officer who timidly offered a mild criticism under an assumed name, there were several surgeons or chaplains lecturing, pamphleteering, or writing articles about conditions in the navy.[57] Staff men seemed to have a freedom that line officers could only dream about, and their revelations further damaged the already low reputation of the service. Like so many other problems, the staff-line controversy was never significantly ameliorated in the Old Navy and festered on until 1898, when staff men were finally given positive rank and engineers were amalgamated with the line.[58]

Only a powerful and traumatic experience could furnish the impetus for the kind of reforms that the officer corps needed to put the navy on a sound managerial footing, and the Civil War served that purpose admirably. Faced with the abrupt loss of most of its Southern officers, the prospect of some extremely tough campaigning, a tremendous expansion, and a technological revolution, the navy had no choice but to shoulder aside the forces of reaction and set its house in order. Consequently, the years 1861 and 1862 saw the most concerted effective naval reform ever experienced by the service. Everything was thoroughly overhauled—promotions policy, retirement, the Navy Department, the navy yards, procurement, and command arrangements in the squadrons and fleets. Even the sacred Articles of War were reissued with some minor modifications.

Although it was unfortunate that the navy had to wait until the Civil War to undertake these reforms, it must be remembered that Old Navy was not really very different from other military organizations of that day. The nineteenth century was preeminently an age of discipline and authoritarian methods of command. None of the other services was "humane" by contemporary standards, and none was run along the lines of modern managerial science. The army's garrison life and disciplinary traditions were so harsh, in fact, that they were held up by at least one commentator as a model for the treatment of recalcitrant slaves on Southern plantations![59] Only the French Navy, under the influence of the Revolution, ever experimented with an innovative disciplinary code, but the results were dismal indeed and soon abandoned.

Personnel administration also was universally characterized by callous disregard of the rights and feelings of individuals. If the U.S. Navy had no provisions for honorable retirement, for promotion based on merit, for equitable treatment of subordinates, or for the preservation of good morale, neither did the services of any other nation.

But in a few areas, the Old Navy was seriously deficient, even by the standards of its time. The attainment of significant achievement in peaceful pursuits by naval officers went almost entirely unrecognized. At the very peak of his career as an oceanographer and cartographer, Matthew Fontaine Maury held the rank, emoluments, and privileges of a mere lieutenant and was all but ignored by his own service. British officers and statesmen, calling on him to pay their respects, were appalled at such indifference. Indeed, during the years 1855 to 1857, Maury was obliged to fight a furious battle simply to be allowed to remain in the navy after the Efficiency Board decided that he was unfit for sea duty on account of an accident that left him with a permanent limp.[60] Adulation, rewards, and recognition went only to those who had distinguished themselves in combat, a dismaying prospect in a service where combats were few and far between. This approach was unnecessarily narrow and uncompromising even for that day and age.

Unusual narrowness was exhibited in another area. Although nineteenth-century military tradition stressed to a high degree the aristocratic nature of commissioned rank, only in the navy of republican America could one find an almost complete absence of officers promoted from the ranks. Entry to commissioned status was held so closely and dispensed so narrowly that there was practically no way a talented petty officer or warrant officer, other than a midshipman, could attain it. Oddly enough, the unsuitability of many of the "young gentlemen" who were able to land midshipmen's berths in the Old Navy was a well-known scandal both in and out of the service.

Finally, the American navy was particularly backward in its arrangements for senior officers. The cutting-off of the rank structure above the grade of captain was done in the name of noble republican sentiments, but its effect on the service was awkward and debilitating. Few other navies were hobbled with such a rudimentary and inadequate command arrangement. The "commodores" fought each other tenaciously for every scrap of professional advantage, every nuance of status, every shred of deference. Their jealousies, feuds, and bickerings caused the Navy Department and the secretaries endless misery.

Perhaps no navy was strong in the area of morale and personnel administration in the nineteenth century. Without a doubt, however, the U.S. Navy was among the most backward and poorly organized of them all.

Chapter II

Disciplinary Tradition
of the Old Navy

When the Civil War ended in 1865, the U.S. Navy was a relatively young service, less than a century old, even if one dates its origins back to the Continental Navy of 1775. Despite its youthfulness, however, it had a tradition of discipline and a system of military law that extended back to antiquity.

In the Ancient World, the best-known and most enduring codification of military law was the *Magistri Militum*, the law of the legions of Imperial Rome. This code, which doubtless drew on customs and traditions as old as warfare itself, recognized distinctions between civil and military law that have endured to our own time. It was based on the simple proposition that "soldiers should fear their own officers more than the enemy."[1] It recognized the principle that military law is intended mainly to take into account the good of the service, not the good of the individual or of society in general. It denied to military men certain fundamental individual rights enjoyed by civilians. The most important of these was the right of an accused person to have his case reviewed by a distinterested tribunal. All tribunals under martial law are interested in the good of the service. The ultimate purpose of military law is not to guarantee any person any particular rights, or due process of law, or set procedures, or even to ensure fundamental justice, but to maintain military discipline.[2]

Only in recent times has the United States, through the Uniform Code of Military Justice (UCMJ), sought to alter the separateness of military law from civil law and to supply military personnel with the same basic rights as their civilian counterparts. The Uniform Code of Military Justice attempts to separate responsibility for the maintenance of discipline from the responsibility that goes with the exercising of command. It also seeks to make military law more concerned with individual justice and more compatible with the constitutional principles that govern society in general.[3]

The movement that eventually resulted in the adoption of the Uniform Code of Military Justice and the repudiation of Roman principles of military law goes back as far as the seventeenth century. In 1671 Sir Matthew Hale, lord chief justice of England, wrote that "Martial Law, being based on no settled principles, is, in truth and reality, no law, but something indulged rather than allowed as a law."[4] Sir William Blackstone, the eminent eighteenth-century legal scholar, believed that the harshness and arbitrary character of martial law could be justified only in time of war, when extraordinary circumstances of national peril require a Draconian approach to the maintenance of discipline and order in the armed services for the good of society as a whole. He maintained that

> if anyone that hath commission of martial authority doth, in time of peace, hang, or otherwise execute any man by color of martial law, this is murder; for it is against Magna Charta.[5]

Another factor that disturbed English jurists was the ban that prohibited the members of a military court from divulging the contents of their deliberations or the vote or opinion of any member of that court unless ordered to do so by the highest authority. This caused military courts to take on an uncomfortably close resemblance to Star Chamber or Council of Ten proceedings, tribunals which are repugnant to the principles of Anglo-Saxon law. Until the advent of the Uniform Code of Military Justice, no enlisted men sat on military courts, and this resulted in yet another violation of constitutional prerogative, the right of trial by a jury of peers.[6]

One of the most interesting and fundamental areas in which martial law differed from civil law was in the nature and number of offenses that carried the death penalty. Although the Georgian codes of eighteenth-century England made extremely liberal use of capital punishment, by the time the twentieth century arrived, only two crimes, murder and treason, could still be punished by death in a civilian court. By contrast, as late as 1949 an American naval court could, at least theoretically, prescribe capital punishment for twenty-two offenses:

— mutiny
— disobedience of orders
— striking a superior officer
— intercourse with an enemy
— unlawfully receiving messages from an enemy
— desertion in time of war
— deserting trust in time of war
— sleeping on watch
— leaving station before being regularly relieved

- willful stranding or injury to vessels
- unlawful destruction of public property
- striking [the] flag or treacherously yielding or pusillanimously crying for quarter
- cowardice in battle
- deserting duty in battle
- neglecting orders to prepare for battle
- neglecting to clear for action
- neglecting to join on signal for battle
- failing to encourage men to fight
- failing to seek [an] encounter
- failing to afford relief in battle
- spying in time of war
- murder[7]

Although Hale, Blackstone, and other members of the legal fraternity were obviously uncomfortable with the system of military law that had evolved by the eighteenth century, military men have always upheld and defended their code as a practical necessity. Nineteenth-century American commentators were particularly adamant. Colonel William Winthrop, a respected authority on American military affairs, wrote:

Courts-martial are not courts, but are, in fact, simply instrumentalities of the executive power to aid him [sic] in properly commanding the Army and enforcing discipline therein.[8]

General of the Army William T. Sherman expressed himself in a similar vein:

The object of civil law is to create the greatest benefit to all in a peaceful community. The object of military law is to govern armies composed of strong men. An army is an organization of armed men obligated to obey one man.[9]

Actually, the status of military and naval law under the Constitution of the United States was spelled out much more clearly than it was under English common law. Article I, Section 8, of the Constitution empowers the Congress to "provide and maintain a navy" and to "make rules for the government of the land and naval forces." Article II, Section 2, provides that the president

shall be Commander-in-Chief of the army and the navy of the United States and of the militia of the several states when called into the actual service of the United States; he may require the opinion, in writing, of the principal officer in each of the executive departments upon any subject

31

relating to the duties of their respective offices, and he shall have the power to grant reprieves and pardons for offenses against the United States except in cases of impeachment.

The Fifth Amendment went one more step in defining the status of military and naval law by stipulating that

> No person shall be held to answer for a capital or other infamous crime unless on a presentment or indictment of a Grand Jury, except in cases arising in the land or naval forces, or in the militia, when in actual service, in time of war or public danger. . . .

These provisions mean that the prerogative of creating and enacting all written laws, rules, and regulations pertaining to the navy rests solely with Congress. The president, working through the Navy Department or, since 1949, the Defense Department, has the power to enforce those laws, to constitute tribunals to try offenders against them who are members of the navy, to oversee the reviewing process and correct the errors or mistakes of these tribunals, and to execute the sentences handed down by naval courts.

Thus, as set up by the Constitution, the naval justice system existed entirely outside of the authority and control of the judicial branch. Military courts were and are courts of limited jurisdiction, not able to try persons outside the services but essentially supreme in their power to try, convict, and sentence members of the armed forces.

That there was, under normal circumstances, no right to appeal the rulings of a military or naval court to the regular judiciary was a well-understood legal principle in the nineteenth century. Nevertheless, it was formally affirmed by the U.S. Supreme Court in the Dynes case of 1857, which established the doctrine that a person serving in the navy gave up his basic constitutional rights for the duration of his service, accepting in lieu of those rights whatever privileges and immunities were granted by the Articles of War and the rules and regulations of the navy.

Frank Dynes, the seaman whose suit before the Supreme Court resulted in this ruling, had been a party to what was apparently a plot to stage a mass desertion from the razee frigate *Independence* as she rode at anchor in New York Harbor in August of 1854. On the evening of the fifteenth, just as the order to draw hammocks was being piped through the ship, several members of a launch's crew overpowered their boat officer, Midshipman Joseph N. Miller, and cast off from the boat boom to pull for shore. As the scuffle in the boat was taking place, four more men burst on deck and rushed out onto the boom, apparently hoping to join the launch and escape with her crew. All four

The *Independence* as a razee frigate. This is how she looked at the time of the mass desertion attempt that ultimately led to the Dynes Case which was argued before the Supreme Court in 1857. (*The Kedge Anchor*, collection of the Nimitz Library)

men fell into the water, however; and only one managed to scramble into the boat, which was pulling frantically for the southern shore of Brooklyn. The other three, one of whom was Frank Dynes, were rescued from the water by the *Independence*'s barge and brought back aboard, where they were confined for subsequent court-martial on charges of desertion.[10]

When his trial came up on 23 September 1854, Dynes waived his right to counsel but entered a plea of "not guilty." Testimony on the part of several petty officers established that he was one of the men pulled out of the water at the time the launch, which had since been found abandoned at the Atlantic Dock in Brooklyn, made its escape. Dynes made no defense statement, and the court quickly found him "not guilty of desertion but guilty of attempting to desert." He was sentenced "to be confined in the Penitentiary of the District of Columbia without pay at hard labor for the term of six months . . . and not to be again enlisted in the Naval Service."[11]

Several of the launch's crew were recaptured and tried for various crimes relating to this incident. Ordinary Seaman David Hazzard, who had drawn his knife on Midshipman Miller, was found guilty of mutinous conduct, raising a weapon against his superior officer, and desertion. He drew a very severe punishment: life imprisonment in the Penitentiary of the District of Columbia at hard labor and without pay.[12] This sentence was mitigated by President Franklin Pierce to last only until the term of his enlistment had expired.[13] Other members of the launch crew received punishments of varying degree, most involving solitary confinement in the cells at the New York Navy Yard and loss of pay.

The crux of the case that Dynes later made against the government was the fact that he was sentenced to serve his term in the penitentiary rather than in the cells of the navy yard. He was turned over to Jonah D. Hoover, marshal of the District of Columbia, and transported to Washington in a steam packet. He completed his sentence and was released sometime in March 1855. On 24 April 1855, his pay was restored to him by Acting Secretary of the Navy Thomas Smith on written instructions from President Pierce.[14]

Dynes may have concluded from this action that he had a chance to collect damages from the government for false imprisonment. He brought suit in the circuit court for the District of Columbia, contending in a writ of error that the naval court had convicted him of a crime not mentioned in the Articles of War—that is, attempting to desert. This meant that Marshal Hoover, in taking him into custody and transporting him to the penitentiary, was guilty of trespass and false imprisonment. The circuit court was not able to resolve the suit, so it was appealed to the Supreme Court and heard during the December term in 1857.

Charles Lee Jones presented Dynes's case, arguing that although desertion was recognized as a crime in naval law, attempting to desert was not "enumerated by the articles for the government of the navy as an offence within the cognizance of a naval court-martial."[15] Jones did allow that perhaps the laws and customs of the sea

> might sanction sub-judicial punishment for attempting to desert, the
> offence being taken as a misdemeanor but on an indictment for felony [a
> defendant] cannot be convicted of a misdemeanor, because the offences are
> distinct in their nature, and of a distinct legal character.[16]

In effect, the naval court had committed a procedural error that would have resulted in its decision being reversed on appeal if it had been a civilian court governed by the usual principles of constitutional law. It had also tried a case when it had no technical jurisdiction over the subject matter.

In his rebuttal, Hoover's lawyer, a Mr. Gillet, reviewed the constitutional provisions and congressional acts establishing the legality and procedures of courts-martial and argued that the court-martial board that had tried the Dynes case had acted entirely within the framework provided by the law and had also followed the principles laid down in various manuals of court-martial procedure. He declared that

Congress specified a limited number of offences, and among them desertion; and then, in the thirty-second article, made provision for all possible cases which could occur in the naval service.

Among the offences which may be committed is the attempt to desert. Desertion is where a person, bound by his enlistment to remain in the service, in violation of his duty escapes from the control of those in command. An attempt to desert is where the motive to desert is conceived and an effort made to carry it into effect, but which is not fully accomplished, owing to want of success, or to a change of purpose. Such an offence deserves punishment in a degree but little below successful desertion. It is clearly one of the unspecified offences provided for in the 32d article.[17]

After reviewing the arguments, Associate Justice James M. Wayne delivered the opinion of the court, which found against Dynes by a vote of six to one. Reiterating the constitutional basis of naval law, Wayne stated:

These provisions show that Congress has the power to provide for the trial and punishment of military and naval offences in the manner then and now practiced by civilized nations; and that the power to do so is given without any connection between it and the 3d article of the Constitution defining the judicial power of the United States; indeed, that the two powers are entirely independent of each other.[18]

Justice Wayne went on to demonstrate that the court-martial was constituted correctly according to naval law and fulfilled all of the relevant legal requirements. He also explained that the verdict "not guilty of desertion but guilty of attempting to desert" was a "partial verdict in which the accused is acquitted of part of the accusation against him, and found guilty of the residue," a procedure well recognized in criminal law.[19]

The Supreme Court did allow, however, that there was some limit to the power that courts-martial held over individuals in the services and that there were circumstances under which redress could be sought in civil courts:

Persons then, belonging to the army and the navy are not subject to illegal or irresponsible courts martial, when the law for convening them and directing their proceedings of organization and for trial have been disregarded. In such cases, everything which may be done is void—not voidable, but void; and civil courts have never failed, upon a proper suit, to give a party redress, who has been injured by a void process or void judgment.[20]

The court that tried Dynes was neither illegal nor irresponsible. It was convened by competent authority and had jurisdiction over the subject matter of the charge. It did not inflict a punishment forbidden by the law. Therefore, Dynes's case had no merit and Marshal Hoover was not answerable to the charges.

Presumably, if Dynes had been able to demonstrate that his court-martial was improperly constituted and conducted in violation of the procedures established to govern such tribunals, its judgment would have been declared void, and compensation for false imprisonment awarded. Given that there was no such finding, naval courts remained like any other court of limited jurisdiction, supreme unto themselves as long as they confined their activities to the adjudication of cases involving naval personnel.

One current legal authority takes a rather uncompromising view of the unique character of military law. Senator Sam Ervin, formerly chairman of the Senate's Constitutional Rights Subcommittee, declared that

> the primary purpose of the administration of justice in the military services, is to enforce discipline plus getting rid of people who think they are not capable of contributing to the defence of the country as they should.[21]

Naval justice is a close relative of military justice. In the American tradition, the army and the navy have always been governed by their own sets of Articles of War, which are essentially the same. Because of the nature of service at sea and the detached character of naval command, naval law has certain dimensions that military law does not need. Naval ships are subject to natural as well as man-made hazards, and the pressures on their commanding officers are unique and unremitting. Only the instant obedience and total subordination of all hands give the captain of a naval ship the kind of control and authority he needs to operate his ship efficiently. As Commodore David Porter stated,

> A man of war is a petty kingdom, and is governed by a petty despot. . . . The little Tyrant, who struts his few fathoms of scoured plank, dare not unbend, lest he should lose that appearance of respect from his inferiors which their fears inspire. He has therefore, no society, no smiles, no cour-

tesies for or from any one. Wrapped up in his notions of his own dignity, and the means of preserving it, he shuts himself up from all around him. He stands alone, without the friendship or sympathy of one on board; a solitary being in the midst of the ocean.[22]

This stark portrait illustrates the powerful and compulsive forces that combined to make the nineteenth-century naval captain the most autocratic of all military officers. He had more power, enjoyed more autonomy, and carried more responsibility than is normal even in military life, and the place where these powers came most definitively into play was in the area of discipline.[23] In the matter of judicial proceedings, courts-martial or courts of inquiry, he had to share some responsibility with brother officers and suffer a review of his actions by higher authority; but in the area of nonjudicial punishment, his powers were intact and absolute. At captain's mast, he functioned as judge, jury, and executioner.[24] The punishments he ordered were carried out on the spot, and there was no appeal to his rulings. If he chose, he could deny the accused a chance to speak in defense of his actions, and the statement "Seaman Jones, you were drunk—twelve lashes" might be all the deliberation devoted to a particular case.[25]

The position of a commodore was even more complex and carried, if anything, even greater responsibility. Technically only a captain himself, although supplied with a courtesy title that put him on a rough par with, but at a decided disadvantage to, the flag officers of other navies, a commodore needed a vast store of patience and judgment to discharge his duties, which ranged from maintaining squadron efficiency to undertaking major diplomatic negotiations. Unless he was fortunate enough to be assigned a flag captain, a commodore had to combine his squadron duties with those of a commanding officer of a large frigate or ship of the line. He was responsible for all courts-martial and courts of inquiry, managed the squadron's movements, saw to the provisioning of its ships, and attended to the morale of his officers and the discipline of his men.[26] Operating thousands of miles from home with no means of rapid communication at his disposal, he was obliged to deal with complicated and awkward situations on the spot, with no reference to or chance of soliciting advice from the Navy Department. In spite of his isolation, all his actions were subject to review upon his return home, and many a commodore faced court-martial or court-of-inquiry proceedings well calculated to spoil the satisfaction that he might otherwise have felt at the end of a three-year commission on a foreign station. Rarely did the army place as much responsibility on its colonels and brigadiers as the navy placed on the shoulders of the men who flew the broad pennant.

In managing and disciplining their lonely commands, captains and commodores relied heavily on the Articles of War and on the customs and traditions that had been developed by an older and larger sea service, the Royal Navy. British martial law, disciplinary practices, and customs were the models upon which American naval law originally formed itself. The British, with their vast experience in mounting naval expeditions and commanding ships of war, had, in their turn, borrowed freely from Roman naval practice. Flogging, irons, keelhauling, and the drawing of firm distinctions between officers and men had their origins on the Roman galleys with their scores of slave oarsmen and a handful of free crewmen.[27]

When the English sea dogs of the Tudor era created the basis of the modern British Navy, most of the Roman practices regarding the administration and management of fleets and squadrons had been forgotten, but the methods by which individual ships were operated and their crews kept in order had survived the transition from oars to sail and from slave crews to ships' companies composed of nominally free men. A sailor of the Tudor navy who suffered flogging, branding, ironing, keelhauling, or confinement on short rations was simply being punished by means that parliamentary acts seldom specified but referred to vaguely as "the ancient customs of the sea service."[28]

It was the work of seventeenth century to evolve the more elaborate disciplinary procedures necessary to ensure the good order and subordination of officers and seamen enrolled in a standing navy. Admiralty courts with special privileges and prerogatives for the adjudication of maritime disputes had existed in England since Plantagenet times. Unfortunately, they had little effect on the conduct of naval squadrons at sea, and the problem was further complicated by the fact that most expeditions of the Tudor era were made up of diverse components—king's ships, private vessels, company ships, and craft belonging to towns, counties, or boroughs. All sailed together but rarely under the firm control of one commander. The twin concept of a national navy and a professional officer corps was in its infancy, and a sense of subordination and obligation of most sea officers to the "good of the service" was even less advanced.[29]

It was in precisely such circumstances that the first recorded court-martial of a sea officer in modern Anglo-Saxon history was held in 1587. In that year, Sir Francis Drake led a naval expedition made up of royal ships and vessels owned by individuals within the city of London to the coast of Spain. It was his intention to raid a certain fortification; but when he gave his preliminary orders, he found his judgment disputed by his nominal vice admiral, William Borough, who commanded the City of London contingent. Borough represented stockholders and speculators who hoped to profit from the plunder of towns and cities, and raiding a coastal fort did not seem to him to promote the interest of his clients. Drake called a council of war in his flagship, denounced Borough, and had his captains vote to relieve him of command. A captain loyal to Drake boarded Borough's flagship, confined him, and took over his duties.

Borough's officers, however, remained loyal to their old commander. That very night they mutinied, released Borough, and set Drake's captain adrift in a ship's boat. Then they sailed for home, taking the entire City of London contingent with them. At home, Borough pled his case in an admiralty court and was reinstated as vice admiral and commander of the city's ships. Drake's action was repudiated by the queen, probably because she did not want to discourage private citizens and corporations from investing in naval expeditions.[30]

Drake was a little ahead of his time when he tried to discipline Borough by means of a group of captains sitting in judgment of another sea officer. It was not until 1652 that the first Articles of War were issued and a specific court-martial procedure was set up to try offenders. In 1653 a tactical code known as the Fighting Instructions was drawn up with the object of imposing some sort of order in the handling of ships during a general action. The Articles of War and the Fighting Instructions received parliamentary sanction in revised form in 1661 with the passing of the First Naval Discipline Act, a code consisting of thirty-seven articles, twenty-five of which were enforced by the death penalty.[31]

Once the Articles of War had been promulgated, the original statutes were added to and enlarged upon, so that a considerable body of naval rules and regulations grew up over the following century. British naval courts-martial began to take on the character of regular judicial proceedings with clear lines of jurisdiction and sentencing. Certain naval officers, especially the port admirals commanding the main fleet anchorages at Spithead, the Nore, Plymouth, and the Hamoage, found that conducting courts-martial and courts of inquiry was becoming a normal feature of their jobs. They became quite adept at staging tribunals and dispensing naval justice. Some idea of the number of cases they heard can be gotten from the fact that between 1688 and 1815 some two hundred "volumes" and six folios of court-martial proceedings were collected, representing possibly fifteen thousand cases.[32]

Obviously the British Navy, as it evolved towards the highly rational and professional service that characterized the Age of Nelson, was building up a vast store of legal tradition. The Articles of War were subjected to periodical review and substantially revised in 1749 in the interest of achieving greater clarity and brevity. A further revision entitled the *Regulations and Instructions Relating to His Majesty's Service at Sea* appeared in 1772.[33]

This rich body of experience in the field of naval justice proved a godsend to the members of the naval committee of the Continental Congress when they sat down to draw up rules and regulations for the navy of the United Colonies in 1775. As an experienced admiralty lawyer and prominent member of the committee, John Adams was given the job of drafting suitable articles of war for the incipient sea service. Being familiar with British customs and traditions, he noted with approval that the British Articles of War were based on the old Roman code:

There was extant, I observed, one system of Articles of War which had carried two empires to the head of mankind. The Roman and the British; for the Articles of War are only a literal translation of the Roman. It

A French seaman is keelhauled for a serious disciplinary offence. Thanks to the foresight of John Adams, who authored the *Articles of War* of 1775, certain harsh and grisly punishments used by European navies never gained a footing in American practice. (*Heck's Iconographic Encyclopedia*, collection of the Nimitz Library)

would be vain for us to seek our own invention or the records of warlike nations of [sic] a more complete system of military discipline. I was, therefore, for reporting the British Articles of War *totidem verbis*. . . .[34]

In actual fact, Adams somewhat oversimplifies his methodology, and modern scholars disagree on the sources of his Articles of War of 1775. Leo F. S. Horan, an authority on the use of corporal punishment in the navy, maintains that Adams copied fourteen of his articles from the British articles of 1661 and modeled eighteen on the articles of 1772, with "but few" taken from the 1742 version. Harold D. Langley, on the other hand, states that Adams drew mostly on the articles of 1661.[35] Whatever the case may be, there is no denying the overwhelmingly British character of the articles Adams proposed. Reminding his colleagues that times were perilous and "nothing short of Roman and British discipline can save us," he submitted his handiwork to the Continental Congress, where it was debated paragraph by paragraph and adopted virtually unchanged in December 1775. The articles were printed and distributed to all captains and commodores and were to go into effect on 1 January 1776.[36]

The Articles of War that John Adams and the naval committee provided the Continental Navy were chosen for their brevity and furnished only a skeletal framework, which was intended to be fleshed out with rules and regulations in the same way that the Constitution is supplemented by statutory law. It is interesting to note that more than half the rules and regulations adopted by the marine committee after 1 January 1776 concerned the welfare of the common seaman, his diet, duties, rights, and punishments.[37]

In the area of punishment, Adams sought to create a new trend by including in his Articles of War an injunction to Continental officers to try humane methods such as making offenders wear badges and collars. Flogging was prescribed for serious offenses but subjudicial punishments were limited to twelve lashes with a cat-o'-nine-tails and court-martial sentences to one hundred lashes. In this way, Adams hoped to banish from American practice such vicious European naval traditions as keelhauling, inflicting death by flogging, shooting men out of a cannon, and other barbarous practices that characterized the older services.[38]

Although to get his idea across Adams chose the very mild method of prescribing flogging for some punishments by name and suggesting fines, forfeiture of prize money, or confinement in irons as alternatives, the lesson apparently sunk in. The judge advocate general's records contain no instances of keelhauling being inflicted on any American naval seaman and only about twenty instances of flogging 'round the fleet, referred to as "whipping through the squadron." Invariably, when a death sentence was handed down by an American naval court, the method of execution was by hanging for seamen and by shooting for marines. The most commonly used alternative to a death sentence was two or three hundred lashes and dismissal from the service. Some use was also made of prison terms at hard labor for offenders who committed serious crimes, particularly after 1850, when flogging was abolished. Consequently, revolting and barbarous methods of carrying out capital punishment never got a footing in American naval tradition, and deadly punishment came to be used sparingly. Only six seamen are known with certainty to have been hanged in the navy between 1799 and 1861: three *Somers* mutineers, two *Ewing* mutineers, and Samuel Jackson. Twenty other seamen and marines were sentenced to death at various times. Nine were pardoned or had their sentences mitigated, seven were probably executed, and four marines were almost certainly shot for desertion during the War of 1812. (See Table III, Chapter V.)

Apparently Roman and British discipline did not succeed in taming the turbulence and curbing the individuality of the colorful and highly irregular Continental Navy. The aristocratic and anti-republican codes of King Charles II and King George II were grossly out of step with the spirit prevailing in Continental vessels, which were often manned by "townies" drawn from seaboard communities and officered by local favorites. These crews could somehow never emulate the atmosphere of iron discipline and total submission to quarterdeck authority that was implied in the Articles of War. John Paul Jones, for example, had a very difficult time indeed with the sullen, privateering-oriented company of Portsmouth-based seamen who shipped on board his *Ranger*. His tenure as commanding officer of the *Alliance* was even more frustrating and for much the same reason: a close-knit crew resentful of him as an "outsider" whose plans were unpopular and not promising in the area of prize money.[39]

Squadron discipline was even more ragged in the Continental Navy. Commodore Esek Hopkins proved unable to maneuver a task force of five ships well enough to capture the British *Glasgow*. The Penobscot Bay Expedition of 1779 degenerated into a full-blown fiasco. This endeavor, undertaken by a motley collection of Continental men-of-war, state navy ships, and privateers, harked back to the days of Drake and seemed to indicate that the lesson learned in the Borough affair of 1587 had yet to be recognized on this side of the Atlantic. Continental commodores like Hopkins and Dudley Saltonstall, who led the abortive Penobscot Bay expedition, were court-martialed and cashiered;

42

but unity, good order, and discipline were elusive qualities in the American Navy. With the coming of peace in 1783, the service was disbanded completely, and the ships and stores were sold at auction.

Fourteen years later, a new U.S. Navy was in being, organized under the auspices of the Adams administration. Rules, regulations, and articles of war were needed once again, and Adams's receptivity to Roman and British discipline was now supplemented by the aristocratic and anti-democratic ideology of the Federalist party. The Articles of War of 1775 were readopted in 1797, and the navy fought the Quasi-War with France under their stern strictures supplemented by rules and regulations drawn up by the individual commanders of the various ships in commission.

Meanwhile, Congress settled down to the task of choosing a permanent disciplinary charter for the navy. Debates over new regulations pitted the anti-aristocratic and anti-navy Democratic Republicans against a coalition of seaboard Federalists who wanted an authoritarian and aristocratic navy and Southern slaveholders who were anxious to see various forms of corporal punishment given legitimacy through their employment in the armed services.[40]

It seemed to the Federalists and Southerners that Adams's 1775 Articles of War were admirably suited to their ideological purposes and to the task of creating a navy that would be orderly and effective, so they were revived as the articles of 1797 and readopted two years later in 1799. Debate continued on a few points regarding the treatment of officers, particularly Article III. This article specified offenses for which officers could be held accountable, namely oppression, cruelty, fraud, profane swearing, drunkenness, and scandalous conduct. The Federalists wanted to delete the right of commanding officers to impose forfeiture of pay without benefit of a court-martial. This was done, and Article XXX was redrafted to read:

> No commanding officer shall, of his own authority, discharge a commissioned or warrant officer, nor strike him, nor punish him otherwise than by suspension or confinement. . . .

This had the effect, at least theoretically, of making naval officers almost immune to routine discipline and punishable in a serious way only by court-martial.[41]

These changes were compatible with the Federalist effort to create an aristocratic and elitist officer corps for the navy; and, they having been duly incorporated, "An Act for the Better Government of the United States Navy" was passed on 23 April 1800. This act, consisting of Adams's first Articles of War plus the changes desired by the Federalist-controlled Congress has been referred to variously as the Articles of War of 1800, the Act for the Government of the Navy, the Act of 1800, or simply the Articles of War. It is the code that generations of naval men have nicknamed "Rocks and Shoals," and it remained in force with a few modifications until replaced in 1950 by the Uniform Code of Military Justice.

The Articles of War of 1800, supplemented by rules and regulations adopted by statute, passed through periodic reissuings and revisions during the nineteenth century. This body of directives, now grown exceedingly complex and voluminous, has been described in one official publication as having the same relationship to the Articles of War as the Old Testament has to the Ten Commandments.[42]

Long-lived as they were, the Articles were as opposed to the genius and spirit of the Constitution as the British articles were to Anglo-Saxon common law. Consequently, they were the target of periodic attacks by legal scholars and civil libertarians. In the nineteenth century, one of the most sustained attacks was made by Herman Melville. In *White Jacket*, he supplements wide-ranging criticism of the navy with many pages of legal and constitutional argument against the Articles of War. In his novelette, *Billy Budd*, he goes even further and builds an entire plot around a miscarriage of naval justice. In both works he is most eloquent in pointing out how arbitrary and inflexible the articles were, and the ease with which judicial errors could be made under them. He traces the monarchal origins of the codes drawn upon so heavily by John Adams, claiming that they represent a violently royalist response to Cromwellian republicanism on the part of the later Stuarts.[43]

Melville was revolted by the absurdity of causing free-born American citizens to give up basic constitutional rights in order to serve in the navy. He felt that no code so at odds with the fundamentally republican character of the United States could long be sustained in an institution as intimately connected with the federal government as the navy. He wrote in a high state of passion, his sensibilities honed to a fine edge by his own searing experience as a topman in the frigate *United States* on a voyage around Cape Horn in 1842 and 1843. Unfortunately, Melville's perspective may have been a little distorted, for the *United States* was an acknowledged "hell ship" in those years, logging the staggering total of 163 floggings during the years he served in her.[44] His ideas on naval justice were out of step with the spirit of his times. The nineteenth century was preeminently an age that respected the sanctity of persons in authority. Being in a position of authority conferred the right to exercise that authority without much thought about right or wrong as long as the letter of the laws, rules, and ordinances were adhered to. Challenges from below were met head-on, exceptions were seldom allowed, inner motivation and reasons for deviant behavior were ignored, and appearances were to be maintained at all costs. Certainly, the most influential molders of the Old Navy's disciplinary traditions were conventional men of their era. The marine committee of the Continental Congress repeatedly exhorted captains to "Use your people well but preserve strict discipline. . . ."[45]

As the first captain to command a major ship in the Federal Navy, Thomas Truxtun was highly conscious of the fact that he was setting an example for his subordinate officers and establishing precedents that would long be perpetuated in the service. He worked hard to create an atmosphere of total subordination and reflexive obedience because he believed that this was the style of discipline that would yield the best results in battle and that all other considerations were secondary to success in action. He strove to make his ship and crew a perfect instrument of his will, issuing detailed instructions to his officers prescribing their conduct in a variety of situations. No officer was to offer an opinion on the working of the ship unless requested to do so. No officer was to sleep on shore without his permission. Officers must be

> civil and polite to every one and particularly so to strangers, for civility does not interfere with discipline: To obey without hesitation is a maxim always practiced by me to my superiors in every point of duty and the same sort of conduct I expect in return by all officers under my orders.[46]

Officers were further enjoined to avoid becoming too familiar with their men and warned to eschew "that detestable vice, drunkenness. . . ."[47]

Truxtun's austere example made a vivid impression on Lieutenant John Rodgers, who, when he attained his own command, elaborated further on the theme and created the "Rodgers System" of maintaining order, which was copied throughout the service. Seeking to keep crews healthy, under good discipline, and hard at work, the Rodgers System called for an absolute minimum of shore liberty, a constant round of "busy work," and judicious use of corporal punishment.[48] Rodgers himself was a popular commander who found it necessary to flog his men only in unusual circumstances. When he commanded the Mediterranean Squadron, 1825–1828, only thirteen floggings were logged in his flagship *North Carolina* in two years.[49] Since the *North Carolina* was a ship of the line with almost a thousand men on board, this record is impressive. Frigates and sloops of war with half as many men often saw a half-dozen floggings in a single week.[50]

Rodgers's achievement on board the *North Carolina* is remarkable also because he was sent out to command the Mediterranean Squadron at a time when discipline on that station was thought to have deteriorated badly. Rodgers, the navy's unofficial leading authority and troubleshooter in matters of discipline, traced the roots of this problem to the general depravity prevailing at Port Mahon, Minorca, the fleet's main operating base.[51] Although he straightened out the ships, the job of cleaning out a decadent southern European seaport exceeded both his talents and his authority. Port Mahon continued to contribute its share of scandal and indiscipline to the fleet for decades.

Of all the early commodores of the Federal Navy, Edward Preble probably took the most individualistic approach to questions of discipline and the administration of naval justice. Since he was by temperament not much of a theoretician, his disciplinary methods were eminently practical. He subscribed generally to Truxtun's dour view that the company of a typical man-of-war was

> a crew of abandoned miscreants, ripe for any mischief or villainy. . . .
> equally destitute of gratitude, shame or justice, and only deterred from the
> commission of any crimes by the terror of severe punishment. . . . the
> pernicious example of a few of the vilest in a ship of war is too often apt
> to poison the principles of the greatest number, especially if the reins of
> discipline are too much relaxed, so as to foster that idleness and dissipation
> which engender sloth, diseases, and an utter profligacy of manners.[52]

Preble was particularly concerned with the question of how best to deal with the relatively few "bad characters" who were to be found in any ship's company. Most sailors were inclined to good behavior, Preble believed; but there was always that hard core of dedicated troublemakers and a somewhat larger group who were ready to engage in mischief if it might go unpunished but who could control themselves in the presence of officers who were determined to keep order. If they sensed any weakness or lack of resolution on the part of their superiors, however, this latter group would become unruly; and that was what made the difference between an orderly ship and a disorderly one. Preble relied on strict but fair discipline to keep these forces within bounds.[53] It is remarkable that this tripartite division of a typical crew into orderly seamen, known miscreants, and opportunists is very close to the social theories of the modern criminologist, James Q. Wilson.

Preble harbored a deep disliking for formal courts-martial and courts of inquiry. In his opinion, too many of them grew out of trivial arguments or dealt with dull and often repeated offenses. What was even worse, formal judicial machinery, with its rules of evidence and opportunity to stage a confrontation between accused and accuser, gave a defendant an altogether too favorable chance of either acquittal or having his sentence mitigated. By keeping as many cases as possible on the subjudicial level, Preble was able to deal with them in his own way without wasting the time and efforts of the officers of his squadron. It is interesting to note that during the years of Preble's Barbary campaign in the Mediterranean, there were very few naval courts of any kind, and the few that were held were virtually unavoidable.

Like the Federalists in Congress, Preble believed in different treatment for officers and enlisted men. He also believed in distinguishing between promising officers and unsuitable ones. He dealt privately with all cases involving officers and took two distinct lines of procedure. If an officer was capable and showed promise, he would counsel him, reprimand him, or confine him to quarters while exhorting him to think over his misdeeds. If, on the other hand, the miscreant was a troublesome officer of little apparent potential, he preferred to pressure him for a resignation, using as a goad the threat of court-martial.[54] A resignation got rid of a bad officer once and for all and better served the interests of the navy than did a court-martial and lighter sentence.

A good example of Preble's arbitrary treatment of officers was the case of Midshipman Thomas Baldwin. While on shore leave in Gibraltar, Baldwin shoplifted a sword knot and, when confronted by a fellow midshipman, drew his sword to threaten his accuser. Preble had had trouble with Baldwin throughout the cruise, and he took this opportunity to persuade him to hand over his warrant and go home. In a letter to the secretary of the navy, he claimed that he merely wanted to save the young man's family from the disgrace of formal proceedings; but most likely he took that course because, had Baldwin faced a court-martial, he would have been given some lighter sentence and would have remained in the service.[55]

In the matter of disciplining enlisted men, Preble's methods were even more arbitrary and uncompromising. Most of their offenses were predictable, an endless litany of drunkenness, disobedience, insubordination, and desertion hardly worthy of the attention of a panel of otherwise busy officers. Knowing full well the regulation against administering more than twelve lashes without formal proceedings, Preble hit upon the device of breaking down every major offense into several subjudicial charges. Then he held a deck court, or captain's mast, and awarded twelve lashes for each offense. When a seaman named Thomas Ayscough, a notorious lower-deck troublemaker, got drunk aboard the frigate *Constitution*, Preble charged him with four offenses growing out of his one binge: drunkenness, embezzlement (of the liquor), disobedience, and neglect of duty. Ayscough got 48 lashes, 12 for each charge. A week later he fed poison to the *Constitution*'s complement of sheep, which were kept to provide fresh meat for the wardroom, and attempted to desert. Preble extracted enough charges here to administer 136 lashes, still without going to the trouble of convening a court-martial. In this way, he contrived to administer almost 200 lashes to one man in several installments without submitting his actions to any sort of review by higher authority.[56]

Preble also staged a flogging 'round the fleet without benefit of court-martial. Seaman John Graves received 300 lashes for desertion by being "whipped through the fleet" while the *Constitution* was blockading Tunis in 1804. In addition to being against the rules laid down in the Articles of War, Graves's punishment was tantamount to a death sentence, but once again no formal proceeding was held.[57]

Another way that Preble evaded the limitations specified on lashes to be administered was by combining modes of punishment. When Marine George Crutch stole a watch while on post and then threw it overboard to escape detection, he was awarded 48 lashes and four months in irons, one of the severest sentences Preble ever meted out. Crutch was, of course, another hard case who was frequently in trouble. He was subsequently court-martialed for sodomy while serving under another captain but was acquitted.[58]

Preble never committed his disciplinary methods to paper, but the men who served under him in the Mediterranean, "Preble's Boys" as they came to be called, apparently took his example to heart and perpetuated them, establishing another disciplinary tradition in the navy. As late as 1850, Melville was explaining the system of redundant charging pioneered by Preble and exposing its illegality and arbitrariness to the readers of *White Jacket*. Preble was, in fact, the very model of "irresponsibility in a judge, unlimited discretionary [latitude] in an executive, and the union of an irresponsible judge and an unlimited executive in one person" that Melville abhorred.[59]

Illegal as Preble's methods were, they were undertaken for the good of the service rather than out of a taste for sadistic vengeance or heavy punishment. He got away with it because his victims were not sympathetic characters and because Congress and the Navy Department were willing in those early days to give commodores on distant stations a fairly free hand. Great care was taken in selecting high-ranking officers for the navy, and there seemed to be a general attitude that the selection process was the best insurance against gross or pointless misuse of authority. This attitude was apparently justified. Few officers pushed things as far as Preble did; but even so, the disciplinary traditions of the navy came to rely perhaps a little too heavily on informal procedures not subject to review.

And so the navy's disciplinary tradition came to be formed of a mixture of highly compatible and complementary impulses. Federalist conservatism and elitist thinking combined with the desire of Thomas Truxtun to live down the motley and disorderly reputation of the Continental Navy, and that further dovetailed with John Rodgers's desire to get the most out of his crews and Edward Preble's hankering for a free hand to deal with obvious troublemakers. These were the unspoken and sometimes misunderstood strictures which along with the Articles of War and the formal rules and regulations made up the navy's disciplinary tradition.

Chapter III

Rocks & Shoals

A careful survey of the origins of the Old Navy's code of discipline makes it clear that it depended on custom and tradition at least as much as it did on statutory law. Indeed, as late as 1945 official naval publications were claiming that customs and tradition were fully as legal and binding as written ordinances.[1] The evolution of the formal mechanisms of naval justice is of major importance, in spite of the strong role of unwritten traditions and derivative Articles of War, because the disciplinary philosophy of today's Navy is, in the main, at odds with that of the pre-Civil War fleet. The disciplinary system in force now, the Uniform Code of Military Justice, relies almost entirely on legal and procedural forms tailored largely to meet the legal requirements of the U.S. Constitution. It was put into effect rather abruptly in 1950, but its antecedents extend back to the first half of the nineteenth century.

For the adjudication of disciplinary cases, the Old Navy relied on three basic tribunals: the general court-martial, the court of inquiry, and the summary court-martial. Minor infractions of discipline were handled at captain's mast, which was informal and often exceedingly brief, and so does not quality as a tribunal.

A general court-martial was composed of from five to thirteen commissioned officers and could be ordered into existence by the president of the United States, the secretary of the navy, the commander of a fleet or squadron, or the captain of a ship. It could try cases involving all grades of naval personnel and all marine officers and enlisted men serving at sea. Its jurisdiction also extended over the officers and men of privateers, several of whom were tried by court-martial during the War of 1812, and midshipmen attending the Naval Academy after its founding in 1845. Cases dealt with by courts-martial were those involving officers accused of offenses that were too serious to be disposed of by suspension from duty or confinement to quarters under the terms of Article XXX of the Articles of War. Enlisted men whose offenses were too grave to be disposed of by a flogging of twelve lashes or its equivalent were also subject to these tribunals.

Courts-martial were grave affairs, conducted with solemnity and ceremony. When one was in progress, a special flag was flown and a gun was fired at the commencement of each day's proceedings. All evidence was submitted or given under oath, and a transcript was made of all proceedings carried out in open court. Accused persons could represent themselves or be represented by an officer of their choice or a civilian lawyer. The navy was represented by the prosecutor, a judge advocate. Judge advocates were regular line officers or civilian lawyers appointed on a case-by-case basis by the secretary of the navy or the commander of a ship or squadron. Every court-martial had a president, whose role was analogous to that of a judge in a civilian court. He regulated the proceedings, ruled on motions, and presided over the deliberations of the other members of the court-martial board. The role of the judge advocate general, with jurisdiction over all naval courts, was the exclusive prerogative of the secretary of the navy except for a brief period from 1865 to 1870, when the press of legal business was so great that a permanent judge advocate general was appointed at the request of Lincoln's secretary of the navy, Gideon Welles.[2]

Every court-martial consisted of two phases. The first phase, during which all opening statements, testimony, cross examination, and summations were heard, was public; the proceedings could be reported in the newspapers and transcripts of them could be published. The second phase began when the members of the court-martial board retired to discuss the case among themselves, arrive at a verdict, and set a sentence. Complete secrecy was the rule at this stage; each member of the board was sworn to silence with regard to its deliberations, the attitudes of the other members, and the identity of those casting votes to acquit or convict. Guilt or innocence was decided by simple majority vote, except in cases where the sentence was either death or dismissal from the service. In those cases, a two-thirds majority was needed to convict. Court-martial boards also had the power to issue contempt citations and award punishment to any person in the navy so cited.

In some ways courts-martial were less formal than civilian proceedings. The accused had the right to object to members of the court and have them removed if he believed they were prejudiced against him. Witnesses and prosecutors could be questioned directly by the judge advocate, the accused person, his counsel, the president of the court, or any duly sworn member of the court-martial board. To assist the officers conducting naval courts-martial, there were directives and procedures spelled out in the Articles of War and the *Naval Regulations*.

In addition, several privately published manuals on court-martial procedure, some of them British, were available. These included Simmons's *Practice*, Macomb's *Practice of Courts Martial*, De Hart's *Military Courts Martial*, and Hough's *Military Courts*.[3] These treatises regulated the conduct of individuals in military tribunals, spelled out the duties and prerogatives of the various court functionaries, established rules of precedence and evidence, and cited guidelines and past rulings for the resolving of in-court disputes and any unusual circumstances that might arise.

All court-martial records and verdicts were reviewed by the secretary of the navy, and his approval had to be secured before a sentence could be carried out, unless the tribunal had been conducted on a foreign station. All death sentences were reviewed by the president, who could, if he so desired, examine other cases as well. Both the president and the secretary of the navy had the power to overrule a guilty verdict, and they had the power to mitigate or set aside punishment, which they often did, especially in cases of severe sentences.

The reviewing process was different in cases involving ships and squadrons on foreign stations. In these instances, the ship's captain or the station commander reviewed the proceedings of the court and either mitigated or carried out the punishments. He did this on his own authority, subject only to a general review of his actions at the end of his cruise or commission. Captains and commodores who were careless or unduly severe in the awarding of punishments abroad were occasionally court-martialed themselves on charges of cruelty, oppression, or inflicting illegal punishment brought by their subordinate officers.

It should be noted here that there is considerable evidence to indicate that courts-martial were much more common in the Old Navy than they are today in relation to the relative size of the service then and now. Courts-martial of enlisted men have changed little over the decades, except that perhaps, before the Civil War, sailors and marines were more often acquitted and the sentences of those found guilty were more likely to be mitigated. Officers found themselves intimately involved with the naval justice system throughout their service lives. The officer corps was small, and the requirements of naval tribunals took up a good deal of its time and energy. It was a rare officer who did not have, at intervals throughout his career, to appear before naval courts as a witness, serve on a court-martial or court of inquiry, and occasionally defend his own actions before a tribunal of his brother officers. In those days courts-martial did not, however, carry quite the same stigma or exert quite the same penalty on an officer's career as they do today. Acquittals were common, sentences for those found guilty were often mitigated or overturned; and since promotion was primarily by seniority, an officer with an adverse court-martial verdict in his record could still count on advancement.

An extreme example of this state of affairs is to be found in the career of Uriah P. Levy. In the course of a service life that spanned almost a half-century, from 1812 to 1861, he was court-martialed no less than seven times on charges that included scandalous, ungentlemanly, or unofficerlike conduct, forgery and falsification, loss of a vessel under his command, contempt of his superior officer, cowardice, disobedience of orders, and provoking and reproachful words, gestures, and menaces. He was never fully acquitted, often reprimanded, and occasionally sentenced to be cashiered. He never left the service, however, and eventually flew his broad pennant as commodore of the Mediterranean Squadron before dying in harness, as head of the Court Martial Board, full of years and very near the top of the navy list.[4]

Admittedly, as the Old Navy's only known Jewish officer, Levy probably owed most of his legal difficulties to the anti-Semitism of his brother officers. Still, by modern standards it is remarkable that he continued to advance through the ranks and attain an important command while trailing such a long train of legal controversy. It was not at all uncommon for officers with less flamboyant proclivities to have been court-martialed two or three times before death or retirement put an end to advancement.

Enlisted men had a good deal less reason and opportunity to cling stubbornly to their naval careers in the face of continual legal difficulties, but even they could and did do so. Perhaps the most notorious offender in this category was Marine George Crutch, who surfaced as one of Commodore Preble's chronic troublemakers in the *Constitution*. Besides the numerous subjudicial punishments heaped upon him by Preble and others, Crutch stood trial four times during a service career that lasted at least seven years. Except for one occasion when he was found innocent of a sodomy charge, he was invariably convicted and suffered heavy punishments, usually fifty lashes or more; yet he was not compelled to leave the service.[5]

Somewhat less formal than a general court-martial was the court of inquiry. A court of inquiry was a fact-finding body appointed by the president, secretary of the navy, commander of a squadron, or captain of a ship. Consisting of three commissioned officers and a judge advocate, it could be used to investigate any question or event where some indication of individual wrongdoing or neglect of duty was evident. It could summon witnesses, administer oaths, and record testimony on the same basis as a court-martial, but it was limited to ascertaining matters of fact. It could forward an opinion but could not decide questions of guilt or innocence nor could it pass sentences or award punishments, except in cases where the charge was contempt.

A court of inquiry was not a substitute for a court-martial, although its deliberations might well result in court-martial action being undertaken by the Navy Department. When this happened, the officers who made up the court of inquiry board could not serve on the court-martial board, although they might appear as witnesses or offer statements before the court. The findings of courts of inquiry were submitted to the secretary of the navy or other convening authority who could act on them or ignore them at will. A record of court-of-inquiry proceedings was submitted to the department, and its contents could be kept secret or made available to the public at the discretion of the secretary of the navy.

A naval court tries a sailor on the quarterdeck. We can assume that this is a routine proceeding for some relatively common offence. The court consists of the minimum number of officers specified by the regulations, and members of the ship's crew have been permitted to look on. Often several men were tried at one sitting. When its business was completed the court adjourned *sine die*, that is, not to meet again. (*Heck's Iconographic Encyclopedia*, collection of the Nimitz Library)

Captain's mast was the navy's most common disciplinary proceeding. All minor infractions of discipline on the part of enlisted men were adjudicated by this device, which was also sometimes referred to as a deck court. Several captain's masts were held each week on board every ship in commission. Charges were brought by a commissioned or warrant officer. The captain heard the case whenever it was convenient and, on the spot, made his decision as to guilt or innocence, mode of punishment, and possible mitigation. No transcript of the proceedings was kept, but the charge and sentence were entered in the ship's log. Since most of the punishments awarded were physical, a surgeon had to examine the offender and certify whether he could withstand the execution of his sentence without suffering death or permanent injury.

Sentences at captain's mast depended heavily on the practice of flogging, which was abolished in the navy by an act of Congress in 1850. Unfortunately, Congress did not provide any alternative to the six to twelve lashes usually imposed for routine transgressions. Naval officers tried to devise alternatives of their own, but none seemed to have the deterrent effect of flogging, except those penalties that could be imposed only by a general court-martial. Since it was manifestly impossible to court-martial every routine offender, the gap that appeared in the naval justice system threatened for a time to destroy naval discipline completely.[6] Faced with this alarming prospect, Congress in 1855 created the summary court-martial, a tribunal more elaborate than captain's mast but less significant than a general court-martial.

A summary court-martial could be convened by the commander of any ship or shore station to consider cases involving petty officers or enlisted men. It consisted of three officers, not below the rank of passed midshipman, and a competent recorder, who need not be an officer, to act as judge advocate. The atmosphere of the tribunal was less formal than that of a general court-martial, but evidence was transcribed and a record of the proceedings had to be sent to the Navy Department. Punishments awarded by the Summary Court-Martial Board were designed to be the equivalent of a severe flogging and included bad-conduct discharges (not to be awarded on a foreign station), solitary confinement in single or double irons on bread and water or diminished rations, ordinary confinement for up to two months, loss of rank, pay, or liberties, and extra police duties. Summary-court proceedings were reviewed by the commanding officer before any sentence was put in effect, and a medical officer was required to certify that no permanent injury to the prisoner's health was likely to result from prolonged confinement on a restricted diet.

This brief summary of the principal naval tribunals shows that the Old Navy had a justice system that was simple and incomplete rather than complex and well developed. As with any system whose written guidelines are sketchy and inadequate, the actual workings of the system took on a Byzantine quality of convolutedness that reflected confused and contradictory forces at work both within and without the navy. To begin with, the responsibility for manning naval tribunals rested entirely on one segment of the navy's population, the regular officer corps. Even during the Civil War, when the volume of cases to be heard rose dramatically, all requests to let volunteer officers serve on court-martial and court-of-inquiry boards were firmly resisted, in spite of the fact that militia officers in the army had the right to do so.[7] There were even some extreme traditionalists in the navy who maintained that staff officers should not sit on disciplinary boards because they were not "fighting" officers.[8]

The quality of the justice that was rendered by naval courts sadly reflected the narrowness of the personnel pool from which the members of court-martial boards were drawn. This can be seen most clearly in cases involving the senior officers of the navy, who constituted a significant disciplinary problem for the Navy Department because of their marked tendency towards insubordination to the secretaries of the navy.[9] Senior officers were somewhat remiss in their observance of Article III of the Articles of War, which forbade "oppression, cruelty, fraud, profane swearing, drunkenness, or any other scandalous conduct," and Article XIV, which provided that "no person in the Navy shall quarrel with any other person in the Navy, nor use provoking or reproachful words, gestures, or menaces. . . ." Ship commanders also habitually violated and allowed subordinates to violate the articles that limited the circumstances under which flogging could be administered and the instruments that it was permissible to use for flogging.[10]

Indeed, this last problem became so prevalent that Secretary James K. Paulding was obliged to issue a Naval General Order which read in part:

> The President of the United States, believing that greater formality in the infliction of such corporal punishments as are authorized by Law may be adopted in the Navy with beneficial consequences, directs that no such punishment shall be inflicted on any person in the service without sentence of a Court Martial, when that is required by Law, or the written order of the Captain or Commanding Officer of the vessel, or Commandant of the Navy Yard to which he is attached, where the authority to cause it to be inflicted rests in the discretion of the Commanding Officer specifying the offence or offences and the extent of the punishment to be inflicted, which

order shall be read and punishment inflicted in presence of the Officers and Seamen belonging to the Vessel or Navy Yard.

And such orders for punishment shall be entered on the Log Book and a quarterly return made to the Secretary of the Navy, stating the names of the persons punished, their offences and the extent of the punishment inflicted, together with such explanations or remarks as the Commanding Officer shall deem necessary to a proper understanding of the case.[11]

Sometimes captains and commodores got into difficulties for such offences as overstepping their authority or taking illegal or unauthorized action while engaged in diplomatic missions, misuse of funds allocated to them for the manning or provisioning of their ships or squadrons, and for timidity, lack of resolution, or overboldness in carrying out the orders of the Department. When brought before courts-martial or courts of inquiry, these men proved remarkably hard to convict or saddle with meaningful punishment. Their peers in rank were reluctant to set precedents which would curb command initiative, and junior officers could ill afford the risk of offending a senior who, even if convicted of wrongdoing, would in all probability remain in the navy and could be counted on to make life miserable for any junior who participated in a court that returned an adverse verdict.

Even when a verdict of guilty was returned, the sentence meted out was likely to be meaningless. The most stringent punishment usually called for five years' suspension from duty with or without some loss of pay. Often the sentence merely read "to be admonished by the Secretary of the Navy" or "to be reprimanded by the President." Since nearly every senior naval officer cultivated political contacts or at least could rely on the congressional delegation of his home state to back him, political pressure was quickly mustered to set aside either convictions or sentences. One commodore who had been found guilty of official falsehood under the most aggravating circumstances was deprived of his command and suspended for three years. He employed his political influence to such effect that an incoming administration relieved him of his suspension, gave him all of his back pay, and placed him back in command of his squadron "as a reward for his outraged feelings."[12]

No mention is made as to just who this officer was, but it might well have been Commodore Thomas ap Catesby Jones. He was court-martialed for his premature "invasion" of California in 1842 and his subsequent efforts to avoid relinquishing command of the Pacific Squadron by eluding his relief for many months. Commodore Jones returned to the Pacific Squadron in 1848, but his tenure in command was once again concluded by a court-martial. This time the principal charge was his use of navy funds to speculate on the San Francisco gold market during the Gold Rush of 1849. Suspended from duty for five years in 1850, the "Contentious Commodore" tried for another reversal with limited success. He was restored to the active list in 1853 and died soon afterwards.[13] In less dramatic cases, admonitions and reprimands were simply set aside by the Department or delivered in the painless form of a private conversation.

The more junior line and warrant officers and staff were in a less advantageous situation. As Lieutenant Matthew Fontaine Maury put it:

> The laws of the Navy are kept in two vials—one of which is closely sealed, and seldom permitted to be opened—the other, large mouthed and convenient, ready at all times with its wrath to be emptied on the younger and therefore weaker & more frail members of the Corps.[14]

Captains and commodores may not have been overly scrupulous about observing the letter of the Articles of War and *Naval Regulations* themselves, but they enforced them to the hilt on their subordinates. Junior officers were charged with a wide variety of offenses ranging from drunkenness and insubordination to vague, catch-all charges like conduct unbecoming a gentleman or scandalous conduct tending to the destruction of good morals, which could be just about anything objectional to a superior. Naval courts trying junior officers were naturally much less afraid of convicting them, and sentencing was more severe. The most common penalties involved suspensions from duty with loss of pay or emoluments for various periods up to five years or dismissal from the service. Junior officers who were suspended often resigned from the navy, especially midshipmen who were young enough to start over again in some other profession.

Junior officers were not without resources of their own when it came to setting aside sentences or mitigating punishments. Virtually all naval officers gained their appointments through congressional political patronage. A penalized or dismissed midshipman or lieutenant had only to petition his mentor or some other member of his state's congressional delegation to rally a faction to see him "done right." Pressure could be applied at the very highest levels, reaching through the congressional naval committees to the secretary of the navy or the president. Court-martial verdicts could be overturned, not approved, set aside, or not implemented, and, on some occasions, a new administration could be persuaded to undo a decision reached by a previous one.

That such affairs were common almost to the point of being routine is illustrated by the case of Passed Midshipman John McIntosh Kell. Kell was court-martialed with three other passed midshipmen for their disobedience of orders of the first lieutenant of their ship during a dispute over the proper duties of a passed midshipman with regard to menial chores. A court-martial found the four guilty and sentenced them to be dismissed from the navy. Returning to his home in Georgia, Kell took his case to Thomas Spalding, a prominent state politician and close kinsman. Spalding, in turn, sent him to Washington with a letter of introduction addressed to Senator John MacPhearson Berrien which said, in part, "I ask you to read the evidences given on these young gentlemen, and if they have been wronged, and if a remedy is within reach, you will best know after such examination." Berrien waited a few months for a change of administrations to bring a fellow Southerner, William A. Graham, to the Navy Department and then petitioned for a review of the case. The court martial's verdict was set aside in time to allow Kell, who had made arrangements in anticipation of the result, to join the company of the steam frigate *Susquehanna* for an expedition to the Orient. In this manner, he and his three companions were back in uniform within less than a year of being cashiered.[15]

That Congress was able to play such a direct and forceful role in the workings of the Naval Justice System was due in part to the smallness and close-grained nature of the federal government in the nineteenth century and because congressmen and naval officers were drawn largely from the same stratum of society. Precedents for congressional interference also existed from the time of the Continental Congress, when the Marine Committee itself conducted many of the Revolutionary Navy's courts-martial and verdicts were voted on by the entire body. Even though the Federal Constitution had taken away some of the authority that the legislative branch had previously enjoyed over routine military operations, Congress still exercised the powers of the purse and controlled most officer appointments, and these prerogatives allowed it to continue to exercise a historical interest in monitoring naval discipline.

The effect of congressional meddling in matters of naval discipline was, predictably, a bad one. Subordination, morale, and discipline among the officers suffered, and abuses multiplied as the opportunistic members of the corps took advantage of the gaps that existed between the inflexible and uncompromising Articles of War and the backstairs maneuvering of Congress. Perhaps the reason why such a chaotic state of affairs existed was because of the ancient and foreign origins of the naval justice system. Nobody really expected a system so arbitrary and unyielding to render justice as freeborn Americans understood it; but rather than overhaul it and make it more compatible with our institutions, it simply became the custom to undermine the system from above, introducing an element of humanity and flexibility more compatible with the American temperament at the cost of orderly procedures and predictable results.

For enlisted men, an entirely different set of assumptions governed the naval justice system. The common sailors of the Old Navy were representative of the lower orders of society in a day and age when class differences were much more pronounced. Since the earliest days of the British sea service, the officer corps had regarded the foremast hands as the dregs of society and worse—as criminals, cutthroats, and potential mutineers.[16] American naval officers were no different; in fact, lines were even more sharply drawn in the ships and squadrons of republican America. The American enlisted man had no entrée into the society of congressmen and bureaucrats. There was no prominent personage to manage his appointment or keep a friendly eye on his naval career. When he was brought before the bar of naval justice, his crimes and offenses were often different in nature from those of the officers and not often conducive to eliciting sympathy. Punishments meted out to enlisted men were not publicized, usually took place out of the public eye, and were administered so quickly that any campaign on the part of a sailor to secure "vindication" or a reversal of a verdict was pointless. It was in dealing with the enlisted men on the subjudicial level that the naval justice system actually displayed the uncompromising and arbitrary character of the Roman-British codes.

There were, however, factors at work which tended to mitigate the harshness of naval discipline even for the lowly sailor. Melville wrongly believed that no American seaman was ever flogged 'round the fleet in an American port because naval officers feared that such a spectacle would infuriate the civilian populace and cause a riot.[17] Likewise, in 1800 at Norfolk, when a court-martial on board the frigate *Congress* convicted several seamen of mutiny and sentenced two of them to be hanged, Commodore Thomas Truxtun mitigated the punishments to one hundred lashes and dismissal from the service in order to spare the civilian population the sight of American seamen dangling from the yardarms of a public vessel.[18] Nearly all death sentences conferred by naval courts-martial involved enlisted men, but most of them were commuted by the President to prison terms at hard labor. In the three certain instances where American seamen were executed by the Navy, two occurred on stations so remote from Washington that presidential intervention was impractical, and one case, the hanging of the *Somers* mutineers, involved the execution of three men at sea by a captain who had become convinced that he had to act to save his ship. Obviously, the force of public opinion was something that the naval justice system had to take into account in its treatment of enlisted men.

The political system also contained persons who were interested in humanizing American naval justice. By the decade of the 1840s, the United States contained reform movements dedicated to a variety of causes ranging from the treatment of prisoners and inmates of insane asylums to the abolition of slavery. The drive to improve the condition of the Navy's enlisted men became part of this movement and spawned, among other things, a powerful movement to abolish flogging as a means of punishment.

In many ways flogging was a natural target for reformers. It was common in almost all American men-of-war, a cruel and revolting thing to witness, and it invariably resulted in at least the temporary disabling of any person undergoing it. In addition, the practice seemed repugnant to America's republican ideology and democratic notions of the dignity of the individual. Civilian government officials taking passage in navy ships became incensed at the continual round of floggings they witnessed,[19] and occasionally an eloquent denunciation or a particularly graphic description of the practice was penned by an articulate sailor and gained wide circulation among the reading public.[20]

By 1850, the movement to abolish flogging in the navy had achieved the status of a *cause celebre*, pitting congressional and humanitarian reformers against the officer corps and their allies in conservative political circles. The reformers eventually scored a victory, and the abolition of flogging became the greatest single change to occur in the navy's treatment of enlisted men until the twentieth century.[21]

Other attempts to reform the navy's justice system were far less successful in the decades prior to the Civil War and centered mostly on the *Naval Regulations*, a body of written articles which supplemented the Articles of War and regulated such routine practices as the issuing of food and liquor rations, the duties of officers and petty officers, the outfitting of ships, and other aspects of service life.

The first set of regulations put into force in the Federal Navy were issued by President Adams in 1798 and bore the title *Marine Rules and Regulations*. This compendium included 116 articles and was supplemented by sets of internal regulations composed and enforced by individual commanding officers. In 1801, President Jefferson's Secretary of the Navy, Robert Smith, recommended that a new set of regulations be drafted. These rules were composed by the Department and circulated among those of the navy's senior captains who were then residing ashore or stationed in home waters. John Barry, Thomas

Truxtun, Richard Morris, and Alexander Murray reviewed the proposals in turn and added their comments and additions. The resulting document was printed and issued to the fleet under the title of *Naval Regulations 1802*.

By 1815 the *Naval Regulations*, which now consisted of 194 articles and had come to be known colloquially as the Black Book, were widely recognized to be in need of revision. They included numerous British codes originally copied by Adams, acts of the long defunct Continental Congress, and additions inserted by the legislative and executive Branches after 1798. Many of them were loosely worded and prolix enough to cause endless confusion.[22] For example, article 10 in the section entitled "Of the Duties of a Captain or Commander" reads as follows:

> 10. As, from the beginning of the campaign, the plan of combat ought to be formed, he shall have his directions given, and his people so placed, as not to be unprovided against any accident which may happen.

The first Board of Naval Commissioners, consisting of Commodores John Rodgers, David Porter, and Stephen Decatur, spent much of its time revising and clarifying these rules; and their work was circulated to the Navy in 1818 in the form of a new set of rules and regulations known as the Blue Book. The result was less than satisfactory. The old regulations, whatever their faults, had been legally approved by Congress and thus had the force of law behind them. The Blue Book, not having congressional approval, was technically illegal in any instance where its provisions contradicted those of the Black Book, so the Navy Department was obliged to follow the Blue Book into circulation with a general order annulling large parts of it because they set aside acts of Congress which had never been repealed.[23]

In 1832 a second attempt was made to reform the regulations, which now consisted of the Blue Book and its modifying circular and portions of the Black Book. A board of senior captains was constituted and produced the Red Book, the contents of which set off a storm of controversy in the navy because the board neglected to provide any limits on the power of prerogatives of commodores and senior captains. The protests of younger captains and junior officers were so vigorous that the Red Book was never fully adopted, leaving the Navy with a confused and almost unworkable tangle of contradictory documents that were its rules and regulations.[24]

With no set of practical rules in force, the various secretaries of the navy took to governing the service by circulars and general orders, "edicts," in the words of Samuel Francis Du Pont, "couched in language unheard of before in official papers addressed to officers and gentlemen."[25] This system of administration further exacerbated an already unhappy situation. A sample of the directives Du Pont was complaining about is among the papers of Isaac Hull. It read:

Navy Department

Sir,
28 October 1840

The Department has been informed that a Private in the Marine Guard on board the U. S. Sloop of War *Cyane* in the Mediterranean was punished with unusual severity for being found asleep on his post at a time when the guard was called upon to perform extremely severe duty.

You will be pleased to furnish the Department with an explanation of the circumstances of this case, and also to report the fact in regard to the duty which has been imposed on the Guard.

I am respectfully yours
J. K. Paulding[26]

These harassments did little to improve the morale of the navy.

Their effect was menacing to true discipline and they were the fruitful sources of heartburnings and reckless despondency . . . it is believed to be a fact susceptible to proof, that in the same squadron, some of them, [i.e., the Departmental circulars] directing important changes, either in the actual construction of the law regulating punishments, or perhaps in the amount of percentage allowed upon issues to the crew, would be in force on one vessel and not on another.[27]

Secretary Paulding made an attempt to rectify this state of affairs in 1840 or 1841. He had an entirely new set of rules and regulations, consisting of nearly eight hundred articles, drawn up and circulated. This document was not the work of an official naval board. In fact, the officers of the navy were mystified as to just exactly who had authored them, but repeated inquiries about them addressed to the Department went unanswered.[28] No congressional approval was ever sought for Paulding's rules, but some of them, presumably those which did not contradict previous legislation, were put into effect in the service.

There was the usual unhappy result. Some of the new rules were useful, but the document as a whole was of uneven quality. Official conduct was overregulated in trivial matters while larger issues were left too much to the discretion of the commanding officers of ships and squadrons. Many of the eight hundred articles dealt with the establishing of different grades of admirals, the punctilio of proposed gun salutes for the projected admirals, and other rules relating to flag officers. Other articles outlined economy measures, the reduction of officer complements on warships, and prohibitions against unnecessary expenditures of powder and shot, presumably during gun drills. Writing approximately a year after the appearance of Paulding's rules, Samuel Francis Du Pont summed up their impact on the navy with the laconic phrase "heartburnings remain & discipline suffers."[29] The entirely to the stupidity of various secretaries of the navy nor was it set of rules and regulations, until the Civil War.

The chaotic condition of the rules and regulations was not due entirely to the stupidity of various secretaries of the navy nor was it attributable entirely to a lack of managerial skills on the part of the officer corps. It was symptomatic of a much deeper problem which was manifested in Congress and rooted in the nation at large. In all truth, there was no consensus in America on the subject of naval discipline. Southerners and Federalists had framed the Articles of War and the navy's first regulations in order to fulfill ideological needs of their own. During the decades after 1815, the North, having shed Federalism, began to move towards a more liberal and egalitarian view of society and towards more enlightened methods of social control. As the sectional and ideological dispute between the North and the South grew deeper and more heated, the question of naval discipline and its reform became a small part of the larger struggle. The Southerners perceived that a liberalization or humanization of naval discipline would give aid and comfort to those forces which opposed the flogging of slaves and the draconian treatment meted out to runaway bondsmen. Northerners felt that if they could liberalize military discipline, it would have the effect of leaving the Southern slaveholders standing in embarrassed isolation as the last remaining practitioners of flogging and arbitrary justice in general.

For these reasons, Southerners and Northerners fought each other to a standstill on the issues of naval disciplinary reform that came before Congress; and with the exception of one major victory for the reformers, the abolition of flogging, nothing could be done to straighten out the navy's system of justice in any comprehensive way. The cause of reform was not helped by the fact that most of the navy's officers categorically opposed any liberalization of the treatment of enlisted men, and some were secretly quite satisfied with the confused and inefficient system of officer discipline which seemed unable to weed out incompetents or bring the discomforts of firm retribution to wrongdoers.

In the decade of the 1850s, reformers from within the navy tried a new tack. In 1855, Commander Samuel Francis Du Pont wrote an informal report for Secretary of the Navy John Dobbin, stressing the need for a sweeping reorganization of the entire Navy Department. Among the many reasons he cited for undertaking such an effort was

> the Discipline of the Navy and the condition of the seamen; and the organization of the Navy Department itself, which requires the Secretary to attend to certain minute details of office—him moreover without the aid of a permanent Judge Advocate & an officer whose duty would correspond with that of the Adjutant General of the Army—both considered as important factors in the organization of the War Dept.[30]

Du Pont never did get a chance to witness the reorganization he spoke of, but his memo apparently struck a responsive chord in the Navy Department. Both Secretary Dobbin and President Pierce were determined to do something about the navy and, in particular, about its unruly officers. Consequently, Du Pont soon found himself, together with fourteen other officers chosen for their interest in naval reform, appointed to the newly created Naval Efficiency Board. The "Plucking Board," as it soon came to be called, had been created by Congress at the urging of Secretary Dobbin to identify all officers in the Navy who were "incapable of performing promptly and efficiently all their duty both ashore and afloat" under the terms of "An Act to Promote the Efficiency of the Navy," which was passed on 28 February 1855.[31] Men identified as unfit or incompetent by the Board were to be either dismissed or retired from the active list.

In providing the members of the Naval Efficiency Board with their instructions in writing, the Secretary of the Navy included one paragraph which left little doubt that they should function as a disciplinary body and recommend for retirement or dismissal those officers who had so far escaped censure for wrongdoing because of lapses in the naval justice system.

> You are required to advance a step further in your examination, and report the names of such officers as you "believe" have become incompetent "from any cause implying sufficient blame on the part of the officers to justify" your recommending them to "be stricken altogether from the rolls." And on this point I venture to suggest the opinion that an officer is to "blame if he has become incompetent from neglect of duty and inattention and indifference to his profession as well as from dissipation and immoral indulgences."[32]

Secretary Dobbin also directed that the full board should deliberate on all midshipmen, passed midshipmen, and lieutenants whose names were brought before it. When the commanders were examined, the lieutenants on the Board would withdraw. Obviously, it was intended that some very deep and dark secrets would be probed and that the honor and reputation of certain individuals would be very much in question.

Undertaken with the best of intentions and with the general goal of resolving personnel problems which had been festering in the navy since at least 1815, the Naval Efficiency Board precipitated a fiasco which eventually imposed upon the naval justice system the greatest challenge and the heaviest caseload ever generated by any single event in the history of the Old Navy. The intellectual and moral limitations of even the most competent of the reform-minded officers of the pre-Civil War era and the looseness and general incompetence of naval administration when confronted with determined resistance from the ranks is graphically illustrated by this unhappy experience.

For fifteen years prior to 1855, the various secretaries of the navy, presidents, naval officers, and other interested parties had advocated the establishment of a retired or reserved list for officers. When repeated attempts to secure congressional action failed, the secretaries were obliged to resort to an unofficial "system" of retirement which was arbitrary and lacked legal sanction. Officers who were physically disabled or far advanced in years, diseased, or disabled by service-connected accidents or illnesses were never sent to sea but were given nominal shore duty or a perpetual leave of absence on reduced pay. Technically, they remained on the active list, however, and eligible for promotion under the strict seniority system then prevailing. Apparently, the Navy Department contrived to pass over certain insane or hopelessly alcoholic officers[33] from time to time but, in general, useless officers got their promotions when their time came, just the same as everybody else.

With the passage of time, the accumulation of unemployable officers became a serious burden on the navy, since they absorbed a large portion of the funds set aside for officer's pay. This was particularly noticeable in the upper ranks. By 1854 there were captains who had not been to sea for thirty years. Of the sixty-seven captains on the navy list, forty were on leave-of-absence pay.[34] It was these officers, plus certain commanders and lieutenants who also seemed to be shirking sea duty, that the Naval Efficiency Board was supposed to evaluate. Midshipmen also came under their purview and were to be examined with regard to their "moral fitness" as prospective commissioned officers.

The fifteen officers of the "Plucking Board" began their deliberations in June of 1855. From the beginning, they adopted the general procedural methods of the deliberative phase of a court-martial. They were sworn to secrecy, could call no witnesses, did not confront the men whom they were discussing, and kept no official minutes or records of their proceedings. Commander Samuel Francis Du Pont did, however, keep a private journal, listing all the cases they considered, excluding those of the captains, which sheds considerable light on the way the Board functioned.[35] Filling two ruled notebooks and devoting a paragraph or so to each midshipman, lieutenant, or commander that the Board discussed, Du Pont's journal shows clearly that the members had little regard for the requirements or orderly procedure and occasionally used their power to pursue private feuds and vendettas.

Starting at the bottom of the navy list, the Board's members considered each name in turn. If any member had reservations about the competence, sobriety, sanity, health, or physical or moral fitness of an officer, he would state his reasons and the rest of the Board would discuss the case, usually drawing on personal recollections of the man in question but occasionally consulting Navy Department records. After this discussion, a vote was taken. If the majority voted to dismiss or retire the man, it was so noted and the Board moved on to the next name on the list. Their judgments were often as harsh as they were imprecise. "Completely insane" or "hopelessly intemperate" or "totally lacking in moral fitness" are phrases which often appear in Du Pont's notebooks, supported by anecdotal material relating to erratic behavior, drunkenness, incompetence, gambling, mistakes, debts, sickness, invalidism, and bad conduct afloat and ashore, both on duty and in private life.

The navy list was short in 1855, as there were only about seven hundred commissioned officers in the entire service. Nearly every officer discussed was personally known to at least a few men on the Board, and some were intimate friends, former messmates, or even kinsmen. In most instances these considerations seem not to have swayed the Board's deliberations. Lieutenant Matthew Fontaine Maury's cousin, Lieutenant William F. Maury, cast the deciding vote in favor of retiring the world-renowned oceanographer on the grounds that his crippled leg, the result of a carriage accident, made him unfit for sea duty.[36] The Board also furloughed the son of one of its members, recommended the dismissal of President Pierce's ward, retired old

Commodore Charles Stewart, who was an uncle of a member, and reserved five men who were intimate friends of members.[37]

What did sway the Board were personal grudges and animosities. Commodore Matthew C. Perry apparently used the Board to continue a vendetta against Commander Cadwalader C. Ringgold that had begun during the expedition to Japan a year previously. Ringgold and Perry had clashed bitterly about the best policy to follow in protecting the lives and property of American merchants during the T'ai P'ing Rebellion in China, and Perry had settled the problem by convening a medical board which surveyed Ringgold as mentally incompetent and ordered him shipped home.[38] When Ringgold's name came before the Efficiency Board, Perry assured his colleagues that the Commander was still "incompetent by reason of insanity":

> The insanity of Comd. Ringgold seemed free from any doubt & whether now cured—or whether able to serve if cured, were points [the] majority did not consider necessary to establish—his usefulness & moral power as an officer were gone, & to risk lives & property on the ocean again after such a warning, struck them as indefensible—

Rem. fr act list Ayes 7

Nays 2

Exc 1 (Com P)

classed on leave 10   [39]

Along with many officers, Ringgold challenged the Board's decision before a court of inquiry, proved his sanity, and won reinstatement in 1857. He served competently throughout the Civil War, winning a Gold Medal for his seamanship in carrying out the rescue of the crew of a gunboat which foundered in a storm in 1863. He retired as a Rear Admiral in 1866.

A further taint on the Board's integrity was the charge that they had selected officers for dismissal or retirement with an eye towards improving their own prospects for promotion. The November 1855 issue of *Scientific American*, whose editors were highly critical of the treatment accorded to Lieutenant Maury, pointed out that 138 officers "black balled" by the Board were senior to its youngest member, while only 46 ranked below him.[40] Senator Iverson of Georgia claimed that as a result of the Board's actions, its lowest-ranking lieutenant, James Biddle, moved forward 139 numbers on the lieutenant's list and that all five of the commanders on the Board advanced to captain. All the captains had advanced in seniority as well; and one, William B. Shubrick, went from number seven to number one and was now the most senior officer in the navy because of decisions made by the Board.[41]

Certainly the Board's deliberations fell with a heavy hand on the upper ranks of the navy. Some 201 officers were directly affected. Forty-nine were dismissed as incompetent. Seventy-one were placed on the retired list with leave-of-absence pay, and eighty-one were placed on a reserved list with furlough pay which amounted to one-half of leave-of-absence pay. Among these men were 52 percent of all the navy's captains and 40 percent of its commanders but only 26 percent of the lieutenants.[42] Much of this seeming imbalance was because health was a major consideration in the Board's deliberations. Problems of ill health were obviously much more common among the older, more senior officers. Nevertheless, since the entire navy had been kept wholly in ignorance of the Board's methods and criteria for the judgments it reached, the results looked highly suspect; and an all too predictable storm of protest developed as soon as the Navy Department acted on its findings.

To begin with, the Board's actions were quickly and all but unanimously interpreted as reflecting on the "honor" and "morality" of the officers selected for removal from the active list. It was a badge of disgrace made even more galling because no accounting was to be forthcoming from either the Board or the Department as to what the decisions had been based on. There were simply the curt, bald statements on Navy Department stationery delivered into the hands of thunderstruck officers. Lieutenant Maury's notice, for example, read:

> The Board of Naval Officers assembled under the Act to promote the efficiency of the Navy, approved February 28th, 1855, having reported you as one of the officers who in their judgement should be placed on the Reserved List on leave-of-absence pay, and the findings of the Board having been approved by the President, it becomes my duty to inform you that as of this date you are removed from the Active Service List and placed on the Reserved List on leave-of-absence pay.
>
> You are however, not detached from the Naval Observatory. I avail myself of the authority of the law to direct that you continue on your present duty.[43]

The groundswell of adverse reaction was not limited to the navy but quickly became public as well. The affected officers, their friends, relatives, and political allies launched a tenacious campaign to have the work of the Board set aside. Criticism of President Pierce, Secretary Dobbin, and individual members of the Board became intense, especially in the southern states. Congress reverberated with angry speeches both for and against the Board; and finally, in January of 1857, a new law, an "Act to Amend 'An Act to Promote the Efficiency of the Navy,'" was passed. This new law gave all officers dismissed, retired, or reserved by the Board the right to request a naval court of inquiry where they could show cause why they should not be removed from the navy list.[44]

One hundred eighteen officers took advantage of this new law, and their chances were further improved by the fact that the Pierce administration left office early in 1857. The incoming Buchanan government was much less anxious to promote naval reform, especially after the depths of heat and passion that the Naval Efficiency Board had stirred up became obvious. A special court of inquiry was set up in Washington, D.C., on 20 February 1857, consisting of three captains and a judge advocate; but its initial progress was so slow that it was soon supplemented by two more similarly constituted tribunals. No confrontation between the aggrieved officers and the original Board members took place, and none of the courts of inquiry attempted to secure records of documents of the Efficiency Board or reconstruct its deliberations on a systematic basis. All that each of the courts of inquiry did was to try to decide independently whether or not an officer appearing before it was fit or unfit for active duty on the basis of individual arguments and evidence brought to its attention by the complaining officer or his representative and the judge advocate.

When the arguments were concluded, the court of inquiry reached a decision by majority vote of its members and passed these results along to President Buchanan, who reviewed each case personally and made the final decision as to whether to uphold the Efficiency Board's original recommendation or go with the new recommendations of the court of inquiry in case of disagreement. In this way, 84 percent of all the officers who challenged the findings of the Efficiency Board received some sort of mitigation of its verdict. Sixty-one officers, one-quarter of the total retired, were fully restored to active duty, while thirty-eight dismissed or furloughed officers had their status upgraded and some of their pay restored.[45]

The discipline and morale of the navy was seriously damaged by the failure of this badly needed but thoroughly botched effort at naval reform. The reinstated officers took their places again alongside men who had been promoted in their absence so that the navy's rolls were even more clogged than usual. Progressive officers were embittered by the failure of their efforts, while the example of officers successfully defying official actions of the Navy Department through the application of political pressure and the playing off of an incoming administration against an outgoing one on a massive scale encouraged further insubordination. Grudges and factionalism, always a problem in the service, became even more pronounced.

The furor of the Naval Efficiency Board controversy had hardly begun to abate when the Civil War broke out. The gradual disintegration of the country was mirrored by a similar disintegration of the naval officer corps, which lost all sense of discipline and cohesion as Northern and Southern officers drew apart, the latter to plot treason and scheme to deliver valuable bases and supplies to the Southern cause,[46] while the former ground their teeth and looked on in helpless fury. No intelligible direction was furnished by the Navy Department during this crisis, and none would be forthcoming until the issue of secession was finally settled. Interestingly enough, the enlisted men were quiet throughout this trying ordeal and few went South when secession came. By contrast, virtually every Southern officer in the navy departed, and many were soon in action as members of the Confederate States Navy.

With the departure of Southern congressmen and officers, sweeping reforms—long postponed by the paralysis of ideological deadlock—came to the navy. Merit promotions, orderly retirement policies, the abolition of the rum ration, the clarification of flag rank and the creation of two grades of admiral, and many other changes were instituted. The *Naval Regulations* were taken in hand again and went through four revisions during the decade of the 1860s in an effort to accommodate all the changes.[47]

Under the stern and watchful eye of President Lincoln's Secretary of the Navy, Gideon Welles, the naval justice system also underwent a substantial change in style, if not in substance. Welles had no patience with inefficiency and no sympathy with the aristocratic pretensions of naval officers. He administered the laws of the navy fearlessly and impartially no matter what the rank or political connections of an offender might be. He had little patience with long, drawn-out courts-martial designed to protect the "honor" or spare the feelings of men of dubious value to the service. He only allowed courts-martial and courts of inquiry when in his judgment there were real questions to be answered, and usually denied requests for naval tribunals on the part of officers who were merely seeking vindication or to overturn an action of the Department.[48] He watched out for instances of naval courts covering up incompetence or culpability, and more than once he rebuked a court-martial board for bringing in a verdict not supported by the evidence presented to it.[49]

The general path followed by Welles was directly contrary to the one advocated by Stephen R. Mallory, Secretary of the Confederate Navy. Mallory's service retained the full panoply of naval justice as it had existed in the Old Navy so that much valuable time and the energies of a disproportionate number of officers were taken up with elaborate courts-martial and courts of inquiry. In this way, the Confederate Navy retained more of the disciplinary traditions of the Old Navy than did the Federal Navy which was its direct lineal descendant.[50]

Welles broke tradition in another area of naval justice. By 1864 it had become apparent that the volume of legal business generated by the greatly expanded wartime navy called for the services of a full-time judge advocate general.

> Legal questions and suits growing out of the transactions of this Department are constantly arising. Some of them involve large pecuniary amounts, and frequently embrace great variety of detail. The cases of courts-martial are numerous, and require scrutiny and careful preparation and revision. The forms and execution of contracts under the provisions of the law demand deliberate and attentive care and consideration. Frauds and abuses on the part of contractors and employees call for investigation and prosecution, and the miscellaneous legal questions which arise are innumerable involving often a vast extent and variety of detail.[51]

Congress responded to Welles's request by authorizing the appointment of a naval judge advocate general on 2 March 1865. President Lincoln appointed William E. Chandler, a civilian from New Hampshire, to this post, and he took office shortly thereafter. Chandler was succeeded by John A. Bolles of Massachusetts on 10 July 1865, and Bolles served until 1870 when the office of naval judge advocate general was abolished and its duties transferred to the Department of Justice.[52]

Obviously, the naval justice system of the Old Navy was but one chaotic element in a service that was poorly organized and badly administered. Its operations were such that few persons could rest assured of its essential fairness, and little satisfaction could be derived from its treatment of disciplinary problems and controversies within the navy. It was capricious, erratic, and bereft of settled principles, as any system administered by unsympathetic and often incompetent persons with no legal training would be. Riddled with political influence, favoritism, and ideological strife, it failed in its basic purpose, to promote discipline and protect the good of the service.

Chapter IV

Naval Discipline in Everyday Practice

It is obvious that the disciplinary system of the Old Navy was highly unsystematic; and before the reforms of the 1860s were promulgated, it tended to fall into greater confusion with each passing decade. Because of the bewildering array of regulations, directives, and modifying circulars in force, any officer or legal scholar attempting to consult its written codes and gain a clear theoretical understanding of naval law was doomed to frustration. The navy's legal code existed on another level, however, separate and distinct from the formal documentary structure; and on this level, its precepts and methods were fairly well understood and reasonably consistent. This more accessible level was that of day-to-day practical application on board the ships and in the squadrons of the fleet, at the Naval Academy, and in certain other special circumstances.

Of course, routine discipline in the Old Navy overwhelmingly referred to shipboard discipline. Shore duty stations were exceedingly rare for all but the most senior officers before the Civil War, and virtually all the enlisted men either served at sea or were temporarily billeted in receiving ships while awaiting assignment to a ship.[1] Navy yards and shore stations usually employed civilian labor, so most of their personnel were not under naval discipline.

Since naval discipline was virtually synonymous with shipboard discipline, its character and form were molded by the conditions of life at sea in a sailing or auxiliary steam-powered man-of-war, conditions which the modern reader would find very confining indeed. To begin with, the nineteenth century wooden warship was crowded almost beyond endurance. The frigate *United States*, for example, mounted fifty-six guns and required six men per gun in action, for a total of three hundred fifty-seven enlisted crewmen. Add to this complement a marine contingent of fifty officers and men and twenty-three commissioned and warrant officers, and the result is a total of four hundred and thirty souls inhabiting a living space measuring $173\frac{1}{4}$ feet, the length of the lower deck, by $44\frac{1}{3}$ feet, the width of the extreme beam.[2]

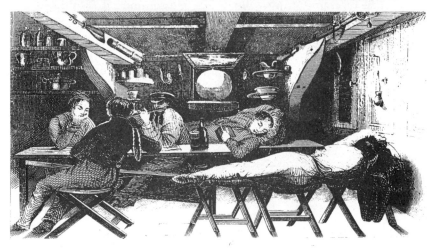

These six views depict living conditions on board a typical sailing man-of-war in the 1840s. Although ships varied greatly in size, the facilities available to the men and the space allocated for them to swing their hammocks in remained pretty much the same. Privacy and creature comforts of any kind are almost totally absent. (*Heck's Iconographic Encyclopedia*, collection of the Nimitz Library)

Within these dimensions the men inhabited two decks, which they shared with the ship's gear, guns, tackle, and stores. When the more spacious officers' quarters and the commodore's great cabin aft were subtracted, each seaman was left with a space 2 feet wide, 6 feet long, and 18 inches high in which to swing his hammock.

Privacy under these conditions was virtually nonexistent, and there were few places that a man could go to for respite during the three years of a normal commission. Leave for enlisted men was unheard of, and shore liberty was granted sparingly and at irregular intervals. "Like pears closely packed," Melville wrote, "the crowded crew mutually decay through close contact, and every plague spot is contagious."[3] Undoubtedly this view of life in a sailing man-of-war is somewhat overwrought, but it does indicate clearly that powerful negative forces were generated by prolonged close confinement; and the function of the naval discipline system was not necessarily to repress all unlawful or immoral behavior, but to keep it out of sight and within tolerable limits. The authority of the officers had to be maintained and the ship kept in readiness for whatever mission she might be assigned.

> The whole body of this discipline is emphatically a system of cruel cogs and wheels, systematically grinding up in one common hopper all that might minister to the moral well being of the crew. . . . Through all the endless ramifications of rank and station, in most men-of-war there runs a sinister vein of bitterness, ... It were sickening to detail all the paltry irritabilities, jealousies, and cabals, and the spiteful detractions and animosities, that lurk far down, and cling to the very keelson of the ship. . . . And though there are vessels that in some measure furnish exceptions to this; and though, in other ships, the thing may be glazed over by a guarded, punctilious exterior, almost completely hiding the truth from casual visitors, while the worst facts touching the common sailor are systematically kept in the background, yet it is certain that what has been said of the domestic interior of a man-of-war will, in a greater or less degree, apply to most vessels in the Navy.[4]

The organizational structure of discipline on board the ships of the Old Navy was identical to that which had evolved in the British Navy since the days of the Stuarts. The captain was the chief disciplinarian, and all the threads of naval authority came together in his hands. The other commissioned officers shared little of this power. They could report offenders to the captain, but Article XXX of the Articles of War expressly stated that the only punishment that lesser officers could assign on their own authority was confinement, and that only in the absence of the captain. In all routine cases, the captain heard complaints, rendered judgment, and passed sentence at captain's mast. Punishments imposed at mast proceedings were entered into the ship's log together with the name and offense of the recipient.

Although all the officers and petty officers were expected to help maintain discipline, there were petty officers whose job consisted solely of police work. These men were the master-at-arms and his assistants, whose number varied according to the size of the vessel. For example, a large frigate usually had a master-at-arms and two ship's corporals, one for each berth deck. A ship of the line typically carried three ship's corporals, while a sloop-of-war might have only one ship's corporal in addition to the master-at-arms. These men were expected to deter wrongdoing by their presence, but they also engaged in detective work. It was they who planned and laid traps to catch the clandestine gamblers who carried on illicit games of chance on the berth decks after lights out, searched for forbidden caches of liquor hidden in the ship, and strove to break up smuggling rings.

The master-at-arms and ship's corporals stood no regular watches and were free to roam the ship at all hours, listening, observing, and conferring with informants recruited from among the crew. Their jurisdiction stopped only with the officers and the marines who were policed by their own noncommissioned officers. Indeed, the work of the Marine sergeants was closely allied with that of the master-at-arms and his men, and they usually formed a mess together with the purser's steward and the ship's yeoman apart from the other seamen and petty officers.

It hardly needs to be added that the master-at-arms and his assistants were highly unpopular men whose work brought them into contact with the most dangerous and unruly members of the crew. They quickly learned not to stand under open hatchways or in places where round shot, marlin spikes, blocks, or other heavy gear could be dropped on them. They also needed to keep a lookout for seamen stalking them with nooses, hoping to lasso and strangle them. Occasionally vengeance was extracted ashore, and more than one master-at-arms was set upon and either killed or castrated by men whom he had harassed during a commission.[5] Informers, when their identity became known, found themselves in similar jeopardy. They often had the head tricing of their hammocks slipped or cut at night after a round shot had been placed under them. Even if the intended victim escaped a broken neck or skull fracture, a miss could serve as a warning.[6]

Whatever the dangers of their positions, the master-at-arms and his mates must have been busy men, because the volume of masts and punishments logged was steady and cases of indiscipline were numerous. Commander Samuel Francis Du Pont kept a notebook listing all the floggings he awarded as commanding officer of the frigate *Congress* on a passage from Norfolk to Callao between 17 November 1845 and 28 March 1846. Du Pont was not reputed to be an unusually strict commander nor one who enjoyed flogging his men, so perhaps his record can be taken as typical of the daily disciplinary activity of an American man-of-war breaking in a newly shipped crew. During the 131 days his notebook covers, Du Pont records 108 floggings, or slightly less than one per day on the average. The actual punishments were usually administered every two or three days so that for the month of December 1845 Du Pont's notebook records forty-one men flogged, as follows:

December	1,	3 men flogged
December	4,	4 men flogged
December	5,	6 men flogged
December	8,	4 men flogged
December	11,	3 men flogged
December	13,	5 men flogged
December	15,	3 men flogged
December	17,	3 men flogged
December	20,	2 men flogged
December	22,	2 men flogged
December	26,	2 men flogged
December	27,	4 men flogged[7]

The offenses that were logged as having earned punishment by flogging were many and varied. Among them were missing muster, fighting, "skulking," lying, being asleep below during watch, being asleep on lookout, disobedience, disrespect, neglect of duty at quarters, being dirty at muster, and "making dirt on the deck."[8] One man, a sailor named Clark, is discussed at some length in Du Pont's notebook, presumably because he stood out as an unusually prominent ship's "bad character."

Previous to punishing this man Clark, I had admonished the crew on many points, upon which for the future I would require more rigid compliance. Having waited with patience for them to [understand] & become accustomed to a man-of-war to become familiar with the laws & [customs] of the service—These remarks were primarily delivered in consequence of a man having been struck, two nights before, in the dark and punched severely in the face. The second offence of this nature—this taking of private vengeance, for suffering injury from one man to another is a feature of the day in our ships of war.

After making clear that Clark was the prime suspect in both cases, Du Pont goes on to describe another of his crimes, the waylaying of a marine on post before concluding

> He is a man of very bad character & gave much trouble in the *Macedonian* last cruise on the C of Africa. In the *Congress* he has caused great trouble in the draft of men he came with from New York and was the cause of a man being drowned. He is undoubtedly an Englishman. He only says he is an Irishman but incidentally an American.[9]

Although Clark pleaded earnestly with Du Pont, hoping to be spared a flogging, the Commander chose to inflict the usual twelve lashes. A pencil note in the margin notes that afterwards "Clark became one of the best men in the Ship."

It should be noted that in flogging his green crew into shape in the time-honored fashion of the navy, Commander Du Pont was also serving as flag captain to Commodore Richard F. Stockton, who was enroute to take up command of the Pacific Squadron. Four years later as Senator Stockton, he led the fight in Congress which resulted in the abolition of flogging, a campaign which pitted him against virtually the entire naval establishment, including Du Pont.

In fact, because of the antiflogging agitation that grew up in Congress after 1846, historians are able to develop a clear picture of routine disciplinary practices in the navy in the pre-Civil War era. For instance, in 1846 and 1847, as a result of a congressional demand for accurate statistics on the use of flogging, the Navy Department reported that a total of 5,936 floggings had been administered on sixty ships during those two years.[10] This averages out to roughly fifty floggings per ship per year, or four per month. Obviously, flogging was the navy's punishment of first resort.

Seen in this light, the figures turned in for Commander Du Pont's *Congress* are extremely high, while those cited for Melville's *United States* in Chapter II are only moderately above average, with slightly less than seven floggings per month. Still, the raw statistics of all floggings in the navy amounted to a staggering total, and the service soon saw that it would be in its interest to drastically reduce the number of corporal punishments coming to the attention of Congress. Therefore, in 1848 only 424 men were reported flogged,[11] a reduction of nearly 86 percent over the average of the previous two years.

Congress was not only interested in the number of floggings, but also in the types of offenses that the navy was using flogging to curb. The data collected for the "Published Senate Document on Flogging in the Navy" lists a variety of offenses considerably broader than those found in Du Pont's notebook. Along with the punishments relating to drunkenness, fighting, disobedience, skulking, theft, cursing, smuggling liquor, and sleeping on watch, there were others of a more exotic nature, including:

Running in debt ashore	12 lashes
Tapping liquor in the spirit room	12 lashes
Stealing poultry from the coop	12 lashes
Doubling the grog tub	6 lashes
Misbehavior at school	6 lashes
Dropping a bucket from aloft	12 lashes
Cursing the ship's corporal	8 lashes
Slow motion in getting into a boat	6 lashes
Being lousy	6 lashes
Selling coffee	5 lashes
Spitting on the berth deck	6 lashes
Dirty and unwashed clothes	12 lashes
Stealing a wig	12 lashes
Spitting on a man	12 lashes
Pumping ship on the berth deck	12 lashes
Being naked on the spar deck	9 lashes
Cursing the master at arms	6 lashes[12]

As a procedural matter, all of these offenses were handled by captain's mast and did not involve court-martial. When floggings were awarded for serious offenses by action of a court-martial, punishments for certain common offenses were fairly uniform. For drunkenness and mutinous conduct the punishment was one hundred lashes, normally mitigated to fifty. For mutinous conduct and disrespect to superior officers, it was eighty lashes mitigated to forty. For desertion, the most common court-martial offense in the navy, the penalty was fifty lashes mitigated to twenty-five.[13]

The practical details of flogging were carefully regulated by Articles III, XX, XXX, and XLI of the Articles of War, both as to the number of lashes that could be administered with and without a court-martial and to the instrument that could be used. Article XXX was particularly explicit on this last point:

> No commanding officer shall on his own authority . . . . inflict a punishment on any private beyond twelve lashes with a cat-of-nine-tails, nor shall he suffer any wired, or other than a plain cat-of-nine-tails, to be used on board his ship. . . .

The plain or "official" cat spoken of was made of nine small, hard, twisted pieces of cotton or flax cord, with three knots in each, fixed to a short, thick, rope handle. Lashes were administered on the bared back, with the recipient secured upright to a hatch grating or triced in the ship's gangway. Punishments were witnessed by all hands with no exceptions, and the favored time for administering floggings was on Sunday after the ship's muster and the reading of the Articles of War.

It has been demonstrated from Preble's time that American naval officers contrived to evade the strictures against administering more than twelve lashes without benefit of formal court-martial proceedings. Equally illegal and even more common was the presence of outlawed whipping devices, such as rope "colts" or "starters," rattan canes and the like, and their frequent use by petty officers. According to Melville, the seamen were

> liable to the "colt" or rope's end, a bit of rattlin-stuff, indiscriminately applied—without stripping the victim—at any time, and in any part of the ship, at the merest wink from the Captain.[14]

He goes on to relate that the colts were used not only by petty officers, who carried them coiled in their hats, but also by officers who wished to chastise a crewman without going to the trouble of reporting to the captain or preferring court-martial charges:

> Nor was it a thing unknown for a lieutenant, in a sudden outburst of passion, perhaps inflamed by Brandy, or smarting under the sense of being disliked or hated by the seamen, to order a whole watch of two hundred and fifty men, at dead of night, to undergo the indignity of the colt.[15]

The illegal use of the colt was certainly one of the problems that inspired the General Order issued by Secretary Paulding cited in Chapter III. The strongest attack on these practices was made by Secretary George C. Bancroft through a series of general orders issued in 1845 and 1846, which apparently curbed colting to a marked degree.[16]

Abhorrent as flogging was to the sensibilities of congressmen and the general public, support of the practice was widespread in the Navy and by no means solely limited to the officer corps. Many seamen approved of flogging, asserting that it was a manly punishment that conferred little lasting disgrace. The men took considerable pride in their ability to endure the lash in silence or without fainting. Willing hands and prudent seamen could take some satisfaction in seeing the ship's troublemakers served in a manner that was at once swift, graphic, and public. Experienced seamen quickly learned how to avoid the lash so that floggings fell mostly on the novices in the crew or on men who shirked their work, gambled or drank excessively, or had trouble controlling their behavior.[17] A ship's company living in extremely close quarters and containing men from all stations in life under the general supposition that "the sea and the gallows refuse nothing" was vitally interested in any force that could maintain effective social control, and flogging seemed to curb all but the wildest spirits.

One reason why seamen generally approved of flogging was because they were decidedly less enthusiastic about some of the other forms of punishment used in the navy. John Adams of the Naval Committee had exhorted the captains of the Continental Navy to experiment with alternate punishments, and Article I of the Articles of War enjoined commanders to

> be vigilant in inspecting the conduct of all such as are placed under their command; and to guard against, and suppress, all dissolute and immoral practices, and to correct all such as are guilty of them, according to the usage of the sea service.

This was an extremely loosely worded article, and it was further supplemented by Article XXXII, which read:

> All crimes committed by persons belonging to the Navy, which are not specified in the foregoing articles, shall be punished according to the laws and customs in such cases at sea.

By custom, these articles gave sanction to such correctives as the stopping of liquor rations, the wearing of badges or marks of disgrace, confinement, ironing, and other similar punishments which the sailors considered worse than a flogging of a dozen lashes.[18] Perhaps even more sobering to the seamen was the realization that Articles I and XXXII gave commanding officers a tacit right to experiment with highly irregular punishments or institute correctives of their own devising which could well turn out to be very painful indeed. Under civilian law, many of the "usages of the sea service" would be considered cruel and unusual punishment of the sort expressly forbidden by the Constitution. When they measured the known terrors of a dozen lashes against the unknown devisings of a captain's imagination, most seamen preferred flogging. Secretary of the Navy Levi Woodbury was but one of many naval administrators and civilian reformers who was simply unable to appreciate this facet of the seamen's minds. In 1831 he wrote to his commanding officers exhorting them to use "pecuniary fines, badges of disgrace, and other mild corrections, rather than the humiliating practice of whipping . . ." as their primary mode of punishment of the errant seamen.[19]

The seamen's fears of Woodbury's "other mild corrections" were confirmed after the abolition of flogging. The officer corps was extremely fearful that the men would become unmanageable and took special precautions to try to stave off mass insubordination from the ranks. While fitting out for his expedition to Japan in 1852, Commodore Matthew C. Perry expressly encouraged his recruiters to pick younger men for his crews, apparently in the hope that they would be easier to handle than older seamen hardened to the lash but now free of its threat. To a friend he wrote:

> The want of legal means for punishing the men for the thousand faults they are daily committing, has weakened the authority of the officers, and Congress may be assured that unless some remedy is applied the Navy as an institution will go to the devil.[20]

Surgeon Charles W. Wheelright of the *Powhatan* echoed Perry's sentiments:

> Everything now is so different from what it was even a few years ago in the Navy. There is no order or system. Officers are dissatisfied and crews disorderly.[21]

Frantically the navy searched for a new mode of punishment to replace flogging. Tattooing, branding, and the wearing of signs had all been suggested and tried before, but after 1850 they were enthusiastically embraced. In addition, new punishments, in keeping with "the laws and customs in such cases at sea," were devised. Sweatboxes, apparently borrowed from Oriental practices, the suspending of miscreants by their necks from the spanker boom for short periods of time, lashing of the thumbs behind the back, tricing men up to the rigging by their wrists, dousing them for long periods with bilge water, bucking and gagging—a traditional Army punishment—and a host of other correctives were all briefly in vogue at one time or another, along with the wearing of strait jackets and long confinements in irons on bread and water.[22] When all else failed, a few officers and petty officers even resorted to the "cat" despite the vigilance of Congress.[23]

Regularity did not find its way back into naval punishment until Congress sat down in 1855 and carefully drew up legislation for the summary court-martial process, together with a list of punishments which could be awarded by that tribunal. Slowly the practice of confining men to the ship's brig on bread and water with full rations every third day for ten-, twenty-, or thirty-day periods by sentence of a summary court-martial replaced flogging as the navy's standard punishment.[24]

Even after the Act of 1855, the devised punishments persisted. In 1862, Senator Grimes of Iowa, head of the Senate Naval Affairs Committee, introduced a bill in Congress to curb the powers of commanding officers to devise cruel and unusual punishments for men not subjected to the summary court-martial process. The Grimes Bill called for limiting punishments for officers to private reprimand, suspension, arrest, or confinement for no more than ten days. Enlisted men sentenced at captain's mast could be awarded a reduction in rating, provided such rating had been conferred by the commanding officer, confinement for ten days, solitary confinement for seven days, solitary confinement on bread and water for five days, deprivation of shore liberties, and extra duty. "No other punishment shall be permitted on board of vessels belonging to the Navy, except by sentence of a general or summary court-martial."[25] Explicit as it was, Senator Grimes's legislation was apparently not enough to do away with certain objectionable practices. In 1872, new regulations and general orders were issued specifically outlawing branding and tattooing, prohibiting the use of sweatboxes, and attacking excessive reliance on thirty days' solitary confinement on bread and water.[26]

Senator Grimes's bill was interesting not only for its attempts to regularize punishments awarded to enlisted men, but also for its expanded provision of minor punishments for officers, the lack of which had characterized navy regulations since John Adams' day. It had become something of a scandal in the Old Navy that there was a wide differential between the treatment of officers and enlisted men who were guilty of the same acts. In 1857, a group of sailors wrote to the editor of the *United States Nautical Magazine and Naval Journal*, complaining that drunken seamen returning to their ship after shore liberty received severe punishments, "but let an officer come aboard dead drunk—which has often been the case this cruise—and nothing is said to him."[27] Senior officers, who were harsh in disciplining enlisted men, often took an indulgent attitude towards junior officers. Rear Admiral Henry H. Bell, commander in chief of the Asiatic Squadron from 1865 to 1867, was a notable martinet who approved many harsh court-martial sentences involving enlisted men; but he had a marked reluctance to punish officers who committed transgressions against the Articles of War or *Naval Regulations*. He let off with short suspensions so many officers accused of drunkenness that he was ultimately reprimanded by Secretary Welles for not ordering courts-martial for two lieutenants accused of intoxication on duty. Bell replied that his ships were dispersed and consequently he could not assemble enough officers to constitute a proper court. Even when he could bring himself to prefer charges, Bell could not seem to make them stick. One young officer, suspended for ignoring regulations laid down for the flagship's deck officers and later court-martialed for insubordination, was merely reprimanded by the Admiral. His career was not injured in the slightest, and he subsequently became a famous battleship commander.[28]

Not all senior officers were indulgent, to be sure. As Melville put it:

> If a captain have a grudge against a lieutenant, or a lieutenant against a midshipman, how easy to torture him by official treatment, which shall not lay open the superior officer to legal rebuke.[29]

Such treatment of junior officers by their seniors probably was common, or at least not unknown; but there was a legal remedy for it. Roughly one and one-half percent of all court-martial charges recorded in the index of the judge advocate general's record of naval courts from 1799 to 1861 are for cruelty and oppression, undue harshness, or illegal punishment.

It is significant to note that much of the differential treatment noted between enlisted men and officers involved drunkenness and conduct ashore. Excessive drinking was the disciplinary plague of the navy, and few, indeed, are the journals of voyages and commissions in the Old Navy and Civil War squadrons that do not mention the intemperate drinking habits of navy men of all ranks.[30] The difference in the treatment of officers and enlisted men lay in the fact that a seaman could be punished each time he was caught drunk, while an officer could only be court-martialed for drunkenness after he had rendered himself chronically unfit for duty or had committed some professional error while under the influence of alcohol.

In the area of shore liberty, differential treatment was—if anything —even more marked. The Old Navy had several major liberty ports around the world, usually in those places where squadrons were home-ported and naval agents and supply depots were situated. These included St. Thomas (Virgin Islands), Aspinwall, Rio de Janeiro, Manila, Shanghai, Hong Kong, Macao, Panama City, Lima, Valparaiso, Porto Praya (Cape Verde Islands), Monrovia, St. Paul de Loando, and Port Mahon in the Balleric Islands.[31] Of all these places, perhaps the most notorious for shoreside indiscipline and deteriorated relationships between the residents and the men of the Old Navy was Port Mahon, which served as home port for the Mediterranean Squadron. Through the courtesy of the Spanish government, the squadron wintered there

The Mediterranean squadron under the command of Commodore John Rodgers sails out of Port Mahon in 1823. In the age of sail the Mediterranean squadron was the most prestigious duty station in the navy. Ship-of-the-line *North Carolina*, frigates *Constitution* and *Brandywine*, and sloops-of-war *Ontario* and *Erie* are depicted here. (United States Naval Academy Museum Library collection)

for several months each year and returned several times during the cruising season to resupply. In this way, the "townies" and the navy men had ample opportunity for prolonged contact.

The seamen, who were granted very little shore liberty in any case for fear of mass desertions, spent most of their brief runs ashore carousing wildly and generally enjoying the services of a community well organized to cater to their vices. From 1840 to 1843, during Commodore Isaac Hull's tenure as commander of the Mediterranean Squadron, he received numerous complaints about his sailors and marines from the Mahonese authorities. They were accused of riding rented horses too fast in the streets, running up debts with the town merchants and refusing to pay them, brawling with the crews of other ships in the squadron, and assaulting Mahonese citizens on the streets and in their homes and places of business.[32] There was no organized shore patrol in those days, and breaches of the peace invariably brought Americans into the jails and courts of the local police, who treated them none too gently. Complaints of false arrest lodged by the United States Consul rested side by side with claims for damages filed by the Spanish.[33] Many a seaman was returned to his ship with stab wounds or broken bones sustained when the Mahonese garrison troops waded into a street brawl or tavern riot with musket butts and fixed bayonets.

The reception accorded the officers was different in some respects, but little better in overall tone. They were granted shore leave much more frequently than the seamen and became patrons of the gambling casinos and public masquerade balls for which Port Mahon was notorious. Some of the officers, like Captain Daniel Patterson, acquired regular mistresses among the courtesans of the town, and there was much indulgence in dueling.[34] Indeed, the shoreside conduct of American officers was so violent that the governor general eventually wrote to Commodore Hull complaining that lieutenants and midshipmen were "in the habit of coming ashore with Pistols, Sword canes, and other weapons, the use of which is prohibited in this Country, not only to foreigners but to citizens."[35] Hull was obliged to write out a general order prohibiting his officers from carrying weapons, other than those prescribed as part of their uniforms—swords for officers and dirks for midshipmen; but the officers were reluctant to comply. In March of 1840, several lieutenants and midshipmen had been attacked while attending a masquerade by citizens and soldiers of the local garrison in a manner that seemed to indicate a prearranged ambush.[36] Later, in 1842, Midshipman J. S. Anderson was waylaid and stabbed to death while returning to his ship after an errand ashore.[37]

Eventually the situation at Port Mahon deteriorated so drastically that Spain requested the American Squadron to remove its ships and shore facilities from Minorca, citing the frequent disorders occurring between the sailors and Mahonese soldiers and civilians. The navy was happy to depart, and a new base was established at Spezzia, Sardinia, in 1846.[38]

Port Mahon was not the only place where shoreside conflict between American naval personnel and local authorities created a diplomatic incident. In Rio de Janeiro, men from the Brazil Squadron were customarily jailed by the police on charges ranging from drunkenness to murder. Once behind bars, they were thrown in with the native prisoners and given nothing to eat until their cases could be heard in a local court. The squadron commodores usually refrained from interfering except to the extent of requesting that the men be judged fairly by the Brazilian court. In October of 1846, however, a particularly aggravated case arose when a group of seamen from the frigate *Columbia* were arrested while being herded back to the ship by an officer after a wild spree ashore. When the officer, Lieutenant Davis, followed the police to protest the detaining of the men, he, too, was arrested and lodged in jail overnight. Commodore Rousseau and the American Consul, Henry Wise, chose to interpret this act as an insult to the flag and retaliated by withholding salutes during a Brazilian national holiday. This, in turn, inflamed the Brazilians; and relations between the two countries were strained for more than a year before the issue was dropped.[39]

Of all the violent behavior patterns that characterized the shoreside conduct of the men of the Old Navy, none was more regrettable or reprehensible than dueling, a practice which ultimately caused the death of thirty-three naval officers between 1798 and 1843.[40] Indeed, almost as many officers died in duels as in combat during the first half of the nineteenth century,[41] and almost all the navy's duels, numbering over one hundred,[42] were fought ashore, often in foreign ports.

Many of these duels could be traced to such evils as jealousy and factionalism within the service, but most were attributable to an exaggerated sense of personal honor which led to pointless quarrels. Senior officers often set a poor example for the juniors, who accounted for most of the passages at arms. Lieutenant Colonel Commandant William Ward Burrows, the first commandant of the marines, for example, once sternly instructed a subaltern who had been struck by a navy lieutenant to "wipe away this Insult." He went on to explain that

> On board the *Ganges*, about 12 mos ago, Lt. Gale, was struck by an Officer of the Navy, the Capt. took no notice of the Business and Gale got no satisfaction on the Cruise; the moment he arrived he call'd the Lieut. out and shot him; afterwards Politeness was restor'd . . .[43]

Theoretically, the practice was outlawed by Article XV of the Articles of War, which stated that

> No person in the Navy shall quarrel with any other person in the Navy, nor use provoking or reproachful words, gestures, or menaces on pain of such punishment as a court-martial shall adjudge.

In reality, this article was one of the most erratically enforced provisions in the navy's code. The only real restraint on dueling in force in the Old Navy was the old British custom which prohibited duels between officers of different ranks because some might resort to it to speed up promotions.

As a result, duels were usually fought over trifles between men who were equals in rank. In 1840, for instance, Lieutenants David D. Porter and S. C. Rowan almost fought a duel over a quarrel that arose when Rowan, senior to Porter in numbers on the lieutenant's list, objected to his passing a dull afternoon at the Hydrographic Office in Washington, D.C., by prodding a drawing board with a pair of dividers.[44] When they were not fighting each other, American officers often dueled with foreign officers and civilians, particularly in Latin America and on the Mediterranean Station.[45]

Although the fighting of duels was abhorred by many progressive-minded officers and naval administrators, only sporadic attempts were made to punish participants under Article XV. Questions of personal honor were held to be much more important than the mere letter of the Articles of War unless the persons involved were very junior officers and their quarrel was particularly silly. Even President Andrew Jackson, himself a noted performer on the field of honor who had fought duels during his army days, confined himself to prohibiting duels only between officers and civilians.[46] He once cashiered three lieutenants for fighting a young Philadelphia doctor, remarking at the time that he would not interfere in duels "between officers whose profession was fighting and who were trained at arms."[47]

One senior officer who recognized the need to make some effort to curb dueling in the navy was, ironically enough, Stephen Decatur, the beau ideal of the "young gentlemen" of the service and a duelist of impeccable credentials. He instituted in his ships a procedure called the "Decatur Plan," whereby he required his junior officers, particularly the midshipmen, to pledge that they would neither give nor accept a challenge without first referring their disputes to him for mature advice and arbitration. The Decatur Plan was widely copied by commanding officers throughout the service in the days before dueling was finally outlawed in the navy.[48]

As with so many other reforms, this had to wait until the Civil War removed the Southern representation from both Congress and the naval officer corps. Dueling had been made a court-martial offense punishable by dismissal from the service in 1857, but it was not until 1862 that the "Act for the Better Government of the Navy" plugged most of the loopholes in the regulations by making it a court-martial offense to send or accept a challenge or act as a second. In 1865, still more comprehensive regulations stipulated that

> No person in the Navy will upbraid another person in the Navy for refusing a challenge to fight a duel. Every person is enjoined to assist in the Honorable Adjustment of any differences that might occur. No disgrace can attach to any one for refusing a challenge, as such a course would be in obedience to law.[49]

In this way the custom of dueling died out in the navy, which has—with perhaps one exception—been free of the practice since the end of the Civil War.

In its heyday, dueling was entirely a business of officers and gentlemen. The enlisted men "fought" much less formally; and their bouts with fists, knives, or marlinspikes were often punished by flogging and even by courts-martial. Since they were as likely to fight on board ship as on shore, their altercations were seen as more menacing to discipline. In this one respect, however, the Old Navy, which made so many informal exceptions to the rules where officers were concerned, allowed the enlisted men an extra legal tradition of their own. If two men who had a grudge would agree to a supervised, fair fight, they could slug it out until a decision was reached one way or another under the guise of an exhibition match. Later they were to shake hands and bury the grudge, and no disciplinary action would be taken. In this way the navy's grudge fight tradition grew up as a counterpart to dueling among the officers and has remained as a device for reducing tensions before they result in infractions of discipline.[50]

It can be seen that in the matter of dueling the midshipmen were the most active participants. In fact, the "young gentlemen" were, as a group, one of the most troublesome and turbulent elements in the navy. They ranged in age from teenage boys to men in their late twenties and early thirties who had passed the qualifying examinations and were awaiting an opening on the lieutenant's list. Although technically warrant officers, they were in a peculiar twilight of status, looked down upon as younger than the other warrant officers but occupying a more privileged position because of their prospects for promotion into the ranks of the executive officers of the navy, prospects which the other warrant holders did not share. Although virtually the only route to a commission in the navy was through service as a midshipman, they were not screened very carefully. Nominations mostly came through congressional patronage, and often the wilder and less dutiful sons and nephews of politically prominent individuals were packed off to sea to keep them out of the public eye until discipline and maturity curbed their spirit. Others were the sons and relations of naval officers maintaining family traditions. These entered the service willingly and often made fine officers.

On board ship, the midshipmen were berthed in their own quarters in the gun room apart from the other officers and the crew. The gun room usually had a rowdy and turbulent life of its own, which included much hilarity and loud skylarking, practical jokes, hazing, bullying, and fighting.[51] The commissioned officers were expected to exercise some control over them but were forbidden to inflict corporal punishment by Article XXX, a regulation peculiar to the American navy inspired by early congressional efforts to strengthen the aristocratic pretensions of the officer corps. The British, whose midshipmen served under similar circumstances, were somewhat more severe and customarily corrected minor faults by bending the youthful miscreant over a cannon and whipping him with a rattan cane. There was no equivalent to "kissing the gunner's daughter" in the American service.

With no legal recourse available to control midshipmen's behavior except confinement or suspension from duty, the navy was obliged to undertake many courts-martial for offenses that would otherwise have been dealt with through corporal punishment. Before 1845, midshipmen were usually tried on charges of drunkenness, neglect of duty, cruelty and oppression, fighting, and disrespect;[52] and the most common punishment was dismissal from the service.

After 1845, the Naval Academy at Annapolis began to function, and the frequency with which midshipmen's names appear in the judge advocate general's index of cases declines markedly. Those whose names do appear are no longer charged with offenses drawn from the Articles of War, but with misconduct or gross misconduct at the naval school. The midshipmen attempted to perpetuate many gunroom traditions at the academy, but continuous close supervision and the institution's demerit system borrowed from the older military academy at West Point created a more confining atmosphere at Annapolis. For the most part, the academy's honor and demerit systems kept the midshipmen out of the toils of the regular naval justice system except for the most aggravated cases, usually involving fights or duels.[53]

The academy's legal system slowly developed into a body of law and custom distinct from that of the navy proper, but it mirrored the image of the larger institution in at least one respect: There were extra legal traditions at the academy which violated the letter of the written code. On paper the regulations were tough, and the midshipmen were treated much more severely than were their counterparts in the British naval school. Academy authorities had little to fear in the way of outside interference; and under the guise of "extra instruction," the midshipmen were subjected to small arms drill in the middle of the night, lined up at attention until a predetermined number had collapsed from fatigue, marched in their underwear in freezing weather, and occasionally lodged aboard a nearby prison ship.[54]

Among themselves, the midshipmen enforced many unwritten traditions by the practice of hazing. Through this unofficial and virtually uncontrolled form of chastisement, new candidates were assimilated into the corps of midshipmen and unsuitable individuals were driven out of the school. Never a gentle means of social control, hazing seemed to reach its nadir of viciousness and unfairness during the unsettled conditions created by the Civil War, when the academy was temporarily situated at Newport, Rhode Island. There Tom Welles, the son of the secretary of the navy, was treated so brutally that he begged his father to let him resign and enter the army.[55]

Hazing at the academy was not usually undertaken to reinforce the formal rules and regulations but could actually be antipathetic to them. It was a way to apply peer-group pressure to individuals who might be tempted to defy the unwritten customs of the corps of midshipmen. For instance, when Alfred Thayer Mahan, out of an excess of zeal for the formal code, reported a classmate for talking in ranks, he was socially ostracized and placed in "coventry" for his entire senior year.[56]

As a means of social control, hazing was much more efficient and effective than the legally sanctioned demerit system,[57] and the example that the academy set by operating on a double standard of conduct and values must have reinforced tendencies which the naval officer corps had already displayed in relation to regulations which were in conflict with the mores of the peer group.

This is not to say that the formal rules of the academy were not severe and exacting in and of themselves, and perhaps unwritten countercustoms were a necessary corrective to an unreasonably harsh formal regimen. Demerits could be imposed for the most minute infractions, but custom saw to it that a certain number of demerits on a midshipman's record was the mark of a gentleman and conferred no disgrace. Behind the facade of iron discipline, the midshipmen found plenty of scope for mischief. John McIntosh Kell spent eight months at the academy in 1847 to 1848 studying to pass his lieutenant's examination, together with other midshipmen who had received their warrants in 1841. The men of '41 had a reputation as an "unruly set of devils to manage. . . ." They rolled thirty-two pounder shot down halls and stairways (the noise was gratifying—like thunder), held all-night drinking parties, fought two duels for which the principals were dismissed from the service, and generally challenged authority so successfully that Secretary Abel P. Upshur was obliged to appeal to their better instincts: "I cannot govern you, young gentlemen; so if you will only govern yourselves I shall be delighted."[58]

The midshipmen of 1841 possessed a great deal of group cohesion. They took a powerful disliking to Professor Henry N. Lockwood, the academy's gunnery instructor, who soon found his practice batteries dismounted and stripped of vital parts, while he himself was hanged in effigy. The class had become highly incensed because they suspected that he was trying to make them learn more gunnery than the previous class had. Ultimately, Lockwood proved unable to complete his course of instruction in the face of this opposition. On another occasion, the entire class armed themselves with pokers and similar blunt instruments and swarmed into downtown Annapolis to investigate the rumor that a fight had broken out between midshipmen and local toughs.[59]

When Kell attended the academy it was only a few years old, and many of its students had spent considerable time in the lawless atmosphere of the fleet's gun rooms before attending. Annapolis remained rough and disorganized throughout the 1850s, and for the first half of the decade of the 1860s the navy was too preoccupied with the Civil War to take it seriously in hand. At the end of the war, a board of visitors, including admirals Farragut and Porter, arrived to inspect the academy and report on conditions there. Porter remained as superintendent, purging the administration and staff, weeding out unsuitable midshipmen, reorganizing the curriculum, overhauling the honor system, setting up an athletic program, and generally transforming Annapolis from a rowdy barracks with classrooms attached into a more comprehensive institution approximating what exists today.[60]

The midshipmen at the Naval Academy constituted but one of the special problems that the naval justice system had to deal with. Another group which found itself under naval jurisdiction were the privateers who operated extensively during the War of 1812. Secretary of State James Monroe, hoping to avoid situations wherein American privateersmen might be mistaken for pirates or create diplomatic incidents by plundering neutral or friendly vessels, requested that Congress provide some means of disciplining them. Congress obliged by passing a special regulation stipulating that

> all offences committed by any officer or seaman on board any vessel having letter of marque and reprisal . . . . shall be tried and punished in such a manner as the like offences are or may be tried and punished when committed by any person belonging to the public ships of war of the United States.[61]

There were British precedents for this provision, written in almost identical language.[62] A further rationalization for putting this segment of the civilian population under the jurisdiction of the Articles of War seems to have been that privateersmen were the closest thing to naval reserves that the country possessed at that time and might be subject to mobilization into the navy in the event of a dire threat to national security.[63]

Courts-martial and courts of inquiry involving privateers reached a peak in 1813 and 1814, with thirty-two cases appearing in the judge advocate general's records index. Privateersmen were charged with mutiny, treason, shameful neglect of duty, firing into a friendly vessel, or plundering a neutral vessel, among other things.[64] On balance, however, there were not too many cases involving privateers, especially compared to the large number of officers and men engaged in this activity during the War of 1812. Naval officers were contemptuous of privateersmen and reluctant to involve themselves in cases they considered ridiculous or trivial. Privateer captains knew little of the Articles of War, often ignored the rules of evidence, and were inclined to make charges that could not be sustained. On their part, the privateersmen soon saw that the Articles of War were unsuitable as rules for civilians engaged in a commercial venture and became increasingly reluctant to involve the navy in their affairs.[65] Congress repealed its privateer act after the War, and since then the navy has seldom exercised legal jurisdiction over persons not in the service.

The navy's role in disciplining privateers was a special case that grew out of singular historical circumstances. In general, the Old Navy's disciplinary problems were remarkably consistent from decade to decade between 1800 and 1861. They revolved primarily around drunkenness, desertion, insubordination, mutinous conduct, neglect of duty, and disrespect to superiors. Assuming that the most commonly lodged court-martial charges represent the navy's greatest disciplinary problems, a table has been compiled in order that a hierarchy of common court-martial offenses can be developed.

There were times when the naval justice system was burdened or challenged by unusual circumstances growing out of historical events. During the Barbary Wars, the War of 1812, the Mexican War, and the Civil War, there were cases of treason, cowardice, and other charges relating to poor performance in battle that did not occur in peacetime. Naval service was often monotonous, but specific discipline problems growing out of monotony were recognized only when the fleet was engaged on extensive blockade duty, as happened during both the Mexican and Civil Wars.[67]

The Civil War era was a major crisis in the annals of the naval justice system. The fleet's personnel strength expanded fivefold, or 526 percent. The regular officer corps actually declined in numbers, however, due to large-scale defections to the Confederacy; so the navy was obliged to commission volunteer officers in such large numbers that by 1865 they amounted to 80 percent of the total officer complement.[68] With this massive new influx of officers and men, the navy was obliged to undertake many diverse and unaccustomed missions, make its final transition from sail to steam, and introduce and operate wholly new and experimental types of ships.

In the course of these events, the navy was saddled with serious morale problems. Many of the volunteer officers were incompetent or unsuitable, drunkenness among all ranks reached serious proportions,

94

Table I. An analysis of charges most commonly made
during courts-martial in the Navy
1799–1861

Offense	Percentage of all charges	Percentage preferred against
Desertion Absence without leave Breaking or escaping arrest	17.7	enlisted men 94.8 officers 5.2*
Disobedience Defiance Insubordination Insolence Disregard of orders or of an order	15.7	enlisted men 65.3 officers 33.7

Scandalous conduct
  tending to the
  destruction of
  good order, morals
  or discipline
Unofficerlike conduct
  or unsoldierlike
  conduct
Ungentlemanly conduct
	10.6	enlisted men 21.6**
		officers 79.4

Contemptuous behavior
  towards a superior
Showing contempt
Disrespect towards a
  superior officer
  or court-martial
  board
	8.9	enlisted men 63.8
		officers 36.2

Drunkenness Intoxication Smuggling liquor Habitual intemperance All other charges relating to liquor	8.1	enlisted men 60.4 officers 39.6

Mutiny
Mutinous assembly,
  words, acts, or
  conduct
Conspiracy to commit
  mutiny
	7.8	enlisted men 91.2
		officers 8.8

95

Table I (cont.)

Offense	Percentage of all charges	Percentage preferred against
Neglect of duty Negligence in the performance of duty	4.8	enlisted men 41.3 officers 58.7

Assault
Assault on a superior
Striking a superior
Assault on a sentry
  or other functionary
  in the execution of
  his office
	4.0	enlisted men 96.2
		officers 3.8

Riotous conduct on board ship Fighting Quarreling Disorderly conduct	3.3	enlisted men 60.5 officers 39.5

Fraud
Embezzlement
Misuse of government
  funds, equipment,
  or property
Signing false musters
	2.7	enlisted men 64
		officers 36***

Gambling Lying Falsehood Larceny Theft	2.5	enlisted men 79.8† officers 21.2
Using provocative or reproachful words Abusive language Profanity	2.5	enlisted men 57.6 officers 42.4

Deserting post in
  battle
Leaving post before
  being properly
  relieved
Sleeping on watch
	1.8	enlisted men 75
		officers 25

Menacing a superior Resisting a superior Drawing a weapon against a superior Menacing	1.8	enlisted men 79.2 officers 20.8

Table I (cont.)

Offense	Percentage of all charges	Percentage preferred against
Cruelty Oppression Undue harshness Illegal punishment	1.4	enlisted men 0 officers 100
Treason Cowardice Timidity in action Failure to engage the enemy	1.2	enlisted men 43.8 officers 56.2

*Officers were never charged with desertion but with absence over leave or breaking arrest.

**Marine enlisted men were sometimes charged with unsoldierlike conduct.

***Pursers and commodores of squadrons are prominently represented here.

†Enlisted men who deserted were often charged with the theft of ships' boats if they used them to escape.

Further Note on Table I: Many other types of charges appear in the JAG Records Index, but none of them amounts to even as much as one percent of the total. For example, charges relating to sex offenses constitute 0.31 percent, charges concerning dueling amount to 0.07 percent, charges involving acts committed while on liberty total 0.4 percent, and charges of treason or sedition constitute 0.4% of the total.[66]

quarrels and friction between the department and hide-bound senior officers developed, and a rapid expansion of the number of black personnel brought integration problems to what had always been a very polyglot and cosmopolitan lower deck.

Specific disciplinary problems of a new or unusual character were particularly noticeable in the Fresh Water Navy which carried on riverine warfare in the western theater of operations. For some time it was under the jurisdiction of the War Department; and although officered by navy men, it was largely crewed by drafts of soldiers from the army. These men were selected from various regiments of the Army of the Tennessee and often included malcontents and other trouble-makers whom officers and sergeants wanted to be rid of.[69] Conditions aboard the gunboats, especially in summer, were extremely unpleasant; and the men were constantly shifted from one ship to another, never getting a chance to "settle in" and identify with one particular command. Since they never operated far from land, desertion reached staggering proportions; and after the major battles had been fought, a monotony of such demoralizing deadliness set in that even junior officers "ran" in significant numbers.[70]

In the Salt Water Navy, problems were of a more traditional nature; but here the reforms instituted in the 1850s and early 1860s had done much to change the face of naval discipline. The seamen's theatricals, so roundly condemned and sparingly allowed in the Old Navy, were now encouraged as a morale booster along with organized sports competitions and music, another outlet formerly taboo in the service.[71] A journal kept by a paymaster's clerk in the frigate *Sabine* during a cruise to the South Atlantic under Captain Cadwalader Ringgold between November 1862 and February 1863 reflects the effect of these changes. Apparently, in the absence of flogging there was less resort to disciplinary correctives and more reliance on leadership. During the four-month period covered by the journal, one man was given a strong public reprimand for tampering with the ship's compass, and a marine named Leary was given a summary court-martial and drew ten days' solitary confinement on bread and water for mistakenly arresting the acting master while he was on sentry duty in the cockpit. Seaman Peter Simons was also given a summary court and drew twenty days' solitary confinement in double irons on bread and water and a forfeiture of one month's pay plus two months' extra police duty with a placard bearing the word "thief" to be hung around his neck on chest and back. His offense was the theft of some clothes. Finally, two men accused of mutinous conduct were tried, again by a summary court. One was given a dishonorable discharge; and the other, who had struck a shipmate with a plate, got ten days' solitary confinement on bread and water with one month's forfeiture of pay.[72]

The frequency with which summary courts-martial were held on the *Sabine* in 1862 and 1863 is of real significance when we compare it with the 108 floggings recorded on board Commander Du Pont's *Congress* during the cruise of similar duration in an almost identical ship described earlier in this chapter. Apparently the trouble and inconvenience of holding a summary court-martial each time a serious penalty was called for had the effect of drastically reducing the number of punishments that came to the attention of the ship's company. One wonders how many more infractions would have been recorded on board the *Sabine* if Captain Ringgold had still possessed the freedom to award twelve lashes at captain's mast on his own authority.

The routine disciplinary practices of the Navy during the nineteenth century reveal a few statistics that give an idea of the volume and trends set by the frequency of naval tribunals between 1800 and 1865. There were a grand total of 4,340 general courts-martial and courts of inquiry, of which 1,420 took place during the Civil War and 2,920 were held between 1799 and 1861. This yields an average of 48 per year; but, as Table II will show, few years were ever average.

Table II. Courts-martial and courts of inquiry in the
Navy on a year-by-year basis from 1800 to 1865

Year	Remarks	Number of naval courts	Total personnel strength—Navy and Marine Corps	Ratio of courts to total manpower
1800	unsuitable officers	15	5,925	1:395
1801	are eliminated	15	3,057	1:204
1802	Preble's years in	1	2,559	1:2,560
1803	command	1	2,042	1:2,040
1804	no remarks	10	2,589	1:259
1805	no remarks	20	3,769	1:188
1806	no remarks	2	1,423	1:711
1807	no remarks	8	2,548	1:318
1808	*Chesapeake* Affair	28	2,488	1:89
1809	no remarks	18	5,398	1:300
			average ratio for decade, 1:707	
1810	no remarks	25	5,598	1:224
1811	no remarks	39	5,920	1:152
1812	no remarks	19	5,945	1:313
1813	includes privateer	39	6,116	1:393
1814	cases	62	8,672	1:140
1815	no remarks	90	7,461	1.83
1816	frequent quarrels	79	6,512	1:82
1817	among officers	67	6,160	1:92
1818	after the War	70	6,105	1:87
1819	of 1812	73	4,753	1:65
			average ratio for decade, 1:163	
1820	no remarks	52	4,559	1:87
1821	no remarks	33	4,814	1:146
1822	no remarks	49	4,505	1:92
1823	no remarks	18	4,754	1:264
1824	Congress complains	28	5,035	1:180
1825	about the number	19	5,186	1:272
1826	of naval courts-	5	5,597	1:1,119
1827	martial	32	5,742	1:179
1828	no remarks	17	5,729	1:337
1829	no remarks	36	5,764	1:160
			average ratio for decade, 1:184	
1830	no remarks	39	5,820	1:149
1831	no remarks	31	5,118	1:165
1832	no remarks	39	6,210	1:159
1833	no remarks	17	6,316	1:371
1834	no remarks	30	6,366	1:213
1835	no remarks	70	6,974	1:100
1836	no remarks	11	6:929	1:630
1837	no remarks	36	10,013	1:278

Table II (cont.)

Year	Remarks	Number of naval courts	Total personnel strength—Navy and Marine Corps	Ratio of courts to total manpower
1838	no remarks	42	8,751	1:208
1839	no remarks	38	8,626	1:227
			average ratio for decade, 1:250	
1840	no remarks	53	9,286	1:175
1841	no remarks	59	9,474	1:161
1842	no remarks	79	12,071	1:153
1843	no remarks	54	11,639	1:215
1844	*Somers* Affair	67	12,189	1:182
1845	no remarks	43	12,217	1:284
1846	no remarks	43	11,298	1:263
1847	Mexican War	66	13:025	1:197
1848	no remarks	88	12,989	1:148
1849	*Ewing* Mutiny	74	12,421	1:168
			average ratio for decade, 1:175	
1850	abolition of	48	9,895	1:206
1851	flogging	127	9,985	1:78
1852	no remarks	81	9,973	1:123
1853	no remarks	91	10,095	1:111
1854	no remarks	70	10,240	1:146
1855	summary courts are	169	10,491	1:62
1856	included for 2 yrs.	227	10,152	1:45
1857	Naval Efficiency	44	11,427	1:260
1858	Board related	40	11,336	1:283
1859	courts of inquiry are not included	27	11,735	1:435
			average ratio for decade, 1:175	
1860	no remarks	47	11,743	1:250
1861	outbreak of Civil	34	30,267	1:890
1862	War	83	35,860	1:432
1863	Navy Rules and	334	41,707	1:125
1864	Regulations	498	60,819	1:122
1865	overhauled	471	62,156	1:131
			average ratio for period, 1:325	

Note on Table II: Of all the numbers recorded in these columns, perhaps the most significant are the ratios which were derived from dividing the number of naval courts for each year into the total personnel strength of the two services that were under the jurisdiction of the Naval Justice System. This is not an entirely accurate indicator, because sometimes more than one naval court was needed to try an individual: that is, a court of inquiry followed by a court-martial. It does tell us *approximately* how many courts were held for each one hundred or one thousand men in the navy during these years. Students of modern military justice will note that these ratios are very high by modern standards. In 1851, for example, one naval court was held for each seventy-eight men enrolled in the service.[73]

The ratio of minor punishments awarded to courts-martial and courts of inquiry held in any given year is difficult to establish, but we do have a few figures available that might give us some insight. We know that there were 109 general courts-martial and courts of inquiry held during 1846 and 1847 and that 5,936 floggings were also administered during those two years. This gives us a ratio of 54.5 minor punishments for each naval court in this two-year period. These figures were collected because Congress was debating the abolition of flogging in 1848. Whether this ratio is accurate for other years would be exceedingly difficult to establish.

Our overview of daily disciplinary practices in the navy between 1800 and 1865 leads us to the conclusion that, after decades of stagnation in customs and methodology, the abolition of flogging in 1850 and the naval reform bills of the 1860s ushered in an era of instability that led to considerable evolution. American naval discipline continued to be conspicuously severe throughout the time period of this study, however; and within the limits set by Congress and the *Naval Regulations*, there was to be no really significant liberalization at all during the nineteenth century.

Chapter V

Mutiny, Desertion, & Murder

In the Old Navy there were many categories of serious crime. Assault on a superior officer, cowardice, sabotage, treason, sedition, fraud, and embezzlement were all offenses known to the naval justice system. There were three categories of naval crime, however, which the navy chose to deal with—at least on occasion—by meting out the death penalty. Between 1799 and 1861, naval courts-martial handed down death sentences twenty-six times as punishment for mutiny, desertion, or murder. In all, fourteen men were sentenced to death for mutiny or mutinous conduct, of whom seven were actually executed. Eight men were sentenced to die for desertion, four of them being marines serving under the command of Master Commandant Daniel Dexter on Lake Erie in 1814.[1] A further four men were condemned to death for murder.

Only three cases involving these death sentences have gained any notoriety among naval historians. The execution of the three *Somers* mutineers in 1842 will probably always be shrouded in mystery and controversy because of the highly unusual circumstances under which the sentence was carried out. The death sentences of two of the *Ewing* mutineers in 1849 were accomplished by less dramatic and more regular procedures, and the hanging of Seaman Samuel Jackson for mutiny on board the sloop of war *St. Marys* off the east coast of Mexico in 1846 presents still another situation. It was apparently perpetrated for the purpose of setting an example for the Home Squadron, whose discipline seemed to be deteriorating under the tedium of wartime blockade duty.[2] Modern jurists might be tempted to call it a case of judicial murder.

When dealing with cases involving mutiny, murder, and desertion, naval courts-martial had an alternative to the death penalty which was used with some frequency. The Articles of War stipulated that "A court-martial shall not, for any one offence not capital, inflict a punishment beyond one hundred lashes."[3] This was taken to mean that if the offense being tried *were* capital but the court did not wish to inflict an overt death penalty, it could prescribe a flogging over the amount of one hundred lashes or even devise a punishment of its own. Between 1800 and 1851, there were forty-nine cases where in excess of

Table III
Death sentences and executions in the Navy, 1799–1862

Case No.	Name	Year Tried	Executed?
I. *Mutiny or Mutinous Conduct*			
JAG 3	Ansel Robinson, Seaman	1800	No
JAG 3	John Carter, Seaman	1800	No
JAG 147	William Johnson, Seaman	1813	Probably
JAG 844	Philip Spencer, Midshipman	1842	Yes
JAG 844	Elisha Small, Seaman	1842	Yes
JAG 844	Samuel Cromwell, Boatswain	1842	Yes
JAG 1016	Samuel Jackson, Seaman	1846	Yes
JAG 1237	Peter Black, Seaman	1849	Yes
JAG 1237	John Black, Seaman	1849	Yes
JAG 1237	Jonathan Biddy, Seaman	1849	No
JAG 1237	William Hall, Seaman	1849	No
JAG 1237	Henry Commerford, Seaman	1849	No
JAG 1320	William Valliant, Seaman	1851	No
JAG 1548	William Thompson, Coal Heaver	1854	No
II. *Desertion*			
JAG 114	Daniel McKenny, Marine	1812	Probably
JAG 172	James Bird, Marine	1814	Yes
JAG 172	James Rankin, Marine	1814	Yes
JAG 178	John Monroe, Marine	1814	Yes
JAG 178	William Bunnett, Marine	1814	Yes
JAG 189	Robert Elixson, Seaman	1814	Yes
JAG 260	Thomas Smith, Marine	1817	Probably
JAG 345	William Bauseman, Marine	1819	No
III. *Murder*			
JAG 2	William Galligher, Seaman	1799	Probably
JAG 252	William Boyington, Marine	1817	Probably
JAG 640	Thomas Allen, Landsman	1836	Probably
JAG 1036	Daniel Davy, 1st Class Boy	1846	No

Note: In listing the eventual outcome of these cases, the following criterion were employed:

"Yes": If it is a historical certainty that the execution took place, or if the death sentence was confirmed by the President or the Navy Department or a commodore on foreign station, the execution is listed as having taken place.

"Probably": If a death sentence was passed by a court-martial board but no documentary evidence survives in the records to indicate whether or not it was confirmed or carried out, it has been listed as probably taking place.

"No": If documentary evidence exists to indicate that the death sentence was commuted by the President or a commodore on foreign station, the execution is listed as not having taken place.

one hundred lashes was handed down.[4] The most severe case was four hundred lashes, later reduced to three hundred, awarded to Seaman John Herring for murder in 1837.[5] The usual practice was to order between 150 and 350 lashes and specify that the miscreant be "whipped through the squadron." In one instance a seaman named John Baptiste was sentenced to receive two hundred lashes, to have the left side of his face and head shaved, to be drummed through the Boston Navy Yard, and dismissed from the service.[6]

Nineteen cases in which a naval court awarded over one hundred lashes saw the punishment mitigated by a reviewing authority, particularly if the sentence was to be carried out in an American port. The practice of whipping men through the squadron, the American euphemism for a "flogging 'round the fleet," seems to have been more popular on foreign stations.

Since the crimes of mutiny and mutinous conduct yield the greatest number of death sentences and many of the severest floggings, a brief history of mutiny in the United States Navy can reveal a great deal about the treatment of capital crimes in the service. In fact, the navy has had only one mutiny in the classic manner wherein a ship's crew actually overpowered its officers and made off with a public vessel. This took place near the Island of Nuka Hiva in the South Pacific early in May 1814. Marine Lieutenant John Gamble and two midshipmen, with a crew of thirteen seamen and six British prisoners, were sailing the prize whaler *Seringapatam* from the Marquesas Islands to Valparaiso, Chile, for a planned rendezvous with the frigate *Essex*. On 7 May 1814, Gamble gave a routine order which was defied by the crew. When he tried to assert his authority by force, he was overpowered, tied up, and locked below with the two midshipmen. After a hasty conference, the mutineers, all seamen from the *Essex* but now joined by the British prisoners, abandoned the three officers at sea in a small boat, together with two loyal seamen. The *Seringapatam* then hoisted British colors and sailed away.

Gamble's boat eventually returned to Nuka Hiva, where he picked up twelve seamen initially left behind, outfitted another whaler, the *Sir Andrew Hammond*, and set sail again for Hawaii. He arrived there after a harrowing voyage of a month's duration, with nearly all of his men sick or disabled, only to be made prisoner by the crew of the British sloop of war *Cherub*. The mutineer's ship was also sighted briefly off Hawaii before disappearing forever into the vast reaches of the Central Pacific.[7]

The mutineers of the prize vessel *Seringapatam* had much in common with the famous *Bounty* mutineers. Like them, their discipline was undermined by a long stay in a tropical paradise, a sojourn which they hoped to prolong by rising up against their officers. Unlike the *Bounty*'s men, however, none of the *Seringapatam* mutineers was ever seen again. Except for one Robert White, even their names are lost to us; and White is remembered only because he had apparently been in trouble in the *Essex* for mutinous conduct during the passage out to the Pacific at the beginning of Commodore Porter's famous cruise.[8]

The records of the Old Navy hold another case that may or may not have been a successful mutiny. In 1846 a small group of men from the sloop of war *Warren* were detailed to sail one of the ship's launches from San Francisco Bay to New Helvetia on the Sacramento River. The *Warren*'s launch was commanded by Midshipman S. W. L. Montgomery and Purser's Clerk John E. Montgomery, both of the sloop of war *Portsmouth*, and carried a considerable sum of cash in the form of gold coins to pay Army troops camped at Sutter's Fort. The launch never reached its destination, and none of its men was ever seen again. California was in an unsettled state, with the authority of the United States only imperfectly established and still highly precarious. Bands of demobilized Mexican troops were at large, and bandit gangs operated with some boldness. Still, other navy small boats were making safe trips on the California rivers. Yeoman Joseph T. Downey, the tart and irreverent chronicler of the voyage of the *Portsmouth*, recalled the general unpopularity of the two Montgomerys, both of whom were the sons of the *Portsmouth*'s commanding officer, Commander John Berrien Montgomery, and speculated that the *Warren*'s men might have done away with the officers and taken the gold.[9] At any rate, some sort of foul play is indicated, because a few years later one of the officer's coats was found being worn by a prostitute in the gold fields east of Sutter's Fort.

Perhaps the true story of the *Warren*'s launch will never be known, but the somewhat similar events which occurred on board the schooner *Ewing*'s boat are a matter of record. The *Ewing* was an armed vessel officered and manned by the navy but operating under the orders of the Superintendent of the Coast Survey. On the evening of 13 September 1849, she was at anchor off Benecia, California. Her commanding officer, Lieutenant William F. McArthur, had entertained some guests at dinner; and late that night a boat's crew under the command of Passed Midshipman William Gibson was detailed to take the party ashore. The California Gold Rush was then at its peak, and all the government vessels in the San Francisco Bay area were observing extraordinary precautions to prevent wholesale desertions on the part of enlisted men who were not immune to the general atmosphere of "gold fever" prevalent at the time. Therefore, Passed Midshipman Gibson, following what had become standard procedure among boat officers on the Pacific Station, brought two pistols with him to keep the boat's crew at bay while the captain's guests were landed.

The trip to shore was successfully completed; but when the boat headed back to the *Ewing*, Gibson unwisely let his guard down and put away the pistols. Almost immediately, two men, John and Peter Black, attacked him and after a brief struggle threw him overboard. The boat then pulled quickly away and headed up Carquinez Strait towards the Sacramento River. Gibson commenced a desperate three-hundred-yard swim to shore, where he was eventually pulled from the water in a half-drowned condition by some bystanders.

Lieutenant McArthur promptly offered a reward of five hundred dollars each for the return of the boat's crew, and two days later they were captured at Pittsburgh while trying to row up river.[10] They were taken to the *Ewing* and quickly transferred under guard to the frigate *Savannah*, flagship of Commodore Thomas ap Catesby Jones, where they were confined in irons while a court-martial board was hastily assembled.

The court-martial began on 8 October 1849 on board the *Warren*. It consisted of thirteen officers, the largest court allowable under the Articles of War. A prominent San Francisco attorney, Hall McAllister, was hired by the commodore to conduct the defense of the accused men at the rate of one hundred dollars per day. The resulting trial lasted for seven days and generated over one thousand pages of handwritten testimony and appended documents. Each defendant was charged with mutiny, desertion, assaulting an officer in the execution of his duty, and theft of government property.[11]

From the beginning, it was obvious that the men were guilty of a major offense; so McAllister concentrated on trying to eliminate the mutiny charge to save the lives of his clients. He argued that the five men—John and Peter Black, Jonathan Biddy, William Hall, and Henry Commerford—had no "actual or previous" intention of making a mutiny or of killing Gibson; but, driven to distraction by "gold fever," they simply wanted to desert. In fact, they had signed on the *Ewing* at Valparaiso with the express intention of deserting as soon as the ship reached California. On the night of the incident, they had hoped simply to rush Gibson and carry the boat when it touched shore; but the officer's vigilance and twin pistols had foiled that plan. Consequently, they had to wait until the boat was back in the stream and Gibson had let down his guard. *Then* they overpowered him and threw him overboard, knowing that he was a good swimmer and within easy reach of the shore. They did not reckon, however, with the effect of the tricky currents of Carquinez Strait combined with the drag exerted by Gibson's bulky boat cloak.[12]

Having explained his clients' conduct on the night in question, McAllister next called the court's attention to the circumstances under which the men had been enlisted in the first place. He related that none of them was an American citizen and that they had all been drunk at the time they had signed articles. This, McAllister claimed, made their "contract" with the navy for three years' service invalid, since it was a well-known legal principle that any contract was not binding on a signatory who was too intoxicated to know what he was doing at the time the agreement was entered into. Since they were illegally enlisted, McAllister maintained, they should not be deprived of their lives.[13]

McAllister and his clients must have sensed that they were making little headway with these arguments. Their next ploy was a signed "confession" by John Black, taking all the blame for attacking Midshipman Gibson on himself and his brother Peter. It was apparently hoped that by taking the blame for the most reprehensible act on themselves, the two Blacks could get the lives of the other three men spared. Finally, the defense called Passed Midshipman Gibson to the stand. He testified that he believed that the prisoners had not actually intended to kill him but only to get him out of the boat.[14]

The court was unmoved by any of these arguments. Perhaps there had simply been too much tension and fear of desertion in the Pacific Squadron for too many months. Some ships had abandoned the practice of running shore boats rather than risk just such an incident as occupied the court's attention. Also there may have been some lingering suspicions about the disappearance of the *Warren*'s launch only three years earlier. The verdict and sentences came back harsh and uncompromising. All five men were condemned to hang.

Commodore Jones then faced a complex dilemma. He was badly frightened by the state of discipline in his squadron and believed that the men needed an example to remind them that naval law would be vigorously enforced. At the same time, the Articles of War plainly stated that no death sentences would be executed in the territorial jurisdiction of the United States unless reviewed and approved by the president. Since Millard Fillmore was thousands of miles distant in Washington, D.C., it would obviously take months to secure the necessary warrants.

Goaded by circumstances, Jones opted to carry out the executions on the practical grounds that the squadron needed a timely object lesson and that California was so remote from the rest of the United States as to constitute *de facto* a foreign station upon which a commodore had the necessary authority to review and approve sentences on his own responsibility. He therefore set the date for the hangings, scheduling them to take place on 23 October 1849. At the last possible moment, he commuted the sentences of Hall, Biddy, and Commerford to one hundred lashes, loss of pay, and confinement at hard labor for the remainder of their enlistments. The two Blacks swung from the fore yardarm of the *Savannah* promptly at 1100 on the scheduled date.[15]

This was not to be the end of the *Ewing* affair. Upon his return to the United States in 1850, Commodore Jones himself stood trial by court-martial on numerous charges relating to his conduct during his cruise in the Pacific, not the least of which was a specification of inflicting illegal punishment on the *Ewing* mutineers. Jones maintained that his situation was unique and extremely dangerous and that two previous secretaries of the navy, John Y. Mason and William Ballard Preston, had given him express permission to conduct his command as a squadron on foreign station. The new secretary of the navy under Fillmore was William A. Graham, and he was not privy to the agreements that Jones had entered into with the two previous secretaries. He intended to hold the "Contentious Commodore" accountable for many irregularities, including this one.[16] Jones ultimately drew five years' suspension from duty.

These three cases—the *Seringapatam* uprising, the disappearance of the *Warren*'s launch, and the *Ewing* mutiny—are the only known or suspected instances in the United States Navy where a "mutiny" progressed to the point where officers were assaulted and a public vessel or craft was diverted from official control. All of the other mutinous incidents that punctuate American naval history stopped short of this point, including the most famous of all, the *Somers* Affair of 1842.

The *Somers* mutiny may not, in fact, have been a mutiny at all. At the time it was being adjudicated, it gave rise to a voluminous literature which did nothing to settle the basic question that still hangs over the whole business. Were the three men condemned and hanged at sea by Commander Alexander Slidell Mackenzie really plotting to capture a U.S. vessel and murder her officers? Or were the three men the victims of an overwrought commanding officer with a hyperactive imagination? Recent authors have written more books on the subject without arriving at a wholly satisfactory conclusion. The case has been analyzed so thoroughly that it is unlikely that any new information will surface. The facts we do know are utterly baffling and include evidence to support either hypothesis.

For example, Midshipman Philip Spencer, the alleged ringleader, was an unstable and undisciplined character. His captain, Commander Mackenzie, was obviously a small-minded martinet with a powerful imagination. The crew of apprentice boys behaved strangely during the *Somers'* training cruise to the west coast of Africa. The strange behavior, however, consisted only of some stampings on the deck, a good deal of tense whispering in odd corners of the berth deck, and some cryptic notes on scraps of paper. The idea that the plotters wanted to convert the *Somers* into a pirate vessel seems absurd; but the *Somers* was, in fact, the fastest ship in the navy and would have made an ideal pirate craft. It seemed that there was deliberate sabotage taking place. A spar was carried away, sails and rigging damaged,

An old Currier print depicts the brig-of-war *Somers* bound for New York with her three suspected mutineers hanging from the yardarms. Cromwell and Small share the starboard yard while Spencer, his body hidden by the foresail, dangles to port. (Beverly R. Robinson print collection, United States Naval Academy Museum Library)

and a topmast sprung. It was also true that the ship was dangerously overrigged, and her gear was very treacherous to handle. Four years later she capsized and sank while on war service in the Gulf of Mexico.

When taking all these factors into account, the impartial scholar who would seek to understand the *Somers* Affair finds himself deadlocked wherever he turns. Perhaps it is best to adopt Samuel Eliot Morison's attitude that "Mackenzie was justified morally if not legally in putting Spencer, Cromwell, and Small to death." This was the finding of Mackenzie's court-martial board, and Morison saw no need at this late date to look further into the incident.[17]

The importance of the *Somers* Affair lies not so much in the validity or invalidity of Mackenzie's actions and suspicions as it does in the ideological factors that governed the attitude of the country and the navy towards it. The year 1842 was the approximate high tide of Jacksonian Democracy. Amid a sea of conflicting emotions created by the advent of the era of the "common man," conservative Whigs confronted "radical" Democrats. Aristocracy was arrayed against democracy, social order and discipline against popular rights, the sanctity of property against the sanctity of life, the safety of society against the right of all individuals to enjoy the advantages of due process of law. Under the glare of publicity generated by the *Somers* Affair, the navy became a potent symbol of the old order and a convenient target for the civil libertarians of that day.[18] The case was pleaded in hundreds of newspapers, pamphlets, journals, and books before the court of public opinion; and ultimately the navy was the loser, suffering a marked decline in the esteem and confidence of the people. Naval discipline became, for a time, a major public issue and a target for reformers, whose work culminated in the major revisions that were put into force in 1850 and 1862.

The *Somers* Affair and Commander Mackenzie's reaction to Philip Spencer's provocation is a significant indicator that the fear of mutiny was part of a naval officer's life in the decade of the 1840s. If so, these fears can be traced back to the beginnings of the Federal Navy. When the first large frigate, the *Constellation*, was being outfitted and manned under the direction of Commodore Thomas Truxtun, the great British mutinies at Spithead and the Nore were only a year in the past. It had come as a shock to American naval officers to discover that whole squadrons and fleets organized on the European naval model could suddenly lose their discipline and become—even temporarily—independent of official control.

Even more ominous was the *Hermione* Mutiny of 1797. In this instance, the ultimate nightmare of the officers of a sailing man-of-war came to full fruition. Cruelly driven by a sadistic commander, the crew of the British frigate *Hermione* rose up against their officers in time of war, slaughtered them ruthlessly, and turned their vessel over to their country's enemies during a cruise on detached service. The *Hermione* was eventually recovered from the Spanish by a raiding party, but her crew had scattered all over the Caribbean and beyond.

As Truxtun undertook the first shakedown cruise of the *Constellation* in the spring of 1798, he established a strict disciplinary atmosphere and a rigorous program of sail and gunnery drill. He noticed a palpable air of sullenness and disaffection settling over the ship. Men gathered in small groups muttering, and soon Secretary of the Navy Benjamin Stoddert received a threatening and disrespectful letter penned on board the *Constellation*.[19] A vigorous search for "ringleaders" quickly turned up a seaman named Hugh Williams, who, upon investigation, turned out to be an ex-crewman and mutineer from the *Hermione*. Apparently Williams had arrived at Norfolk on a merchant ship returning from the Caribbean and had signed on the *Constellation* after a three-day run ashore. From Williams, Truxtun's officers learned that the Spanish authorities had put most of the *Hermione*'s crew to work on rock piles and salt pans on the vague pretext that they were prisoners of war, or at least not wholly trustworthy. Faced with this sort of treatment, most of them had eluded the Spaniards and shipped out of the Caribbean on neutral vessels under assumed names. Some of them were seeking safety in the United States.[20]

Truxtun knew the details of the *Hermione* Mutiny and believed that her captain, Hugh Pigot, was guilty of extreme brutality and gross bad judgment as an officer and leader. Still, he could not condone any act of violent mutiny coupled with treason in time of war. Williams was clapped in irons and turned over to the British consul at Norfolk.[21] This was not, however, to be Truxtun's only brush with incipient mutiny nor the only time that the American Navy felt reverberations from the *Hermione*. In May of 1800, a seaman named William Ash got drunk at sea and harangued the crew of the frigate *Essex*, then under the command of Captain Edward Preble. Ash urged them to attack the officers and eliminate them "as we did on board the *Hermione* and serve them right." Preble quickly arrested Ash and confined him in irons. Four months later he was still in confinement when he penned a letter to his captain asking to be released on the grounds that he was drunk and not actually a mutineer in his heart.[22]

At about the time of the Ash affair, Truxtun was exercising the duties of Senior Naval Officer Present at Norfolk. Captain James Sever, the unpopular and incompetent commander of the frigate *Congress*, reported that mutiny was being "actively plotted" on board his ship. Sparked by Sever's refusal of an issue of candles at dinner and goaded by the fact that they could look around the anchorage and see that other ship's crews had candles, the men staged a loud protest, which Sever broke up by using the Marine detachment. Eight supposed ringleaders were collared, including a midshipman named Prince.[23]

Sever immediately appealed to Truxtun to convene a court-martial, but the Commodore was oddly hesitant. Sever was also having trouble with his officers, and his ship had been dismasted in a gale on her shakedown cruise. Writing to Secretary Stoddert, Truxtun complained that ". . . the prejudices against Captain Sever—are very great—indeed I fear his Idea of discipline is not correct—Discipline is to be effected by a particular deportment much easier than by great severity."[24] Stoddert wrote back in annoyance:

> As Commander of the Squadron, you might have ordered a Court-Martial at once, without appealing to me, & I am sorry you did not do it. I do not like this method of appealing to the head of the Department by officers, who are themselves Competent to the object of the appeal.[25]

On this uncordial basis, the trial of the *Congress*'s mutineers got under way. Truxtun chose as judge advocate one Robert Taylor, a civilian lawyer whom he described as "A member of the Legislature of this state—he is a good Federalist and has talents necessary for the occasion in question—"[26] The surviving transcript for the trial is extremely jumbled and often illegible, but the results of the court-martial were most unsatisfactory to Captain Sever. Midshipman Prince was dropped entirely from the proceedings, probably as the result of family pressure. Seaman Benjamin Davis was acquitted of all charges, while four other men—Andrew Robb, William Brown, John Davis, and John Wilson—each received seventy-two lashes. Ansel Robinson and John Carter, accused as ringleaders, were sentenced to hang; but in reviewing the case, Truxtun mitigated the death penalties to one hundred lashes and dismissal from the navy.[27] Writing once more to Secretary Stoddert, Truxtun confided that he believed most of the trouble aboard the *Congress* was due to the incapacity of Captain Sever, whom he described as "not regularly bred to the sea," meaning, perhaps, that he was a political appointee. To make his annoyance clearer, Truxtun informed the secretary that he was drafting most of the *Congress*'s crew into the frigate *Chesapeake*,[28] thus leaving Sever sitting at anchor in Hampton Roads in a dismasted and deserted command.

When the *Congress* got to sea again, rerigged and with a new crew, Captain Sever experienced another mutiny scare. Surgeon Samuel L.

Marshall had warned him that some of the bread which was being fed to the men was spoiled and unfit for consumption. The captain, who admitted before witnesses that he had "an aversion to the gentlemen of the lancet," declared that the bread was fit to eat and ordered it issued until it was all consumed. This resulted in bitter protests from the crew. Dr. Marshall's advice was further ignored in the case of a Lieutenant Burns, whom Sever had ordered confined to his quarters for punishment. Marshall believed that continued close confinement of Lieutenant Burns would endanger his health. When Sever persisted in the punishment, Marshall criticized the captain's conduct in the wardroom, comparing Sever to Hugh Pigot of the *Hermione*.

This found its way to Sever's ears, and the doctor was quickly charged with five offenses related to the propagation of mutinous behavior among the crew. The fourth charge, in particular, accused Marshall

of having made use of language, in the Ward room, of the U. S. Frigate Congress, declaring your *Warm Approbation*, of the *Mutinous, Murderous Conduct* of the Crew of His Majesty's Frigate *Hermione*—which *conduct* is highly injurious and tends not only to the entire *destruction* of *all order* and *discipline*: but also renders *insecure* the lives of Officers serving on board Ships of War.[29]

During the ensuing trial, the court explored fully the allegation that Marshall was advocating a *Hermione*-style mutiny on board the *Congress*.

Question. (By the court to Lieutenant Seaton) Do you remember to have heard Doctor Marshall make any observations relative to the crew of the *Hermione*, and of what nature?

A. He remarked that he thought the conduct of the crew—relative to the Commander of that ship, right—I do not know whether he alluded to the Americans [i.e., impressed seamen on board the *Hermione*] alone, or to the whole crew.

Seaton's testimony and that of other witnesses indicated that the wardroom officers of the *Congress* had been generally discussing whether or not American seamen impressed into the *Hermione* were morally guilty of mutiny and liable to prosecution for the crimes committed on that ship. Marshall maintained that he did not approve of the conduct of all the *Hermione*'s crew but did feel that its American component was fully justified in throwing off the bonds of British naval discipline and authority. Sever had apparently been fed a garbled and inaccurate account of this wardroom conversation.[30]

In his defense summation, Marshall declared that

> The Circumstances which attended the Mutiny on board the *Hermione*, were totally different from any thing that can possibly happen in our navy.
>
> We have not adopted the Barbarous custom of impression [*sic*] unsanctioned even by the Laws of Great Britain. We hold out a handsome and ample compensation to the men who enter our service. . . .[31]

He went on to explain that in his view men who had been freely enlisted were liable to correction for improper conduct in a way that would not be the case

> if they were compelled to enter the service—contrary to their own judgement & inclination. [Impressed men] Could not be properly considered amenable for improper conduct as their will was never consulted in their situation.[32]

Whether because of his lofty argument, his playing on the anti-impressment sentiments of the court, or because of the distrust and prejudice against Captain Sever, Marshall was acquitted of all charges and returned to duty.

The next reference to the *Hermione* to surface officially came from the berth deck rather than the wardroom and was consequently even more fundamentally alarming. In the late spring of 1804, Captain Samuel Barron of the frigate *President* received an anonymous letter stating that

> The horrid usage that has been carried on in this ship by the principal officers is enough to turn any man's heart to wickedness—We are kept on deck from 3 O'clock in the Morning 'til 8 at night—there is no regulations in any one thing, we have been on deck several days without one bit of victuals and durst not look for it.—We cannot wash a single article for fear of being cut in two—you expect everything done at a word—there is no allowance made for our freezing day and night, but the time will come when you will drive all thoughts other out of our minds—tyranny is the beginning of all mischief & is generally attended by bad doings at the latter end—Any Commodore or Captain that had the least feeling of thought would not suffer this horrid usage, it is almost impossible for us to live— The President is arrived at such a pitch as to exceed the *Hermione*—Some of our friends in America & other parts shall know of this shortly & in time we hope to get redress. deth [*sic*] is always superior to slavery—We remain your unhappy slaves.[33]

This rambling and ill-constructed letter must have struck Barron and his officers as the worst kind of mutinous threat. A determined investigation eventually led to a seaman named Robert Quinn, who pleaded guilty to a charge of mutiny based on the authorship of the letter. The court-martial proceeding was brief. The court decided to crush Quinn with a punishment that would set an example for the rest of the navy. He was sentenced to have his head and eyebrows shaved, to be branded on the forehead with the word "mutiny," to receive 320 lashes, wear a white cap with a label, and to be drummed on shore under a gallows in a boat towed stern first.[34] An officer who witnessed Quinn's punishment wrote:

> I have no idea that he [can] survive the whole of it, but must die under the operation. It is to be sure, most cruel punishment, but the existence of the Navy require it.[35]

Captain John Rodgers presided over Quinn's trial and punishment, which took place at Hampton Roads, Virginia. No documents survive to indicate that the sentence was ever reviewed by President Jefferson or his Secretary of the Navy, Robert Smith. Perhaps neither man cared to sign his name to such a warrant.

An officer who wrote an anonymous and mutinous letter at about the same time fared somewhat better than Quinn. Midshipman William Reid of the frigate *John Adams* was court-martialed for drunkenness, participating in a mutinous and seditious assembly, and writing a false and malicious letter to Commodore Samuel Barron.[36] Midshipman Reid had apparently been having considerable difficulty in getting along with his superior officers, particularly Lieutenant George Kearny. Kearny testified that Reid had been drunk on one occasion when he was supposed to be helping to break out a kedge anchor. Another time he allowed a watering detail under his direction to become intoxicated while filling casks ashore. His "mutinous and seditious" assembly apparently consisted of carrying rum to the enlisted men in his watch, singing songs with them, and persisting in this behavior after having been warned not to fraternize with the seamen. His greatest crime was to write a letter to Commodore Barron accusing Lieutenant Kearny of the death of a man named Starbuck who had sickened and died a few weeks after having been flogged by the Lieutenant's order for slowness in answering a hail.[37]

Although the letter in question was unsigned, Reid had bragged to several acquaintances, including enlisted men, that he intended to write it; and this formed the basis for his conviction on the charges. He was sentenced to be deprived of his warrant and dismissed from the navy, but implementation of the sentence was to be delayed until it could be reviewed by the president. The condition of the record of this proceeding, like that of most of the navy's earliest court-martials, is very poor, with many illegible pages and items either missing or out of order. Since there are no further documents, it is impossible to know if Reid was actually dismissed.

Although it is evident that the navy was preoccupied with mutiny during the first decade of its existence, it was not until 1812 that a man was actually sentenced to death for that crime. In that year Seaman William Johnson of the ketch *Despatch* was tried for mutiny after brawling with two officers on a wharf at the Norfolk Navy Yard. The circumstances of this incident are confused. Apparently, Johnson was in the hospital at the Yard and left his ward without permission to go aboard the *Despatch* to pick a fight with Ordinary Seaman James Durety, who had offended his brother on some earlier occasion.

Johnson must have been either drugged or drunk, because his subsequent actions indicate extremely erratic behavior. He was fighting with Durety when Midshipman Enoch Lowe, commanding officer of the ketch, tried to break them up. Johnson immediately turned on Lowe and challenged him to come on shore and fight him, cursing him roundly in the process. When Lieutenant Walter Anderson came on deck, Johnson challenged him to a duel with pistols and declared that he was "as good as any man in the Navy Yard."[38] The two officers gave Johnson a severe beating and dragged him to the guardhouse, where he was double ironed and gagged until a trial could be convened by Captain John Cassin, commandant of the navy yard. Captain James Tarbell presided at the court-martial.

Johnson's only defense was that he had been "so violently beaten about the head by Mr. Anderson that he was confused and did not know what he said or did."[39] Witnesses disputed this and claimed that Johnson was very specific in his verbal abuse of the two officers, declaring that he was "as good an officer as [Mr. Lowe] was nor that he did not care for Mr. L. nor any other officer further than civility." He also offered to "whip all on board the Ketch."[40]

The court decided that Johnson's actions fell under Article XIII of the Articles of War and sentenced him "to suffer death by hanging at such time and place as his Excellency the President of the United States may direct." The president seems not to have chosen any time or place or, if he did, the document has been lost. All that remains in the record is a tart note to Captain Cassin from the Navy Department which reads:

Sir:

I have received the copy of the proceedings of a Court-Martial held by you on board the Frigate *Constellation* at Norfolk on the 17th instant.

I request you to inform me under what authority you conceived yourself authorized to convene such a Court-Martial.

[Signature obliterated][41]

There is nothing to indicate whether or not Johnson was hanged. Although he was charged with mutiny, it is obvious that he was not guilty of that crime in its usual sense but rather of mutinous conduct or assault upon an officer or even disrespect and disobedience.

The Johnson case clearly shows that some naval officers were inclined to use mutiny and mutinous conduct charges loosely. For this reason many of the courts-martial listed in the judge advocate general's records with mutiny or mutinous conduct among the charges do not actually represent mutinous activity in the sense that the word is understood by laymen. A good many of them are really assault cases or disobedience and disrespect directed towards officers by enlisted men. Since the Articles of War made these crimes punishable by death, it is possible that mutiny or mutinous conduct charges were simply tacked on in order to make a greater psychological impact on the court-martial board and provide an example for restless crews.

Such a case was that of Seaman Samuel Jackson of the sloop of war *St. Marys* during the Mexican War. In the summer of 1846, the *St. Marys* was part of Commodore David Connor's Home Squadron which was engaged in the tedious close blockade of the unhealthy and largely barren east coast of Mexico. Under these conditions, morale deteriorated until the commodore became worried about the state of discipline in his command. He decided that the squadron needed an example. Seaman Jackson seemed the logical choice when he knocked down the officer of the deck and cursed and reviled him. Jackson had hidden a pair of shoes under a gun carriage during an inspection, and the officer of the deck had found them and kicked them overboard. Jackson, a hot-tempered Irishman serving in the navy under an assumed name, exploded in rage and assaulted the officer.[42]

Although such an offense could merit the death penalty, the Articles of War permitted the court to assign a lesser punishment, and it was customary to do so in cases like this one. The *St. Marys*, unfortunately, had the reputation of being a disaffected ship, her crew being unusually sullen and difficult to manage. Therefore, Commodore Connor took the role of prosecutor (that is, as the officer preferring the charges) and added a charge of "mutinous and seditious words" to Jackson's indictment. He also took steps to let the court-martial board know that he expected a death sentence.[43]

The court obligingly returned the verdict and sentence that the commodore wanted. Connor then arranged for the execution to take place where he believed it would do the most good. Samuel Jackson was hanged from the fore yardarm of the *St. Marys* on 17 September 1846 at the fleet anchorage at Anton Lizardo in full view of the entire squadron.[44] Because he was executed at the behest of Commodore

Connor and for his convenience rather than for reasons germaine to his particular offense, the hanging of Seaman Jackson is a reasonably clear case of judicial murder. Occurring a mere four years after the *Somers* executions, it attracted surprisingly little notice outside the service.[45] The Home Squadron's crews remained under good discipline for the rest of the Mexican War.

When all the known mutinies that took place in the navy are accounted for and when all the instances where an enlisted man attacked or threatened an officer and found himself facing mutinous conduct charges in lieu of assault or disrespect indictments, there still remain a few instances where the crews of naval vessels staged work stoppages or engaged in collective defiance of official authority. While comparatively rare, these actions perhaps come closer to the classical concept of mutiny than anything else that happened in the navy, with the exception of the *Seringapatam* Incident.

The first of two such incidents which appear in the records took place on board the frigate *Constitution* at Hampton Roads in 1838. Commodore Jesse Duncan Elliott had brought the ship home from a three-year cruise in the Mediterranean with a wide assortment of art objects and valuables stowed in the hold. In addition, most of the available space on the gun deck was taken up by jackasses and other livestock stabled in temporary pens between the guns. All of this cargo was the personal property of the commodore, and the animals were particular objects of hatred among the crew because they had taken up much of the *Constitution*'s already cramped living space.

The men expected to be discharged upon arrival at Hampton Roads. Commodore Elliott, however, delayed the paying off of the men and turned them to unloading the animals and cargo, which included two massive marble sarcophagi. This consumed an entire working day, and that night the men rioted after getting drunk on whiskey smuggled from shore. They surged up the hatchways to the spar deck, where they beat up a mulatto sailor and defied the orders of the ship's lieutenants to return to the berth deck. They ran about the decks yelling for several hours, attacked the master-at-arms, and drove him to take refuge in the wardroom pantry.[46] Finally they quieted down of their own accord and returned to their hammocks.

The next day the men were discharged and the incident would have gone unreported and unrecorded except that several officers, who had been feuding with Commodore Elliott during the cruise, saw a chance to damage his reputation and strengthen other charges that they were bringing against him concerning his methods of commanding the Mediterranean Squadron. In 1840, Elliott was court-martialed on numerous charges; and among them was "witnessing a mutiny and not doing his utmost to suppress it." Lieutenants Charles H. McBlain and Bushrod Hunter both testified that Elliott had been aboard the *Constitution* on the night of the riot, together with his flag captain, Commander William Boerum. However, they failed to support the ship's lieutenants in their efforts to get the men below except to order them to "go forward" after they had chased the mulatto sailor into officer's country.[47]

Obviously, Elliott was not anxious to confront his rebellious crew. Transporting his animals and unloading his cargo was what had triggered their uprising. Any investigation of the incident would lay him open to charges of transporting private property in a public vessel; and since the men were due to be discharged anyway, Elliott apparently hoped to suppress the whole affair. Perhaps if he had not alienated so many of his officers on the cruise, he might have been able to accomplish his objective. He filed no report and made no log entries. When confronted by the court two years later, he could only bluster and deny that what had taken place amounted to a mutiny. The court acquitted him of the charge relating to this incident, but found him guilty of enough others to sentence him to four years' suspension from duty with loss of pay for the first two years.[48]

A somewhat similar incident took place on board the frigate *United States* of the African Squadron in 1849. The *United States* was the flagship of Commodore George Read and was commanded by Captain Joseph Smoot. These two officers and the first lieutenant, George A. Prentiss, were bitter personal enemies. At the end of the cruise, Lieutenant Prentiss was court-martialed on charges brought by Smoot and Read which grew out of the three-cornered, running feud. As a defense measure, Lieutenant Prentiss filed countercharges against his captain and commodore of "witnessing a mutiny and doing nothing to suppress it."[49]

The "mutiny" in question occurred in the harbor of Port Mahon, where the *United States* had called for victualing after a long and unrewarding search for slavers in the Bight of Benin. The crew wanted shore leave and an advance on their wages. Captain Smoot assembled them on deck and informed them that he would not make any funds available. At this point the men began to shout that they would sell their clothes to get money if none were forthcoming. Smoot replied that they could "sell their clothes and be damn'd."

The next morning, the crew assembled on the gun deck, triced up the hatchway ladders, and refused to do duty. The alarmed Prentiss reported the mass protest to Commodore Read, but the flag officer refused to get involved and ordered Prentiss to take up the problem with Captain Smoot. Smoot was in his lodgings ashore, and it was an hour before he came on board. Once returned, the captain took the necessary steps to safeguard the officers and public property. He paraded the Marine detachment, issued them powder and ball, and called for representatives from the crew, whom he commenced to bargain with. The men restated their demand for ten dollars in advance money to spend ashore. Smoot offered them eight dollars, claiming that the ship did not have sufficient funds aboard to cover the larger advance. After prolonged negotiation, the crew settled for eight dollars and permission to sell their pea jackets. The mutiny, or work stoppage, was over. The men swarmed into the boats and hurried ashore, leaving in their wake a scandalized Lieutenant Prentiss, who lost no time in writing a letter to the Navy Department describing the incident. He called it mutiny and accused the captain and commodore of not helping to suppress it.[50]

When Smoot and Read found out about Prentiss's letter, they composed their own differences long enough to suspend the lieutenant from duty and filed charges of falsehood against him. At the trial, Captain Smoot defended his actions by claiming that what had taken place was, in fact and law, not a mutiny. He pointed out that there was no legal definition or description in the *Naval Regulations* exactly defining just what did constitute mutiny. Thus, a captain was free to decide for himself if his crew was mutinous; and he, Smoot, thereby declined to designate the crew of the *United States* as having been in a state of mutiny.[51]

Lieutenant Prentiss countered this argument with great resourcefulness. He agreed that no court had ever laid down an exact definition of mutiny as it applied to a ship of war, but he cited a federal court opinion derived from a case involving a merchant vessel, which reasoned that

> a crime of mutiny or revolt, consists not in simple disobedience of orders, nor in the mere exhibition of turbulence or violence, but in organized and concerted resistance to lawful authority, aiming at the subversion, for even a brief period of time, of the power of those legally entitled to command.
>
> Actual disobedience of some order given is not necessary to constitute the offence of an endeavor to make a revolt. If the crew have combined together to disobey orders, and to do no duty the offence is complete by such combination, although no orders have been subsequently given. But a simple refusal by one or more to do duty does not amount to the offence unless it is done by a common combination, or to effect a common purpose. In short, the parties must act together and with the intention of mutual encouragement and support.[52]

Prentiss claimed that this doctrine applied to naval vessels as well as merchant ships and that the incident aboard the *United States* fulfilled the requirements stated in the opinion.

The court-martial board reached a mixed decision in the case of Lieutenant Prentiss. He was found guilty of disobedience and disrespect but not of having stated a falsehood. He was sentenced to be reprimanded in general orders, a meaningless penalty in those days. Captain Smoot and Commodore Read were never called upon to stand trial for their actions. Therefore the incident, which obviously grew out of the bad feelings that existed among the three men, reached a conclusion that was unsatisfactory to all parties. Prentiss had not been able to embarrass his superiors, and they had not been able to ruin him.

The uprisings on the *Constitution* in 1838 and the *United States* in 1849 were both ventilated in naval courts after being officially unreported by the captains of the respective ships. This leads to speculation as to how many similar close encounters with mutiny or work stoppages might have occurred and been successfully covered up. It is possible that the work stoppage and occasional riots may have been an unofficial means of relieving tension that was condoned by many officers, at least to the extent that they went unreported if no lasting harm was done.

We do know that under certain circumstances commanding officers expected their crews to become restless and insubordinate and generally did little about it. This was particularly true when enlistments expired before the end of a cruise. The men had a right to demand discharge at the expiration of their articles even if this meant releasing them in a foreign port. A captain would then find himself confronted with the prospect of shipping unreliable foreign seamen or completing his cruise woefully shorthanded. Faced with such a choice, some commanding officers arbitrarily extended the enlistments of their men, who then retaliated by becoming intractable and insubordinate; and the officers were obliged to tread very softly.[53]

In 1839, Commodore Nicholson penned a letter describing just such an impasse on board the razee frigate *Independence* on the Brazil Station: ". . . the men are in a great state of excitement and insubordination, many of them having refused to do duty."[54] A ringleader was found and a court-martial convened to try him for mutiny. However, since the man's enlistment was officially expired, the court decided that they could not legally punish him.[55]

Naval officers were also vigilant to detect signs of mutinous assemblies among their crews. Joseph Downey, the *Portsmouth*'s diarist, skirted on the edge of a mutiny charge because he belonged to a small clique of clandestine drinkers who met secretly in the ship's storeroom, of which Downey had a key, to plot mischief and determine ways to harass the officers. They were so successful that morale aboard the *Portsmouth* plummeted, and the ship was filled with rancor. As a result, Downey was disrated from yeoman to seaman.

In the spring of 1846, the *Portsmouth*'s first lieutenant, John S. Missroon, decided to make some use of the former yeoman's literary talents. Several crewmen had been subjected to courts-martial, and their right to submit written defense statements had been denied by the officers sitting on the tribunals. Missroon wanted Downey to compose bogus defense statements to be attributed to the defendants and inserted into the records so that it would seem that all due process had been observed. Downey was a clever man with a gift for satire. After some resistance, he consented and produced a set of statements that were impudent and hilarious burlesques of the proceedings. These he read aloud to his storeroom cronies, and eventually the word spread all over the ship that he was ridiculing the officers and undermining their authority in the eyes of the crew.[56]

When these facts became known to Lieutenant Missroon and Commander John B. Montgomery, they seized Downey and confined him to a makeshift brig while they petitioned the commodore to try him on charges of insubordination, suspected mutiny, and improper use of official documents while the Pacific Squadron was assembled at Mazatlan, Mexico. Of course, the officers were on poor ground. They knew it and Downey knew it. Commander Montgomery had written a delicately worded letter to Commodore John D. Sloat, hoping to get a court-martial authorized without going into embarrassing details concerning the true nature of the charges against Downey.

The commodore took two weeks to reply, during which the defiant and unrepentant Downey harassed Missroon as best he could from his place of confinement, the sail locker situated on the *Portsmouth*'s foredeck. Eventually the commodore's letter arrived; but to the chagrin of the ship's officers, it only stated that Sloat "could not discover in them [the charges and specifications] sufficient cause to bring [Downey] before the Court." Montgomery was authorized to investigate the case himself and either keep Downey confined until the next time the squadron could be assembled or punish him in his own way.[57] Montgomery arranged a captain's mast, with himself as president and Lieutenant Missroon as the prosecutor. Downey was found guilty of mutiny, insubordination, and lying, given twelve lashes, and warned never again "to touch pen or pencil to paper." The punishment was logged as retribution for lying and insubordination.[58]

Perhaps the Downey affair best illustrates the loose way that the officers of the Old Navy used charges of mutiny to cover a multitude of lesser offenses which in their eyes threatened their status and image rather than the actual safety of their ships. It is ironic that the closer an incident came to actually resembling a mutiny, the more reluctant officers were to identify it as such. In direct and willful violation of orders during a protest over the abolition of flogging in 1850, some two or three hundred men refused duty and walked off the frigate *Brandywine*.[59] This was the beginning of a grave disciplinary crisis that resulted in numerous complaints of insubordination, defiance of authority, and serious irregularities that persisted until 1855. No court-martial or court of inquiry was ever convened in the *Brandywine* affair. In fact, only one case of collective indiscipline can be found in the records of the judge advocate general for this period.

In August of 1852, the sloop of war *Cyane* was lying at anchor in Hampton Roads. The night of 9 August passed uneventfully. But when dawn broke on the morning of the tenth, the officers discovered that a chair and several swabs had been hoisted to the head of the fore royal mast and that a large portion of the white stripe that delimited

Because of a traditional reluctance on the part of naval officers to report confrontations with their crews that stopped just short of open mutiny, we may never know just how many times a scene similar to the one imagined by the artist Howard Pyle was enacted on the quarterdecks of American warships. (Copy of a painting by Howard Pyle in the print collection of the United States Naval Academy Museum Library)

the gun ports on the port side had been smeared with coal tar. Obviously some portion of the crew had used this method to publicly disgrace the *Cyane* and her officers.

The Senior Officer Present at Norfolk lost no time in convening a court of inquiry "for the purpose of ascertaining the perpetrators of certain acts of indiscipline" on board the *Cyane*. In addition to this, the court was also instructed to investigate the apparent negligence of the various officers who had been on watch when the vessel was being defaced.[60] Each of the officers who had stood anchor watch on the night in question was called in turn, and each declared that he had seen and heard nothing. The night had been blustery and stormy, but apparently nothing unusual had occurred in any watch.

Stymied here, the court began a general inquiry into the methods of discipline used on board the *Cyane* and into the background of some of the ship's "bad characters." Lieutenant Theodore F. Green, the executive officer, testified that the *Cyane* had been in a poor state of discipline ever since a draft of men had arrived from the frigate *St. Lawrence*. The *St. Lawrence* had just completed a long cruise on a foreign station, and her crew was looking forward to the mass discharge that usually marked the end of a long voyage. Several of her men still had some time left to serve to make up a full three years. These were sent to the *Cyane*, which was shorthanded. The *St. Lawrence* men quickly filled the ship with disaffection and repeatedly pestered the *Cyane*'s officers to give them their discharges to which they felt they were entitled.[61] The day before the defacing incident, two *St. Lawrence* veterans, Mark A. Lewis and George Lewis, had been caught drunk and were disrated to landsmen as punishment.

The court now commenced to ask specific questions about disciplinary policy:

> *Question.* (by the court to Lieutenant William D. Hurst) Do you think it is possible since the abolishment of the cats to discipline a man-of-war's crew?
>
> *A.* As far as I have had an opportunity of judging and from my experience, I think a ship's crew cannot be properly disciplined without flogging.
>
> *Q.* (by the court to Surgeon Solomon Sharp) What are the methods of punishment in use aboard the *Cyane*?
>
> *A.* Tricing the men up on the inside of the rigging by their wrists and legs, making them sit on the outside of the rigging, stopping their grog, and confinement in irons.
>
> *Q.* Are these punishments adequate to prevent offences in the service, if not, why not?
>
> *A.* I think they are not, because they are inflicted without proper form and tend to irritate and exasperate the men.[62]

All of the *Cyane*'s officers echoed Surgeon Sharp's observations. Petty officers also complained about the irregular methods by which the punishments were inflicted. Lieutenant H. A. Harrison testified that they were ineffective in deterring offenses "Because [the men] think themselves illegally punished by these means and such punishments only tend to irritate and make them worse."[63]

The court seemed to be on the verge of dropping the investigation into the specific events of the evening in question in favor of a general diatribe against the abolition of flogging. However, on the third day of the proceedings an anonymous note was delivered to the court.

> The Boy Bailey has been heard to say he knew who black'd the white streak. I did not hear him myself: It was mentioned in my presence, perhaps there's the clue to the whole mystery.[64]

Thomas Bailey was duly called before the court but would not or could not relate anything. The author of the note, a seaman named Peter Lines, was found; and he claimed his information came from another seaman, one George Gearnee. When called to testify, Gearnee, likewise, denied knowing anything.

After four days of proceedings, the court opined that it could not accurately fix blame for the incident on any party, and it judged that discipline on the *Cyane* was as good as on any other ship in the navy "and as efficient as it is in the power of the officers, under the present system to maintain. . . ." This was followed by a general broadside concerning the state of naval discipline:

> The Court is of the opinion and regretfully report, that the origin of these violations of discipline, is to be ascribed in great measure to the removal of those wholesome restraints which are imposed on the vicious by the judicious exercise of corporal punishment: that the acts referred to were acts of malice and mischief, perpetrated in all probability by dissatisfied and discontented persons, and that the system of punishments, at present authorized, and in use, is inadequate to maintain good order and discipline in the service, and that, in its inefficiency, it tends directly to the fostering of such insubordination and offences.[65]

This complex of problems was essentially resolved by the introduction of the summary court-martial procedures in 1855, but the regular officers of the navy continued to be most circumspect in their use of the term "mutiny." Not until the Civil War, which brought a great influx of volunteer officers unaccustomed to the nuances of naval customs into the service, do we hear of it again. The judge advocate general's index for the years 1862 to 1867 contains proceedings relating to two incidents: a "mutinous riot and affray" aboard the supply

Gunner William Myers, one of a handful of lower deck folk artists from the age of sail, depicts a flogging on board the sloop-of-war *Cyane*, circa 1843. This is a unique visual rendering of the scenes so vividly described by Melville who sailed before the mast in the frigate *United States* in the same year. (Print collection of the Nimitz Library)

barque *Fernandina* in April of 1862[66] and a "mutiny" in the war steamer *Western World* in February of 1863.[67] In each case the charges of mutiny were filed by acting volunteer officers, and in each case the regular officers who sat on the court-martial boards refused to acknowledge that mutiny had indeed taken place.

In all probability, the court's judgments were correct. In the *Fernandina*, the captain had been attacked by some of his men while trying to break up a drunken brawl. He then called upon his officers to support him and after arming himself returned to the scene of the disturbance and restored order. In the melee, a seaman was shot and killed by the captain. In the opinion of the court:

> There was not at the time of the shooting of John Hillman, nor had there been, anything which could be called a mutiny on board the ship, nor did the officers who witnessed what occurred on deck, regard the ship as in a state of mutiny, except the Captain, who seems so far to have lost his self-possession as to magnify the noise of three drunken men into a mutiny. . . . It was this entire misapprehension by the Captain of the nature of

the disturbance which alone extenuates the gravity of his fault in shooting John Hillman, which was wholly unjustified by any real existing danger to himself, or to the ship.[68]

The captain of the *Western World* had a stronger case. While he was ashore, a delegation of petty officers and crewmen approached the executive officer and stated that they would no longer serve under the captain and urged him to assume command. When the captain returned to the ship, his executive officer said nothing about the incident; but the crew staged a work stoppage and informed the captain that they wanted a change of command. He then went below and tried to rally his officers to put down the "mutiny." Few of them cooperated, until he threatened them with prosecution. The captain then mustered the crew, read them the Articles of War, and got them to return to their work. Later some of them were court-martialed for mutinous conduct.[69]

Judging from the number of death sentences handed down for it, mutiny must have been the most frightening category of naval crime known to the officers of the Old Navy. It is apparent that the possibility of mutinous uprisings in American naval vessels was most common in the smaller ships and boats and in vessels on detached service. This was certainly the case of the *Seringapatam* and perhaps of the *Warren*'s launch as well. Real mutinies were rare, however; and what was usually prosecuted as mutiny under the Articles of War was often something else: mass desertion in the case of the *Ewing*'s men or individual disaffection, as in the case of Robert Quinn and Samuel Jackson. Work stoppages such as occurred in the *Constitution* and the *United States* actually resemble the classical definition of mutiny more closely, but it can be seen that the charge of mutiny was only made in these cases by subordinate officers seeking to embarrass a commanding officer for reasons of their own.

The offense which most closely follows mutiny in the number of capital sentences prescribed was desertion. This was the most vexing and annoying offense that naval officers had to cope with. Unlike mutiny, desertion was quite common, accounting for more courts-martial than any other category of naval crime; and it continues to this day to be the navy's greatest single disciplinary problem.

The captains and commodores of the early navy were both baffled and chagrined by the propensity of their men to desert. After several of the *Constitution*'s crew had absconded into a British man-of-war at Gibraltar in 1805, Commodore John Rodgers penned the following General Order:

The Commodore cannot but express his concern and regrets that an incident should occur which compels him to order the infliction of Punishment on Individuals serving under his Command, both painful and degrading to the Seaman and Soldier, but viewing the Crime of desertion, particularly from the service of the United States, where Seamen have so many advantages over those in any other Service as a crime of the *Blackest* Kind and justly inviting the most exemplary punishment, and being determined never to pardon crimes fraught with such fatal consequences to the Service, nor to mitigate in the smallest degree the Punishment annexed by Law to such crimes; In consequence of having approved the sentence of the Court-Martial decreed against John Graves, John Pindar, Stephen Keith, Henry Bruin, and Michael Penny [i.e. 180 lashes and to be whipped through the squadron] orders the same to be executed this day on the Display of Signal for punishment.[70]

The crime of desertion, however, was not always taken this seriously. After American officers had become more used to the shock of seeing men deserting in droves, even in favor of service in British ships, they generally settled down to a less draconian view of the problem. Seamen were, after all, mostly drawn from a large pool of seafarers who drifted more or less casually from one ship to another and passed easily from naval to mercantile service and back again. The qualifications needed for enlistment on a sailing man-of-war were minimal, and men who "ran" could be easily replaced. On occasion, the men who deserted into foreign men-of-war were replaced by other fugitives. Once Commodore Preble, busy encouraging British deserters to enlist into the *Constitution* at Gibraltar, discovered with shock that one of his own acting midshipmen, John Bartell, was helping Americans to desert into H.M.S. *Termagant*. Apparently the men had won Bartell's sympathy by claiming to be British, just as the deserters Preble was encouraging claimed to be Americans. An unofficial investigation indicated that Bartell had gone so far as to make arrangements with the British to have the *Termagant*'s berth shifted to a mere cable's length off the *Constitution*'s port quarter for the express purpose of enticing deserters. Preble was not fond of courts-martial, and he refused to order one in Bartell's case. He was promptly discharged as "unfit for duty" and unceremoniously sent home.[71]

The first person to be executed for desertion by a naval court was Marine Daniel McKenny, who left his post at the Norfolk Navy Yard in May of 1812. Recaptured the following month, he was quickly found guilty and sentenced to death. In addition to this, McKenny was assessed by the court for the expenses occasioned by his desertion. The sentence stipulated that McKenny be shot by a firing squad.

President Madison ordered the execution of the sentence suspended for thirty days, after which it can be assumed, since there are no further notations, that it was carried out.[72]

It is perhaps significant that McKenny was executed on the eve of the War of 1812. That conflict saw desertions reach alarming proportions, particularly during 1814. In that year, the only seaman ever to be executed for desertion was shot to death at Sackets Harbor, New York. This was an erratic drunkard named Robert Elixson, who had managed no less than four attempts to desert in just six months. He first "ran" from the sloop of war *Ontario* on 15 January 1814 in Baltimore Harbor. Making his way to Philadelphia, he reenlisted in the navy under the command of Lieutenant Joseph McPherson, who was recruiting seamen to serve in Commodore Isaac Chauncey's squadron on Lake Ontario. During the trip overland from Philadelphia to Sacket's Harbor, Elixson deserted twice but was recaptured. Arriving at his destination, he was sent aboard the sloop of war *Superior* and once more "deserted from under the sentry's charge from on board the *Superior* on the seventh day of June last and was brought back on the tenth day of the same month."[73]

Elixson's trial was brief, his defense feeble. When asked why he had deserted so many times in such a brief period

> he stated that it was owing altogether to liquor and that when he got too much he did not know what he did—it set him sort of crazy—and having nothing further he was remanded and the Court cleared.[74]

The excuse fell on unsympathetic ears.

> having taken into serious consideration, the profligate repetition of the Prisoner's offences, in extenuation of which nothing hath been offered, the dangerous frequency of this offence, and the alarming consequences attending to the naval service of our Country, we reluctantly resolved to exert the power delegated to [us] by the law and endeavor to deter others from thus withdrawing their services from the state in this season of national peril—the court doth therefore Adjudge and Sentence the said Robert Elixson to be
>
> Shot to death
>
> at such time and on board such vessel of war as Commodore Isaac Chauncey . . . may direct . . .[75]

President Madison approved the sentence of the court in August 1814.

The most severe crackdown on desertion to occur during the War of 1812 took place not among the salt water squadrons but on the Great Lakes. In the spring and summer of 1814, Master Commandant

Daniel Dexter, commanding the United States Naval Forces on Lake Erie, executed four marines for desertion. In a very short court-martial proceeding held at Erie, Pennsylvania, on 4 June, Corporal James Bird and Private James Rankins were tried for leaving their posts after having been detailed to stand guard over the naval storehouse. In enumerating all of the charges and specifications against the two men, Judge Advocate George Lawton took particular pains to stress that Bird and Rankins had taken solemn oaths and enlistment bounties "and enjoyed all the Benefits arriving from having joined the [Marine] Corps."[76]

Perhaps not realizing that they were on trial for their lives, the two marines simply pleaded guilty and threw themselves on the mercy of the court, which swiftly sentenced them to "suffer death, the time and mode of executing the above to be decided by the Secretary of the Navy." Secretary B. W. Crowninshield promptly sent word back to Dexter that President Madison had confirmed the sentences and stipulated

> that the said Corporal James Bird and Private James Rankins be forthwith shot to death upon the deck of the U. S. Brig *Niagara* with all the solemnity due the occasion previously announced in a general order throughout the Squadron.[77]

Two months later another pair of marines were tried on board the *Niagara* for desertion. Privates John Monroe and William Bunnet had been reported by Marine Lieutenant Benjamin Hyde for absenting themselves during an overland march while campaigning in the vicinity of Lake Erie. The records of this case are fragmentary, and the usual endorsements and appended documents are missing. However, Master Commandant Dexter and Judge Advocate Lawton succeeded in securing another death sentence, and it is probably safe to assume that Monroe and Bunnet were executed.[78] If all the executions did take place as indicated by the records, then Daniel Dexter has the distinction of presiding over more executions than any other officer in the history of American naval jurisprudence. George Lawton becomes the "deadliest" judge advocate, and Secretary Crowninshield signed more death warrants—six in all between 1814 and 1817—than any other secretary of the navy.[79]

The navy did not persist in executing seamen for desertion after the Elixson case. Two more marines, however, received death sentences for desertion. Private Thomas Smith apparently was shot for this offense in March 1817.[80] The cycle was not broken until the sentence of Private William Bauseman, condemned to be shot for desertion in September of 1819, was commuted by President Madison to one year's imprisonment at hard labor.[81] After the Bauseman case, there were no more death sentences handed down for desertion until the Civil War.

Nevertheless, desertion continued to be a serious problem. In simple cases, the usual punishment was fifty lashes; more if there were aggravating circumstances. The standard punishment of fifty lashes had been established in the case of Michael Debrod, a seaman who deserted from the frigate *John Adams* in March of 1801 at Cap Francois, Haiti. Debrod had fled from a boat detail with four other men and hidden out in the town for three days before being recaptured. He and all his companions pleaded guilty, and all received identical sentences—fifty lashes and forfeiture of wages.[82]

During the War of 1812, the standard penalty was increased to one hundred lashes, but fifty lashes were still used in cases where the court was not entirely sure of its ground. For example, Seaman William Gordon was given fifty lashes for attempting to desert from the Boston Navy Yard in September 1814. Gordon was one of the crew of the ill-fated frigate *Chesapeake*. He had been returned to Boston in a cartel ship together with a large group of *Chesapeake* sailors who were lodged in a receiving hulk. On the day of his return, Gordon was arrested by a midshipman, who charged that he was roaming at large in the town when he should have been enroute from the cartel to the hulk. Nothing was done about this infraction, but the next evening he was found "loitering" near the navy yard fence with another seaman. He was arrested on suspicion of plotting to desert, since the vicinity of the fence and gate were off-limits to sailors after sundown.[83]

At his court-martial, Gordon claimed that he was the victim of trumped-up charges. In a written statement, he explained that all of the *Chesapeake* men had expected to be granted shore liberty; but Gordon's arrest coupled with the disappearance of several men from the first liberty party had caused the others to be confined to the yard. Angered, they took out their resentment on Gordon, the only miscreant still within reach, by alerting the navy yard officers that he was planning to run. He was thus under covert surveillance; and when he approached the fence in the course of strolling in the yard compound, he was apprehended.[84] The court must have decided that the *Chesapeake*'s crew needed an example. It sentenced Gordon to receive fifty lashes.

Another case typical of the Navy's policy toward desertion in wartime was that of Ordinary Seaman Thomas Gardner. Gardner ran from the frigate *Constitution* in Boston Harbor on 26 September 1813. A year later he was discovered serving in the privateer *Surprize* out of Salem. As an explanation of his actions, Gardner offered the excuse that when he had left the *Constitution* he had not intended to desert.

Several of his companions, however, had persuaded him to "run." After that, fear of punishment had kept him away. He made no mention of better wages and conditions aboard the privateer, but the court was obviously aware of these factors. Gardner was returned to the *Constitution* and given one hundred lashes.[85]

Although the punishments were less severe in the decades from 1815 to 1861, the Navy continued to experience desertion on a large scale. A few cases chosen at random give some perspective on the problem. On 12 July 1828, Seaman William Miors and several other members of a boat's crew deserted from the ship-of-the-line *Delaware* in Messina, Sicily. A party of officers from the ship hunted the men down and returned them under arrest the next day. On 25 July they were all court-martialed together with three more men who had tried to "run" from the schooner *Porpoise* at Valletta and also a midshipman who was accused of "ungentlemanly conduct."[86] Testifying against Miors, Midshipman Charles Beverly claimed that he had left him and another seaman as boat guards while he took a working party ashore to collect casks of beef and limes. When they returned, the boat guards were gone; and in the ensuing confusion, a few other men contrived to slip away.

Midshipman J. S. Carter next took the stand to describe how Miors had been recaptured. It seems that a citizen of the town had rowed out to the *Delaware* and offered to take a party of officers to the place where the deserters were hiding. This offer was accepted, and the Sicilian led them to a house about three miles from the center of town. Here the officers took the two boat guards. The informant was paid twenty dollars for his tip, which was later extracted from the pay of Miors and his companion. When Carter's testimony was concluded, Miors threw himself on the mercy of the court, which sentenced him to fifty lashes and forfeiture from his pay of the expense of his recapture. All of the other men before the court for desertion drew identical sentences.

The convicted seamen penned a joint appeal to the commodore of the Mediterranean Squadron, stating that they had only meant to take "french leave" so that they could have an overnight "frolic" ashore. Consequently, upon reviewing the case, Commodore William Crane mitigated the sentence, appending a note to the record which read:

> With the hope that the example may produce the proper effect, the punishment awarded by the above sentence is mitigated to three dozen lashes, in the manner prescribed: the remainder of the sentence is approved.[87]

Desertion was still being handled the same way two decades later, when Freidis Sturgeon, a landsman, "ran" from the war steamer *Union* at Pensacola, Florida, on 19 August 1844.[88] Captured in Mobile and returned to the *Union*, Sturgeon pleaded guilty at his court-martial even though the court "cautioned and counseled" him to withdraw his plea and defend himself against the charge. Heartened perhaps by the court's interest in him, Sturgeon requested that he be allowed to call a character witness, Purser Charles Murray of the *Union*. Murray testified that Sturgeon was one of the best men in the ship and that he had been in close confinement since his capture a month previous to the trial. Murray also mentioned that Sturgeon had been billed $41.60 for the cost of his recapture.[89]

Sturgeon then submitted a defense statement explaining that he had originally enlisted on the ship of the line *Pennsylvania* and had served two and one-half years in her before being drafted to the *Union* against his will. Objecting to service in a steamer, he had tried several times, without success, to get himself reassigned to the *Pennsylvania*. Taking into consideration his mulcted pay and time spent in the brig, the court gave him a mere twenty-five lashes.[90]

In the 1850s, the sentencing procedure for desertion underwent a considerable change because of the abolition of flogging and the introduction of the summary court-martial system. On 9 March 1856, Ordinary Seaman John Winter Smith deserted from the sloop of war *St. Marys* at Mare Island, California. He was tried by a summary court together with another deserter, Landsman John Hoover. Smith made no defense of his actions and pleaded guilty to the charge, his second attempt to desert from the *St. Marys*. He was sentenced to solitary confinement in double irons on bread and water for thirty days, loss of pay for three months, and extra police duty for one month after his release from confinement.[91]

The court next turned its attention to Hoover, who put up a better fight. After getting one officer removed from the summary court on the grounds that he had preferred charges against him once before, Hoover pleaded guilty but submitted a written defense statement, maintaining that

> When I deserted from this ship, I had no intention to desert entirely from the Naval Service, as I had no dislike of any of the officers, neither do I complain of any ill treatment, being solely induced by feelings of mortification consequent upon having been tried on a previous occasion, and being the first and only one up to the time of my desertion. In conclusion, I beg to throw myself on the mercy of the Court.[92]

Two tars languish in irons in an impromptu brig. Most of the navy's sailing men-of-war had no regular place of confinement. Empty storerooms, odd corners of the orlop deck, and even screened off spaces between the guns were used in lieu of cells. (*Heck's Iconographic Encyclopedia*, collection of the Nimitz Library)

Apparently, it paid to present *some* kind of defense to a summary court, even an incoherent one like this. Hoover drew thirty days' solitary confinement on bread and water, lost his pay for only one month, and received no extra police duty.

These examples show that ordinary desertion cases were routinely conducted after the War of 1812 without any serious consideration of the death penalty except in unusual circumstances. On 10 January 1845, Seaman John Sweeny, who had been found guilty of desertion and theft, was sentenced to receive two hundred lashes, forfeit all pay due him, be discharged from the service and never permitted to enter it again. To make sure the sentence stuck, the court stipulated that "a description of his person . . . be sent to all recruiting stations."[93]

The Sweeny case was unusual. While the sloop of war *Preble* was cruising off the slaving grounds on the west coast of Africa, she encountered the British barque *Dominica* aground and abandoned on Folle Reef. Commander Thomas W. Freelon of the *Preble* quickly organized a salvage party, which consisted of twenty men led by Lieutenant William Pinckney and Passed Midshipman John Clemson. Sweeny was among the men chosen to go.

Although the sea was calm, the area was often subjected to sudden weather changes. Once Pinckney had boarded the wreck, he ordered Sweeny and two other men to row the launch out a safe distance from the reef and anchor. Instead of doing this, Sweeny and his companions hurriedly set a lug sail and made off with the boat and all her arms and gear "to the value of nearly two thousand dollars."[94] Sweeny ignored repeated gunfire and recall signals from the salvage party. The three deserters were eventually picked up by the U.S. storeship *Erie* and taken to Puerto Grande, Cape Verde Islands. Meanwhile, back at Folle Reef, the weather changed suddenly and a heavy ground swell developed, which gave Lieutenant Pinckney and his men some anxious moments before the *Preble* could take them off.[95]

Sweeny's court-martial was long and featured a massive amount of detailed testimony. He pleaded not guilty, chose one of the *Preble*'s midshipmen, John S. Man, as his defense counsel, and made a vigorous effort to reduce the seriousness of the charges. There was no lack of evidence to establish that Sweeny and his compatriots had made off with the boat. Sweeny claimed that he had acted under the influence of alcohol. He maintained that the *Dominica* carried a partial cargo of rum and that Pinckney's men had broached it, and many of them were drunk as well. He further asserted that when he made off with the launch, there was no danger to the salvage party and that the peril which subsequently developed was due entirely to the poor judgment and bad seamanship of Lieutenant Pinckney.[96] Just possibly, this spirited defense saved Sweeny, whose actual name was John Smith, from a death sentence.

As a significant problem within the naval disciplinary system, desertion was overwhelmingly an enlisted man's offense. Officers who deserted or absented themselves from their ships or stations without authorization were almost never charged with desertion, even though their actions may have resembled those of enlisted men. Usually, the charge against officers who had apparently "run" read "disobedience of orders," "breaking arrest," or "absent over leave." "Deserter" was considered too demeaning a label to apply to an officer.

An example of this rule is the case of Midshipman Lewis M. Wilkins and Acting Midshipman John S. Patterson.[97] These two officers had been put in charge of a launch belonging to the frigate *Brandywine*. While on an errand in the harbor of Callao, Peru, they left the boat tied to a wharf and absented themselves for several days, only returning to the frigate after they had been tracked down by the first lieutenant and ordered back on board.[98] They were subsequently court-martialed on rather vague charges of neglect of duty and unofficer-like conduct.

The two men pleaded guilty but asked to be allowed to call witnesses to testify about their general character and attention to duty on board the *Brandywine*. When the request was granted, they called Captain David Deacon, commanding officer of the frigate and president of the court that was trying them. Deacon, under examination by the two midshipmen, told the court that both had been generally well thought of on board the ship. One wonders if Wilkins and Patterson were not perhaps trying to use their commanding officer to undercut his first lieutenant who had originated the charges and was thus officially the prosecutor in the case.

Whatever their motives, the tactic did little good. Midshipman Wilkins was sentenced to be dismissed from the navy, while Acting Midshipman Patterson ". . . in consideration of his youth and inexperience and the bad example of his senior in whose company the acts complained of in the charges were committed" was sentenced to lose the date of his warrant, be confined to his ship for six months, to have his sentence read before the assembled midshipmen of the squadron, and to be reprimanded publicly by the commodore. Upon review, the portion of the sentence relating to the loss of Patterson's warrant date was remitted.[99]

Obviously, desertion was a very serious problem for the navy and one that its officers were inclined to punish severely. Still, the number of deserters was so great that it would have been unacceptable to the public and probably extremely impractical as well to impose a death sentence or its equivalent on every deserter that the navy managed to recapture. Even in wartime, only a few deserters were executed, and then only after the problem had reached alarming proportions. In adjudicating desertion cases, naval courts never made any effort to find out why the men brought before them had tried to desert. In no other category of naval crime was the question of motive so often ignored. This is particularly interesting when it is remembered that many of the desertions were undertaken not by individuals but by groups of men. Indeed, some desertions were carefully planned and had all of the outward appearances of jailbreaks or escapes from prisoner of war camps. The affair that brought Frank Dynes to the bar of naval justice was an example of this tendency.

Of course, it is possible that most navy men considered the causes of the high rate of desertion that the navy endured to be self-evident. The atmosphere on board ships was one of extreme severity coupled with serious overcrowding, low pay, and highly restricted personal freedom and autonomy. That some men could not endure these conditions for a full three years was perhaps too much of a commonplace to be worthy of notice. Officers simply seemed to view the tendency of their men to "run" whenever a good opportunity offered as one of the more or less routine vexations of service life. Recaptured deserters were perfunctorily court-martialed and punished, for the most part by the routine and only moderately severe sanction of fifty lashes.

The final category of naval crime that yielded death sentences was that of murder. Unlike mutinous conduct and desertion, murder was a rare occurrence in the Old Navy and represents a very small percentage of the cases listed in the judge advocate general's index of courts-martial. Yet, four men were sentenced to death for deadly assault or murder between 1799 and 1862. The very first death sentence ever passed by a naval court was for murder.

Like desertion, murder was exclusively an enlisted man's crime. Officers dueled with some frequency, and a good many were killed; but after one abortive attempt, the victors of duels were never tried for murder. This tradition was established by the case of Midshipman F. Cornelius de Kraft, who had killed a fellow midshipman, William R. Nicholson, in a duel at Syracuse, Sicily, on 18 September 1804. Dueling in the Mediterranean Squadron had become a serious problem, so the Navy Department decided to make an example of de Kraft and ordered that he be court-martialed for murder. After a long wait, de Kraft was given a preliminary hearing before the Secretary of the Navy, and there was every indication that strong action would be taken. However, Congressman John Hopper Nicholson of Maryland, a relative of the dead midshipman, wrote to the Department explaining that the duel was a fair passage at arms and there was no need to prosecute de Kraft. After a decent interval, he was restored to his squadron and resumed active duty.[100]

The de Kraft case created an unofficial precedent or tradition which prohibited the prosecution of duelists for murder, although a few were later tried under Article XV of the Articles of War:

> No person in the Navy shall quarrel with any other person in the Navy, nor use provoking or reproachful words, gestures, or menaces, on pain of such punishment as a court-martial shall adjudge.

This was an exceedingly feeble approach to the problem and did little to curb dueling.

Aside from dueling, there is no record of any officer in the navy killing another officer in an act of cold-blooded murder, premeditated or otherwise. There is also no case of an officer murdering an enlisted man, although there are cases of officers being tried for negligence or even manslaughter. This occurred when an enlisted man died under accidental circumstances that indicated negligence or carelessness on the part of the officer.

There was a tradition in the navy, begun by Lieutenant Andrew Sterett of the *Constellation,* which involved officers killing men who deserted their posts in battle. Midshipman David G. Farragut was actually given orders to hunt down and execute three men who were trying to escape from the *Essex* while it was being battered to pieces by a British squadron near Valparaiso, Chile, in 1814. This was, however, never called murder. Also, according to the judge advocate general's index, no enlisted man in the Old Navy ever succeeded in killing an officer, although such a crime was attempted on a few occasions. When this happened, the perpetrator was tried either for mutiny, mutinous conduct, or assault upon a superior officer with intent to kill. If found guilty, he was sentenced to three or four hundred lashes, the equivalent of a death sentence, unless the court had some doubt about his sanity.

Consequently, the classic navy murder case always involved two enlisted men and usually grew out of a petty quarrel that escalated into premeditated violence resulting in the death of one of the principals. This pattern is exemplified by the navy's first murder case. One night in 1798, Seaman George Galliger was seated on a match tub at the forward end of the berth deck of the brig *Eagle.* Apparently Galliger had a loud conversation with some cronies. Seaman John Buckley told him to quiet down lest he wake up some officer. Galliger refused. The two men scuffled. Galliger drew a knife and stabbed Buckley twice. Galliger then threw his knife away and allowed himself to be restrained by onlookers.[101]

At his court-martial, held on board the frigate *John Adams* at Bassaterre Roads, Guadalupe, Galliger pleaded not guilty; but the preponderance of eyewitness testimony was conclusive, and he was sentenced "to be hanged by the neck from the Fore yard arm of the U. S. Brig *Eagle.*"[102] There is no further notation on the records of the proceedings, but it is probable that Galliger is the first man ever to be executed in the navy. His trial was held on 9 November 1798.

The next man to be executed for murder was Landsman Thomas D. Allen of the frigate *John Adams.* He was tried on 8 May 1836 for the murder of Thomas Noland, another landsman, while the two were ashore on liberty on Minorca. The Allen case had obvious psychological overtones which the navy court, perhaps in keeping with the spirit of the times, chose to ignore.

Allen and Noland were apparently wandering drunkenly through a field on the outskirts of Port Mahon when they got into an argument over whether or not to return to the ship. Noland terminated his part of the argument by lying down with his head pillowed on a rock and going to sleep. Allen then picked up another rock, weighing perhaps forty pounds, and dropped it on Noland's head. Making his way back to the *John Adams*, he confessed his deed to Captain Silas Stringham. Led by Allen, a party from the ship returned to the field and recovered the corpse.[103]

Except for the trivial dispute and his drunken condition, Allen could give no reason for his actions. Character witnesses at the court-martial described him as quiet and withdrawn, and Allen himself testified that when he was drunk he became irrational and often had suicidal impulses. Yet he was to outward appearances rational and coherent and seemingly "sane" by the standards of the times. In his defense statement, he described himself as "suffering from partial derangement occasioned by sickness," subject to "nervous excitement," and "of a melancholy temperament." He further explained that in the grip of his derangement he was tempted to commit "Excesses."[104] In the light of modern psychology, Allen seems to resemble a classic case of manic depression.

He certainly baffled the members of his court-martial board. In concluding the trial, they wrote:

> The Court have sought with anxiety to establish a plea of insanity on behalf of the Prisoner or some mitigating circumstance in his favor, But the charge and specification are too clearly established against him to permit the Court to doubt. The Court are willing to believe that the crime was committed under the influence of intoxication, for nothing that occurred between the Prisoner and the deceased has come to the knowledge of the Court that would otherwise account for it.[105]

With their minds set against Allen's insanity plea, the court sentenced him to hang, but there are no further documents or notations among the records of the proceedings to indicate whether or not he was ever executed.

That the death penalty did not always follow axiomatically from a navy murder trial is shown by the case of Seaman John Herring. In November 1837, Herring attacked one Thomas Hyland, rated as a Boy, while in the grip of a drunken rage. The incident took place on the frigate *United States*, cruising in the Mediterranean. According to witnesses, Herring's assault on Hyland was motivated by another seaman, who told him that Hyland wished to fight him. Herring rushed on deck to seek out Hyland and found him asleep under the boat booms. He immediately began to kick and pummel the groggy Hyland, who attempted to struggle to his feet while pulling off his jersey. He was thus off balance when Herring struck a heavy blow that knocked him backwards into the hatchway, but managed to grab a coaming and hold on. Herring then picked up a length of rope and began to lash Hyland's hands and shoulders, forcing him to let go and drop perhaps twenty feet through another open hatch on the gun deck and into the frigate's hold.[106]

Herring was immediately apprehended by the first lieutenant, Z. G. Johnson. In his intoxicated and highly agitated state, Herring swore that "he hoped it would be the *death* of him [Hyland] and that he would be hanged for it." When told that Hyland was lying at the bottom of the hold badly injured, Herring declared that "He wished the Son of a Bitch might die and then he would be hanged." The next day Hyland died. By that time, Herring had sobered up and regretted his action.[107]

His regrets did not prevent his waging a vigorous defense at his subsequent court-martial. He chose the Reverend Thomas R. Lambert, chaplain of the *United States*, as his defense counsel. Lambert began by invoking a series of legal technicalities borrowed from civilian jurisprudence to delay the proceedings. Since an inquest had been held to ascertain the facts immediately after the death of Hyland, Lambert argued that the official court-martial of Herring was actually the second trial for the same offense and therefore illegal under the double-jeopardy provision of the common law. When this maneuver was rejected on the grounds that the preliminary inquest had not reached any verdict but merely remanded Herring to custody, Lambert refused to plead his client and continued to raise objections to the legality of the proceedings.

The court overcame Lambert's objections one by one, and ultimately the case was heard. Eyewitnesses established the facts so conclusively that Herring could not escape responsibility for Hyland's death. The defense concentrated on demonstrating that there had been no previous bad feeling between the two men and that Herring was drunk when he made his fatal attack.[108] This tactic at least gave Lambert the means to forestall the death penalty. He reverted quickly to his professional persona as a chaplain and penned a long defense memoranda, citing the evils of alcohol and the base passions it aroused. He warned the court to arrive at a

> decision which shall not render miserable the remainder of your lives, a decision upon which you may reflect without dread in the hour of death, a decision which heaven may approve.

He maintained that Herring should not suffer death for an act committed in a drunken rage and under a false impression, one that he was already doomed to spend the rest of his life regretting.[109]

The court may or may not have been swayed by Lambert's moralistic eloquence. The charge was reduced to manslaughter, but Herring was awarded the stupendous total of four hundred lashes. Upon review, Commodore Jesse Duncan Elliott reduced this total to three hundred lashes but specified that he should be flogged 'round the fleet at Port Mahon and his sentence read on each vessel.[110]

From these three cases, which are typical of the relatively few murders that occurred in the Old Navy, we can see that the cases which the navy chose to label as murder had very little significance as "military" offenses. That is, they were the sort of crimes which could just as easily have occurred in civilian life—a drunken quarrel leading to bloodshed between two individuals who were social and legal equals in the eyes of the law. Had these crimes involved an enlisted man murdering an officer, or even a petty officer, they would then have taken on military "significance" because they could have been construed as an attack on authority, hence mutiny, or mutinous conduct, or assault upon a superior officer, crimes which had no counterpart in civilian law but which were critical to the disciplinary structure of any military organization.

In surveying the Old Navy's use of the death penalty, it is interesting to note that marines bore a heavy share of the navy's capital punishments, particularly for desertion. It is also interesting to note that the navy's use of the death penalty was arbitrary, capricious, occasionally irregular, and almost always justified by the "good of the service" rather than by the merits of the cases. The hanging of Seaman Samuel Jackson is the clearest example of these tendencies, but the four marines shot by Master Commandant Dexter constitute the most ambitious program of executions so undertaken.

A nebulous area connected with the navy's use of the death sentence is the record of forty-nine instances wherein naval courts sentenced men to receive in excess of one hundred lashes in lieu of an overt death penalty. It is well known in naval history and tradition that one hundred or more lashes with a cat-o'-nine-tails could easily cause the death of an individual so punished and that it was likely to permanently impair the health of any person who managed to survive it. The judge advocate general's records indicate that some of the men sentenced to receive more than one hundred lashes had their punishments mitigated to one hundred lashes or less by higher authority. Still, approximately thirty seamen did receive in excess of one hundred lashes, many being "whipped through the squadron" in the process. The records are silent concerning how they withstood this treatment. If no special measures were taken to keep them alive, it is a certainty that some of them died under the lash and that others were permanently crippled.

Some may, in fact, have been sentenced to this sort of exceptionally severe flogging in the actual expectation on the part of naval authorities that they would not survive. Because of this situation, we may never know exactly how many *de facto* death sentences were imposed by naval courts-martial and subsequently carried into effect. It is certain, however, that the Navy's use of the death penalty between 1800 and 1862 was not as sparing as historians have heretofore believed.

Chapter VI

Dishonor & Disgrace

The first priority of the naval justice system between 1800 and 1861 was to establish and maintain a high degree of discipline and subordination in the naval service. Second only to this, however, was a singular level of concern for the professional and personal honor of the service and for naval personnel, especially officers. No less than twelve articles of the "Act for the Better Government of the Navy of 1800" cover the offenses of treason, sedition, cowardice, failure to join in battle, premature surrender, desertion of a post of duty under fire, the pillaging of prisoners, collusion with an enemy, defection to an enemy or rebel power, and the proper conduct of naval personnel as prisoners of war. All acts violating the strictures of these articles were punishable by death or such lesser sentence as a court-martial might see fit to impose. Between 1800 and 1861, no naval officer or enlisted man was ever sentenced to death for any of these offenses, although there are courts-martial in the records relating to each one of them.

In matters of personal honor, the naval justice system went beyond these articles and concerned itself with conduct, particularly on the part of officers, that could be considered personally dishonorable, even if it was irrelevant to the professional or official conduct of an individual. The judge advocate general's records contain many cases of unofficerlike conduct, ungentlemanly conduct, falsehood, quarreling, and scandalous conduct that are directly related to questions of personal honor or morals. Indeed, one of the most popular and commonly used charges was scandalous conduct tending to the destruction of good morals, a broadly construed catchall that might involve anything from disagreeable manners in the wardroom to the most aggravated frauds and embezzlements, gross falsehoods, insubordination, and improper conduct. In many cases, scandalous conduct was a popular charge to tack on to more specific accusations because it could be proved or sustained more easily than a specification relating to a discrete act. Scandalous conduct charges served another function, that of regulating quarrels between officers. Eventually, the act of bringing such charges came to replace the practice of dueling, especially among the junior officers.

Chronologically, the first courts-martial for violations of the navy's code of honor related to the treatment of prisoners taken during the Quasi-War with France. Article IX of the Articles of War provides that

> No person in the navy shall strip of their clothes, or pillage, or in any manner maltreat prisoners taken on board a prize, on pain of such punishment as a court-martial shall adjudge.

In the summer of 1800, several Haitian prisoners captured on board the privateer *Vengeance* charged that Master Commandant David Jewett had pillaged them of twenty thousand dollars while transporting them to the United States.[1] Likewise, Captain George Little of the frigate *Boston* was accused of mistreating the officers of the corvette *Berceau*. At his court of inquiry, Captain Little's counsel argued persuasively that his client's honor was at stake merely because the enemy's "brawny bodies were not handled with the delicacy and decorum in a maid of honor undressing a Queen." The Frenchmen complained in their turn that "we were examined in those parts which delicacy forbids to name, in pursuit of money!!!"[2] Jewett's case was immediately decided in his favor, perhaps because his accusers were mulattoes; but Little's inquiry board recommended a court-martial.

During the ensuing tribunal, the French prisoners, all of them regular officers in the French Navy, deposed that they had been robbed of money, watches, personal jewelry, buttons, handkerchiefs, musical instruments, knee buckles, and other trinkets and that Little had appropriated three black "boys" from the *Berceau*'s crew and made personal servants of them. In the ensuing testimony, all of the French witnesses held to this story, while every American witness disputed it and swore that no pillaging had taken place.[3] Noting the two sets of mutually exclusive testimony, Captain Little's counselor penned a long defense summation, declaring his client innocent of everything, from defrauding the United States Government of captured booty to harsh treatment of the prisoners. He played on the emotions of the court, stressing the grasping and piratical nature of French naval personnel, in whose coffers

> upon examination would be found not merely a few contemptible baubles but an accumulation of all the American spoil which avarice urged by fury has been able to grasp from the merchant, the sailor, the fisherman . . .

He wound up his summation by characterizing the trial of Captain Little as one calculated to give aid and comfort to the enemy.[4] Obviously, the sympathies of the court were not with the French. The judge advocate confined himself to a reading of Article IX, and the court quickly and unanimously exonerated Captain Little, characterizing the Frenchmen's charges as "malicious and ill founded."[5] No other pre-Civil War naval officer was ever tried on charges of maltreating prisoners.

The next serious controversy to arise concerning the honor of the service involved the question of premature surrender. Although it is not generally realized, Captain William Bainbridge surrendered the frigate *Philadelphia* to the Tripolitans on 1 November 1803, before any of his men had been killed or wounded and before the ship had been seriously disabled by enemy gunfire.[6] Even greater sensitivity to the issue of precipitate surrender was engendered by the *Chesapeake-Leopard* affair. In the Old Navy, every officer who surrendered his ship to an enemy had to undergo a court of inquiry, and there are a surprising number of cases which date principally from the War of 1812. Some of these instances show that, contrary to modern naval tradition, under certain circumstances it was routine practice for American naval vessels to strike their colors without first exchanging fire with the enemy. If an enemy vessel was considerably larger and better armed, and if it were capable of decisively outsailing its American opponent, and if it managed to bring the Americans under its guns, surrender without resistance was definitely sanctioned by naval law and custom. An officer surrendering his vessel under those circumstances could look forward to a full vindication by a court of inquiry provided he had behaved well under the pressures of the chase and upheld the honor and reputation of the service while in captivity.

An excellent example of such a surrender is the case of Lieutenant John D. Henley, who struck the brig *Viper*, twelve guns, to the British frigate *Narcissus* off the Passes of the Mississippi on 17 January 1813. In a perfunctory manner, the court of inquiry, comprised of Captain Thomas Trigg, Commandant of the New York Navy Yard, and two lieutenants, sought to establish whether or not the *Viper* had had a chance of escaping her larger adversary. Henley explained that he had fallen in with the Britisher while trying to enter the Mississippi for the purpose of stopping a bad leak. The *Narcissus* first blocked Henley's entrance to the river and then used a two-knot advantage in speed to outsail the *Viper* and bring the Americans under her broadside. As soon as the British captain hailed him, Henley fired a gun to his disengaged side and hauled down his colors.[7] During the chase, the *Viper* had thrown four guns overboard to lighten the ship but kept the rest to fight any attempt to board her on the part of the *Narcissus'* tender.

With these facts established, the court next inquired into those matters which were of paramount concern.

Table IV. Warships of the United States Navy
that surrendered to enemy forces without resistance, 1798–1823

Case No.	Vessel (And Number of Guns)	Year	Taken by (And Number of Guns)
—	*Baltimore* (24)	1798	Two British frigates, 55 men impressed
JAG 25	*Philadelphia* (36)	1803	Tripolitan gunboats
JAG 43	*Chesapeake* (36)	1808	HMS *Leopard* (56)
JAG 119	*Nautilus* (16)	1812	British squadron off New York
JAG 136	*Viper* (12)	1813	HMS *Narcissus* (36)
JAG 139	*Vixen* (12)	1813	HMS *Southampton* (36)
JAG 204	*Rattlesnake* (16)	1815	HMS *Leander* (56)
JAG 205	*Frolic* (22)	1815	HMS *Orpheus* (36)
JAG 404	*Gunboat #158*	1823	Fired upon, boarded, and searched by Spanish sloop of war

Question. [by the court to Sailing Master Daniel Mooran] Did Lt. Henley at all times during the chase do his utmost to preserve the vessel under his command & to support the honor & dignity of the American flag?

A. He did, He appeared to do everything the whole of the time to make his escape after he found the enemy was a Frigate.

Q. Was there any impropriety of conduct on the part of the officers and crew or any of them during the entire chase or at the time of or after the surrender?

A. None.[8]

Since all the testimony of the other witnesses corroborated that of Sailing Master Mooran, the court decided that Henley had done all that could have been expected of him and absolved him from the necessity of having to stand trial by court-martial.

A similar but slightly less complimentary verdict was rendered by another court of inquiry in the case of Master Commandant James Renshaw. Renshaw had surrendered the brig *Rattlesnake*, sixteen guns, to H.M.S. *Leander* (56) off Halifax, Nova Scotia. The *Rattlesnake* had been on a long commerce raiding cruise in European waters and was steering to make a landfall at the entrance to Penobscot Bay. Unfortunately, cumulative navigational errors conspired to put Renshaw badly off his reckoning and brought him into the vicinity of Halifax, where he fell in with the *Leander*. The *Rattlesnake* had been chased several times previously and had thrown all of her big guns overboard in the process of eluding a British frigate off the Azores. Nevertheless, she had managed to capture several prizes. Consequently, she was both disarmed and undermanned; and when the *Leander* outsailed her, Renshaw struck.[9]

The members of the court of inquiry questioned Renshaw closely, indicating that they believed that he should have sailed to a French port to reprovision and procure new armament before starting home. They implied that his not having done so showed lack of initiative. Renshaw replied that he had considered doing this and had actually sailed to within a day's run of the French coast when he spoke with the master of a merchant ship, who informed him that Napoleon had suffered severe battlefield reverses and was near collapse.[10] Armed with this intelligence, Renshaw decided to bring his depleted command home without further delay. The court could find no evidence to indicate any doubts about the captain's loyalty, coolness, or bravery. They simply decided that errors had been committed but that the *Rattlesnake* had not been lost through intention or neglect. The errors enumerated were that Renshaw had not carried through his original plan to go to France and his faulty navigation.[11] He was not recommended for court-martial.

The same court that tried Renshaw also looked into Stephen Decatur's surrender of the frigate *President* and Captain Joseph Bainbridge's loss of the sloop of war *Frolic*. Although the *Frolic* had surrendered without resistance, the court found no errors in judgment and opined that "Captain Bainbridge conducted himself with perfect coolness and self-possession and with the courage becoming an officer and a gentleman." It further declared that "the *Frolic* was not lost through the fault, intention, or negligence of Captain Bainbridge." The sloop had been surrendered to the British frigate *Orpheus* off the Bahamas on 20 April 1814.[12]

The surrender of small vessels of war to powerful enemies seemed to cause the navy few qualms, but the striking of a large frigate to an enemy of roughly similar force was, understandably, quite another matter. For this reason, the two greatest controversies concerning premature surrender on the part of an American vessel concern the unlucky frigate *Chesapeake*. Commodore James Barron's surrender of this ship to the H.M.S. *Leopard*, a considerably larger vessel, is an issue which still rankles naval traditionalists. As recently as 1967 a new article appeared in the United States Naval Institute *Proceedings* reexamining the incident and its subsequent court of inquiry and court-martial. Many of the earlier treatments of the *Chesapeake-Leopard* affair reflect the conviction that Barron dishonored himself by not fighting or by not being ready to fight and by his conduct under fire. This attitude is reinforced by the verdict of his court-martial board, which suspended him from duty for five years. Although he subsequently returned to active service, he could never fully vindicate his conduct in the eyes of his contemporaries.

Recent scholars have been much more inclined to examine the quality of Barron's court-martial proceedings, and particularly the role Stephen Decatur played in them. Decatur was an outspoken critic of Barron's actions. Indeed, he was so prejudiced against the commodore that he sought to be relieved of duty as a member of the court-martial board because by his own admission he could not render dispassionate justice. A shortage of officers of sufficient rank to try a senior captain kept him on the court, however; and the result was what is now considered an obvious case of scapegoating.[13] Even after the trial, as Decatur's star rose in the service, he used his power and prestige to continue to bait and goad Barron, with the result that the two men fought a duel in 1822 which proved fatal to the brilliant, young commodore.

Decatur's name is intimately connected with another notable incident concerning the *Chesapeake* which is likewise tainted with a hint of scapegoating. This time the principal victim was Midshipman William S. Cox. Cox had joined the *Chesapeake* at the express invitation of Captain James Lawrence only a few days before she sailed out to engage the *Shannon* on 1 June 1813. During the hasty preparations for this battle, Cox was appointed acting fourth lieutenant and put in charge of a division of guns. At the time of his appointment, Cox knew little of the ship or of his men. When the battle commenced, the well-drilled British crew made it a particular point to keep the *Chesapeake*'s quarterdeck swept with canister and musketry. Consequently, Captain Lawrence and the first, second, and third lieutenants were all felled by a single blast of fire just at the moment when they were trying to rally a boarding party. Thus, with the two frigates lying yardarm to yardarm and in a moment of supreme confusion, command of the *Chesapeake* suddenly devolved upon Midshipman Cox. Shortly afterwards, the British boarded and carried the ship and captured her crew.

Once the prisoners had been exchanged under a cartel, a court of inquiry was set up to delve into the loss of the *Chesapeake*.[14] As the senior surviving officer, Third Lieutenant George Budd would naturally have been the principal object of the investigation; but Midshipman Cox was the most senior officer to have gone through the battle unwounded, so the court quickly came to focus its attention on him.

As testimony accumulated, a confused picture of the action emerged. Cox had not been part of the boarding party which Lawrence had organized prior to the battle. He had been at his station on the gun deck when he heard the bugle signal for the boarding party to assemble on the spar deck. Since his division of guns was on the disengaged side of the ship, he left his station and hurried to the assembly point, calling on his men to follow. His intention was to reinforce the boarding party; but few of his men went with him, and he arrived on the quarterdeck virtually alone. He was just in time to see the fatal volley of canister sweep through the assembled boarders and strike down all of the principal officers. Cox rushed to Lawrence's assistance. Believing that he heard the captain ask to be helped below, Cox helped support him and saw him to his cabin. Here he was found by a messenger

The famous battle between the *Shannon* and the *Chesapeake* was fought off Boston Harbor in 1813. The loss of the *Chesapeake* was the most humiliating defeat ever suffered by the Old Navy. Under the deliberately misleading charge of neglect of duty, several of her officers and crew were tried for cowardice. (United States Naval Academy Museum Library collection)

from Lieutenant Budd, who informed him that he was now in command. He attempted to regain the quarterdeck, only to discover that the British had carried it. He dashed forward looking for a hatchway that would admit him topside, but everywhere his path was blocked by American seamen trying to get below and take refuge on the gun deck. He was not able to regain the spar deck before the *Chesapeake* struck.[15]

It should have been obvious that the *Chesapeake*'s improvised command structure and her newly enlisted and undrilled crew had been thrown into chaos by the extraordinary events of the battle. The court of inquiry, however, chose to ignore these mitigating circumstances and recommended that several of her officers and men be court-martialed on charges revolving around cowardice and premature surrender. Midshipman Cox was to be the principal defendant. Captain William Bainbridge, who had chaired the court of inquiry, opined that Cox should be the only officer censured for his conduct during the battle because

> being stationed in Command of the second Division on the main deck: That when there, and the enemy boarding or on the brink of boarding, he left the deck to assist Capt. Lawrence below and went down with him from the spar deck to the berth Deck [and] did not return to his division; but went forward on the gun deck; that while there and the men were retreating below he commanded the men to go to their duty without enforcing their commands.[16]

Acknowledging that the real reason for the loss of the *Chesapeake* was that so many of her officers fell at the critical moment when the boarding party was being formed, the court was willing to give Cox some benefit of the doubt:

> as a Court of Enquiry allows an accused person no opportunity of vindicating his conduct, the members of this Court trust that their opinion on the conduct of Lieutenant Cox may not be deemed conclusive against him, without trial by Court-Martial. . . .[17]

A court-martial was duly convened under the presidency of Captain Decatur, who was then in command of the frigate *President*, lying blockaded at New London, Connecticut. Once again, Decatur, who had been in close touch with Bainbridge during the court of inquiry, made statements that indicated that he would not be an impartial judge. He was determined to hold Cox responsible for the loss of the *Chesapeake*.[18] The charges drawn up by the Navy Department included cowardice, disobedience of orders, desertion from quarters, neglect of duty, and unofficerlike conduct. The specifications made it clear that all of these charges were extracted from Cox's actions between the time he left the gun deck and the moment the ship struck her colors, perhaps five minutes in all.[19]

As the court listened to the testimony of eyewitnesses, it slowly became obvious that very few of them could contribute significant evidence against Cox. Only Lieutenant Budd seemed to have seen and heard virtually everything. It was Budd, for example, who disputed Cox's claim that Lawrence had asked him to help him below when he was wounded. Budd maintained that Cox had admitted to him while they were prisoners in Halifax that Lawrence had ordered him not to leave the quarterdeck, strongly implying that helping Lawrence below was merely an excuse to get away from the battle. Budd also testified that, after he was wounded, he had sent several messengers to find Cox and notify him that he had become the *Chesapeake*'s commander and that Cox could easily have returned to the quarterdeck if he had been prompt in replying to Budd's summons. He was also highly critical of Cox for leaving his division.[20]

One other witness was able to furnish a bit of damaging evidence against Cox. Midshipman Delozier Higginbotham had encountered Cox at the forward hatch where he was trying to regain the deck against a torrent of American seamen who were pouring below as the British boarding party was securing its possession of the spar deck. Higginbotham asked Cox if he should "cut down" the retreating Americans in conformity with the customs of that era, but Cox replied "no, it is no use."[21] This testimony formed the basis for a second specification under the unofficerlike conduct charge, which accused the defendant of

not doing his utmost to aid in the capturing of the *Shannon* by animating and encouraging, in his own example, the inferior officers and men to fight courageously and in denying the use of coercive means to prevent the desertion of the men from their quarters, and not compelling those who had deserted from their quarters to return to duty.[22]

Cox made a vigorous and determined defense of his actions, but he did his cause little good by confronting the court directly with the accusation that they were offering him up as a scapegoat, "a sacrifice to heal the wounded honor and reinstate the naval pride of the nation." He further maintained that "had the events of the contest been different, many of these very acts . . . would have enhanced my merit in the public estimation."[23] During cross examination of witnesses and in his defense summation, Cox urged the court to consider the actions and motives of Lieutenant Budd. He asked how, in the heat of battle, the senior officer and acting commander of the *Chesapeake* could have been so minutely observant of his every action. He speculated about the reason why Budd was anxious to turn over command to him at the very climax of the engagement. His own explanation was that Budd was overly concerned with his own safety; and seeing the engagement going against the Americans, he did not want to be in command at the final moment when the deck was carried and the frigate surrendered.[24]

Concerning the propriety of deserting the quarterdeck in order to assist the wounded Lawrence below, Cox allowed a tone of scorn to creep into his statement. Recalling that he and Lawrence were intimate friends and had been together in battle before, he compared his actions to those of Captain Thomas Hardy at Trafalgar:

> Was the man on whom Nelson leaned when he was wounded and who helped him when he died, a coward? or a deserter from his duty? or was it ever said that a Sailor would have done as well?[25]

As president of the court, Decatur was disturbed by the lack of witnesses to corroborate the testimony of Budd and Higganbotham. Writing to Secretary of the Navy William Jones, he lamented that

> These charges appear from the summary alone to be founded in several instances on the testimony of a single witness. It is certainly desirable if these facts are provable that they should be established by more than one witness if there be more to the same facts. . . .[26]

Unfortunately, no other witnesses could be produced who had any clear recollection of Cox's conduct during the few critical minutes under investigation. In the end the court sustained only vague charges of neglect of duty and unofficerlike conduct. Cox was exonerated of all charges relating to cowardice, disobedience, or desertion. He was sentenced "to be cashiered and rendered forever incapable of serving in the navy."[27]

President Madison approved the verdict of the court, but Cox kept trying to have the case reopened until his death. In 1952, a great-grandson succeeded in getting the proceedings reviewed by the House Armed Services Committee. Cox was fully vindicated by that body and restored to the navy list as a lieutenant, with his service record terminating on the date of his death, 17 October 1874.[28]

After disposing of Cox, the same court went on to try several other members of the *Chesapeake*'s crew. Two midshipmen were court-martialed, one for having been repeatedly drunk in captivity and one for giving his parole and then "prowling" about the town of Halifax under an assumed name. Two petty officers and twenty-one seamen had joined the British Navy, and there were a few cases of enlisted men treating the officers with contempt while in the custody of the enemy. Two enlisted men, Gun Captain Joseph Russell and Bugler William Brown, were tried for cowardice because of their conduct during the battle.

Of all these cases, perhaps the most interesting concerned the bugler. William Brown had played a critical role in throwing the *Chesapeake*'s crew into confusion by deserting the quarterdeck just at the time he was to sound the signal for "away boarders," which would have sent the men gathered in the waist by the previous assembly call into battle. Brown, a free Negro, was represented by a civilian lawyer, who offered the following defense:

> I would suggest as a subject worth some enquiry whether the negro is not naturally inferior to the white man in those qualities which go to make up courage. If so the shipment or enlistment of every negro is presumed to be made with a knowledge of the fact, and no other duties should be required of them than such as nature has qualified them to discharge.
>
> God has made the prisoner too insignificant a being on whom to visit the loss of the *Chesapeake*. If his accidental exertions might have saved the ship, he would not have had the credit of it, nor would he have been entitled to it. And if you decide otherwise, and charge the whole misfortune to one who could barely comprehend his simple duty, other nations will laugh at the little subterfuges to which we resort, and instead of enlarging our naval fame we shall belittle our national character.[29]

Apparently the court held a higher opinion of the inherent capabilities and accountability of Negro seamen. William Brown was sentenced to receive three hundred lashes and "to be mulcted of all his pay now due and which may accrue to him during the remainder of his service." President Madison mitigated this to one hundred lashes and loss of all pay.[30]

Continuing its uncompromising attitude towards the *Chesapeake*'s men, the court next tried Midshipman James W. Forrest for cowardice, neglect of duty, and drunkenness on specifications so flimsy that ultimately only the drunkenness charge was sustained, and that because Forrest pleaded guilty to it. Adopting a tone of extreme severity, the court proceeded to

> pointedly express [their] abhorrence of a vice destructive of morals, ruinous to the individual; and disgraceful to the public service; and sentence the prisoner to be cashiered with the perpetual incapacity to serve in the Navy of the United States.[31]

Since this was not the usual sentence for drunkenness on the part of a young warrant officer, it was obvious that Midshipman Forrest had been punished for cowardice after all.

Only Midshipman Henry P. Fleshman was able to find some evidence of sympathy on the part of the court. Charged with "Imposition & unofficerlike conduct after capture by the enemy," Fleshman was allowed to explain why he had given an assumed name in taking the parole offered by the British at Halifax. He had been captured previously and held at Halifax before being exchanged in a cartel. He had not given his parole on that occasion but had lost his certificate so declaring. When he was again captured, he was afraid that he would be permanently imprisoned as a parole violator, so he assumed the identity of another midshipman named William Brown, who had left the *Chesapeake* before the battle but whose name was still on the muster roll.[32]

Still presided over by the implacable Decatur, the court found

> in the conduct of the prisoner, in Halifax, a departure from the principles which should characterize every officer, and should never be compromised for personal convenience; but in consideration of his youth and inexperience, and his good conduct in the action sentence him to be publicly reprimanded in such a manner as the Honorable Secretary of the Navy shall direct.

Secretary Jones quickly replied, stipulating that

> The Sentence is approved and the President of the Court directed to reprimand Midshipman Henry P. Fleshman upon the quarterdeck of the United States Ship *President* in such a manner as he may deem most impressive and effectual.[33]

From the lengthy proceedings that grew out of the *Chesapeake* debacle, it can be seen that in the eyes of their contemporaries the crew of that unfortunate vessel failed in two areas of conduct considered significant to the prevailing concept of naval honor. First, they did not successfully withstand the test of battle with an opponent of equal strength; and, second, they did not acquit themselves well as prisoners of war.

In the Old Navy, there was one other instance when the behavior of American naval prisoners of war broke down significantly. When Captain William Bainbridge's men were being held for ransom in Tripoli after the surrender of the *Philadelphia*, five enlisted men collaborated with the Tripolitans, telling malicious lies about their fellow prisoners, participating in punishments meted out to them, and helping the Bashaw's men to build gunboats and fortifications. These collaborators, whose conduct actually constituted treason, were John Wilson, rated as quartermaster, Peter West and William Godby, ship's carpenters, and Thomas Prince and Louis Hexner, seamen.[34] They were called "the Apostates" by the rest of the crew and characterized as having "turned Turk," especially after Hexner embraced the Islamic faith. They proved especially adept at supervising forced labor gangs made up of the *Philadelphia* seamen.[35]

Strangely enough, although these actions were well known to all of the officers and men of the *Philadelphia*, none of the "Apostates" was ever tried by court-martial, even though all of them were eventually delivered back into the navy's hands when Bainbridge's crew was exchanged in 1805. William Godby was even called upon to testify at the court of inquiry that investigated the circumstances under which the *Philadelphia* was lost. As a ship's carpenter, he described various scuttling measures which he had carried out, such as the boring of holes in the ship's bottom. Throughout the court of inquiry, held under the presidency of Commodore Preble on board the *Constitution*, all mention of the conduct of the prisoners in captivity was scrupulously avoided. No questions relative to it were asked by the court, and no information was volunteered by the witnesses.[36]

Although the navy's main concern seemed to be to track down instances of misconduct and cowardice in defeat, a few cases grew out of successful actions. Lieutenant Edward R. McCall of the brig *Enterprise* brought charges against Sailing Master William Harper for cowardice apparently displayed during the engagement with H.M.S. *Boxer* on 5 September 1813. McCall, who had taken command of the *Enterprise* when Captain William Burrows was wounded, specified that Harper had screamed, "By God, we shall all be killed" when he thought the *Enterprise* was about to be raked, "thereby unsettling a number of marines stationed upon the quarter deck," and that he later deserted his post near the helm and tried to shelter behind the foremast and under the heel of the bowsprit. Harper was further charged with trying to induce McCall to haul down the colors even though the action was going well for the Americans.[37]

During the court-martial proceedings, several witnesses testified that Harper was an unpopular officer, and one man declared that before the battle was joined he had told the Sailing Master to his face that he hoped he would be killed during the engagement.[38] Under these circumstances, it is possible that Harper might have suspected an attempt on his life would be made by *Enterprise* crewmen under cover of the engagement.

As the trial progressed, the case against Harper was damaged by information elicited by the defense during cross examination of the prosecutor, Lieutenant McCall. It developed that once the battle had been concluded Harper was immediately appointed Prize Master of the *Boxer* and no charges of misconduct were made against him until some twenty-four hours after the fact.[39] In his defense summation, Harper further stated that none of the *Enterprise*'s men, including McCall, had ever been in battle before. In the heat of the action, these inexperienced witnesses had simply misunderstood his actions, for which he had valid explanations. He emphatically denied that he had ever wanted to haul down the colors, pitting his word directly against that of Lieutenant McCall on that specification.[40] Apparently not wanting to spoil the luster of the *Enterprise*'s victory, the court unanimously found Harper not guilty.

The practice of not pressing misconduct charges growing out of victorious engagements was also adhered to in the case of Captain Jesse Duncan Elliott. During the Battle of Lake Erie, Elliott commanded the brig *Niagara* and during a critical juncture failed utterly to support his commodore, Oliver Hazard Perry, hanging back while the flagship *Lawrence* took the fire of several British vessels. This incident gave rise to a later controversy between the two men which resulted in Perry bringing charges against Elliott for spreading falsehoods, cowardice, negligence, and disaffection under fire. The charges were acknowledged by Secretary of the Navy Smith Thompson on 3 October 1818 and forwarded to President Monroe, who apparently decided to quash them for political reasons. No court-martial was ever authorized, and all the documents supplied by Perry subsequently vanished except for a copy of the charges and specifications later found among the Decatur papers.[41]

Another abortive attempt to press charges related to a scandal growing out of alleged cowardice was the effort to prosecute Franklin Wharton, the Lieutenant Colonel Commandant of the Marine Corps. In this instance, a navy court-martial board was convened under the presidency of Commodore Charles Stewart in the summer of 1817. Since the actions in question had taken place on land, during the Battle of Bladensburg, Wharton successfully challenged the right of the navy court to hear his case.[42] Jurisdiction was transferred to an army court, which found him innocent of the charges.

Between 1815 and 1846, the United States was at peace except for skirmishes with minor principalities and primitive peoples. Consequently, there are few cases of cowardice recorded in the judge advocate general's index for these years, and those that are there relate to trivial matters. For example, Commander Uriah P. Levy was charged with cowardice, among other things, by his executive officer while he was in command of the sloop of war *Vandalia*. The specification states that Levy called one Antoine Collins

> A citizen of Pensacola, a blackguard, or a damned blackguard or apply[ed] words to that effect to him, and then suffer[ed] the said Collins to wring his nose severely, without making any resistance.[43]

In another instance, Captain William C. Bolton of the frigate *Brandywine* was accused of cowardice in several newspapers because he apparently abandoned his squadron and returned home with his ship during the diplomatic crisis with Great Britain over the Maine Boundary Dispute of 1841. A court-martial found Bolton guilty of disobedience of orders and sentenced him to be reprimanded privately.[44] His brother officers dealt with the accusations of cowardice by writing letters to the offending papers explaining Bolton's actions in terms of the strategic situation that prevailed at the time. In one of these letters, Commander Samuel Francis Du Pont pointed out that in the event of hostilities with England, the American Mediterranean Squadron, to which the *Brandywine* had been attached, would have had to face "16 sail of the line, with war steamers, frigates, and sloops by the score." Bolton, Du Pont maintained, would have been compelled either to surrender without resistance or allow himself to be blockaded in some neutral port. To demonstrate that Bolton was not wanting in courage, Du Pont cited his conduct at the Battle of Lake Erie some twenty-seven years earlier.[45]

Apparently, the Mexican War gave rise to only one officially recorded instance of questionable conduct under fire. On 17 November 1847, Commander Thomas O. Selfridge commanded U.S. naval forces ashore at the Battle of Guaymas, successfully defending the town against a Mexican attempt to retake it after its capture the previous month. Despite the successful outcome of the engagement, Selfridge's conduct during the battle slowly developed into a scandal; and on 3 November 1851, a court of inquiry was held to investigate his "conduct on the occasion of the engagement with the enemy at Guaymas, in Mexico . . ."[46] These proceedings had been instituted by the Navy Department to examine charges made by Lieutenant William Taylor Smith, who believed that he had witnessed cowardly behavior on the part of Commander Selfridge which had gone unreported at the time.

On the day in question, Selfridge, who was commanding officer of the sloop of war *Dale*, had landed a force of some seventy men at Guaymas for the purpose of surveying damage to the fort there and searching the town for Mexican troops. The landing party, which was equally divided between sailors under the command of Lieutenant Smith and marines under the direction of Lieutenant Robert C. Tansill, left the ship's boats at the town wharf and, accompanied by a boat's cannon for artillery cover, occupied the fort and began to advance on the town.

As they approached the central square or plaza, a volley of musket fire suddenly erupted from a nearby house. Both Smith and Tansill ordered their men to take cover along the sides of a street and looked to Commander Selfridge for orders. To their astonishment, they saw him running hard in the direction of the wharf. About halfway there, he was met by a seaman who hoisted him on his back and carried him the rest of the way to his boat.[47]

Neither Smith nor Tansill had been told what the object of the landing was, so Smith sent his second in command, Midshipman James P. Houston, to find Selfridge and request orders as to how to proceed or what to do next. When Houston caught up to Selfridge, he was already in his boat, exclaiming in an agitated voice, "I am fainting, give me water, oh God, what will become of my family, shove off or they will be down upon us." He gave no intelligible orders to Houston; but the boat pilot, a Mr. Davis, told him to go back and order Lieutenant Smith to "give it to them," or words to that effect.[48]

Smith and Tansill exchanged fire with the Mexicans for a little while and then retreated back to the fort under cover of a bombard-

The sloop-of-war *Dale* lies anchored off La Paz during the Mexican War. In a setting similar to this one, her commanding officer, Thomas O. Selfridge, laid himself open to charges of cowardice under fire when he abandoned a shore party he was leading after taking a wound in the foot. (United States Naval Academy Museum Library collection)

ment by the *Dale*'s guns. The enemy then abandoned the town, and the entire landing party returned to the *Dale*. As Lieutenant Smith came on board, he remarked to the executive officer, Lieutenant Edward M. Yard, "that Com. Selfridge had run on the first fire and left the shore without giving him a single order."[49] By that time Selfridge was down in his cabin being treated by the ship's surgeon for a painful wound in his right foot which he had sustained in the initial volley and which had caused his precipitate retreat.

After listening to all the eyewitness testimony, the court, which was presided over by Commodore John P. Sloat, sought to establish just how disabling the foot wound was and whether or not it alone could explain Commander Selfridge's conduct. For this purpose, the testimony of several surgeons who had treated Selfridge at various times was enlisted. All of the expert medical testimony was essentially similar to that of Assistant Surgeon John Rubenstien [sic], who explained that the musket ball had grazed Selfridge's calves, entered the foot from above, followed an erratic path, damaging bones and tendons, and finally passed out again.

Question. [by the court to Surgeon Rubenstien] Would it be the probable effect of such a wound, at the time it was received, to derange and shock the nervous system generally so as greatly to impair the mental as well as physical energies?

A. Yes it would.

Q. Was not the condition of Com. Selfridge such, when he was brought on board, as to require immediate surgical aid, and would it have been prudent to have deferred such aid?

A. It was necessary that he should receive immediate surgical aid, and it would not have been prudent to have defer[red] such aid? [sic]

Q. Would such a wound be likely to incapacitate an officer for command when first received, and in what degree would it probably affect his control over his own actions?

A. It would be likely to incapacitate a majority of persons for command and likewise it would, in a great many instances, destroy one's self control. Different men are differently affected by gun shot wounds.

Q. How far would such a wound be likely to affect the use of the foot for locomotion?

A. Not in a very great degree at the immediate time.[50]

In this court of inquiry, the role played by the judge advocate was a small one. Both Commander Selfridge and Lieutenant Smith were represented by counselors who handled most of the cross examination. Lieutenant Smith's lawyer made a determined effort to demonstrate that in spite of his wound Selfridge should have remained at his post and continued to direct his men. Several examples of prominent Army officers who had taken foot wounds and continued to exercise command were brought before the court.

The combined depositions of the several surgeons, all of whom agreed with Dr. Rubenstien, weighed heavily, however. When all of the proceedings had been concluded, the court delivered itself of the opinion "That [Commander Selfridge's] conduct on the occasion referred to should *not* injuriously affect the character and standing of the said Com. Selfridge."[51] This finding was reviewed and approved by Secretary of the Navy William N. Graham on 10 December 1851.

No further major cases of cowardice can be found in the judge advocate general's records until the advent of the Civil War. This is understandable, since the years from 1848 to 1861 featured little in the way of combat action for the navy. Of the small number of cowardice cases which did arise, it is difficult to arrive at any firm interpretations which might link them together in a pattern. This is because the sampling is too limited and the circumstances of the individual cases—ranging from the surrender and loss of a major warship, the *Chesapeake*, to the pulling of an officer's nose on a Pensacola sidewalk—are too varied. The only time a person suspected of cowardice was ever convicted and punished on *any* charge was in the context of a defeat that resulted in severe humiliation and loss of prestige for the service. It is indicative of the fear and dread and awe that naval officers held for accusations of cowardice that no officer charged with it was ever found guilty of it. Commodore Barron and Midshipman Cox came the closest, each having surrendered a major warship; but they were found guilty only of negligence or neglect of duty and related specifications. It was the stigma of cowardice, not the legal finding of it, which remained with them for the rest of their lives.

It is obvious, however, that the navy was very inconsistent and unsophisticated in its treatment of cowardice. There is more than a hint of scapegoating in both of the affairs involving the frigate *Chesapeake*. On the other hand, serious questions involving the surrender of the *Philadelphia* before she had suffered any significant casualties or battle damage and the conduct of Sailing Master Harper of the *Enterprise* were almost completely glossed over.

It must be remembered, of course, that the battle experience of the Old Navy was very limited. There were few general fleet actions. Ship-to-ship duels were limited only to the years between 1812 and 1816, when Commodore Oliver Hazard Perry took the Algerian frigate *Mashuda*, and to the era of the Quasi-War. This meant that American officers were relatively unseasoned in battle in comparison to British or French officers and consequently may have had difficulty deciding what sort of behavior was reasonable. Since there were few surrenders of American naval vessels, courts-martial had few precedents to guide them in determining just when an honorable surrender, especially one occurring after a hot action, was or was not justified.

One fact does stand out. In contrast with the usages of the Modern Fleet, the Old Navy did recognize the right of the commanding officer of a badly outgunned and tactically trapped or outsailed warship to surrender without firing a shot. Table IV of this dissertation attests to the number of captains who took advantage of this custom. The idea that a naval vessel must go down fighting and with her flag flying no matter what the odds against her are is a product of the steam and steel navies of the twentieth century.

It is also noteworthy that although there were significant instances in which enlisted men deserted their posts during a battle, particularly during the *Chesapeake-Shannon* action and the last fight of the *Essex*, the most vigorous prosecution of suspected cowards was reserved for officers.

In many ways, the treatment of treason followed a pattern similar to the one established in the adjudication of cowardice cases. Technically, the enlisted men from the *Philadelphia* who collaborated with the Tripolitans and the *Chesapeake* men who joined the British Navy in 1813 were all traitors, but they were never tried. In all probability, the War of 1812 must have produced many more "turncoat" seamen from among the naval prisoners taken by the British, but nothing was ever done about them. Perhaps the "honor" of the enlisted man was held in much lower esteem than that of his superiors so that very little effort was made officially either to impeach or redeem it.

Among the officers, treason was naturally a much more serious matter. Fortunately, the Old Navy had little or no trouble with treachery among its officers until the years 1860 and 1861. On the eve of the breakup of the Union, many officers of southern birth violated their oaths and conspired, either actively or passively, to deliver naval stations, stores, ordnance, and other public property to the forces of the seceding states. After having undermined the authority of navy yard commanders and given material aid to "rebels" in direct violation of Article X of the Articles of War, almost all of these officers escaped court-martial and punishment by the simple act of resigning their commissions. President Buchanan's Secretary of the Navy, Isaac Toucey, meekly accepted sixty-eight such resignations, much to the disgust of incoming Secretary Gideon Welles. Welles was anxious to initiate wholesale arrests and trials of these officers on treason charges. Indeed, upon taking office, Welles promptly set up a special bureau, headed by Captain Silas Stringham, to review all of the navy's remaining officers and vouch for their loyalty.[52]

Welles's policies speeded up the process of resignation until, in the Secretary's own words, 322 officers had "traitorously abandoned the flag."[53] Seventeen more officers stationed at the Norfolk Navy Yard were dismissed by the Secretary in a vain attempt to be rid of them before they could seriously interfere with the destruction of the workshops, ordnance, and ships located there.

Ironically, the only result of Welles's actions was that among the few officers who were tried for treason were those who had remained loyal and tried to do their duty as best they could under the circumstances. When Commander Henry Walke, the commanding officer of the supply ship *Supply*, brought a shipload of refugees into New York Harbor, he was tried for disobedience of orders, and a special effort was made by the judge advocate to question his loyalty. Likewise, Commodore James Armstrong was court-martialed for his role in the surrender of the Pensacola Navy Yard to Florida militia forces. He was charged with neglect of duty, disobedience of orders, and conduct unbecoming an officer; but in reality, he was suspected of treason.

Perhaps the Walke case best illustrates the confusion and hysteria that characterized the naval command system at that time. Commodore Pendergrast of the Gulf Squadron had ordered Walke to take his ship to Pensacola, load coal and stores, and return to the squadron anchorage at Vera Cruz. When the *Supply* arrived at Pensacola, the base was surrounded by Florida militia troops, as were three nearby Army posts —forts Pickens, Barrancas, and McCrea. Armstrong had orders to deliver supplies to the army posts. He hoped to commandeer the *Supply* and use her for this task. After much confusion and indecision, Walke allowed Armstrong to supersede his original orders and send the *Supply* to the forts.[54] When Walke returned from this mission, he found the Pensacola Navy Yard in rebel hands. Conferring with Armstrong under a flag of truce, Walke received further orders to embark some 151 Navy and Marine officers, enlisted men, navy yard civilians, and their dependents, and carry them to a northern port.

Walke chose to make for New York, arriving there on 4 February 1861, nineteen days out of Pensacola. Upon his coming to anchor off the New York Navy Yard, still more confusion ensued. A rumor had preceded him into port alleging that the *Supply* carried a secessionist raiding force bent on sabotaging the navy yard and its facilities. On his part, Walke was afraid that secessionist forces hidden on shore might make an attempt to rush the *Supply* and use her to escape south.

For these reasons, the commander refused to make the normal calls ashore, and a boarding party subsequently set out from shore to board and take the *Supply* by force. After some initial resistance, the shore party managed to get on board; and Walke and his passengers were put through the indignity of a minute personal search before any of them were allowed to land.[55] Deeply suspicious of Walke, who was a Virginian by birth, the Navy Department quickly preferred charges of disobedience of orders against him and used these as a pretext to scrutinize his behavior for signs of disloyalty.

The specification under the charge made it clear that the official reason for holding the court-martial was to investigate why Walke had not carried out his original instructions to carry coal to the Gulf Squadron. The situation prevailing at Pensacola was examined in great detail, along with Walke's resupply mission to the army forts. In his defense, which was printed and publicly circulated by the Navy Department, Walke cited what should have been obvious: that in the highly unusual situation prevailing at the time, it was necessary to depart from a slavish adherence to official orders and make liberal use of discretion and initiative. To have insisted on delivering Commodore Pendergrast's coal and abandoned Commodore Armstrong to his fate would have been unacceptable.[56]

The court agreed in part but could not bring itself to fully vindicate Walke. He was found guilty but sentenced merely

> To be admonished by the Secretary of the Navy—the mild sentence which the court has passed is occasioned by the peculiar and extraordinary circumstances in which Commander Walke was placed.[57]

Old Commodore Armstrong did not fare as well as Walke. After a lengthy court of inquiry "into the circumstances connected with his surrender of the Navy Yard at Pensacola," he was court-martialed on charges of neglect of duty, disobedience of orders, and conduct unbecoming an officer.[58] The resulting trial was long, the testimony repetitious and highly tedious, and very little was accomplished. In the end, a deep personal tragedy was inflicted on the old commodore, who had served the navy faithfully for fifty years.

The story that emerges actually impeaches the government rather than the commodore. When he was cited for disobedience of orders, Armstrong demonstrated that he had no orders, only vague directives to cooperate with the army commanders in the eastern Gulf area, "exercise caution" and "maintain vigilance," all of which he had done.[59] He was charged with the protection of public property but had no orders to remove or destroy it. Some of his officers were obviously disloyal. Indeed, it was his executive officer, Lieutenant Francis B. Renshaw, who actually hauled down the flag over the commodore's protests, afterwards resigning his commission and joining the rebels.[60]

The Navy Department seemed particularly incensed that Commodore Armstrong had not made a fighting defense of the navy yard with the forces available to him. Armstrong explained, however, that he had only a small detachment of marines, a few enlisted artisans, and a handful of loyal officers when he surrendered. His batteries were mounted facing the bay rather than the gates of the yard, many of the gun carriages were rotten, and critical parts had been stolen. These conditions had made it futile in his judgment to try and oppose the several hundred armed Florida troops that menaced him.[61]

Not mentioned in the transcript of the trial, but equally compelling, was simple exhaustion and confusion on Armstrong's part. An elderly officer intending to spend a few remaining years of service in undemanding shore duty, he was suddenly confronted with the complete collapse of all institutional power and authority. He looked for orders and received none. He gave orders and was ignored. Some of his officers were openly disloyal, some secretly so. The habits of a lifetime of service in a rigidly structured and moribund environment had not equipped him for such trials and tribulations. In vain, he pleaded for acquittal, to be allowed to live out his few remaining years in good standing in the service to which he had devoted a half-century. Instead he received five years' suspension from duty with loss of pay for the first half of said term and was reprimanded by the Secretary of the Navy in General Orders.[62] He was never formally accused of treason, but it is hard to escape the conviction that to some extent he suffered in the place of all the actual traitors which the department would have liked to prosecute if they had been within reach.

It can, perhaps, be argued that it is not fair to characterize as treason actions taken under the impact of impending civil war, with all of the unsettled emotionalism and divided loyalties which prevail at such times. Still, Article XII of the Articles of War specifically covers even this eventuality.

> Spies, and all persons who shall come or be found in the capacity of Spies, or who shall bring or deliver any seducing letter or message from an enemy *or rebel* [italics inserted] or endeavor to corrupt any person in the navy to betray his trust, shall suffer death, or such other punishment as a court-martial shall adjudge.

Writing four decades after the events of 1861, Charles Oscar Paullin, a pioneer historian in the field of naval administration, proposed that a distinction should be made between those officers who straightforwardly resigned from the Old Navy without trying to harm or cripple it and those who remained in the service while actively or passively cooperating with rebel forces and helping them to secure stores, munitions, ordnance, and bases for future use against the United States. Such men, Paullin maintained, had dishonored themselves both legally and morally and constitute a sizable corps of naval traitors.[63]

Given the confused circumstances of the times, Paullin's judgment may be harsh. If the years 1860 and 1861 are excluded from the reckoning, the navy's record is remarkably free of traitors throughout the nineteenth century. During the Civil War only one obvious naval traitor emerged, in the person of Acting Master Daniel W. Glenny. A native of Connecticut, Glenny was a volunteer serving as commanding officer of the war steamer *Rattler*, operating in the lower Mississippi River. In 1864, he arranged with Confederate officers to deliver his ship and crew to the rebels for two thousand dollars cash, one hundred bales of cotton, and command of a blockade runner.[64]

Unfortunately for Glenny, his frequent trips to the plantation of one Joshua James, where he met and parleyed with his Confederate contacts, excited the suspicion of the *Rattler*'s officers and men. On the day of the planned betrayal, they were able to frustrate their captain's purpose to the extent that the *Rattler* was holed on a snag, blown ashore, and burned before the rebels could take possession of her. Glenny was arrested but escaped before he could be court-martialed, and apparently made his way to the Confederate lines. He was never captured nor was he tried *in absentia*.[65]

If acts of treason were rare in the navy before 1861, the charge of sedition was significantly more common and was used against both officers and enlisted men. Often it can be found coupled with charges of mutinous conduct or rendered as mutinous and seditious words. An examination of a sampling of sedition cases shows that most of the enlisted men laid themselves open to this charge by cursing or criticizing their superior officers or the navy in general. Officers—especially junior and staff officers—who made disparaging remarks about their commanding officers or about the navy were also liable to sedition charges. As used by the navy, this charge had little to do with loyalty to the flag or nation. Often it was preferred after some hasty remark had been made in a moment of anger, frustration, or while the offending individual was drunk or in a state of violent agitation.[66]

Another category of behavior in which both officers and enlisted men could bring disgrace upon themselves concerned homosexuality and relations with the opposite sex. In both areas, the service was much more rigorous with officer offenders than it was with enlisted men who violated the navy's largely unwritten codes in these matters. In general, the navy made no effort to regulate the heterosexual activities of enlisted men at all, aside from denying most of them feminine companionship while they were at sea or lodged in a receiving ship or shore station. Apparently, the U.S. Navy never followed the old British custom of allowing "wives" to visit crews confined in ships anchored in American ports. On the other hand, at least one officer who married an "unsuitable" woman was investigated by a court of inquiry; and three officers were prosecuted for bringing women of low repute into their ships to live with them.

The extent and nature of homosexual activity in the Old Navy is one of the major question marks in its social history. Precise evidence in the form of records, documents and statistics is almost wholly lacking. Aside from four court-martial cases listed in the judge advocate general's index, there is only a report submitted to Congress in 1847 which details some 5,936 floggings for subjudicial offenses which were administered in sixty naval vessels during the year 1846. Of these floggings, five were clearly for homosexual activities, three being entered as sodomy, one as "improper conduct too base to mention," and one as "filthy and unnatural practices." Thirteen other log entries list offenses such as filthy conduct, "gross misconduct to boys," and "improper conduct on the berth deck," which may be circumlocutions for sodomy.[67]

Unfortunately, log entries are very stark and give no real idea of the social attitudes and disciplinary practices that the navy held and employed in relation to homosexuality. For this reason, the court-martial records, scanty as they are in this area, provide our only insight into these matters.

The navy's first court-martial for sodomy was held on board the *Constitution* in the Mediterranean in 1805. According to the testimony, Marine Private George Crutch waylaid a seaman identified simply as "Geregano" and attempted to sodomize him. A friend of Geregano's, Seaman Dominico Otesio, woke up Marine Sergeant James P. Mix and told him what was happening. Mix, together with Sergeant James Reynolds, immediately went on deck and found

> George Crutch on the Spars between the boats, with his Pantaloons down, and shirt above the Navel, on top of Geregano; he [Mix] immediately run his hand down between them & felt the Penis of George Crutch. —it appeared to him by the feel that Crutch had no connection with Geregano but was about making the attempt and that Geregano had his shirt above his waist.[68]

166

This testimony was substantially corroborated by Sergeant Reynolds, who added that he had found the two men together and "held them in that situation until I was joined by Sgt. Mix." The officers hearing the case must have been embarrassed or revolted by the frank details of the testimony. They asked only if Crutch appeared intoxicated and, receiving a negative reply, cut off all further deliberation and unanimously voted to acquit him of the charge. No attempt was ever made to explain this rush to reach a verdict so at odds with the testimony offered by the two sergeants, but it was nevertheless routinely approved by Commodore John Rodgers.[69]

A much more thorough and detailed case involving a homosexual theme was that of Lieutenant Owen Burns of the frigate *Potomac*. He was examined by a court of inquiry to determine the truthfulness of ". . . certain reports in Circulation on board the said Frigate *Potomac* prejudicial to the Character of Lieutenant Owen Burns. . . ." The recording clerk in the Navy Department later reduced this tentative charge to a simple accusation of "masturbation," which appears in the judge advocate general's index.[70]

As the court of inquiry, which was held on board the *Potomac* in Naples Harbor during September of 1835, listened to the testimony of witnesses, it developed that a former seaman named Thomas Cumming, then living ashore in Naples, had circulated stories through the ship that Burns was having illicit intercourse with two of the ship's boys. When called to testify, both boys related that Lieutenant Burns had demanded that they masturbate him in his cabin.

> *Question.* [by the court to Andrew Hansen, ship's boy] Did you ever frig Lt. Burns?
> *A.* Yes—
> *Q.* How often?
> *A.* Five or six times.[71]

Hansen asserted that on one particular night Burns had called him to his cabin and ordered him to "put my hand close to him," threatening that if he did not "I might suffer the consequences—after I had satisfied his desires I went on deck."[72] John Williams, the other ship's boy involved, claimed that Burns had approached him but had not been able to get him to perform any sex act. In addition to these witnesses, John Julian, a ship's boy on board Lieutenant Burns's previous ship, the schooner *Shark*, testified that he also had refused to "frig" Burns at his request although he "asked me almost every night to do it."[73]

Perhaps the most revealing facts were exposed when Thomas Cumming testified. He claimed that he had discovered what was happening when Hansen complained to him that Burns was "molesting" him. Burns sought to impeach the credibility of Cumming by calling Captain Joseph Nicholson, Commanding Officer of the *Potomac*. Nicholson testified that all of the witnesses against Burns were persons of poor reputation and character. He related that Cumming and Hansen were known to be lovers and had once been caught having intercourse between two cannons on the gun deck. Nicholson had handled that incident in what may have been a standard navy practice, discharging Cumming immediately and sending him ashore while retaining Hansen with the intention of letting him go at the next port of call "so as to keep them separate."[74] Apparently Cumming's motive in making trouble for Burns was to disgrace the lieutenant, get Hansen discharged at Naples, and reclaim him as his lover.

Burns continued to defend himself energetically. He called Surgeon George T. Terrill to testify that he had been treating the Lieutenant for a venereal infection. Terrill had prescribed genital baths in cold water and ordered Burns to refrain from any sexual activity.[75] Burns then explained that he had called the boys to his cabin for the purpose of giving him the baths required by the surgeon.

The court of inquiry obviously did not relish the task of arriving at a verdict concerning the Burns case.

> We now approach the subject with great diffidence and with great regret, as we are led to believe that Lieutenant Burns must, from his conduct [have] laid himself liable to improper impressions as well as improper remarks from those of his inferiors who have been permitted to approach him to discharge their domestic duties; and we take leave to observe that an officer ought at all times in our opinion, [to] be placed above suspicion or the shadow of reproach.[76]

Commodore Daniel T. Patterson was equally reluctant to confront the full implications of Burns's actions. He chose instead to furnish him with a letter authorizing him to leave the squadron and expressing his confidence in the "entire innocence" of the Lieutenant.

This attempt to sweep the proceedings out of sight and get rid of Burns quietly drew a protest from the members of the court:

> We have congratulated ourselves that our duty in this disagreeable affair ceased with our report to the Commander in Chief of the Squadron; but, as he subsequently gave Lieutenant Burns permission to leave the Squadron at Naples, furnishing him with a letter expressive of his belief in Lieutenant Burns entire innocence "of all and every charge," [sic] we feel ourselves called upon as officers having a common interest in the honor and respectability of the Naval Service to declare in the most decided manner

our belief that Lieutenant Burns is not worthy of holding a commission in the Navy.[77]

This missive had its effect. Commodore Patterson ordered that Burns be publicly reprimanded. There are no further notations to indicate whether or not Burns later left the squadron or the service.

An interesting sidelight to the Burns case was the testimony of Captain Nicholson regarding the treatment meted out to Cumming. When he was told that Cumming was molesting Hansen, Nicholson had sent a couple of petty officers to investigate. They discovered the two men in the act and reported back to the captain, who then decided unilaterally on a course of action. Nothing was recorded and no formal procedure was followed. When Cumming was put ashore at Naples, he had a simple discharge and was technically not guilty of any offense. This made it possible for him to come before the Burns court of inquiry and offer testimony.

The next suspected homosexual to be tried by the navy was Seaman Daniel Lupenny of the sloop of war *Marion*. The specification attached to his sodomy charge reads that

the said Daniel Lupenny did on or about the evening of the 2nd of February [1840] go to the hammock of Henry Phinney 2nd class apprentice boy . . . . and did by threatening his life force the said boy to admit him to his hammock and did then and there consummate upon the body of the said boy the Crime of Sodomy.

The charge was preferred by Lieutenant William Pearson of the *Marion* and was accompanied by a second specification in which it was alleged that Lupenny overpowered a sentry in the brig eight days later, returned to Phinney's hammock, and stabbed him twice with a sheath knife.[78]

Lupenny plead not guilty and requested Lieutenant John W. Moore to act as his counsel. The first person to testify was the victim, Phinney. He claimed that on the night in question, Lupenny, who generally slept next to him on account of their muster roll numbers being consecutive, woke him up "and asked me to let him bugger me." Phinney refused, and the resulting argument woke up two other seamen, James Flint and Ben Dyer. These men promised Phinney to report Lupenny next day at mast. This they did, with the result that Lupenny was arrested and consigned to the brig.

When Phinney completed this story, a member of the court asked him if he were a "chicken" of Lupenny's, to which the apprentice replied, "no."[79] Continuing with his testimony, Phinney contradicted the specification by claiming that Lupenny had never threatened him and had not actually consummated the act of sodomy described. Since he was asleep at the time of the stabbing, Phinney could not identify Lupenny as the man who had done that either.

Flint and Dyer were called next and offered testimony that was in conflict at a number of points. Flint claimed to know nothing about sodomy, attempted or otherwise. He maintained that he had only reported Lupenny for making a disturbance on the berth deck. Dyer, on the other hand, claimed that he had heard Lupenny ask to be allowed to sodomize Phinney and reported that there had been an act of intercourse between them on another occasion. Dyer claimed that Phinney was trying to put Lupenny off by claiming to be sick when he and Flint intervened.[80]

The defense was able to challenge this contradictory evidence successfully, even seeking to discredit Dyer by claiming that he had been "overfond" of a boy named Robbins during the *Marion*'s cruise. The stabbing incident had taken place under circumstances that made it impossible to conclusively identify Lupenny as the wielder of the knife. Therefore, the court had only the overpowering of the sentry and Lupenny's escape from custody as clear proof that he was guilty of anything. From this act, a charge of insubordination had been extracted and added to the sodomy charge; and this is what Lupenny was finally found guilty of.

The process of selecting this sentence took a form not normally seen in naval courts. The judge advocate polled the members publicly after the guilty verdict had been reached, suggesting various combinations of punishments. For example: "Shall Daniel Lupenny who hath been found guilty of insubordination receive fifty lashes with the Cats and be transferred to the Flag Ship and it was decided in the negative." After seventeen such proposals, the court agreed on fifty lashes and dismissal from the navy. The president of the court then protested on the grounds that fifty lashes was too many and that Lupenny should not be discharged on a foreign station. The commodore of the Brazil Squadron, to which the *Marion* was attached, overruled these objections and the entire sentence was confirmed.[81]

Five years elapsed before a naval court heard another case involving homosexuality charges, and once again the suspect was an officer. On 10 April 1845, Midshipman Joseph Miller of the frigate *Savannah* received an anonymous note reading:

> Sir: The Midn. of this ship becoming acquainted with your conduct (under cover of night)—during May—1844 have deemed it necessary—(with their own good standing in the Service—and as a duty toward themselves—)

to make it known to the executive officer of this Ship—that it might be duly investigated by him.

Should your memory fail you & it be necessary for them to give you an account of your own deed—they will do so—

Miller promptly made inquiries about this arch and somewhat juvenile note and was rewarded the following day with yet another.

Sir: At your request we herein state the charges, which we lay against you—

You are charged sir with having (during our stay in this port [Callao] about the ninth of may—1844—Crept Staethily [sic] & under cover of night) to Mr. Griffin's hammock—and, then while that gentleman was asleep, removed the bedclothes—from his person and taken his Penis—as it appeared—in your hands—for what purpose, we are at a loss to imagine.

Respectfully, the
Steerage Officers[82]

Upon receipt of the second communication, Miller immediately petitioned Commodore John Sloat to convene a court of inquiry, while the steerage officers carried out their stated intention of reporting him to the *Savannah*'s executive officer. Since the event referred to in the charge was supposed to have taken place a year previously, Sloat was obviously suspicious of the accuser's motives. In instructing the members of the court, he charged them to find out

if the accusers have sufficient testimony to justify them in preferring a Charge of so disgraceful a nature against an officer of heretofore unblemished reputation; and should the court consider the grounds insufficient, they are directed to express their opinion fully as to the conduct of the persons that have made the accusations.[83]

When the case was heard, the accusers turned out to be six midshipmen and one purser's clerk, all of whom slept in the steerage with Miller. On the advice of the court, they appointed two of their number, Midshipman George C. Morgan and Midshipman A. C. Jackson, as spokesmen. Miller conducted his own defense. As testimony accumulated, it developed that Midshipman Griffin was the victim but that the accusations were being made most energetically by another midshipman named Phenix. Miller's alleged conduct had been a topic of steerage conversation for almost a year, a sort of family secret among the warrant officers, but had not emerged publicly until Miller and Phenix had quarreled over an unrelated matter. Griffin testified that he had been visited in his hammock and had his genitals "handled" on several occasions and that the last time he had awakened in time to see Miller ascending a hatchway ladder some four feet distant. Griffin also mentioned that previous to this he had caught a seaman doing the same thing to him and that this man, identified only as "Squibb," had been discharged together with a boatswain's mate for "taking liberties" with the officers.[84] Another midshipman named Genet also testified that Miller may have put a hand in his hammock.

When the evidence against Miller was concluded, it was found to rest only on these incidents. It was, however, abundantly clear that Miller was highly unpopular with his messmates because "his manners were disagreeable." Nearly all of the midshipmen considered themselves his enemies; but at least one, Harrison Hough, broke ranks with the others over the accusation before the court, withdrawing from the case and writing Miller a letter of apology.

The three lieutenants who constituted the court of inquiry were not impressed with the case made by the *Savannah*'s warrant officers. After hearing all of the evidence offered, they began a merciless grilling of the principal accusers that uncovered what amounted to an adolescent conspiracy to bait the unpopular Miller. In its summation, the court unanimously declared that

> This testimony clearly discovers Midshipman Genet and Midshipman Phenix to have been the prime movers in this conspiracy. . . .
>
> It exhibits [Phenix] in the treble capacity of *agitator—*of *Prosecutor* and of *Persecutor*, endeavoring by all means to gratify a *vindictive animosity* towards Midshipman Miller regardless of *his own promises* and the appeal of Midshipman Griffin and his friends *who had imposed and who still desired* and *urged silence* on the subject. Nor does the testimony of Midshipman Phenix appear worthy of *the least credit*.
>
> Of Midshipman Genet the court consider it necessary . . . to remark that the evidence of *a strong personal animosity* towards the accused, taken in connection with the manifest *discrepancies* between his testimony and his relations of the same occurrences according to the deposition of other witnesses, some of whom were his confidential advisors, prevent the court from attaching *the least weight or credit* to his testimony.

The court designated Miller as "a deeply injured man" and expressed the collective opinion that the whole matter should have remained "completely out of sight."[85] Commodore Sloat approved this verdict without further comment.

Interestingly enough, this attempt to discredit an officer by flimsy charges and insinuations of homosexuality is paralleled in that same year and in the same squadron by an effort on the part of several seamen to disgrace Yeoman Joseph Downey of the *Portsmouth* in much the same way. Downey had been moved by the plight of one of the ship's boys who was being persecuted by some older shellbacks, and developed a close friendship with him in the course of functioning as his protector. Downey's enemies, of whom there were many, reported him to the first lieutenant for being "overfriendly," but the officers declined to look into the matter.[86]

The final case in the records of the Old Navy relating to a homosexual offense involved one William Kieth, rated Captain of the Top, who was tried before a summary court-martial on 10 April 1856 for "Indecency and drawing a knife on the boatswain's mate" in the sloop of war *Germantown*.[87] Eyewitness testimony established that Kieth had managed to become intoxicated and was trying to climb into the hammocks of various ship's boys on the berth deck, when he was confronted by Boatswain's Mate John Oliver and several other men. Oliver manhandled Kieth roughly in the course of preventing him from molesting Landsman Charles Smith and told him "he was a dam'd rascal for such dirty conduct." This started a shouting match which Oliver terminated by hitting Kieth. The topman then went on deck and reported Oliver to the marine sentry stationed on the quarterdeck. Meanwhile, Oliver reported Kieth to the berth deck sentry. Once again the two antagonists confronted each other, this time in the presence of the two marines and such other witnesses as had been attracted by the disturbance. In the course of an exchange of violent language, Kieth suddenly drew his knife but was quickly disarmed and led away to the brig before he could strike with it.[88]

As had occurred before in the Crutch, Burns, Miller, and Lupenny cases, the summary court flinched from the prospect of finding a man guilty of homosexual behavior. Kieth was found guilty only of drawing his knife against Oliver. In reviewing the proceedings, Commander William Lynch was obviously relieved that the issue of attempted sodomy had been evaded.

> In reviewing these proceedings, I am gratified by the acquittal of William Kieth, from the first and gravest part of the specification. . . .
>
> I think it proper also to remark that if Oliver had struck Kieth at the moment when he thought he detected him in the attempt to commit an unnatural crime, it would have been [a] palliation of his infringement of the law; but according to his own testimony the blow was given for offensive language only, and as he [Oliver] thereby made himself amenable to severe punishment, he is directed to be put in double irons.

Lynch mitigated the original punishment meted out to Kieth by the court to five days' solitary confinement on bread and water.[89]

From Lynch's review of the Kieth case, it seems clear that he was serving notice to his petty officers not to trouble him officially with accusations of homosexual conduct. Settle it on the spot, with a blow if necessary, but don't come aft with it, he seems to be saying. Turning the verdict against Oliver and clapping him in irons certainly must have alerted the other petty officers as to just how determined their commanding officer was to spare himself from exposure to this particular aspect of life on the berth deck.

That Lynch's behavior was fairly commonplace on the part of naval officers seems to be borne out by careful study of the other sodomy cases previously examined. When rumors of berth deck homosexuality began to circulate within a ship or when an incident was reported, it was always petty officers who were sent to investigate—never commissioned or warrant officers. When the guilty parties were apprehended, they were supposed to be quietly reported to the commanding officer, who either gave them twelve lashes, logging the punishment vaguely as retribution for "filthy conduct," or discharged them and put them ashore at the first opportunity without recording anything on paper. In those instances when homosexual activity, for some reason or other, was officially reported so that it became a matter of record, a court-martial was held. In these cases, the officers comprising the court-martial boards betrayed their disgust and loathing for the duty assigned them by simply refusing to grapple with the issue of homosexuality. They either voted to acquit without waiting to hear much of the evidence, or they found the defendant guilty of some other charge and assigned him a punishment for that. Consequently, not one navy man was ever convicted of homosexuality by a formal court-martial, although a few might have been punished more severely for the charges that they were found guilty of because they were suspected of being involved in sodomy.

When an officer was a defendant, the case was much harder to handle quietly. A court of inquiry was convened, with obvious and unmistakable reluctance, and in the case of Midshipman Miller, with an ominous warning from the commodore that the prosecutors had better be very certain of their grounds. The evidence was presented to court of inquiry boards which displayed open hostility and skepticism towards the witnesses and were obviously looking for any reasonable excuse to acquit the defendant and close out the proceedings. It was only in the case of Lieutenant Burns that the issue of homosexual behavior could not be avoided by the court, so the commodore attempted to accomplish the evasion through the reviewing process. No officer was ever convicted of homosexuality.

In *White Jacket*, Herman Melville gave a literary confirmation to what the records reveal, relating that evils were practiced among the crew of his semi-fictional frigate *Neversink* that were so direful that they will hardly bear even so much as an allusion. The sins for which the cities of the plain were overthrown still linger in some of these wooden-walled gomorrahs of the deep. More than once complaints were made at the mast of the 'Neversink' from which the deck officer would turn away with loathing, refuse to hear them, and command the complainant out of his sight.[90]

On another page, Melville continued his treatment of homosexuality in the navy in typically obscure nineteenth-century fashion, with allusions to "the suppressed domestic drama of Horace Walpole" before finally bidding, in the manner of his archetypical officer of the deck, that the landsman should "guardedly remain in his ignorance" and "forever abstain from seeking to draw aside this veil."[91]

Although homosexuality was largely a taboo subject within the naval justice system, heterosexual activities were confronted much more frankly, particularly in those instances when a junior officer's sex life violated naval regulations. In one particular area, an odd double standard was practiced in the navy, especially in the years prior to the War of 1812. Although it was expressly forbidden in the Black Book, key senior petty officers and warrant officers from the technical departments could take their wives to sea with them on a clandestine basis. The journal of Midshipman Henry Wadsworth related that when one of these "wives," the consort of James Low, rated captain of the forecastle of the frigate *Chesapeake*, gave birth to a baby while the ship was cruising in the Mediterranean in 1803, a full broadside was fired in hopes that the resulting shock would facilitate the delivery. When christening time came, Midshipman Melancthon Taylor Woolsey, who had stood godfather for the infant, arranged a "handsome collation of wine & Fruit." The baptism was held under the direction of the ship's chaplain, the Reverend Alexander McFarlan; and as Mrs. Low was indisposed, a Mrs. Hayes, "the gunner's Lady," acted as hostess.

> The other Ladies of the Bay—The Forward most part of the Birth Deck [sic]—viz. Mrs. Watson: the Boatswain's wife, Mrs. Myres the Carpenter's Lady—with Mrs. Crosby the Corporal's lady; got drunk in their own Quarters out of pure spite—not being invited to celebrate the Christening of Melancthon Woolsey Low.[92]

Because of the secretive nature of the practice of taking wives to sea, we have no way of knowing if the five ladies residing on the *Chesapeake* represent more or less than the usual number. There is little to indicate whether or not women went to sea in vessels smaller than a frigate.

It is clear, however, that the privilege of enjoying feminine companionship at sea was not extended to junior officers. Between 1809 and 1819, one lieutenant and three midshipmen were court-martialed for keeping a prostitute on shipboard and sleeping with a prostitute on shipboard. The first three cases were all close together chronologically and similar in nature. They involved junior officers commanding gunboats on the lower Mississippi River during 1809 and 1810. In each case the "prostitute" in question had lived on board the vessel for a considerable time, sharing the cabin with her lover. None was discovered until their presence on board had been betrayed to the squadron commander through the device of an anonymous letter.[93]

The first case to be tried was that of Lieutenant John B. Nicholson, commanding officer of gunboat *No. 58*. Nicholson had commissioned his vessel at Baltimore and sailed her down Chesapeake Bay to Norfolk, where he apparently met a woman of low reputation and offered her passage to New Orleans. After a call at Havanna, *No. 58* arrived at New Orleans and joined the gunboat squadron then stationed on the lower Mississippi. Soon thereafter an anonymous letter arrived at the Navy Department in Washington, D.C.

> Sir: I embrace the now offering opportunity of informing you of my unpleasant situation on board of the Boat with Lieut. John B. Nicholson as Master's Mate and it is all in consequence of one the Common Prostitutes of Norfolk which he brought out in the Boat with him, and to inform you that we are all hands liked to famished to death for want of water on the passage in consequence of her having expended about one gallon per day washing her face and hands three or four times per day. And that all this time we lay in the Havanna she must have one of the people on shore to attend her, . . . and to inform you, Sir, that there was never peace nor quietness after she came on board and I expect that I shall have to quit the navy in consequence of her which I must say I am very sorry of it, and I think the gun boats have come to a very high pitch when they are commanded by Common Prostitutes . . .[94]

Nicholson was tried in November 1809 at New Orleans. During the proceedings, the writer of the anonymous letter identified himself as William Fleetwood, Master's Mate and Second in Command of *No. 58*. He testified extensively concerning all the charges he had made in his letter, and other witnesses came forward to corroborate most of his statements. In addition to the items previously mentioned, it was further demonstrated that the woman, who is never identified by name, used her influence over Lieutenant Nicholson to have men flogged and disrated.[95]

Nicholson's defense was lengthy but dwelt mainly on procedural technicalities. It was ignored by the court, and he was found guilty of "absolutely unmorally and Scandalously Keeping a prostitute of the vilest class on board his vessel to the destruction of discipline and the dishonor of an officer."[96] He was sentenced to be "cashiered and rendered forever incapable of serving in the Navy." In reviewing the case, President Madison remitted the part pertaining to Nicholson's future disqualification from naval service.[97]

Although Nicholson had been cashiered in disgrace, his example had apparently convinced two of his fellow gunboat captains that feminine companionship in the cabin was a reasonable proposition. Midshipman Thomas C. Magruder of *No. 16* and Midshipman William Peters of *No. 5* each took a young lady on board sometime in the fall of 1809. The presence of the women was not detected until the following spring, when Commodore David Porter received another anonymous letter complaining about both of them and especially about Peters's consort, whose actions were "particularly adapted to destroy not only the harmony of the officers but to create the most painful dissatisfaction among them, as well as the men belonging to the different gun vessels here."[98]

Peters was court-martialed first, on charges of keeping a prostitute on his vessel and oppression and cruelty. The specification for the second charge clearly stated that it related to "cruelty and mistreatment of his crew at the instigation of the said prostitute."[99] During the trial the court concentrated on trying to prove three major points: that the woman had lived on board; that she was indeed a professional prostitute; and that she had instigated cruel and oppressive treatment of the crew.

The testimony of several witnesses confirmed that the woman, Fanny Martin of New Orleans, had lived with Peters in the cabin for at least nine months. Two witnesses established her *bona fides* as a prostitute by claiming to have seen her residing in a house of "ill fame" in New Orleans the previous summer. Only one witness, Purser's Steward Newton Berryman, who was then serving on Magruder's gunboat *No. 16*, was willing to testify that Fanny Martin had instigated cruel or oppressive punishments on board *No. 5*. No other witnesses would confirm that testimony.[100]

Midshipman Peters defended himself energetically. He admitted that he had kept the girl on board but claimed that no lasting harm had been done thereby. He maintained that "occasional indulgence in dalliance with the fair sex need not necessarily be construed as harming the interests of the Navy or demoralizing its men." Finally, in an obvious reference to Nicholson, he observed that

As to keeping a woman on board the vessel under your respondent's command—he urges in excuse or justification *Example & Precedent,* of those superior in rank and older in service than your respondent.[101]

The court was not impressed with these arguments to the extent of allowing Peters to keep his Fanny on board, but it chose not to be severe with him. He was acquitted of the charge of cruelty and sentenced to be reprimanded for the remaining offense.

The court, oddly enough, decided to charge and punish one of its principal witnesses. Purser's Steward Berryman was accused of giving false testimony in relation to the unproved charge of cruelty and was sentenced to thirty-nine days' confinement in wrist irons on board gunboat *No. 5.* Perhaps this action can be explained by the tone of the court's questioning of Berryman. Obviously they suspected that he had written the anonymous letter, and it could be that they were angered by his persistent denials of authorship.

Magruder was tried next, also on a charge of cruelty and oppression in addition to the one relating to the prostitute. Perhaps the treatment of Berryman by the previous court chilled potential witnesses, because none could be found who were willing to talk about punishments or other improper treatment instigated by Magruder's paramour, identified only as "Charlotte," on board *No. 5.* Magruder was, like Peters, found guilty only of the first charge and sentenced to a reprimand.[102]

After these three trials, there were no more such cases until 1819, when Midshipman Robert N. Nichols was examined by a court of inquiry for "sleeping with a prostitute on shipboard" and "marrying a prostitute." These accusations were made by Captain M. T. Woolsey, Commodore of the Lake Ontario Squadron, on the grounds that Nichols, who commanded the schooner *Jones,* had "disobeyed a standing order of this station that no officer shall keep a prostitute on ship Board."[103] As judge advocate for these proceedings, Woolsey named James Brooks, the chaplain of his flagship.

The investigation revealed that the woman in question, one Hannah Damewood, was a resident of Sackets Harbor, New York. Her family was of a disreputable character, and she herself had been discharged from domestic service in Captain Woolsey's house because he had found her "lazy and filthy and supposed to be dishonest."[104] She had gone on board the *Jones* to nurse Nichols through an illness and had spent several nights together with him in the cabin. At the conclusion of the "illness," Lieutenant Nichols married her in a ceremony presided over by a local justice of the peace.

When Woolsey heard about the marriage, he testified that he made strenuous efforts to persuade Nichols "to resign from the service and leave the country so as not to disgrace the service and his brother officers." Nichols defended himself by disputing that Hannah had ever slept with him on board ship and also by claiming not to be legally married to her, but the Captain was able to substantiate his charges with witnesses. Several members of the *Jones*'s crew specified the number of nights Miss Damewood had spent in the cabin, and the judge who had performed the marriage ceremony described it to the court.

In delivering its opinion, the court of inquiry came down partially on the side of Captain Woolsey.

> . . . it appears very evident . . . that the female to whom [Nichols] is allied, is an improper character—I conceive therefore that he has disgraced himself as an officer and a gentleman by his alliance, destroyed his reputation, and placed an unmoveable stigma on his character—The charge of having violated a standing order of Captain Woolsey's, relative to keeping prostitutes on ship board, in my opinion, is not fully proven
>
> (signed) [Master Commandant] John T. Newton

The court adjourned without further comment and without recommending a court-martial.[105]

With the conclusion of the Nichols case, there are no more instances of officers keeping women on board ship, and it is obvious that the practice of allowing petty officers to be accompanied by their wives died out, as well, either during or just after the War of 1812. Cases involving officers' relations with women are exceedingly rare in any case. After 1819 the sole representative of this category of offense is a court of inquiry held in San Francisco in 1849 to determine "the truth of certain serious allegations lodged against Lieutenant Joseph W. Revere of the U. S. Navy by James G. Sawkins, a citizen of the United States."[106] Revere had been carrying on an affair with Sawkin's wife, using her to loot her husband's bank account and eventually abducting her from her residence after the cuckolded spouse had returned from the gold fields. When located by the jealous husband, the couple had sworn out a false affidavit in a San Francisco civil court to avoid prosecution by a civilian magistrate. These were dishonorable doings from the navy's point of view, and the court of inquiry recommended that Revere be court-martialed; but apparently he never was. There is no notation to indicate how or why this came about.[107]

From this survey of cases of cowardice, treason, homosexuality, and relations with women of low repute, it is evident that courts-martial and courts of inquiry dealing with charges that could bring serious disgrace to officers were relatively rare. In that era of dueling with pistols and swords, it was dangerous to question the honor of an officer and gentleman in a serious way. Men avoided it if they could. Also, society was much more tightly knit then, and even the rumor of dishonor could ruin a man's prospects for the rest of his life if the issue were one of importance.

Alternatively, cases that could reflect mild dishonor or which grew out of trivial affairs were common. Officers were charged with scandalous conduct or one of its many variant specifications because of incidents which grew out of personality clashes, disputes, insults exchanged during arguments, or grudges which festered during close confinement on long cruises. Among the enlisted men, marines were occasionally charged with unsoldierly conduct, which could cover anything from cowardice to irresponsibility. Navy enlisted men were sometimes charged with sedition, but this invariably meant merely that the offender had been overheard to make some remark critical of the navy or one of its senior officers.

As employed by the naval justice system, all of the scandalous-conduct-related charges were used with great latitude. The foundation for most of them rested with Article III of the Articles of War:

> Any officer, or other person in the navy, who shall be guilty of oppression, cruelty, fraud, profane swearing, drunkenness, or any other scandalous conduct, tending to the destruction of good morals, shall, if an officer, be cashiered, or suffer such other punishment as a court-martial shall adjudge; if a private, shall be put in irons, or flogged, at the discretion of the captain, not exceeding twelve lashes; but if the offence require severer punishment, he shall be tried by a court-martial, and suffer such punishment as said court shall inflict.

The judge advocate general's records contain a vast array of courts-martial which feature scandalous or ungentlemanly conduct charges. It is beyond the scope of this work to examine them in detail and to explore all of the different ways in which this type of charge could be used. They were, for example, paired with all of the more specific offenses enumerated in Article III and could accompany other behavior-related offenses as well. There are a certain number of cases, however, where the charge stands alone or nearly so. One example of each kind of usage has been selected to give some insight into the myriads of similar cases which dot the court-martial index.

On 28 February 1849, Passed Midshipman John P. Hall stood trial on charges of scandalous conduct unbecoming an officer and a gentleman, willful and malicious falsehood, habitual disrespect and contempt for superiors and for the rules and discipline of the navy, and combining with another passed midshipman to oppose the lawful order of Captain Silas H. Stringham.[108]

The Hall case was replete with violent personality clashes. The midshipman had quarreled with Captain Stringham over the banning of wine and liquor from the wardroom of the sloop of war *Warren* and been court-martialed for it at Callao in March 1848. He had written a disrespectful letter to a Lieutenant Simmonds in the *Warren* and had been court-martialed for that at Monterey, California, in October 1848. The February 1849 court-martial grew out of "a vituperative paper, offered & used by him in abuse of the privilege of a written defence" during the October trial at Monterey.

The prosecutor in this affair was Commodore Thomas ap Catesby Jones, who took serious exception to that part of Hall's defense summation wherein the defendant maintained that he had

> been in the Navy of the United States for eight years and has never known a difficulty until after being brought under the influence of the command of the present chief of the U. S. naval forces in the Pacific.[109]

Hall had read some law before entering the navy, and during this latest tribunal he showed himself to be a most resourceful and uncompromising self-advocate. He raised every possible legal objection to the propriety and validity of the proceedings. He argued that the principal witnesses were absent, that Commodore Jones lacked the approval of the Navy Department to convene the court, and that he was being prosecuted "contrary to the spirit of the institution of the United States Navy by which a Commodore is required to protect and not abuse or abase his Junior Officers."[110] Finally, Hall proclaimed:

> it is contrary to the Spirit of the Laws of the United States Navy . . . that a Commanding officer who is the prosecutor, shall appoint the court and review the proceedings thereof, and in the present instance especially where the charges are of the gravest nature and preferred in a manner to leave no person room to doubt that they are preferred entirely through bad feeling without reference to justice or truth.[111]

This line of argument must have been calculated to bait Commodore Jones, who had already accused Hall of "an inordinate desire to show off a little law reading before a court-martial."[112] After studying the latest document penned by Hall, the Commodore unburdened himself in a letter to Commander Stribling, the president of the court.

> Formerly it was the practice of naval courts-martial to require the accused to submit his written defence to the Judge Advocate for correction and for the Judge Advocate to strike out and so modify as to divest the defence of all superfluous and offensive matter.

Jones maintained that he had never previously agreed with this practice but that in Hall's case it should have been done.[113]

As the trial proceeded, Hall underlined his conviction that the court was illegal and incompetent by refusing to call witnesses or cross examine those called by the judge advocate. The court eventually found him guilty of the first charge only and sentenced him to be dismissed from the navy. Commodore Jones, perhaps knowing that scandalous conduct convictions were frequently reversed upon appeal to the Navy Department, bitterly condemned the court for not finding Hall guilty of the other charges as well. This was no idle gesture. Eight months later, President Taylor sent the Secretary of the Navy a brief note which read:

> The Sentence of the Court-Martial dismissing Midshipman John P. Hall from the Navy of the United States is disapproved.
>
> (signed) Z. Taylor
Oct. 3rd, 1849[114]

A case where the charge of scandalous conduct tending to the destruction of good morals stood alone was that of Commander Robert Ritchie. The charge had been preferred by Captain Samuel Francis Du Pont and was triggered by a dispute which grew out of a ruling by the Naval Efficiency Board of 1855, of which Du Pont was a member.

The board had decided that Ritchie should be retired from active service because of the general state of his health and particularly because he had a tendency to experience severe hemorrhages.[115] No accounting or explanation of the board's action was ever made to Ritchie, however; and he assumed, like most of the other officers removed from the active list, that someone had blackguarded his reputation. Eventually he became convinced that Du Pont had done it and began to refer to him as a "liar," "coward," and "scoundrel" in conversations with other officers in and around Washington, D.C. Finally, Ritchie confronted Du Pont in person and repeated the recriminations to his face, whereupon Du Pont brought the charge because

> the said assertations and language of the said Ritchie [were intended] to bring on a quarrel or duel between him and the said Du Pont, and tend also to impair the efficiency and independence of tribunals, such as the said Board, constituted by law for public purposes and to deter members of such boards or tribunals from the conscientious discharge of their duties.[116]

The Ritchie trial, as was typical of most tribunals involving scandalous conduct, became a drawn-out affair which ended inconclusively.

Testimony showed that Ritchie had asked Du Pont if he had anything to fear when he had first discovered that the Naval Efficiency Board was deliberating his case. Du Pont had answered, "No, your bill is as clear as that of any man's in the navy."[117] Du Pont's personal notes recording the board's deliberations show that this statement was correct when it was made. The original intention of the board had been to retain Ritchie on active duty, and it had so voted. Much later someone brought up the problem of Ritchie's hemorrhages; and upon those facts becoming known to it, the board reversed its previous finding.[118] Since all deliberations of the board were secret, this could not be explained to Ritchie, who naturally began to suspect that Du Pont had purposely deceived him.

Although Du Pont was in a position to understand why Ritchie made his personal attack on him, he was determined to demonstrate that the Commander's behavior was impermissible no matter what the provocation may have been, and that it was damaging to the reputation of the service for officers to go around calling each other liars, cowards, and scoundrels. Ultimately the court agreed in part with Du Pont. Ritchie was found guilty, but the verdict of the court exonerated him of many of the specifications filed with the charge. He was sentenced "to be reprimanded by the Hon. Secretary of the Navy at such time and place as he may think proper."

Secretary John C. Dobbin took advantage of the court's torturous logic and equivocal decision to disapprove the verdict. In a letter to the court he explained that

> I think the Court erred in finding that the offensive words were not used "publicly"; My opinion is also that they erred in excluding certain testimony which would have tended to enlighten them as to the other important specifications. Notwithstanding, therefore, the correctness of their finding as to the *charge*, and without in the least reflecting on the integrity of the Court, the general action and the sentence do not accord with my views so as to make me feel satisfied to approve.[119]

In other words, Dobbin believed that Ritchie was guilty to a greater degree than the court's verdict indicated; so he disapproved the verdict and sentence, which had the practical effect of removing even the mild penalty previously assessed. To anyone not privy to the correspondence between the Secretary and the court, Ritchie had been declared innocent upon review.

Now it was Du Pont's turn to agonize over the significance of an official action of the Navy Department. Dobbin did nothing to ease his mind of the suspicion that an officer of inferior grade who had insulted him repeatedly under the most aggravated circumstances had been supported in that course of behavior by none other than the secretary of the navy himself. In a brief note written in his own hand, the secretary merely informed Du Pont that

> I have carefully examined the proceedings of the court & considered fully the course which in my opinion the whole case & the good of the service requires me to pursue. The Proceedings are not approved & the Sentence not confirmed.[120]

Du Pont was left to vent his rage and frustration in letters to his wife and friends.

Perhaps the incredible conclusion of the Du Pont-Ritchie controversy can be taken as typical of the callous and indifferent way that the Navy Department and the naval justice system treated its officers when they brought questions of personal honor and deportment before courts-martial and courts of inquiry. In matters as significant as the surrender of the *Chesapeake* and as trivial as the squabbles between Midshipman Hall and Commodore Jones, the naval justice system indulged in scapegoating, allowed simple justice to be set aside by arbitrary whim, intimidated and punished witnesses, and even let plainly guilty men go free rather than grapple with unsavory facts and indelicate matters. In the handling of scandalous conduct cases, so numerous and diversified that they defy easy analysis, there were stunning irregularities in verdicts, sentences, and acquittals. These irregularities made the naval justice system resemble almost a blind lottery where questions of personal honor are concerned. In this regard, it was hardly a legal system at all, but more like a mere caricature of a system.

Chapter VII

Disrespect, Disobedience, & Drunkenness

During the years between the Quasi-War with France and the Civil War, the United States Navy was known for the extraordinary strictness of its shipboard discipline. The behavior of American naval seamen was minutely regulated; and punishments, although not unusually cruel or sadistic by the standards of the times, were handed out freely. The merest sign of hesitation in carrying out an order was enough to merit several stripes with a petty officer's "colt." Petty offenses which found their way into the logbook—the wearing of dirty clothes, spitting on the deck, or urinating out of a gunport—easily merited from six to a dozen lashes with the cat-o'-nine-tails.

It is, in fact, an interesting feature of America's maritime tradition that close punitive disciplinary control was also a feature of life on merchant vessels under the Stars and Stripes. The publication in 1840 of Richard Henry Dana's *Two Years Before the Mast* marked the first serious attempt to examine the conditions under which American merchant seamen worked, and it detailed many brutal practices used by merchant marine officers to maintain discipline. By the end of the nineteenth century the sadistic masters and "buckoo" mates of the surviving Cape Horn square riggers had become a national scandal.

In the Old Navy, two categories of offenses stood out as the most common and troublesome disciplinary problems which had to be regularly and routinely dealt with. Drunkenness and other offenses related to liquor accounted for more subjudicial punishments than any other category of crime, and there were enough serious liquor-related problems to make drunkenness one of the more common court-martial offenses, as well. The other category of disciplinary offenses which appears frequently on both subjudicial punishment rolls and in the judge advocate general's list of courts-martial is disrespect and disobedience. Indeed, charges of disobedience and disrespect are more common than those related to any other offense known to naval law with the exception of desertion.

185

The treatment of disrespect and drunkenness cases poses certain problems for the modern researcher, since both categories of offense existed on both the subjudicial and the judicial level. The principal difficulty lies in trying to determine why some offenders received summary justice while others were subjected to the full panoply of a naval court-martial. Records of subjudicial proceedings are largely limited to ships' logbooks, which merely list the name, offense, and punishment inflicted. Court-martial records are much more detailed, but the cases themselves reveal little in the way of a consistent pattern. Some men committed serious offenses related to disrespect or drunkenness, but others were brought before the courts on relatively trivial specifications. In any case, there are literally hundreds of courts-martial listed under both categories.

Another problem posed by these offenses is that the court-martial records tend to give a distorted picture as to who was committing them. It was much more difficult to administer summary justice to an officer than it was to an enlisted man. Consequently, officers are over-represented in this study because they were more likely to be court-martialed while an enlisted man was more often logged, flogged, and forgotten. In the judge advocate general's index of cases, approximately two enlisted men were court-martialed for disobedience or disrespect for each officer tried. Roughly the same ratio holds for drunkenness.[1] It is probable that far more enlisted men were punished for disrespect and drunkenness on the subjudicial level, but the records do indicate that officers committed these offenses with surprising frequency.

Interestingly enough, the first example of a court-martial for disrespect and disobedience involved an officer, Surgeon Charles Webb of the brig *Eagle*.[2] Dr. Webb had been reprimanded by his commanding officer, Lieutenant William Bunbury, for beating one of his loblolly boys, stabbing a wardroom servant with a fork, and flogging a boatswain's mate with a piece of wood. Although ordered to stop administering punishments without authorization, Webb refused to comply. He told Bunbury "that he would whenever it suited him Flogg [sic] any man onboard."[3] Thereafter, the surgeon began to speak disrespectfully of Bunbury to the other officers of the *Eagle*, calling him the "damndest scamp in the Navy" and asserting that "he did not know his duty," was "unfit to command," and "did not know how to treat gentlemen with Commissions."[4] Finally, within a few days after receiving Bunbury's warning, he waylaid the petty officer whom he had originally flogged and kicked him severely.

At the court-martial, it turned out that there were eyewitnesses to all of these events. Eventually, practically every officer and petty officer

186

in the ship contributed testimony against Webb. Faced with the unanimous hostility of his shipmates, the surgeon penned a written defense which he read before the court in lieu of calling any witnesses on his own behalf. In it he declared that both the loblolly boy and the wardroom servant were mulattoes and "notoriously saucy." He had punished the former for stealing medical supplies and had thrown a fork at the latter because he was slow in serving the officers at dinner. It was simply an accident that the fork had lodged in the man's chest. The boatswain's mate, Henry Jenks, had been disrespectful to the doctor, who merely struck him twice with a small piece of wood. On the second occasion, Webb had kicked Jenks because he stepped on his hand while descending a companionway ladder.

With regard to his remarks about Lieutenant Bunbury, Webb claimed that

> they were not done with the smallest intention of injuring the character of Capt Bunbury, or to make an unfavorable impression on the mind of any one present, and that it was entirely the effect of intoxication, having that day had the pleasure of dining on board the Commodore's ship, with the Gentlemen of the Wardroom.[5]

The court declined to credit Webb's arguments that beating mulatto crewmen was an act of no consequence and that his attacks on Jenks and remarks about Bunbury were unimportant. He was unanimously found guilty and sentenced to be cashiered. This verdict was reviewed and approved by President Jefferson on 10 July 1800.[6]

There are undercurrents in the Webb case that seem to indicate that the results were not entirely unsatisfactory to the surgeon. Possibly he wanted a quick discharge and felt that being cashiered was faster than waiting for a formal resignation to be accepted. Another officer who may have had this in mind was Midshipman Robert Ward. On 22 April 1811, Ward was tried by a court-martial for disrespect to his commanding officer, Lieutenant Henry E. Ballard of the schooner *Enterprise*. The court found him guilty; but as his services were urgently required on board, he was only given a severe reprimand and ordered to make a formal apology to Ballard.[7]

Six months later, Ward was on trial again, this time for scandalous conduct and mutinous language. Apparently, Lieutenant Peter Blakley of the *Enterprise*, in a moment of exasperation, had called Ward a "Dam'd little rascal." Shortly thereafter, Ward went ashore in charge of a watering party, which he promptly deserted, taking refuge in a hotel and refusing to come back aboard the *Enterprise* until he had received an apology from Blakely. A series of acrimonious notes were exchanged between ship and shore before Ward was finally led back on board by another lieutenant who was acting as an intermediary. At his second court-martial, Ward offered no defense or explanation of his actions whatsoever, and it was quickly decided that he should be cashiered.[8]

Of course, not all officers who stood trial for disrespect were merely looking for a way out of the service. There were also cases that arose out of suspicion and misunderstandings rather than defiance and provocative behavior. On 20 December 1819, James Terry, Sailing Master of the ship of the line *Washington*, was court-martialed for disobedience of orders and disrespect to a superior officer after he had failed to report for duty after being ordered to do so by Commodore Isaac Chauncey. When he finally did come on board, he absented himself frequently, also in apparent defiance of the commodore's wishes.[9]

At the trial, the *Washington*'s surgeon, Dr. John A. Dix, testified that Terry invariably claimed to be sick whenever he left the ship. He went on to state that none of the ship's doctors had ever seen Terry exhibit any symptoms and that whenever they called at the sailing master's house to examine him he was out. Other witnesses, who had carried messages from Chauncey to Terry, confirmed Dr. Dix's testimony. It was also mentioned, however, that Terry was possessed of a generally good reputation for competence and character.[10] Finally, Terry produced his own private physician, who explained to the court that the sailing master had been under his care for approximately six weeks, during which he suffered from an intermittent "high inflammatory fever" and experienced at least one epileptic fit.[11]

The court ruled against Terry, primarily because of his failure to inform Commodore Chauncey about his health problems. Taking into account his "previous and continuing ill health," they gave him a relatively light penalty, suspending him from duty, pay and emoluments for six months.[12]

On at least one occasion, an officer stood trial for disobedience on the basis of charges that were politically motivated. On 13 October 1834, Lieutenant Edward B. Babbit stood trial on charges of ordering alterations on a vessel under repair without the knowledge or consent of his commanding officer, unwarranted assumption of authority, unofficerlike conduct, neglect of duty, and disobedience of orders.[13] These accusations were brought by Commodore Jesse Duncan Elliott, then commandant of the Boston Navy Yard.

During this trial, several days were spent in explaining the events that had given rise to the charges. It eventually became clear that they had all arisen during a period when Commodore Elliott was absent from the yard and Lieutenant Babbit, as his executive officer, was in temporary command. The court was impressed mainly by the trivial nature of Elliott's complaints. Babbit's "unjustified alteration" of a vessel consisted of fitting warping chocks to the gunwales of the sloop of war *Erie*. His neglect of duty offense consisted of the way he had managed the removal of ballast from the frigate *Potomac* prior to docking her. When pressed by the court, the commodore could not demonstrate how any harm had been done to either ship by Babbit's actions.[14]

After many pages of ridiculous testimony had been recorded, the court began to shift its focus and call witnesses to testify as to what motives lay behind Elliott's prosecution of his second-in-command. Babbit, after all, was an officer of twenty-five years' seniority and highly regarded in the service. Ultimately, two theories emerged. One was that some years previously Babbit's brother, also a lieutenant in the navy, had died while trying to carry out an order given by Elliott under circumstances that seemed to indicate some carelessness or negligence on the commodore's part. Perhaps for this reason Elliott harbored a bad conscience towards his executive officer or felt threatened by his presence in the yard.[15]

The other explanation proposed was even more damaging to Elliott. Witnesses had been hinting that his enmity towards Babbit was of a "political" nature throughout the trial. Finally, by means of leading questions put to various witnesses by the court, it became clear that Elliott had left the yard in Babbit's charge while he had gone to Washington, D.C., to visit President Andrew Jackson and that while he was gone someone had contrived to saw off the effigy of Old Hickory which the commodore had caused to be fitted to the frigate *Constitution* as her figurehead. News of this act of political vandalism had reached Elliott while he was busy professing his undying loyalty to the Jacksonian faith and caused him acute embarrassment.[16] He had returned to Boston in a rage, apparently determined to recoup his prestige with the administration at the expense of the first convenient scapegoat.

Elliott was by now a highly unpopular officer both within the navy and among many citizens of Boston. As typical naval officers, most of the court were presumably of the Whig persuasion and not terribly downcast about the fate of the *Constitution*'s figurehead. Babbit was acquitted of every charge.[17] Elliott continued to command the Boston Navy Yard, however; and in the end, his administration became notorious for his frequent clashes with his officers, the arbitrary character of his disciplinary methods, and his general lack of favor within the city of Boston.[18]

Elliott was not a man to be deterred by setbacks. Throughout his career, he continued to bring disobedience and disrespect charges against his subordinates, even though the results were often highly unsatisfactory from his point of view. In March of 1838, for example, he was serving as commander in chief of the Mediterranean Squadron when a court of inquiry was convened to investigate Chaplain Thomas Lambert, who was suspected of writing an anonymous and disrespectful letter impugning his conduct in a dispute with Lieutenant Charles G. Hunter.

The Hunter affair grew out of a horse race that was held at Port Mahon and attended by many officers from the squadron. Both Elliott and Hunter had entered animals in one particular heat. The race was close, and in his excitement Lieutenant Hunter claimed a victory for his horse. The commodore, who was mounted on a mule, immediately rode up to where Hunter was standing and vigorously disputed the results of the race, claiming that his horse had been the first to cross the finish line. When Hunter refused to accept Elliott's judgment, an argument ensued during which the commodore accused the lieutenant of "separating the Honor of an officer from that of a Gentleman." Hunter protested this slur on his honor and so enraged Elliott that he raised his cane and would have struck Hunter with it if he had not been restrained by spectators. Hunter was suspended from duty and confined to his quarters.[19]

Smarting over this humiliation, Lieutenant Hunter wrote a letter of protest to the Secretary of the Navy. Elliott found out about the letter and ordered Hunter's court-martial for disrespect and treating with contempt his superior officer. Unfortunately for the commodore, the court failed to convict Hunter of either charge. Elliott then resolved to try the lieutenant again, this time on the basis of remarks he had made during the previous court-martial. He called his flag secretary, Mr. Wells, and Chaplain Lambert to a meeting and explained his plans to them, directing Lambert to search through various manuals of court-martial procedure and find rules or precedents for such a proceeding. Wells was ordered to comb the muster lists of the squadron and prepare a list of "reliable" officers to constitute the court-martial board.[20]

These tactics revolted Lambert, who was a former legal student, to the extent that he wrote an anonymous letter to the Secretary of the Navy referring to the "villainy" of Commodore Elliott and describing in detail his machinations in the Hunter case. He closed this missive by recommending that Elliott be court-martialed upon his return to the United States.[21] A copy of the letter was sent to Elliott, who was able to deduce the identity of its author. Confronted by the court of inquiry, Lambert admitted that he had written it. Although they were armed with this knowledge and the eyes of a vengeful commodore were upon them, the court of inquiry professed itself unable to form any opinion or make a recommendation for a court-martial. Clearly the officers of the Mediterranean Squadron had resolved to blunt their commodore's disciplinary tactics by a policy of noncompliance with his known and expressed desires.

Despite the example set by Commodore Elliott, not all charges of disobedience and disrespect lodged against officers were of an insubstantial nature. For instance, on 26 September 1831, Lieutenant Victor M. Randolph of the sloop of war *Boston* was tried for disobedience of orders, treating with contempt his superior officer, and neglect of duty. These charges were preferred by Master Commandant George Washington Storer and all derived from instances in which Lieutenant Randolph had made some error in seamanship or professional judgment. He had, among other things, once let go an anchor after being ordered to hold it in a crowded harbor. On another occasion, while serving as officer of the deck in Gibraltar Harbor, Randolph had failed to notice that an anchor cable had parted until the *Boston* had almost fouled another vessel. The final mistake, which had exasperated Storer to the point of preferring charges, occurred while the *Boston* was simultaneously tacking and shaking a reef out of the spanker sail. Randolph was in charge of the mizzen halyards and braces. At the critical moment when the *Boston* was crossing the eye of the wind, he failed to cast off the spanker vangs and the lee mizzen topsail brace. This had the effect of throwing all of the mizzen sails aback so that the *Boston* missed stays and fell "in irons." Captain Storer was obliged to struggle desperately to get his ship under control again and prevent damage to her rigging. During the ensuing confusion, he noticed Randolph lounging about the quarterdeck and appearing "to be quite indifferent to the duty going on"; so he ordered him below, relieved him of duty, and preferred charges.[22]

Lieutenant Randolph plead not guilty to the charges. Nearly all of the witnesses called helped in some way to sustain his plea. Franklin Jameson, the *Boston*'s first lieutenant, testified that he had never seen or heard any disrespectful or contemptuous behavior directed towards Storer by Randolph. He also remarked, under questioning by the defense counselor, that Storer was in the habit of giving orders indistinctly and in a low tone of voice.[23] Other witnesses who testified concerning the technical details of Randolph's errors in seamanship said much the same thing. This testimony made it impossible for the court to determine whether Randolph was really an incompetent and disobedient officer or whether he was simply missing key orders through the fault of his commanding officer.

One thing that the testimony of witnesses did clearly establish was that after Randolph was relieved of duty and confined to his quarters he adopted a very stiff and formal demeanor towards Storer which the latter chose to interpret as "contempt." The court was obviously at a loss as to what to make of the case. Their verdict reflected a total confusion of mind and procedure. They found Randolph not guilty of disobedience or neglect of duty but cited him for contempt. He was sentenced to be reprimanded by the commodore of the Mediterranean Squadron and dismissed from the *Boston*. It was further stipulated that this sentence should be read publicly on board every ship on the station. Having done this much, they proceeded to undermine their own verdict and sentence with a supplementary statement claiming that

> as it appears to the Court that the misconduct of Lieut. Randolph arose more from his erroneous ideas as to the proper relation existing between a junior and his Commander when in the execution of the duties of their respective office than from any malicious, or insubordinate spirit—and from a knowledge of the gentlemanly and correct deportment of Lieutenant Randolph, the Court recommend a remission of that part of the Sentence which relates to dismission from the U. States Ship *Boston*.[24]

Another fruitful source of disrespect and disobedience cases grew out of the sometimes difficult relationship between staff and line officers in the Old Navy. Staff officers occasionally found themselves being prosecuted by lieutenants, and in such instances the question of rank and precedence was acute. An excellent illustration of this problem was the case of James M. Green, surgeon of the frigate *Brandywine,* who stood trial on 15 February 1841 as the result of a violent personality clash with Lieutenant Richard L. Pinckney. In his enthusiasm to prosecute the surgeon, Pinckney preferred a barrage of charges, including

> menacing, disrespectful & contemptuous conduct to a superior and commanding officer, Unofficerlike, seditious, and insubordinate conduct, and tampering with the midshipmen—of disobedience of orders and neglect of duty—improper conduct and treatment to a diseased and sick man—additional charges: disobedience of orders, gross neglect of duty, and nonperformance of duty as a surgeon—misrepresentation and Lying.[25]

It is interesting to note that Pinckney was first lieutenant of the frigate. The actual commanding officer of the *Brandywine* stood aloof from the proceedings and never offered testimony.

The court quickly discovered that most of the specifications supporting the charges made by Lieutenant Pinckney grew out of his personal enmity towards Surgeon Green. The unusual accusation of "tampering with the midshipmen" concerned the surgeon's attempt to draw several of them into his quarrel with the First Luff by insinuating that those berthing in the starboard steerage were not being treated as well as the inhabitants of the larboard steerage.[26] The charge relating to mistreatment of a patient represented a direct jurisdictional conflict. Quartermaster Benjamin Thompson had been certified as fit for sea duty by Surgeon Green over the objections of Lieutenant Pinckney, who believed that he was too ill to go to sea. The lieutenant had proved correct and it became necessary to send Thompson ashore. Green made the necessary arrangements and put Thompson into a shore boat, once again over the objections of Pinckney, who maintained that the weather was too rough. Thompson testified that the boat had nearly capsized and that he had finally been landed in a thoroughly drenched and chilled condition.[27]

The final charges, concerning neglect of duty, misrepresentation and lying, turned out to be related to Surgeon Green's efforts to impede or hinder Pinckney's attempts to draft his initial charges. First he refused to turn over the accounts and records of his department, thus leading the lieutenant to charge that he was not keeping them properly. Next he misinformed Pinckney about countercharges that he was drafting, telling him that he was relying on memory alone when in fact he had kept a written record of incidents relating to their feud.[28]

A large number of witnesses was called to testify, few of whom could furnish any detailed information about the specific charges leveled against Surgeon Green. Many of them did provide anecdotes and additional information, however, because Pinckney and Green were both in the habit of criticizing each other to third parties, particularly midshipmen. Acting Midshipman James Nicholson, for example, testified that once, when he heard that Green was sick, Pinckney had declared "a dozen with the cats is the best medicine for him, the son of a bitch."[29] On his part, Surgeon Green was fond of asking various warrant officers if they had noticed "that Mr. Pinckney was rather more fond of liquor than the other lieutenants."[30]

The testimony makes it clear that Green was a passionate and indiscreet man and that Lieutenant Pinckney was determined to use his superior status and authority as a line officer to break him and drive him out of the navy. In assessing punishment against the surgeon, the court took note of this undercurrent and remarked that

> In passing this light sentence [public reprimand and dismissal from the squadron] the Court have taken into consideration the many extenuating circumstances, and the vexatious nature of the several charges that were wholly unsubstantiated: For example, the evidence adduced to sustain the fourth charge, [improper conduct and treatment to a diseased man] reflects much more on the Prosecutor than on the accused; for it was the duty of the former to have countermanded the order for conveying the sick man on shore, entertaining the views he did, as to the impropriety of the measure. The Court furthermore, cannot refrain from [commenting] upon the aggravating procedure of bringing a charge of falsehood without positive proof to sustain it.[31]

Another instructive case involving a surgeon was that of Washington Sherman of the sloop of war *Dale*. Charges of disrespect and disobedience were preferred against him by Commander William McBlair. The point at issue between the two men was the size and healthfulness of the punishment cells on board the ship. As provided for in naval regulations, the only serious check on the authority of a commanding officer to carry out minor punishments was the surgeon's willingness or unwillingness to certify that the corrective measures contemplated would not permanently impair the health of the prisoner.

Dr. Sherman had resolved to use this power to mitigate a number of punishments which he considered "Cruel & inhuman & not Contemplated by the Law."[32] He was particularly concerned about the size and location of the cells because the *Dale* was cruising on the West Africa Station, a notoriously unhealthy duty station where insect-borne fever diseases combined with a debilitating tropical climate to produce a high rate of mortality among naval personnel. Also at issue, although it was never specifically acknowledged, was the character of the cells themselves. From the dimensions given for them and from the way they were employed, they were not proper brig cells, but actually "sweatboxes." In a covert way, Surgeon Sherman was really attacking his commanding officer's right to use sweatboxes as an instrument of discipline.

The Sherman case was tried on 2 August 1858 at the West Africa Squadron's home port of Puerto Praya in the Cape Verde Islands. It is noteworthy that all of the other surgeons in the squadron signed and submitted a statement expressing their support of Dr. Sherman, while the surgeon of the flagship, the senior medical man present, served as his defense counselor. This pitted them against nearly all of the line officers, who signed a similar statement of support for Commander McBlair.

The specific punishments at issue had been imposed on two seamen by a summary court-martial and consisted of the men spending the night in the *Dale*'s detention cells with their hands and feet triced behind them in double irons. Sherman testified that the cells, specially constructed at the order of Commander McBlair, were too small to either stand up or sit down in, had inadequate ventilation, and were located too close to the galley range. He also stated that one of these men had become violently ill and that when word of this spread around the ship, McBlair had threatened to double the punishment of any man who tried to report himself sick after spending a night in the cells.[33]

When his turn came to testify, McBlair made no effort whatsoever to refute any of Sherman's statements. Instead, he based his whole case against the surgeon on the fact that he had made unauthorized use of the captain's clerk of the *Dale*, one William Morgan, to copy out a letter that he sent to the commodore protesting the condition and uses being made of the *Dale*'s cells. This, McBlair contended, constituted "Treating with contempt his Superior Officer" and made Sherman guilty of disobedience and disrespect.[34]

The court was obviously receptive to this tactic, but the defense counselor insisted that they should at least visit the *Dale* and inspect the cells. Ultimately they did make a trip out to the ship to look over the cells and take measurements. As a result, Surgeon Sherman was found guilty as charged and sentenced to be dismissed from the squadron. Having delivered themselves of this verdict, the court proceeded to declare that, while the cells were generally normal and healthy, it would be desirable

> as a matter of prudence, rather than as a matter of absolute necessity, that the position of the "cells" on board the *Dale* be removed from the present location within the influence of the Galley, to the space amidships, abaft the fore-hatch, now occupied in part by an "Hawser Reel."[35]

Otherwise, the court maintained, the punishments meted out on board the *Dale* were "necessary proper and legal."

When the proceedings of the Sherman court-martial were reviewed by the secretary of the navy, the verdict was summarily overturned. In a terse note to the commodore of the West Africa Squadron, Secretary Isaac Toucey noted that none of the members of the court had signed the official transcript of the trial except the judge advocate and the president. This oversight was the responsibility of Commander John

S. Missroon, the president of the court. Because of it, Surgeon Sherman was restored to duty on board the *Dale*.[36]

In comparison to those cases which involved officers, the trials of enlisted men for disobedience and disrespect were neither as lengthy nor as complex and thus not nearly as instructive. Nevertheless, there are scores of them in the judge advocate general's records. Many more cases were dealt with on the subjudicial level without benefit of formal proceedings. In many cases the offenses of enlisted men who were court-martialed for disobedience and disrespect were not significantly different from those of men who merely received summary justice at captain's mast. In general, a disrespectful enlisted man was court-martialed only if his offense had been especially flagrant or aggravated and witnessed by a large number of bystanders.

One of the earliest cases involving an enlisted man was that of marine George Crutch. This was the fourth and last court-martial this incorrigible character faced. On 13 February 1811, he was tried for intoxication, disobedience of orders, and contempt on the complaint of Master's Mate Champion Wood, commanding officer of gunboat *No. 21* based at New Orleans.[37] According to the specifications and testimony of Wood, Crutch had attempted to go ashore for the purpose of drawing his pay from the naval storehouse while intoxicated. Wood had stopped him at the gangway and ordered him to go below until he had sobered up. Perhaps an hour later, Crutch came on deck with two other marines, both of whom were also drunk, for the purpose of relieving the sentries on post. When Wood noticed the state they were in, he ordered them all below; but the marines refused to go, loudly demanding to be put on post. During the resulting scuffle, Crutch rushed Wood and threatened him with his cutlass. Several crewmen moved to restrain him, but his companions supported him with drawn bayonets. Finally, with the help of a large crowd of bystanders, the three marines were subdued and confined below decks in irons.

In his defense, Crutch stated that he was following the positive orders of Corporal William McTamnay to relieve the watch, and in his drunken state he had not realized that Wood had countermanded the order.[38] McTamnay testified that he had ordered Crutch and his two companions to go on post not realizing that they were unfit for duty because he himself was drunk at the time.[39] The court dealt severely with Crutch and his codefendants. No stranger to the cat, the recalcitrant leatherneck was sentenced to receive one hundred lashes. Private John Rivo, one of the codefendants who had threatened several seamen with a bayonet, also received one hundred lashes plus six months' imprisonment at hard labor with a ball and chain and dismissal from the service. Corporal McTamnay was disrated.[40]

One case which represents an interesting feature of naval justice was that of William Bounds, a carpenter's mate serving at the Boston Navy Yard in 1819. Although Bounds's case was clearly a matter of disrespect or contempt, he was actually tried on a charge of seditious words. According to the testimony of witnesses, Bounds was being transported in a boat along with a working party that had been assigned by Commodore Isaac Hull to carry out repairs on the ship of the line *Independence*. Bounds was uneasy about the arrangements made by Hull for paying the men for this work; and his immediate superior, Carpenter Nehemiah Parker, tried to placate him by declaring that the commodore had promised to compensate them promptly. Upon hearing this, Bounds muttered rather loudly, "He be damned—I know him of old. I have not forgot the work I have done on other ships at the Navy Yard."[41]

This remark was overheard by an officer, Midshipman Charles P. Derby, who reported it to Hull. The commodore quickly organized a court-martial, which convened on 6 January 1819. Bounds's only defense consisted of a denial that his remark had been directed at Hull. He pointed out that he had not used the commodore's name at any time. The testimony of several witnesses made the context of his statement so obvious that the court had little trouble arriving at a guilty verdict. Bounds was given twenty-five lashes and disrated to the rank of seaman.[42]

The Bounds case and several others make it clear that as a matter of naval usage, sedition charges had little to do with lack of patriotism or disloyalty to the nation. Instead, they were closely akin to disrespect and contempt charges and were used when a seaman or officer made a disparaging remark about the navy, his ship, or one of his superiors that was not intended to be heard by anyone who might be inclined to bring charges. Sedition charges usually came about because someone heard a remark he was not supposed to or because some comment was reported to higher authority contrary to the expectations of the speaker. It can be speculated that often only a blurred and unclear distinction existed between seditious words and the usual grousing and complaining that is a feature of life in every service.

Judging by the number of cases contained in the judge advocate general's file, direct disrespect on the part of an enlisted man towards an officer was perceived as a much greater problem than sedition and accounted for a much greater number of courts-martial. Most officers with any experience and seasoning must have realized that their subordinates would do some clandestine grumbling and that as long as care was taken to preserve outward forms of deference little harm was done and the disciplinary atmosphere of the ship remained wholesome. When, on the other hand, the dissatisfaction or disaffection of the men began to take the form of open defiance or disrespect, then a serious threat to duly constituted naval authority could be perceived. If immediate action were not taken, the problem would mushroom inexorably until the very safety of the officers and the ship was in doubt. For these reasons, it was much more essential to follow up quickly on any act of open disrespect. A prompt and public arrest must be made, a solemn military court assembled amid all the pomp and panoply of firing a special gun and displaying a special flag, and a severe and highly physical punishment administered before an assembled crew. It was the example that counted. Hushed whispering and clandestine grousing was of minor significance. It may even have served as a useful safety valve. Open defiance, with its implied challenge of legal authority, was intolerable.

Despite the fact that punishment for even minor acts of disrespect was swift and highly physical, there are a surprising number of instances when enlisted men, perhaps goaded into recklessness by the pressures of life afloat, actually cursed officers to their faces or refused to obey orders. One of the more aggravated cases was that of Seaman William Bambury of the frigate *Constitution* who was tried on charges of contempt and disrespect in May of 1841. According to the specifications, Bambury first accosted Midshipman Silas Bent over being denied a ration of grog during "up spirits." After arguing with the warrant officer for some time, Bambury abruptly declared, "I want my grog. I'll be damned if I won't have it." When Bent still refused to issue the ration, Bambury raised his fist to him and shouted, "By God, I will have it!"[43] Bent did not report Bambury immediately, and the seaman was able to procure a grog ration from some other source. He returned to the midshipman and, holding the cup of liquor aloft,

> did in an insolent, disrespectful, and contemptuous manner address the said Midshipman Bent in the following language, viz "Here's not to your good health but to your good manners: Sir—I have a particular regard for some of you *coves* and shall remember you."[44]

This outburst attracted the attention of Lieutenant William Smith, who spoke sharply to Bambury and received in reply a torrent of abuse. The specification quotes the seaman as exclaiming, "God damn

—Kiss my ass—Kiss my bloody ass!"[45] The remaining record of Bambury's court-martial is brief and fragmentary. No record of a defense statement and no testimony of eyewitnesses survives. For punishment he received thirty-nine lashes with the cat-o'-nine-tails.

One case of clear-cut disobedience that can be cited is that of Seaman John Thompson, who was court-martialed for refusing to participate in extra gun drills on board the sloop of war *Plymouth* at anchor in Rio de Janeiro in November 1851.[46] On the day the incident took place, regular gun drills had been concluded and the crews had been dismissed from quarters. For some reason, extra drill was assigned to the crews of guns eight and nine, and Thompson was ordered to take over as a gun captain by his division officer, Lieutenant E. C. Bowers. Thompson first refused to accept the leather belt that served as the badge of office for gun captains and, when threatened by Lieutenant Bowers, thereafter declined all duty whatsoever, claiming "it was his watch below and he would not exercise." Bowers remonstrated with him, but he steadfastly refused to serve the gun.[47]

Thompson's behavior was, in the words of Lieutenant Bowers, "cool, deliberate and defiant." He was immediately lodged in the brig. Some idea of his motivation can be gained from the testimony of one of his guards, Marine Corporal James Mulholland. According to Mulholland, Thompson confided that he believed he had "broke out of the navy" and was beyond the reach of naval authority. He reasoned that since flogging had been abolished, the *Plymouth*'s officers would have no choice but to discharge him if he refused to take orders.[48] Obviously, Thompson had sickened of navy life and the procurement of a discharge had been his principal goal.

Throughout the court-martial, Thompson continued to harbor the misconception that he was in little danger of serious punishment other than immediate discharge. He refused counsel and merely explained his behavior by stating that he had no criminal intentions in defying Lieutenant Bowers. He merely wanted to protest what he believed were too many drills in his watch below.[49]

Unfortunately for Thompson, his superiors were still nervous about the effects of the abolition of flogging. They prescribed a punishment designed to teach him an object lesson about the effectualness of those penalties still in use. He was sentenced to three months' solitary confinement in double irons on bread and water, loss of all pay, and discharge from the navy at the expiration of his time in the brig. The court further stipulated that if his ship were at sea when the sentence expired, punishment would be continued until after arrival at the next port of call. To make sure that their message was clear to other would-be discharge seekers, the sentence was ordered to be read aloud on board every ship in the Brazil Squadron.[50]

The next most numerous category of charges to be found in the judge advocate general's records after disobedience and disrespect are those relating to drunkenness. In addition to the formal courts-martial that were adjudicated cases involving drunkenness, there were also a vast number of subjudicial punishments awarded for this offense or charges related to it. In fact, as has been said before, drunkenness constituted that navy's greatest single disciplinary problem. At least until 1862 a significant portion of the enlisted men were confirmed alcoholics who had entered the service for the sake of the grog ration. Although the liquor was not dispensed in great quantities and was always mixed with water so that it could not be saved up, the grog ration gave endless trouble. However, most of these difficulties could be dealt with on the subjudicial level.

Many liquor-related offenses involved efforts on the part of the men to secure illicit supplies of intoxicants. Attempting to break into the spirit room, bribing petty officers to provide extra rations of grog, smuggling contraband liquor from shore, attempting to brew alcoholic concoctions and distribute them on board, and profiteering from the sale of liquor substitutes such as eau de Cologne were all offenses known to the officers of the Old Navy.

The officers were also painfully aware that the thirst for liquor among the men was a dangerous force that could compromise almost any operation if precautions were not taken to keep the men sober. Whenever some extraordinary event occurred—a shipwreck, a landing party, or something else which disturbed or disrupted shipboard routine, some of the men were certain to procure liquor and drink themselves into a condition of utter uselessness if not actual insubordination. The crust of naval discipline was hard but thin. Any unsettling happenstance could break it, and the catalyst for such a crisis was invariably liquor. These breakdowns were covered by Article XLII, Section 2, of the Articles of War, which reads as follows:

> *And be it further enacted,* That in all cases, where the crews of ships or vessels of the United States shall be separated from their vessels, by the latter being wrecked, lost or destroyed, all the command, power, and authority, given to the officers of such ships or vessels, shall remain in full force as effectually as if such ship or vessel were not so wrecked, lost, or destroyed, until such ship's company shall be regularly discharged from, or ordered again into the service, or until a court-martial shall be held to inquire into the loss of such ship or vessel. . . . and every officer or private

who shall, after the loss of such vessel, act contrary to the discipline of the navy, shall be punished at the discretion of a court-martial, in the same manner as if the vessel had not been so lost.

One specific case that serves as an example of the dangerous thirst for liquor is that of the crew of the sloop of war *Yorktown*, which struck a reef and foundered off Mayo Island in the Cape Verdes on 6 September 1850. The *Yorktown* had driven onto the reef in the early morning hours. Her crew had only enough time to launch the boats and make a landing through the surf on a nearby beach before she broke up and sank. By salvaging gear and sails that had washed ashore, Commander John Marston was able to organize an encampment near the principal village of the island to house his crew until a relief vessel could arrive.[51]

Although the liquor normally carried by the *Yorktown* had been lost in the wreck, the Mayo Islanders lost no time in selling large quantities of the local "agua ardiente" to the crew; and many of them became disrespectful, abusive, and unmanageable under the influence of this potent beverage. First Lieutenant Thomas R. Rootes testified that the ship's cook, Edgar L. Lear, "was drunk several times, and neglected his duty in not cooking provisions for the men, agreeably to my order, and quarreling with the men at the same time."[52] Another seaman, John Smith, entered the tent of Lieutenant J. M. Frailey the morning after the wreck and reviled him, declaring:

> You are all a set of damned sons of bitches, and had it not been for you
> . . . the ship would not have been lost. I could navigate her a damned
> sight better myself, by dead reckoning.

Frailey and another lieutenant shoved Smith out of the tent and gagged him with a piece of wood to shut him up. They noted that he was very drunk at the time.[53]

Among the men who became serious disciplinary offenders on the island were some who had been troublemakers on the ship, as well; but others, particularly petty officers, had been reliable and well-behaved before the wreck. Once ashore amid unfamiliar surroundings and supplied with liquor, they changed character completely. With the epithet "sons of bitches" constantly ringing in their ears, Commander Marsden and his lieutenants decided to forbear any serious attempt to restore discipline or curb the men's drinking for the present. They allowed them to solace themselves to the extent that "Nearly all of them indulged too freely in the use of ardent spirits; and many were drunk the greater part of the time they remained there."[54]

Since it was obviously impractical to court-martial the better part of a whole ship's company for drunkenness, the court of inquiry which made the initial investigation of the *Yorktown* incident stated that

> considering the Circumstances under which they were thrown ashore, with the loss of everything but the cloths [sic] they wore, at the time, the court trusts it will be excused for naming only those who were guilty of other offenses besides drunkenness.[55]

Nine names of enlisted men were handed down for court-martial on the charge of acting contrary to the discipline of the navy. All nine were chosen because they had compounded their drunkenness with other offenses and also because they had been ship's "bad characters" even before the wreck. After rather brief and perfunctory tribunals, eight of them drew one month's solitary confinement and loss of pay. The ninth, ship's cook Edgar Lear, got two months' solitary confinement and loss of pay.[56]

In addition to the *Yorktown*'s crew, there are many other cases in the judge advocate general's records which involve enlisted men charged with drunkenness under far less dramatic circumstances. Often the charge was paired with another, representing an act which the seaman had committed while under the influence of alcohol, such as an assault or a gesture of defiance or disrespect. Most of these cases are of little intrinsic interest, being repetitious in nature and all too predictable as to verdict and punishment. Men accused of drunkenness were rarely tried with scrupulous care or allowed to stage elaborate defense campaigns, although there were occasional acquittals.

Under certain circumstances, of course, drunkenness was not a naval crime. Shore liberty was granted very infrequently; but on those rare occasions when it was possible for the men to go ashore, the expectation was that many would return to the ship drunk, with clothes torn, and bearing the marks of fights and riots. The officers of the deck merely recorded the return of each man in the logbook. A man returning in reasonable condition was logged as "CS," meaning clean and sober. A drunk was logged as "DD," which stood for drunk and dirty. A drunken libertyman had one rather interesting prerogative that had grown up with the practice of granting shore leave. He was expected to conduct himself as best he could in the presence of the gangway watch; but upon reaching the gun deck, he was allowed to curse the officers, the ship, the navy, or any other institution in the vilest language he was capable of uttering with impunity. This practice was called "gundecking" and constituted one of the few ways which the men of the Old Navy had for releasing pent-up emotions.[57]

Another habit of returning libertymen was that of attempting to smuggle liquor on board for later consumption at sea or to sell for profit. There were a variety of methods that were favored. Sometimes the men made "snakes," long tubes which were fashioned out of the intestines of cattle or sheep and filled with liquor. The would-be smuggler coiled them around his ankles and calves under the flare of his bell-bottomed trousers and simply walked on board. Other tricks included hiding containers in the bodies of dressed poultry or baskets of potatoes, dropping snakes into water casks, or having a bumboatman attach one to the anchor cable for later retrieval by a swimmer from the ship.[58]

The most ambitious smugglers hatched elaborate schemes which involved sending whole barrels of whiskey on board disguised as casks of paint, turpentine, or linseed oil. In 1842, Chaplain Charles Rockwell described an incident wherein a group of sailors doctored several casks by filling them with whiskey, olive oil, and white paint. Once brought on board and stowed in the paint locker, the oil rose to the surface while the paint settled to the bottom. A long straw inserted into the cask allowed the men to draw off the whiskey which occupied the middle.[59] This practice of drawing hidden liquor out of a cask or other container by means of a straw was known among the sailors as "sucking the monkey." Unfortunately, Reverend Rockwell declined to mention how the men were caught in this particular instance. It would also have been interesting to learn how their digestive systems withstood the mixture of whiskey and paint once the dregs of the liquor had been reached.

In *White Jacket*, Melville described yet another ingenious scheme whereby the fictional *Neversink*'s master-at-arms and several other petty officers regularly smuggled liquor on board in bogus parcels addressed to the ship's officers. These were packed with containers of liquor ashore and delivered on board by paid messengers. The master-at-arms would intercept them at the gangway and promise the officer of the deck that he would inspect them for contraband and deliver them to the addressee. Once below decks, the package was actually delivered to a confederate, who arranged to distribute the goods among the thirsty seamen at a considerable profit.[60] We don't know if Melville actually witnessed this smuggling ring in action or merely heard about it happening on some other ship and incorporated it into his narrative.

Melville's credibility in these matters might be suspect because he was, after all, writing a semifictional account of navy life. The judge advocate general's records, however, contain an even more bizarre scheme involving Purser McKean Buchanan. Buchanan was investigated during February and March 1841 for contriving to arrange for a short supply of whiskey to be stowed on board the frigate *Constitution* at the outset of a cruise to the Pacific. When the whiskey supply failed, providentially just as the ship was beating around Cape Horn, the purser and his steward began to sell the crew bottles of eau de Cologne at prices ranging from twenty-five cents to one dollar per bottle. Some seventy bottles were consumed by the crew, although some of the purser's customers later testified that the toilet water was unsatisfactory as an intoxicant.[61]

Purser Buchanan was prosecuted with great zeal and determination by Commodore Alexander Claxton, who suspected him of falsifying his accounts, purchasing rotten tobacco, stealing flannel shirts and yard goods, and overcharging the crew for shoes and handkerchiefs as well as profiteering in the sale of the eau de Cologne. Claxton admitted that he harbored an abiding hatred of all pursers and was so intent on crucifying Buchanan that he attended the court of inquiry day after day to cross examine witnesses personally even though he was dying of a "wasting illness." He managed to accumulate 342 pages of evidence derived from testimony before he expired at sea on 8 March 1841. After his death, the court of inquiry, which apparently did not share the commodore's righteous wrath, quickly closed down the investigation, merely reporting for the record that "the whole matter under the Inquiry is of a confidential and unofficial character."[62]

Although drunkenness was undoubtedly most common among the enlisted men, it was also a serious problem among the officers, as well. The first court-martial ever held under the Articles of War of 1800 involved charges of cruelty, drunkenness, and sleeping on watch lodged against Lieutenant James B. Cordis of the frigate *Constitution*. Midshipman James Pitts testified that Cordis was in the habit of coming on watch after having consumed so much liquor that he had difficulty in staying awake. Once he had been caught asleep on deck by the first lieutenant. Another time Pitts was sent to him with a message while he was supposed to be on watch and found him instead sleeping in his cabin. When asked if he were certain that Cordis was asleep, Pitts replied that "he could plainly hear him snore."[63] Cordis called upon most of the other officers of the *Constitution* to bear witness as to his good character and managed to win an acquittal on this occasion.

After the Cordis case, there were many more instances in which officers were accused of excessive drinking, habitual intoxication, drunkenness, or intemperance. A typical case is that of Lieutenant James E. Legare. In 1826, Lieutenant Legare was court-martialed for drunkenness and frequent intoxication. He was found guilty and sentenced to a reprimand.[64] Reassigned to a new ship, the schooner *Shark*, Legare figured in a violent quarrel with another lieutenant during which he abused him verbally, drew his sword on him, and challenged him to a duel. The commanding officer of the *Shark* arrested him and preferred charges of quarreling, riotous conduct, and drunkenness, both ashore and afloat. He was put ashore at the Pensacola Navy Yard under parole to await court-martial.

While he was languishing under house arrest at Pensacola, Legare decided to resign from the service. He penned a letter to the Secretary of the Navy, maintaining that

> The unbecoming manner in which I have been treated since I left the ship to which I was ordered by the Department in January last obliges me to state to you that I can no longer submit to such oppressive conduct, I find myself compelled to quit the service of my country in which I have been upwards of fifteen years, and engage in one in which more regard is paid to justice honor and independent feelings, I therefore tender you my resignation.
>
> But though engaged in a foreign service [i.e. the Mexican Navy] the flag of my native country shall never be violated and one of my warmest wishes shall be to see the navy of the U. S. in a prosperous condition and purified from the abuses now too generally practiced by venal and corrupt authority.[65]

In December of 1826, having unburdened himself of his sentiments, Legare departed for Mexico without waiting for a reply or reporting his intentions to the commandant of the navy yard.

By May 1827, Legare had been detained through the cooperation of the Mexican Government and returned to Pensacola, where he went on trial with the charges of writing a disrespectful letter to the secretary of the navy and breaking his arrest replacing the original complaints lodged against him by the captain of the *Shark*. Since breaking arrest and writing a disrespectful letter were graver charges than drunkenness and riotous conduct, it is evident that the court wanted to concentrate on these charges. No doubt it was felt that they would be easier to prove and provide more of a basis for ejecting Legare from the navy.

Legare pleaded not guilty, claiming that his letter was not in fact disrespectful and explaining that he thought he had relieved himself of the obligation to remain under arrest by resigning. The court found him guilty only of the first charge pertaining to the disrespectful letter and sentenced him to be dismissed from the navy.[66] Upon reviewing the case, President Adams discovered numerous procedural errors and omissions. These included failure to try Legare on the original charges, failure to provide legal evidence of the terms of his arrest, and failure to establish the limits of his confinement while awaiting trial. "But," the President wrote, "although for these cases it is necessary to disapprove the proceedings of the Court, no doubt is entertained of the criminality of Lieut. Legare, nor of the propriety of dismissing him from the Service."[67]

What made the Legare case typical of so many others involving drunkenness on the part of officers is that his overindulgence in alcohol soon led him into other difficulties. Eventually, charges relating to his intemperance became only part of his difficulties with the naval justice system. There are relatively few cases wherein an officer was tried solely for intemperate habits. More commonly, the navy waited for a known alcoholic to make some other professional error that could be combined with chronic drunkenness to make a stronger case. There are, however, a few instances in which hard-drinking officers were subjected to courts of inquiry which investigated only their intemperate habits.

One example is the case of Lieutenant Junius T. Boyle, who was investigated on 13 January 1851 with regard to his conduct as commanding officer of the storeship *Southampton*. The court was particularly concerned in establishing whether or not Lieutenant Boyle had ever appeared to be "laboring under the influence of liquor" while exercising his command responsibilities. It also wanted to know whether or not he, while drunk, had improperly granted shore liberty to the crew and whether or not he had ever granted extra liquor rations to the crew in violation of navy regulations. The testimony gathered from officers and men who had served under Boyle in the *Southampton* was contradictory, but at length enough evidence emerged to satisfy the court that he was a "confirmed drunkard." Deploring the example that he had set for the other officers under his command, they stated that in their opinion "Lieut. Boyle's conduct has rendered him unfit to command said storeship."[68] Presumably, Boyle was subsequently relieved of his command. If so, he may be the only officer in the Old Navy to lose his command on account of excessive drinking.

Another officer, Lieutenant Hillary H. Rhodes, has the distinction of being perhaps the only officer to be officially denied promotion on the grounds that he was "addicted to habitual intemperance" and therefore not fit to exercise an independent command.[69] The court of inquiry that was formed to look into the Rhodes case produced a long and detailed transcript that sheds much light on the way the navy regarded its alcoholic officers. It had its beginning on 5 July 1851. On that date, Rhodes, who after thirty years of continuous service had reached the top of the Lieutenant's List, received the following letter from the Secretary of the Navy:

> Sir, The position of your name in the Navy Register, entitles you to promotion to the grade of Commander according to the rule of seniority.
>
> But it has been suggested to the Department that you are so addicted to the vice of intemperance as to be unsuited to perform the duties and to be entrusted with [a] command in that office at sea.
>
> You will therefore please inform the Department whether this allegation is denied to the end that in such event a Court of Enquiry may be ordered for the information of the Department and the President before proceeding to fill the vacancy now existing.[70]

The Navy Department retained a prominent Washington attorney, Charles Lee Jones, to serve as judge advocate. His strategy was to call upon numerous witnesses who had known Lieutenant Rhodes and were familiar with his habits and reputation during his service career. Rhodes's current commanding officer, Commodore W. E. Ballard of the Washington Navy Yard, led off. He related that he had seen Rhodes only three times during his tenure of command and that on two of these occasions he was drunk to the point of incoherence. He maintained that Rhodes's reputation around the navy yard, where he had served for several years, was that of an habitual and confirmed drunkard.[71]

Commodore Lawrence Kearney had been Rhodes's commander during his last tour of sea duty as a watch officer in the flagship of the East India Squadron from 1843 to 1844. Kearney testified that he had noticed Rhodes's drinking habit and had been worried about it. He felt, however, that the squadron could not dispense with his services because "there were other officers on board in worse condition than himself." At that time Rhodes was drinking to such an extent that Kearney testified that "I am of the opinion that intemperance was habitual with him."[72]

Jones next called several commanders and asked them, as men who held the rank to which Rhodes aspired and who knew him personally and by reputation, whether they thought him fit to carry out the duties of that grade. To a man, these witnesses advised against promoting the lieutenant. For example, Commander Theodore Bailey, upon being sworn, made the following deposition:

> I have not seen Lieutenant Rhodes, within the last seven years. I served with him in the frigate *Constellation* for about two and a half years, or perhaps a little more or less. He was then given to habits of intemperance. I know nothing of his habits since.

Question. [by the Judge Advocate] Were his habits of intemperance a subject of notoriety or general remark on board the frigate, and what reputation did he have on board the frigate and in the Navy generally, for temperance or the reverse?

A. His habits of intemperance were then a matter of notoriety and general remark, and he bore the reputation of an intemperate man.

Q. [by Lieutenant Rhodes] Did the habits to which you say Lieutenant Rhodes was addicted interfere with the discharge of his official duties?

A. They did interfere with the efficient discharge of his duties.

Q. [by Lieutenant Rhodes] Did you ever see Lieutenant Rhodes intoxicated whilst on duty?

A. I have, but day or date I cannot recollect.

Q. [by the court] From your knowledge of Lieutenant Rhodes and from his general character in the navy, do you think he is fit to be a commander?

A. I do not.[73]

After various senior officers had testified, a large group of lieutenants who had been shipmates with Rhodes were called to the stand. From them there emerged a graphic and ribald picture of a man who had been drunk repeatedly both ashore and afloat on every voyage for at least twenty years. Rhodes had missed watches often and frequently reported himself unfit for duty, especially after a spell of shore liberty. Lieutenant Matthew F. Maury told of encountering him reeling drunkenly in the streets of Washington. Another witness recalled a time when two midshipmen got Rhodes drunk and put him on a donkey, which carried him careening through the streets of Port Mahon at a full gallop. On another occasion during that particular cruise on the Mediterranean Station, Rhodes disgraced himself by getting drunk at a wardroom party given for British officers at Gibraltar.

Rhodes could provide no witnesses in his own behalf, and his efforts to cross examine hostile witnesses did him little good. His only counterattack was made in his defense summation. He asserted that he had a weak head for alcohol so that only a few drinks rendered him helpless. He also related that he had a speech impediment which caused people to believe he was drunk when in fact he was not. On the advice of his civilian counsel, Rhodes also initiated a series of legal maneuvers based on the premise that the court of inquiry was illegal and invalid. It was an investigation into his general habits and character, which were no business of a naval court. To be legal, it would have had to be an inquiry into a specific incident or offense against the Articles of War. In fact, Rhodes could look back on a naval career entirely free of any official censure or recorded professional errors.[74]

These arguments carried very little weight when compared to the avalanche of testimony recorded by the court. Alluding not only to this mass of information but also to the fact that Rhodes had attended the court of inquiry and actually questioned witnesses while in a state of doubtful sobriety, the court ruled

> that Lieutenant Rhodes is now, and has for a long tract of years past, been addicted to habitual intemperance: That his habits in that respect, are in themselves of a disqualifying tendency and unfit him for promotion to the grade of Commander in the Navy.[75]

No mention was made about what should be done with Rhodes. Presumably, he was free to remain in the service until he saw fit to retire voluntarily or died.

Boyle and Rhodes were unique in that they were among the very few officers whom the navy ever used an official naval court to investigate for drunkenness. As such, they represent the only visible manifestation of what was really a much deeper problem. There were many other drunken officers who managed to remain hidden from official view, probably because they never received commands or became eligible for promotion and managed somehow to avoid any serious mishap. They were not, however, unknown to their brother officers; and capsulized accounts of their service reputations are available through the minutes of the deliberations of the Naval Efficiency Board recorded unofficially by Commander Samuel Francis Du Pont. Here are two representative examples of officers that the board recommended dismissing from the service on account of drunkenness:

> No. 126 Charles Gray, Del. (Passed Midn.)
>   Drunkard—Drank in the Vincennes & was a sot in the East Indies—drank also in the West Indies—Three members testified to his intemperance, Buchanan, Pendergrast, & Page—Also Com Perry went strongly against him —has been met very drunk in Philad. since the Board has been in session— he was sent home from the *Southampton* for drunkenness
>   And,
> No. 188 James Bruce, Mass. (Passed Midn.)
>   Sailed with Captain Pendergt [Pendergrast]—an indifferent officer Capt. P would not give him a letter, drinks—passed his examination however. Was ordered to the *Columbia* again—recommenced drinking—would get tight ashore, and once broke his liberty for a week, this only 18 months Since—Finally got into an ugly scrape when drunk & had a piece of his upper lip bitten off—tolerably smart but crooked & decidedly given to intemperance.

The board unanimously voted to remove both men from the active list and drop them from the Navy Register.[76]

To gain some perspective on the navy's approach to the problem of alcoholism, it should perhaps be noted that the service mirrored the general tendency of nineteenth-century thought, which held that drunkenness was a moral and ethical problem and that habitual intemperance was the result of a defect in character. It was not until 1908 that a naval doctor, H. G. Beyer, first introduced the idea that alcohol was addictive. In 1914, a civilian psychiatrist, William A. White, suggested that psychiatric therapy should be made available to seamen who had drinking problems. It was not until 1971, however, that the navy actually undertook rehabilitation programs for alcoholics, under the "Armed Forces Drug Abuse and Drug Dependence, Prevention, Treatment and Rehabilitation Act." In the contemporary navy, alcoholism is still a major concern, affecting perhaps 38 percent of all naval personnel. It has now been recognized as a health problem rather than a disciplinary matter.[77]

Disobedience, disrespect, and drunkenness were without a doubt the Old Navy's most commonplace disciplinary problems. In this brief survey of some of the many hundreds of cases relating to these offenses which can be found in the judge advocate general's records, it can be seen that a careful study of courts-martial for disrespect, disobedience, and drunkenness can reveal much about the true state of relations between the officers and the enlisted men and about relations between brother officers. Indeed, the entire body of cases contained in the judge advocate general's files comprise an incomparable source of raw data about the social history of the navy. Because they are so numerous and cover so many different kinds of cases and so many different sets of circumstances, the disrespect, disobedience, and drunkenness courts-martial are probably the single most valuable references within the files for the reconstruction of the navy's social history.

These cases also reveal a great deal about the differential treatment of officers and enlisted men by the naval justice system. To be prosecuted for disrespect, disobedience, or drunkenness, a seaman had but to commit one simple act and it was immediately followed up by an arrest, trial, and punishment. An officer, on the other hand, had to commit *repeated* offenses before he was accorded such treatment; and sometimes even then he escaped censure, as did Lieutenant Rhodes, until such time as his condition became a matter of acute embarrassment to the service. It was implicit in those days, as it is now, that officers were expected to maintain a higher standard of deportment than enlisted men; but it can be seen from the disobedience and drunkenness cases that an officer who chose not to hold himself to the desired standard could expect to get away with quite a bit of substandard conduct. Apparently, all he had to do was somehow avoid putting anything disrespectful in writing, making a professional error which resulted in damage to his ship, or threatening a brother officer with bodily harm, and he could look forward to a long career in the navy. Since promotion was slow and by seniority, his professional prospects were as good as those of an exemplary officer unless he was, like Lieutenant Rhodes, an obviously hopeless and untrustworthy individual.

Chapter VIII

Neglect of Duty, Assault, & Theft

Among the more routine disciplinary problems that confronted the Old Navy, disobedience, disrespect, and drunkenness easily accounted for the greatest number of court-martial cases and subjudicial proceedings. These three categories of naval crime were closely followed by three others: neglect of duty, assault, and theft. Taken together, offenses in these categories add up to about 15 percent of the total number of courts-martial recorded in the judge advocate general's index for the years 1800 to 1861.[1]

As with the offenses examined in the previous chapter, officers tend to be overrepresented among the courts-martial and courts of inquiry recorded and filed by the Navy Department because most of the enlisted offenders were tried on the subjudicial level. Since cases involving officers are generally more fully developed than those involving enlisted men, they will likewise predominate among those examined here.

In one category, however—that of assault—cases involving enlisted men will predominate. This is because assault was overwhelmingly an enlisted man's offense. Unlike merchant marine officers, naval officers rarely assaulted seamen. Naval punishments for minor offenses were much more routine. Also, petty officers with colts and rattan canes were almost always on hand to administer chastisement for infractions of the rules or instances of disrespectful or defiant behavior. Likewise, because they were also bound by the rules and assumptions governing conduct among "gentlemen," officers seldom assaulted one another, preferring either to fight formal duels or bring court-martial charges as a means of settling grudges.

In contrast, the enlisted men settled most of their disputes with fists. Sometimes fights between enlisted men were staged with official sanction so that two berth deck enemies could resolve a feud and entertain the ship's company in the process. More often, however, the seamen fought spontaneously or waylaid each other. When this happened, either a subjudicial punishment or a court-martial could be resorted to, depending primarily on the whim of the commanding officer. One category of assault that almost always resulted in a court-martial was an incident in which an enlisted man assaulted an officer. An assault upon a petty officer might also merit a judicial tribunal, but this was by no means inevitable. On occasions when a weapon was employed, the charge read not only assault but assault with intent to kill, and the punishments meted out were only slightly less drastic than those assessed for mutiny or murder.

One of the earliest cases of an enlisted man assaulting an officer involved the ever-unpopular Lieutenant James B. Cordis. While serving as First Luff of the frigate *Congress*, Cordis was obliged to pen the following letter to his commanding officer, Captain James Sever:

> Sir, the charge respecting Partrick [sic] Brown, (Ordinary seaman), of which I enter'd a Complaint—is as follows—when calling him to account for his Quarrell [sic] with (Hugh, ordinary seaman) Dunbar—he attempted to colar [sic] me the first attempt I clear'd myself, by knocking him down—the second attempt he accomplished—which obliged me to call for my side arms—and soon disengaged myself—the men surrounding me were supporting me as much as possible—
>
> The Insult receiv'd from him Obligates me to request of you a Court-Martial.[2]

The court-martial board, whose proceedings have since disappeared entirely from the judge advocate general's records, decided that Brown was "Guilty of a great Violation of the Laws & Discipline of the Navy of the United States." They noted in mitigation of his offense that he had shown great contrition and gave him a relatively light punishment of forty eight lashes.[3]

The Brown case and others indicate clearly that most assaults on officers took place under confused circumstances and at a time when the perpetrator was in a state of extreme agitation, usually as the result of fighting with another seaman. For instance, on 11 July 1805, Seaman William Bothick of the frigate *Constellation* stood trial for striking a midshipman and knocking him off a companionway ladder. The circumstances were that Midshipman Nathaniel Goodwin together with the frigate's master-at-arms were descending the ladder to the berth deck to investigate a report that there was a fight in progress. They found the place in turmoil; and while Goodwin was standing on the ladder, someone struck him and quickly vanished among the hammocks, where it was impossible to apprehend or identify him.[4]

Commodore John Rodgers immediately offered a reward of two hundred dollars and an immediate discharge from the navy to any person who could identify Goodwin's assailant. The offer of a discharge is interesting. Usually it was thought of as punishment and coupled with a flogging. In this case, however, the commodore must have intended to preserve his berth deck informer from the vengeance of his messmates. A day after the reward had been posted, a seaman named Mark Clark came forward and named Bothick. Although Clark repeated his accusation at Bothick's court-martial, it did not sit well with the board. No other witnesses could be found to corroborate Clark's story. Deciding that "there is some mystery in [Clark's manner of giving evidence] which ought to be clear'd up . . . ," they recommended an investigation of his conduct. Meanwhile, Bothick was acquitted.

Bothick's court-martial board then reconstituted itself as a court of inquiry. Having been drawn from other ships in the squadron, members of the court did not know about the commodore's offer of a reward; but they soon found out. Under severe questioning, Clark admitted that he had informed on Bothick only for the sake of the money and had no idea who had really assaulted the midshipman.[5] Clark defended his actions by claiming that he was "very drunk" at the time he reported Bothick and had not really intended to perjure himself or commit fraud. The court of inquiry let him go without recommending a court-martial. Perhaps they reasoned that he would probably be a berth deck outcast for the remainder of the *Constellation*'s cruise and that this was punishment enough.

A slightly more straightforward case was that of Seaman John Jones III, who was tried for assaulting Midshipman Edward Le Roy in October 1834. Le Roy was walking on the quarter-deck of the ship of the line *Delaware* when he heard an officer pursuing a man who ran aft and descended the steerage ladder. Le Roy joined the chase and collared the man, who turned out to be Jones. The officer of the deck then ordered him to take his prisoner to the orlop and confine him. As the party was going below, Jones suddenly turned on Le Roy and punched him, saying, "take that, you damned son of a bitch." Another midshipman, James Riddle, quickly came to Le Roy's aid; and together they subdued Jones and put him in the brig. The seaman was by now cursing and threatening both officers.[6]

Jones conducted his own defense and waged a vigorous, if inept, campaign to mitigate the charges of mutinous language and assault on an officer lodged against him. He questioned Le Roy and Riddle and tried to get them to agree that he was drunk when the blow was struck. They refused to so testify. He asserted that he had really aimed his blow at the master-at-arms, who was also part of the chase, and had never intended to strike Le Roy. He called on several members of the *Delaware*'s crew to confirm that he was drunk and had merely struck out at random, but none of his witnesses would admit to knowing anything. When he began to call marines to testify as to his good conduct in the brig, the court became noticeably impatient and ordered him point-blank to submit his defense summation so that the trial could be concluded.[7] Ultimately, Jones was found guilty and sentenced to receive 150 lashes and to be "whipped through the squadron at such time and in such manner as the Commander-in-Chief may direct."

There were few cases of an enlisted man deliberately assaulting an officer. An example of such an instance was the trial of Seaman James McDermot, who was tried on 8 August 1848 for attacking and wounding with a knife Passed Midshipman Henry C. Hunter in the naval storehouse at Spezia, Sardinia.[8] According to several eyewitnesses, a working party from the frigate *United States* under the command of Midshipman Hunter had gone to the naval storehouse to draw supplies. While his men were in the warehouse assembling casks and boxes, Hunter sat down in the anteroom to chat with Harlow Spaulding, the naval storekeeper, and Purser's Clerk Philip Henriques. Suddenly McDermot rushed Hunter from behind and began to stab him about the head and arms with his sheath knife. The other two men in the room grappled with him; but he broke away, ran out of the building, and jumped into the harbor. He was pursued by the ship's boat that had been waiting for the supplies and quickly apprehended.[9]

McDermot's attack made a grave impression on the officers of the *United States*. His court-martial was convened so quickly that it had to be adjourned immediately to give the prisoner twenty-four hours in which to prepare his defense as prescribed by naval regulations. Upon being reassembled, the court first established the facts of the assault and then proceeded to try to discover the motive behind it. As testimony accumulated, it became clear that McDermot was very drunk. About fifteen minutes before the attack, Hunter had noticed him and accused him of being "staggering drunk"; but McDemot denied it. While working in the warehouse, the prisoner was heard to mutter several times that "he would kill him" and "that he was willing to be hung or killed for killing him" and "that he was going to kill him for getting people into trouble."[10] Storekeeper Spaulding heard these remarks and ordered him to be quiet. Purser's Clerk Henriques testified that McDermot had been making similar statements ever since the previous day, when Hunter had reported another seaman for a disciplinary infraction.[11]

In his defense statement, McDermot declared that he was "still unconscious of having assaulted Mr. Hunter." He maintained that

> If I did do it, it was done in a moment of mental madness and delirium, to which I have been sometimes subjected ever since the injury of my head from a fall on shipboard from aloft, and brought about by excitement and especially from drink.[12]

He also claimed that he had no prior grudge against Midshipman Hunter.

The court found him guilty of assault upon a superior officer with intent to kill and sentenced him

> to receive no further pay from the United States, to be taken to the U. S. in irons and to suffer solitary imprisonment for life in the Penitentiary at Washington or elsewhere as the President of the U. S. may direct.

A postscript was added to this sentence noting that the court had considered imposing the death sentence on McDermot but was deterred from doing so by doubts about his sanity.[13]

The proceedings of the McDermot court-martial were reviewed by Commodore George Read and disapproved. Maintaining that "writers on Criminal law have laid it down that drunkenness is rather an aggravation than a mitigation of crime," Read stated that if the court really believed that McDermot was insane "from any other cause than that produced by liquor," then he ought to have been acquitted and recommended for consignment to an insane asylum. The commodore noted that he had "neither the power nor the means given him to carry such a Sentence into effect" and indicated that he would keep McDermot in confinement until he could consult with the Secretary of the Navy about the ultimate disposition of the prisoner.[14] There were no further notations appended to the transcript of the McDermot case. Presumably, he was eventually returned to the United States and institutionalized.

The action of Commodore Read in disapproving the decision of the court in the case of Seaman McDermot reflects some of the caution that naval officers had about submitting their judicial actions to the scrutiny of the secretary of the navy and the president. When they sat on disciplinary tribunals, naval officers became—at least for a brief period—judges. It is part of the general legal tradition of the United States that all judges should be subject to some reviewing authority with the power of reversal in cases where illegal or improper procedures have been followed or where sentences are not in line with customary practice. For naval courts, the secretary of the navy and the president formed the reviewing authority, and the squadron commodores were the filter through which the cases were passed on their way to Washington.

The attitudes towards naval justice which the secretary and the president held were very likely to be those of civilian-trained lawyers. This is because many presidents and secretaries of the navy were lawyers by training or at least had become familiar with normal civil jurisprudence during the course of their years in public life. They knew in principle that military law was different from the civil codes they were accustomed to; but, as the remarks they appended to some of the cases they reviewed clearly show, they did not know exactly how it was different. They frequently overturned convictions on legal technicalities or principles that were common in civilian law but had no counterparts in the Articles of War.

Also, it must be admitted that, because they were made up of amateur legalists, naval courts sometimes made procedural errors; and these were occasionally cited by a secretary of the navy or president as grounds for a reversal of a verdict or mitigation of a sentence. It must not be forgotten, either, that the high officials of the executive branch of government were all of them politicians. In reviewing naval courts-martial, they often came under political pressure to revise or mitigate a court-martial's verdict or sentence. Many officers had prominent friends in Congress or in state politics. To set aside a verdict as a political favor was quite simple. In such cases, the president or secretary was sovereign. There was no authority to review *their* actions or appeal them on behalf of the navy. This is still the case today.

In addition to assaults carried out by seamen upon officers on a one-to-one basis, instances wherein a group of men attacked an officer or petty officer were not unknown to the Old Navy. Yeoman Joseph Downey related an incident that took place among the naval detachment that helped garrison Los Angeles, California, for a brief period during the Mexican War. The sailors, who were drawn from among the crews of the sloops of war *Portsmouth* and *Cyane,* were housed in barracks and employed in building fortifications. At night they got drunk and indulged in rowdy behavior in their quarters. Noting that the men were getting out of hand, Lieutenant William B. Renshaw of the *Cyane* tried to restore discipline by invading the barracks nightly and carting some of the drunks off to the guardhouse. One night he appeared in company with a midshipman and tried to arrest several men. Someone doused the lights, and in the dark all of the men whom Renshaw had collared escaped. Enraged, the lieutenant stormed at the men in the barracks and threatened to discipline all of them. In reply, the room quickly filled with the sound of seamen hooting and "black-guarding" Renshaw, who drew his pistols and "swore he would shoot, where he heard the next sound come from, let him hit innocent or guilty, he cared not which."

Unfortunately for Renshaw, the sailors were also armed. They fired three muskets at the lieutenant, who was obliged to drop to the floor and crawl out of the room on his hands and knees, leaving his weapons behind. The nameless midshipman, more concerned with honor and dignity, fired both of his pistols randomly into the room and walked out after his superior. Perhaps because he was embarrassed or ashamed to admit that he could not control his men, Renshaw never reported the incident; and no action was taken against the sailors.[15]

In another instance, five men were court-martialed on a charge of mutinous conduct and language after an angry confrontation between some of the officers and crew of the sloop of war *Decatur* in 1854 ended with an assault on the master-at-arms. The record of the trial contains no information concerning the reason why the incident took place, but it does note that it was terminated when five men were ironed and ordered confined. Under the direction of the master-at-arms, Ephriam Denis, a detachment of the *Decatur*'s marines was engaged in lashing the men down between the guns when Ordinary Seaman Richard Biddle managed to break loose momentarily. With his wrists and ankles in irons, he butted Denis severely and knocked him to the deck. While he was down, the other prisoners kicked him severely before the marines could restrain them and rescue him.[16]

A court-martial board made up of officers from the Pacific Squadron heard the case in the spring of 1854. Alarmed by the suspicion that the *Decatur* incident was the result of an incipient mutiny, they deliberated imposing the death penalty on Biddle, whom they regarded as the principal culprit. They lacked the two-thirds majority vote necessary to impose such a sentence, however; so they sentenced all of the men to ten years at hard labor in the Washington, D.C., penitentiary. President Pierce reviewed the case and mitigated the term of imprisonment to the remainder of each man's enlistment, a matter of a little more than one year.[17]

In general, assaults perpetrated by seamen on petty officers and other seamen were probably common in the Old Navy. Such cases, however, are not often found in the judge advocate general's records because they were primarily handled on the subjudicial level. Thanks to the short-lived practice of recording the proceedings of summary courts in the Navy Department's file during the years 1855 and 1856, some representative cases can be cited.

One of these is the trial of Seaman Philip Miller, who attacked and severely beat Boatswain's Mate George Brown while the two were ashore on liberty from the sloop of war *St. Marys*. Both men had been drinking at the New Bedford House Inn at Talcahuaui, a small port in the Hawaiian Islands. As they were leaving, Miller suddenly turned on Brown and began punching and kicking him severely, saying, "now you son of a bitch, I have got you," or words to that effect. At the summary court, which was held the day after the incident, Miller explained that Brown had been falsely reporting him to the commanding officer for negligence in performing his duties. Miller had confronted Brown and offered to fight him on shore, and the two men had agreed to meet while on liberty for that purpose. Brown had, however, taken the opportunity to arm himself with a pistol and a knife. Faced with this array of hardware, Miller backed down. He invited the boatswain, who had bragged repeatedly about his prowess as a fighter, to drink with him. He stood drinks until Brown had overindulged to the point of becoming seriously intoxicated and then proceeded to beat him up.

The summary court found Miller guilty but gave him the comparatively light sentence of deprivation of shore liberty for the remainder of the cruise and extra police duty "in consequence of the extenuating circumstances exhibited by the evidence on the part of the prisoner."[18]

Another case involving an assault upon one sailor by another is that of Bernard McGill, who was charged with making an "unprovoked and outrageous attack upon a seaman." In this instance, McGill and his victim, Seaman Henry Richardson, were frying fish on the galley range of the sloop-of-war *Saratoga*. For some reason, which was never clarified, McGill demanded that Richardson leave the galley. Richardson refused; and the resulting argument attracted the attention of the master-at-arms, who informed McGill that Richardson "had as much right to be there as he did" and ordered the two men to "knock off quarreling." When Richardson had completed his task and left to go forward, McGill followed him and hit him very hard from behind. He then seized Richardson's right hand and severely bit the forefinger.

The summary court quickly established that neither man was drunk, that Richardson had apparently said or done nothing to provoke McGill, and that he had not defended himself when attacked. McGill threw himself on the mercy of the court and received two months' loss of pay.[19]

The rarest type of assault case in the records is that which involves an attack upon an officer by another officer. There are a few cases of assaults between officers, however, which grew from highly unusual circumstances.

Perhaps the most complicated case was that of Lieutenant Joshua R. Sands, who was accused of "mutinous and insubordinate conduct, treating with contempt his superior officer, being in the execution of his office [and] not using his best exertions to prevent the destruction of public property by others." The specifications further stipulated that Lieutenant Sands "did violently assault and take Hold of Commodore Isaac Chauncey his superior officer in the execution of his duty."[20]

From the statement of Lieutenant Sands and the testimony of eyewitnesses, a thorough reconstruction of this incident is possible. The lieutenant's father and brother claimed title to a strip of waterfront land adjacent to the New York Navy Yard. This title was disputed by the Navy Department, which ordered the commandant of the yard, Commodore Chauncey, to build a fence around the parcel. After the fence had been completed in November of 1827, the two civilian members of the Sands family showed up one day with hammers and handspikes and commenced to try to tear it down. This brought Chauncey to the scene together with several marines and yard workers and Lieutenant Sands, who was then stationed at the yard.

A violent confrontation took place between the commodore and the elder Sands. Amid loud threats and exclamations, Chauncey drew his sword and pistol. Upon seeing his father threatened, Lieutenant Sands interposed himself roughly between the two men, jostling Chauncey in the process. In his rage and agitation, the lieutenant declared "that he did not care a damn for his commission and that he would throw it in the face of those who gave it, before he would have his rights invaded."[21]

In his defense summation, Lieutenant Sands stressed that his father's claim to the land was more valid than the navy's, and therefore Chauncey was carrying out an illegal seizure. This implied that his orders were unlawful in this instance and Sands was thus not bound to obey them. In effect, because of the illegality of what he was trying to do, Chauncey was not "in the execution of his office." Therefore, the "assault" that Sands made upon him was personal and not in defiance of the commodore's naval authority. Furthermore, Sands maintained, he had tendered his personal apology to Chauncey and it had been accepted.[22]

The court refused to concern itself with the conflicting land claim. There was enough eyewitness testimony to establish that Sands had committed all of the acts listed in the charges and specifications. On the strength of this evidence, he was found guilty and sentenced to be cashiered; but in consideration of the peculiar circumstances of the case, he was "recommended to the mercy of the President." Upon reviewing the proceedings of the tribunal, President Adams upheld the verdict of the court but remitted the penalty.[23]

In another instance some three decades after the Sands affair, Passed Midshipman J. W. Bennett of the steam frigate *Susquehanna* was charged with assaulting his superior officer, Lieutenant Randolph, while ashore at Kowloon during Commodore Matthew C. Perry's cruise to Japan in 1853.[24]

The origins of the quarrel between Bennett and Randolph lay in a dispute that had taken place several months earlier in the wardroom. Lieutenant Randolph, as mess caterer, had neglected to provide a seat for Bennett at a formal dinner; and Bennett, perhaps sensitive because of his indeterminate status as a passed midshipman, took offense. In a heated exchange, Randolph accused Bennett of impertinence, and Bennett called the lieutenant a liar. Randolph then struck Bennett, who would have returned the blow had he not been restrained by his messmates. Commander Franklin Buchanan suspended both officers but restored them to duty after extracting a promise from each man not to pursue the quarrel on board the ship.[25]

On 28 December 1853, Bennett encountered Randolph ashore and approached him, stating that "as he had been laboring under the stigma of that blow for some time, he had come ashore for the purpose of asking [Mr. Randolph] to give him satisfaction."[26] Randolph refused to accept the challenge, and Bennett struck him lightly with his cane. The two men grappled briefly until Randolph informed Bennett that he was "a sick man." Bennett then let go, whereupon Randolph said, "you have struck your superior officer and I will report you to Captain Buchanan." Bennett replied, "I do not wish to be misunderstood. I merely wish to insult Mr. Randolph."[27]

The primary concern of the court was to establish whether or not Bennett actually meant to fight a formal duel with Randolph and if the lieutenant had either waived his rank and privileges or invoked them to avoid Bennett's challenge. Randolph testified that

> Bennett approached me, he stated to me in words as nearly as I can recollect, that he understood that Captain Buchanan did not hold us responsible for anything that might occur whilst not actually on board the ship and that as he had pistols with him he was desirous of settling some little difficulty which had occurred some months previous, and invited me to go on the Cauloon [Kowloon] side for that purpose . . .[28]

After digesting the testimony, all of which was substantially in agreement, the court found Bennett guilty, not of the original charge, but of quarreling. He was sentenced to be "publicly reprimanded by the Commander in Chief in such manner, and at such time and place as he may deem proper, and [be] dismissed from the squadron." In a further comment on the case, the court explained their verdict in these terms:

> The Court having by this sentence shown their sense of the great offence against Naval Law committed by Mr. Bennett, do yet in consideration of the previous provocation he had received, and the extenuating circumstances disclosed in the testimony, recommend such mitigation of the sentence as may appear proper to the Commander in Chief.

Commodore Perry chose to mitigate the sentence considerably. Bennett was not reprimanded at all and merely removed from the *Susquehanna* and sent to another ship in the squadron.[29]

After assault, one of the most common categories of offenses that figure prominently in the judge advocate general's records and related to routine disciplinary offenses was that of theft. Theft took many forms in the Old Navy; and in one way or another, cases involving thefts, frauds, or embezzlements included personnel ranging in rank from the most senior commodores to the lowliest landsmen. As they do in the instance of assault, the judge advocate general's records give a distorted picture of the distribution of this crime since most of the enlisted men caught in acts of theft were tried and punished on the subjudicial level. Article XXVI of the Articles of War provided the justification for this. It reads:

> Any theft not exceeding twenty dollars may be punished at the discretion of the captain, and above that sum as a court-martial shall direct.

Since most thefts perpetrated by enlisted men were minor, they came under the jurisdiction of the various commanding officers, and little effort was made to record the mast proceedings. Theft cases involving officers were usually tried by court-martial because the sum or value of the goods involved often exceeded twenty dollars and because of the questions of personal honor at issue.

It is also noteworthy that theft cases, like others involving officers, were much more complicated and interesting than those concerning enlisted men. Since they were in positions of trust and responsibility, officers had opportunities to indulge in many forms of peculation, profiteering, currency speculation, fraud, diversion of government stores, funds, and property, and even misuse of naval personnel for private gain. Enlisted men, on the other hand, tended to be limited to simple thefts of money or property and some categories of government stores, such as boats, liquor, sailcloth, and the like. Their cases were straightforward and easy to dispose of.

It is difficult to gain a perspective of the incidence of theft among the enlisted men. Since so many enlisted thieves were punished on the subjudicial level, we have no real means of ascertaining just how much theft went on in a typical nineteenth century man-of-war. Melville, speaking from personal experience in only one ship, claimed that theft was so pervasive a fact of life on the berth deck that

> To enumerate all the minor pilferings on board a man-of-war would be endless. With some highly commendable exceptions, they rob from one another, and rob back again, till, in the matter of small things, a community of goods seems almost to be established; and at last, as a whole, they become relatively honest, by nearly every man becoming the reverse. It is in vain that the officers, by threats of condign punishment, endeavor to instill more virtuous principles into the crew; so thick is the mob, that not one thief in a thousand is detected.[30]

The moralistic author of *White Jacket* goes on to describe the activities of organized rings trained to waylay crewmen known or thought to be carrying quantities of coins in neckbags which the sailors called monkeybags. Men who secreted valuables in the linings of their hammocks ran the risk of having them slit open from below while they slept. As the victim fell through, he was pinioned while the seams of the hammock were gone over, the whole action taking place on the crowded berth deck after lights out.[31]

Occasionally, an enlisted thief found himself facing the entire panoply of naval justice. On 4 October 1853, Ordinary Seaman John Monohain was court-martialed for entering the medicinal storeroom of the frigate *Constitution* "and [taking] therefrom, two bottles of wine, the property of the U. S. Government." He had been caught by Hospital Steward John N. Falk and Landsman Abraham Johnson, who testified that they had found him with one bottle in his hand and one in his shirt. Upon being challenged, Monohain had tried to persuade the two witnesses to let him go and remain silent about his attempted theft. Failing that, he had informed them that he was on an errand for one of the officers. After the testimony was concluded, Monohain declined to make a defense statement. He was sentenced to forfeit twenty dollars of his pay and lose his liberty privileges for twelve months.[32]

The unusual thing about the Monohain case was that a full-dress court-martial was held in a theft incident when all the parties involved were in the navy. The majority of other theft cases wherein enlisted men were court-martialed involved the victimization of a civilian by a sailor. This was in accord with Article XXVII of the Articles of War, which provided that

> If any person in the navy shall, when on shore, plunder, abuse, or mal-treat any inhabitant, or injure his property in any way, he shall suffer such punishment as a court-martial shall adjudge.

An example of a court-martial held under this article is that of two marine privates, Frederick Smitley and John Murray. These two men were charged with "a breach of the 27th Article" of the Articles of War for stealing a sheep from one "John Kelso, Esquire, of the Borough of Erie on or about the 11th Ultimo [i.e., 11 May 1817]."[33]

Smitley and Murray were prosecuted by Master Commandant Daniel Dexter at the express request of Kelso, who also served as the principal prosecution witness. Smitley immediately plead guilty, but Murray elected to try to defend himself by putting all the blame on his companion. Three witnesses, including Dexter, testified that Murray had helped to steal, butcher, and eat the sheep. Both men were sentenced to receive thirty lashes and to repay the cost of the animal.[34]

Another case where an enlisted man was court-martialed for stealing from a civilian was that of John Brown IV, of the steamer *Allegheny*. On 1 June 1848, Brown was part of a boat's crew which took a party over to conduct an inspection of the American merchant schooner *Juliet*, then at anchor in the harbor of Rio de Janeiro. As the naval boarding party was about to leave the schooner, her master confronted the lieutenant in charge of the detachment and reported that one of his men's sea chests had been broken open and that a gold ring, watch, and slung shot were missing. While this was taking place, Acting Midshipman John J. Laughlin noticed Brown apparently hiding something in the launch. When he was approached by the officers, he was seen to throw the slung shot overboard. The boat was searched and a handkerchief containing the watch and ring was found tied under the thwart that he had been sitting on.[35]

Brown was taken back to the *Allegheny* and, after a brief hearing at captain's mast, was given a dozen lashes and made to wear a placard saying "Thief! take care of your bags." Apparently, the *Juliet*'s crew were determined to exact more retribution than this and complained forcefully to Commodore George Storer of the Brazil Squadron. Storer ordered Brown court-martialed on a charge of theft, with himself acting as prosecutor.

During this proceeding, Brown defended himself with great vigor. He declared that since he had already been tried and punished by his commanding officer, the court-martial constituted double jeopardy and thus violated his rights as an American citizen. He maintained that nothing reported stolen had been found on his person and that only the relatively worthless slung shot, consisting of a quantity of lead musket balls in a pouch with a length of rawhide thong attached to form a crude sort of blackjack which he was seen to throw overboard, linked him with the crime. He attacked the character and motives of the *Juliet*'s crew, reminding the court that they were suspected of being slavers.[36]

The court completely ignored all of the arguments put forward by the prisoner. Brown was found guilty and sentenced to receive seventy-five lashes, "equal portions to be given on each ship in the squadron then in port," and to continue wearing the placard. Upon reviewing the proceedings, Commodore Storer remitted the flogging.[37]

Simple cases of theft involving officers were as rare as they were common for enlisted men. Those that existed nearly always turned out to involve midshipmen, and many were the result of false and malicious accusations. In one such instance, Midshipman Nicholas Marchand was accused of stealing some combs from a fellow passenger on board a merchant vessel. When a court of inquiry looked into the accusation, which was made by the passenger's mulatto serving girl, it uncovered a complicated chain of events involving petty theft among servants, the ransacking of the ship by pirates, and the planting of incriminating articles in Marchand's baggage. Ultimately, all of the accusations were traced to the serving maid, known by everyone to be untrustworthy and prone to thievery. Marchand was exonerated.[38]

Among senior officers simple theft was unknown, but there were a surprising number of cases that involved complicated schemes to defraud the government, embezzle funds or stores, or misuse supplies and manpower. Commodores and captains commanding navy yards and squadrons were particularly susceptible to charges of this nature and often suffered the indignity of being found guilty. The resulting punishments were more embarrassing than exacting. No doubt the situation of some crusty old quarterdeck autocrat caught in a particularly ridiculous peculation provided a highly gratifying measure of comic relief to the usual grim drama of navy life. Such cases were long, drawn-out affairs featuring exquisitely detailed testimony. The juicy tidbits of scandal that leaked out must have amused everyone—except, perhaps, the red-faced, old mossback in the dock.

Consider, for example, the situation of Commodore Jesse Duncan Elliott. During his court-martial in 1840 on multiple charges of fraud, embezzlement, the transporting of private cargo in public vessels, cruelty, and oppression, thousands of pages of testimony were taken delving into every aspect of his command of the Mediterranean Squadron from 1837 to 1839.[39] The most ribald and unrestrained aspect of this tribunal came to center on Elliott's embarking a score of Barbary jackasses on board his flagship for transportation to the United States. The judge advocate probed exhaustively all of the multifaceted aspects of procuring, caring for, transporting, and off-loading jackasses, using the labor of naval personnel, victualing the beasts with public stores, and erecting stalls for them between the guns, which effectively turned the flagship into a defenseless livestock transport. When asked to explain his actions, the commodore, whom everyone suspected of attempting to restock his farm in Maryland at government expense, could only testify lamely that he had intended to make the animals a gift to the nation "to improve the domestic breed."[40]

Even more interesting was the case of Commodore Thomas ap Catesby Jones. After completing his harrowing tour of duty on the Pacific Station in 1849, Jones returned home to face a court-martial that lasted from 16 December 1850 to 1 February 1851. The court probed every aspect of Jones's conduct from the hanging of the *Ewing* mutineers to his use of government funds to speculate in gold dust.[41] This last was a most singular endeavor. Jones had apparently appropriated the entire contents of the Military Contribution Fund, some $10,643.09. Originally, this was remitted to his care by the Mexican Government as part of the war indemnity agreed upon to settle claims against Mexico at the conclusion of hostilities in 1848. With this cash he purchased gold dust and nuggets in San Francisco for later resale in New York.

In his gold dust machinations, Jones was taking advantage of the fact that raw gold was worth less than its equivalent weight in coined money in San Francisco. Once purchased cheaply, it could be sent to New York and sold for a much higher price. Through the flagship's purser, Joseph Wilson, Jones had the entire amount of the Military Contribution Fund turned over to his personal care and used it to buy 275¼ ounces of gold. He put this precious cargo on board the supply ship *Lexington* and sent it to New York consigned to his brother, who had instructions to dispose of it on the New York market. With the proceeds of this sale, Jones intended to replenish the fund and pocket several thousand dollars in profits.[42]

Of course, Jones not only needed an obliging purser to carry out this scheme, but he also found it necessary to ignore repeated demands from the Navy Department that he submit detailed accounts of the uses to which he put the funds in his care. It was the intention of the secretary of the navy that the money should be used to help defray the expenses of the squadron as an economy measure for the department. Since the funds were not available for this purpose because of the commodore's actions, serious misunderstandings had arisen in Washington.

Commodore Jones fought his case hard, contesting every shred of hostile testimony. Unfortunately, he had been on trial for irregular procedures before, and the court, although bound to hear him out in deference to his rank, seniority, and heroic conduct during the War of 1812, had little sympathy. He was found guilty of attempting to defraud the United States, of neglect of duty in failing to account for the funds under his care, and of scandalous conduct tending to the destruction of good morals. He was sentenced to be suspended from duty for five years and to lose all pay and emoluments for half of the period of his suspension.[43] He retired to his home, where he passed the remaining years of his life writing acrimonious letters to the Navy Department. He died in 1855 after being restored to active duty two years earlier.

Although the commodores of squadrons on foreign stations were commonly involved in frauds and embezzlements, perhaps the most fruitful vineyards for peculating senior officers were the navy yards. The administration of the naval shipyards of the early nineteenth century was one of the Old Navy's most obvious failures. High costs, inefficient labor, wastefulness, and misuse of materials and resources all combined to fix hostile congressional and public attention on the navy yards and render them contemptible in the eyes of military men and civilians alike. Consequently, they were a major source of courts-martial and courts of inquiry involving frauds, thefts, embezzlements, and misappropriation of labor and materials. Usually it was the commandants of the various yards who bore the brunt of these proceedings.

A more-or-less typical case was that of Captain Samuel Evans, commandant of the New York Navy Yard in 1823. Evans was court-martialed for misuse and theft of public property. A total of fifty-four specifications, most of them contributed by civilian employees of the yard, detailed numerous diversions of public stores and materials. This included the selling of government-owned supplies and fittings to private shipping interests, the use of government-owned small boats to operate a ferry service for Evans' private gain, the building of a ferryboat for Evans' private use with government labor and materials, and the diversion of lumber and workmen to build an addition to Evans' home.[44]

The resulting trial was a long one. The evidence was copious, the testimony detailed in the extreme. Whole pages of account books and ledgers were admitted as evidence and laboriously copied into the transcript of the proceedings. Evans' defense of his actions was equally complex, sometimes obscure, sometimes plausible, ultimately damning. He was found guilty of "blending his private and public concerns" and sentenced to receive a reprimand from the secretary of the navy. Secretary Samuel Southard chose to warn him solemnly of the dangers of "the blending of public with private concerns," and the issue was closed. Apparently nobody was hard-hearted enough to suggest that Evans should give up his post.[45]

Such obscure and unremarkable officers as Samuel Evans and Captain Thomas Tingey, the notoriously corrupt commandant of the Washington Navy Yard, were not the only men to succumb to the temptations that abounded in the shipyards. Even such an illustrious hero as Isaac Hull gave way to temptation and had to stand trial for diverting labor and materials to his personal use while he was commandant of the Boston Navy Yard in 1822.[46] It was not the navy's way to punish such transgressors rigorously, however, much to the disgust of certain economy-minded congressional critics; and the records show no instance where a yard commandant was ever removed from his post. There was no provision made for a fiscal watchdog in the Navy Department, at least until the advent of Gideon Welles and Benjamin Franklin Isherwood during the Civil War; and in the absence of any dedicated, technically well-versed public servants, corruption flourished.

Another category of theft-related offenses that seems to have been part of the legacy of the navy in the days of sail were those that involved pursers and their principal assistants, the clerks and stewards. The purser of a sailing man-of-war was a staff officer of considerable power and influence. He was the chief storekeeper, principal fiscal officer, head clerk and accountant, victualer, and vendor of both vital and luxury consumer goods to the officers and crew alike. Under the Old Navy's archaic accounting system, pursers had almost unlimited opportunities to indulge in either small-scale graft or large-scale embezzlements. Pursers could, for example, speculate in currency, profiteer in the sale of slops and dunnage to the crew, lend money at exorbitant rates of interest, or short weight the ship while purchasing supplies and provisions, to name just a few of their more common machinations.

Before the advent of a regular wage for pursers, which was instituted in 1840, they were actually *expected* to make up their pay out of the profits of their various enterprises. Even relatively honest pursers were expected to clear thousands of dollars in personal profits from the activities of a single voyage in a large frigate. Indeed, Melville relates the tale of one purser who was reputed to have amassed the sum of fifty thousand dollars during a cruise in a ship of the line on the Mediterranean Station.[47] It is no wonder that pursers were often distrusted by the line officers and referred to as "nipcheeses" among the crew.

There are a few instances of pursers or pursers' stewards being court-martialed for irregularities before 1840; but the principal effort to regulate their activities through the mechanism of courts-martial comes after the institution of the regular stipend, which was originally pegged at $3,500 per year, or twice the wage of a naval lieutenant. There can be little doubt that after they had been granted regular wages, pursers were held to a much stricter standard of accountability. Not all of them were successful in making the transition.

One such individual was Pursers' Steward S. Henriques on board the frigate *Potomac* attached to the Home Squadron. On 6 February 1856, a court of inquiry was convened by Commodore Hiram Paulding at the request of Captain Levin M. Powell to determine whether or not Henriques was lending public money to the crew at usurious rates of interest.[48]

Twelve enlisted men were called to testify, all of whom had borrowed money from Henriques. The system used by the steward was a simple but ingenious one. He had complete charge of the *Potomac*'s payroll and on paydays disbursed all funds to the crew. When a man wanted to borrow, he simply requested a sum from Henriques, who advanced it, theoretically from his personal funds. On payday, he deducted the sum borrowed plus interest from his debtor's wages and pocketed them directly. In short, he was operating a loan service using what may or may not have been his personal cash reserves but insuring the security of his investments by his control of the disbursing of public money. Although he enjoyed a security for his loans that the most discriminating bank would have envied, the interest he charged was painfully high, amounting to 25 percent compounded every two weeks. Bernard M. Fowler, Captain of the Forecastle, testified that he borrowed the sum of $27.50 and was charged $2.50 in interest on his next payday less than a week later. He also related that Henriques had quoted his interest rate in advance of the transaction, and it had been clearly understood that the money involved was from private funds but that repayment would be by means of payroll withholding.[49]

It was upon this point that the court was particularly anxious to focus:

> *Question.* [by the court to Charles Fisher, Coxwain] Did you consider the money you obtained from Mr. Henriques as an advance on account of your pay: or simply a private matter between you and him?

A. I knew it was not the government that speculated on my pay, but I expected to pay Mr. Henriques for it by signing for it on the Pay Roll. I wanted the money & was willing to pay the per centage to get it.[50]

Throughout the inquiry, Henriques maintained that all of the money lent out was his own and that he had been engaged in running such a loan service in every ship that he had been assigned to in seventeen years of naval service as a steward. The court was still dubious. Purser Hieskill, Henriques' immediate superior, testified that his steward had "never had the Key to the Public Chest" but that he was responsible for making all disbursements to the officers and crew and thus routinely had between three hundred dollars and six hundred dollars in public funds in his possession at any one time.[51] It was impossible to establish whether or not Henriques had illicitly used some of this money to provide himself with lending capital.

Perhaps the most damaging aspect of Henriques' lending activities was that he carried them on in a secretive manner. Captain Powell testified that the pursers' steward had no specific authorization to lend money and certainly none to collect his debts by instituting a payroll withholding. Henriques had been in business for at least six months before Powell had become aware of what he was doing and issued a written order putting a stop to it. Immediately after that, he had requested a court of inquiry.[52]

Henriques must have sensed that the opinion of the court would go against him. Before the inquiry could be concluded, he submitted his resignation from the navy, thus putting himself beyond the reach of a court-martial. He did, however, submit a formal defense asserting that he had never lent any public money on his private account.[53] After considering both the resignation and the continued protestations of innocence on the part of the defendant, the court delivered itself of the following opinion:

> The Evidence taken Establishes the fact that the Purser's Clerk of the Frigate *Potomac*, Mr. S Henriques has been in the Habit of making payments on advance to the crew without authority from the Captain & [reimbursing] himself out of the money due them from the government [at] a premium of usurious interest of 25 per cent.
>
> Upon their application he has habitually let them have money, whether public or private taken the amount with 25 per cent premium in his hands & procured them receipt for both the payment & premium on the Pay Roll of the Ship, the men fully understanding the terms of the arrangement.[54]

Since Henriques had already resigned, there was no court-martial.

The Henriques case involved the sort of semi-illegal sharp practice that pursers were particularly known for. A much clearer instance of criminal wrongdoing was that of Purser J. B. Danforth of the steam frigate *Cumberland*. He was tried at Puerto Praya on 5 June 1858 for "Fraudulently selling United States Government Provisions and other Public Stores" and "Fraud against the United States." Among the many detailed specifications were accusations of selling uniform clothing at prices above those established by the Navy Department, selling wardroom stores and provisions to the officers at higher prices than those authorized, smuggling ship's stores ashore at ports of call and selling them for personal gain, purchasing supplies and provisions for the ship in smaller quantities than those listed in his accounts and pocketing the difference. The profits accruing to Danforth from these transactions ranged from twenty dollars to sixty dollars each.[55]

There were two specifications that were particularly grave because they involved currency manipulations, and in one case the sum involved was quite large.

> Charge 2, Specification 4: In this, that the said Purser Danforth did, at Sierra Leone on or about the seventh of January . . . . sell a United States Government Bill of Exchange on Messers Baring Brothers Co. of London for the amount of three thousand pounds sterling, for which the said Purser J. B. Danforth received the sum of thirteen thousand six hundred and eighty dollars of which [he] . . . placed to the credit of the United States government only twelve thousand nine hundred and sixty dollars, thereby defrauding the United States government of seven hundred and twenty dollars. . . .

The specification went on to describe in detail how Danforth had split the profits of this sale with an American consular official at Sierra Leone. Another specification explained how Danforth had used 180 British sovereigns to pay the *Cumberland*'s bills at the port of St. Paul de Loando, exchanging them at the rate of five dollars per sovereign when the normal exchange rate was $4.80. "This allowed him to divert 20¢ on each sovereign to his own pocket, $36 in all."[56]

When confronted with these charges and specifications, Danforth immediately indicated that he wanted to plead guilty. The court warned him that they would sentence him on his plea alone and that if he had any defense he should present it. Danforth opted not to call witnesses or to cross examine his prosecutor. Instead, he submitted a statement in which he asserted that he was inexperienced and ignorant of the regulations and procedures of the navy. He had been advised by other pursers in the West Africa Squadron and by his own pursers' steward, M. L. Tubb, that the practices of overcharging for supplies and speculating in foreign currencies were common and necessary to insure that there would be sufficient funds to cover all accounts at the end of the *Cumberland*'s commission.

Danforth further stated that when he finally realized that he had been misled and took the trouble to familiarize himself with the regulations, he admitted his errors to the commodore and begged to be allowed to make good all of his peculations. He also offered to resign, but this had not been allowed and he found himself facing charges instead.[57]

After fully describing all of the irregular practices which the other pursers on the station had told him about, Danforth threw himself on the mercy of the court, begging them to consider his aged parents and "a young and innocent wife dependent upon my future efforts for support."

The court was unmoved. It sentenced him to "be cashiered, and to be considered forever incapable of any further employment in the service of the United States and to forfeit all pay and subsistence due him." The sentence was approved by the commodore; but when the transcript was forwarded to Washington, President Buchanan noted that, like the record of the Sherman trial described in the previous chapter, it had not been signed by every member of the court-martial board. This seems to have been another oversight on the part of Commander Missroon, who had presided at both trials. The president appended a tart note calling attention to this fact and mitigated all of the penalties imposed by the sentence, merely accepting Danforth's resignation.[58]

From this brief survey of cases involving theft, it is clear that this particular category of offense took many forms in the Old Navy and that the higher the rank of the perpetrator and the more complex his scheme was, the more likely he was to escape any serious punishment. With some exceptions, the same rule also holds true for our next category of naval crime: neglect of duty and negligence in the performance of duty.

As is the case with the modern fleet, the Old Navy experienced a certain number of mishaps, accidents, losses of ships, and injuries to personnel that were the result of carelessness or incompetence. Any officer or enlisted man who was suspected of being the cause of such an occurrence could be tried under Articles XIX and XX of the Articles of War.

Article XIX   If any officer, or other person in the navy, shall, through inattention, (a) negligence, or any other fault, suffer any vessel of the navy to be stranded, or run upon rocks or shoals, or hazarded, he shall suffer such punishment as a court-martial shall adjudge.

Article XX   If any person in the navy shall sleep upon his watch, or negligently perform the duty assigned to him, or leave his station before regularly relieved he shall suffer death, or such punishment as a court-martial shall adjudge; or, if the offender be a private, he may, at the discretion of the captain, be put in irons, or flogged not exceeding twelve lashes.

The provision for enlisted men in Article XX is probably the reason why officers were generally more likely to be court-martialed for neglect of duty than seamen. Among the enlisted men, the crime of sleeping on watch is common and was apparently punished on both the judicial and subjudicial levels, depending on the consequences of the act and the attitude of the commanding officer. Marine enlisted men were more vulnerable to neglect of duty charges because much of their work involved standing guard over valuable stores or prisoners and patroling berth decks or otherwise policing the sailors. If government property was stolen or prisoners escaped, the marine sentries posted to guard them could be accused of negligence.

One case that serves as an example of this trend is that of Marine Privates James Watson and John Brody. Brody had been assigned to duty as a sentinel at the guardhouse of the Pensacola Navy Yard. On the night of 12 May 1827, he was found "in a recumbent position" by his relief, Private Watson. It was also noticed that two prisoners then confined in the guardhouse, Seaman Uriah Coddington and Marine Private John Adams, had escaped. Although Watson gave the alarm, the two escapees were not recaptured; so the two guards were court-martialed—Brody for sleeping on his post and Watson for neglect of duty in that he had not given the alarm promptly.[59]

The records of this trial are incomplete and in considerable disorder, but the incident can be reconstructed. Apparently the two prisoners had managed somehow to divest themselves of their wrist and leg irons and made their exit by forcing a back window of the guardhouse, which was a rather rudimentary log structure. The night they escaped was windy and a heavy surf was running, which provided sufficient noise to cover their escape.

In his defense summation, Brody called attention to the fact that the marine detachment at Pensacola was doing strenuous duty. He himself was a mess cook in addition to his normal round of guard duty obligations. On the night of the escape, he had been fatigued and had sat down to rest. He denied, however, that he had been asleep and pointed out that Watson would only testify that he had been in a recumbent position and not to his knowledge actually sleeping.[60] The specification that Watson had not been prompt in sounding the alarm was also challenged and turned out to be unsupportable. Ultimately the court acquitted both men, attributing the escape to the fact that the log cabin was not a proper guardhouse and indicating that there had been no provable neglect on the part of the sentries.

Another incident that involved a seaman is of particular interest. On 7 July 1818, Ordinary Seaman Jacob Johnson was court-martialed for putting his ship in hazard, the only charge of that type to appear in the judge advocate general's index of cases. The specification maintained that while serving in the frigate *United States* in the Mediterranean he had

> Wickedly and mischievously cut; hacked and wounded the Breechings of Eight of the Main Deck Guns of the said frigate thereby rendering them useless and the guns unmanageable and thus impairing and reducing the force and defense of the said Frigate.[61]

This action caused grave concern because cutting the gun breechings of a sailing man-of-war was not really an act of negligence but of sabotage. During the Napoleonic Wars, British seamen had, upon rare occasions, cut the breechings of their ship's guns as a surreptitious protest against naval discipline. Such an act was taken as a sign that mutiny was brewing among the crew.

The officers of the *United States* launched a vigorous investigation and eventually the ship's carpenter came forward and informed the first lieutenant that Johnson had confided to him that he was responsible. Other witnesses from among the crew also testified that rumors circulating in the ship likewise named Johnson as the culprit. Although they were nervous about coming to a verdict wholly on the strength of hearsay evidence, usually inadmissible in naval tribunals, the court found Johnson guilty. Upon hearing this judgment, the prisoner then confessed voluntarily, swore he was drunk at the time he vandalized the guns, and threw himself on the mercy of the court. He was sentenced to receive one hundred lashes and forfeit all pay and subsistence.

In reviewing the case, Commodore Charles Stewart expressed his regret that the verdict of the court had been arrived at wholly through hearsay evidence and a confession made only after the prisoner no longer had any hope of acquittal. Nevertheless, he approved the punishment and added that "It is desired that [Johnson] be not again taken into the navy service by any officer under [this] command."[62]

For the most part, the navy assumed that except in the case of marines who allowed prisoners to escape or seamen who engaged in acts of sabotage, there was little to be gained by court-martialing sailors for professional errors. A dozen lashes for carelessness or negligence awarded at captain's mast was sufficient in most instances.

With officers, more was at stake. The negligence of an officer could have grave consequences, and it was much more important to weed out negligent or careless officers earlier in their careers. If such men were allowed to remain in the navy, they would either rise to positions of great responsibility or clog up the Navy Register, unemployable and yet fully entitled to continued pay and promotions under the rule of seniority. For this reason, neglect of duty charges bore down most heavily on the midshipmen, particularly before the establishment of the Naval Academy and the regularization of officer procurement procedures. There are myriads of cases of neglect of duty involving midshipmen and passed midshipmen in the judge advocate general's index of cases; and in nearly every instance, when a guilty verdict was reached, the penalty was dismissal from the service.

The problem of unsuitable midshipmen was compounded in the earliest years of the navy by the fact that many officers in higher grades were also unsuitable. As the first ships joined the fleet, personnel from commanding officers on down had to be recruited. There was at that time very little systematic appreciation for the nuances of personnel selection. The result was that a few ships, the smaller brigs and schooners being the most prominent among them, went to sea with officer contingents that were quite incapable of discharging their duties properly.

One such vessel was the brig *Experiment*, which was commissioned under the command of Lieutenant William Maley for service during the Quasi-War with France and against the picaroons in the Caribbean. Commodore Richard Dale was obliged to hold a court of inquiry after receiving a torrent of complaints and countercomplaints from the *Experiment*'s captain and other officers. Maley's officers accused him of drunkenness, cowardice, theft of property taken from prizes, and numerous irregular practices. On his part, the lieutenant commanding submitted his journals, which recorded the derelictions of his subordinates, particularly the watchkeepers. They habitually slept on duty, one actually allowing the *Experiment* to collide with the frigate *Boston* through sheer inattention, and were often found drunk when called to relieve the deck. They insulted Maley to his face and, he charged, several had proven cowardly under fire.[63]

Even the senior petty officers were careless and negligent. A pirate barge escaped when the gun crews proved unable to fire a broadside because the gunner had neglected to charge the powder horns. The marines let Maley down by failing to fire on command a volley into an enemy craft. They had forgotten to provide themselves with ammunition. The ultimate disgrace occurred during a hot engagement with several barges full of picaroons. Seven guns were put out of action after their breechings failed.[64]

After reviewing the proceedings of the court of inquiry, Commodore Dale wrote ruefully to Secretary Stoddert that he believed Lieutenant Maley, although an "excellent seaman," was otherwise totally unfit to command a warship. He had hoped that action might be delayed until the crew's enlistments had expired and the ship could be paid off. The obvious mismanagement of the *Experiment*, however, had demanded an inquiry.[65] No further notations survive in the documents relating to this case; but presumably Maley and perhaps some of his officers as well were persuaded to resign their commissions.

Dale had even more perplexing difficulties with Captain Hector McNeil of the frigate *Boston*. During a cruise to the Mediterranean in 1802, McNeil commanded his ship with such disregard for the formalities of the naval service as to indicate his utter incomprehension of the requirements of his position. He sailed the *Boston* according to his own whims, leaving some of his officers behind at ports of call. Once he abducted three French naval officers who had come aboard the ship to visit at Toulon. He habitually violated quarantine regula tions. Ultimately, he fell in with an entire squadron of Tripolitan ships that were pursuing a Neopolitan frigate. Calling his crew to quarters, he went into action against the Tripolitans and shot them to pieces. His own ship suffered considerable damage and heavy casualties, but McNeil filed no official report of the action. After upwards of a year of cleaning up the messes McNeil left in his wake and tendering apologies to outraged foreign governments, the commodore finally complained to the secretary of the navy, and McNeil was relieved of his command by order of President Jefferson.[66]

After these early eccentrics had been weeded out, the remaining officers achieved a higher standard of professionalism and the navy became more stable. From about 1805 onwards, problems relating to commanding officers declined greatly, and they were usually tried for negligence or neglect of duty only if their ships were lost or severely damaged during their tenure in command. Of these cases, perhaps the most noteworthy is that of Captain John T. Newton of the steam frigate *Missouri*.

The *Missouri* was the navy's newest and most powerful steam war ship when she burned and sank in Gibraltar harbor on her maiden voyage in April 1844. The fire which destroyed the ship was caused by a broken glass demijohn of turpentine, the contents of which leaked from the engineer's storeroom into the fireroom, soaked into some felt cloth covering the main steam chests, and was set afire by an open flame lamp.[67] Testimony by the ship's engineering officers established that the turpentine had been stored contrary to standing orders and had been hidden in the engineer's storeroom because the black gang did not want to go all the way to the regular paint locker whenever they needed mineral spirits. Further testimony revealed that they had also been violating standing safety regulations by using an open flame lamp while overhauling the steam chests and repacking the stuffing boxes when the fire broke out.[68]

The court of inquiry decided that the loss of the *Missouri* was due to negligent practices and blamed the unsafe stowage of turpentine and the use of naked flame lamps on the engine room crew. None of this was, of course, directly the fault of Captain Newton; but the loss of the

The spanking new steam frigate *Missouri* burns in Gibraltar harbor in ". . . the first case arising under the steam marine." An illegally stowed glass jar of turpentine broke and leaked into a compartment where the engineers were overhauling steam chests by the light of an open flame lamp. (United State Naval Academy Museum Library collection)

Missouri was a hard blow to the navy. Someone had to be accountable other than a few despised engineers. Consequently, it was decided that Newton should stand court-martial for negligence.[69]

The specifications listed under the charge dealt mainly with safety violations. The embarkation and stowage of turpentine in glass jars and in an improper place, the failure to keep the fire pumps in good order, allowing a naked light to be used in the engine room, the failure to hold sufficiently rigorous inspections to enable the commanding officer to discover unsafe practices, and the failure to enforce internal safety regulations were all cited.[70] The testimony at the court-martial was more extensive and detailed than that at the court of inquiry. The outfitting of the *Missouri*, her voyage, the fire, and its aftermath were all exhaustively explored with the help of many witnesses. Perhaps the most interesting information to be gained from this mass of information was the consistent pattern of deception employed by the engineering staff. For a long time, they had managed to keep their captain in ignorance of the many safety violations they were committing in order to make their jobs a little more convenient and easy.

In his defense summation, Newton argued that it was the negligence of his subordinates rather than himself that had caused the loss of the ship. He had taken all reasonable precautions and done his duty as called for in the naval regulations. How, he asked, could he be held responsible for turpentine jugs willfully concealed from him and stored in violation of his standing orders by an act of deliberate disobedience on the part of his engineers?[71]

Newton's arguments were quite reasonable; but the navy was new to steam engineering, and the court apparently believed that a greater degree of responsibility on the part of commanding officers was called for. Although they made no direct statement to this effect, Newton was found guilty and sentenced to two years' suspension from duty. In reviewing the case two months later, President Tyler wrote that

> An important principle having been settled in this case [i.e., the doctrine that commanding officers are ultimately responsible for the actions of engineers as well as deck officers] and the measure of punishment being altogether secondary to this, the first case arising under the steam marine—and considering that there is nothing implicating in the slightest degree the naval standing of Captain Newton, I direct the remainder of his punishment to be remitted.[72]

No mention of the possibility of courts-martial for the offending engineers was ever made.

The light penalty assessed against Captain Newton for the loss of the navy's most valuable warship seems weak compared with contemporary policies that mandate nothing less than the ruination of an entire service career for a commanding officer who loses a ship under accidental circumstances. Actually, even in more orthodox cases, when all the fault rested with the captain and his deck officers, the navy was more lenient in the years prior to the Civil War than it is now. An example of this is the case of Commander G. T. Pearson, who was court-martialed for the loss of the sloop-of-war *Boston* off Eleuthera Island in the Bahamas on 15 November 1846. This wreck occurred because Pearson had elected to use a somewhat risky method of navigation known as "running down the reckoning." On the night in question, he had laid down a course calculated to bring the *Boston* to a point about one mile north of Eleuthera at 0500. Pearson had assumed that the ship would make an average speed of three or four knots on a southerly course while passing down the east coast of Great Abaco Island. His night orders called for the officer-of-the-deck to notify him at 0500 or whenever the ship had run thirty miles from her position at 2000 the previous evening. It was Pearson's intention to change course at that time and steer clear of Eleuthera by way of the Northeast Providence Channel.

During the night, the *Boston* encountered several squalls on her southward passage. For this reason, her speed was increased and she actually covered the thirty-mile course laid out by Pearson in eight hours instead of nine as anticipated. The squalls also prevented the watch officers from taking bearings on Hole in the Wall Light, which was obscured by rain and mist for most of the early morning hours. Consequently, the *Boston* arrived at her course change point at approximately 0400, just when Lieutenant Francis L. Haggarty was being relieved as officer-of-the-deck by Passed Midshipman Henry Rolands. Rolands kept the deck for forty-five minutes and was just preparing to send a messenger to wake the captain when the ship struck bottom.[73] All hands were called, and the coming of the dawn revealed that the *Boston* was aground on a reef, surrounded by rocks and shoals. She was pounding severely in heavy surf and there was no chance of saving her. The north shore of Eleuthera was less than a half-mile distant, due south.

After reconstructing the events leading up to the wreck with great care, the court of inquiry delivered the opinion that the loss of the *Boston* was "attributable to incompetence on the part of Commander George T. Pearson, in running the ship in for land in squally weather, at night." Lieutenant Haggarty was censured for not calling his captain after the ship had run thirty miles, and Passed Midshipman Rolands was declared negligent for not determining his position when he relieved the watch.[74]

The Navy Department ordered a court-martial but preferred charges only against Commander Pearson. Haggerty and Rolands participated as witnesses, but no charges were preferred against them even though the court of inquiry had indicated that they shared responsibility with Pearson for the loss of the *Boston*. The commander was formally charged with "improper navigation of a vessel of the navy under his command."[75]

In making his initial defense statement, Pearson charged that the loss of his ship was entirely attributable to the fact that both Haggarty and Rolands had failed to carry out the instructions he had written in the night order book. Questioning by the judge advocate on this point brought forth the fact that it had never been the custom on board the *Boston* for the deck officers to actually read and initial the captain's order book. They merely repeated his instructions orally to their reliefs at the end of each watch. Testimony by Lieutenant Haggarty and other witnesses also established that Commander Pearson had been on deck frequently throughout the night supervising the shortening of sails during the squalls. He therefore had direct knowledge of all the conditions prevailing, and his frequent appearances apparently led the watch officers to assume that the night orders were correspondingly less significant since the captain knew most of what was happening on deck.[76]

In his defense summation, Pearson kept insisting that his watch officers had "flagrantly" violated his standing orders and maintained that ". . . the loss of the *Boston* is to be attributed to the total neglect of my orders, and to no other cause. . . ." The court refused to accept this line of reasoning. Pearson was found guilty of being "imprudent" rather than negligent. He was sentenced to be "suspended for one year and admonished by the Secy. of the Navy to be more prudent in the future."[77]

It can be seen from the results of the Newton and Pearson trials that the Old Navy was not unduly severe with officers who made errors and lost ships. It was not until the advent of the Civil War that naval officers first came to be vigorously prosecuted for incompetence and effectively driven out of the service if they made serious errors. This was because many of the acting volunteer officers who entered the navy at that time proved to be incompetent, and the navy was obliged to act very harshly towards them, often cashiering them summarily without so much as a court of inquiry or even an informal hearing. If volunteer officers were being treated this way, it was hardly defensible to continue indulgent treatment towards regular officers who made similar mistakes. The tradition of effectively ending the careers of officers of doubtful competence, having gained its first foothold during the Civil War, has remained in the navy ever since.

Many of the acting volunteer officers who served in the engineering branch were a particular disappointment to the department. They were dealt with so summarily that on occasion an injustice was perpetrated. An example of one such case is that of Acting First Assistant Engineer Henry E. Rhoades, Jr., who was serving as chief engineer of the steamer *Sonoma* when she vainly pursued the Confederate raider *Florida*. The chase lasted some thirty-four hours, during which the engineers were exhorted to "crowd all steam." On several occasions, Rhoades protested that the prolonged forced draft steaming would cause an explosion; but his caution was directly overruled by the captain, who told him, "your duty is to obey orders, mine to capture or destroy the *Florida* at any risk." Despite such heroic efforts as throwing sides of bacon into the fireboxes to make a hotter conflagration and generate more steam, the *Florida* escaped and the *Sonoma* limped into New York with crippled engines. A survey revealed that the boilers had to be completely retubed. Five weeks later, Rhoades received a letter from the Navy Department baldly stating that

> A report of the examination of the machinery of the gunboat *Sonoma* shows that it has been seriously injured in consequence of your neglect of duty. You are therefore dismissed [from] the service, and you will, from this date, cease to be an Acting First Assistant Engineer in the Navy.[78]

> [signed] Gideon Welles

Even during the Civil War, however, the treatment of negligence cases was far from consistent. In January 1863, Commander John Downes of the war steamer *Cuyler* ran short of fuel in the Gulf of Mexico and brought his ship into port by burning his spars, gun carriages, and other wooden furniture, as well as lumber purchased from a passing merchantman. "And for all this," Welles noted in his diary, "sends me a dispatch complaining of his engineer and preferring charges against him without any seeming consciousness that he was responsible himself, or blamable."[79] A court-martial found Downes guilty of negligence and sentenced him to be dismissed from the service.[80] Welles commented that

> The sentence is severe but correct, though the punishment may be mitigated. It is necessary, however, to correct a rising error among a certain

class of officers who are inclined to relieve the commander of a ship of responsibility—a pernicious error that would, if acquiesced in, demoralize the service. That his engineer was at fault was doubtless true, but the commander must make hmself acquainted with the condition of his vessel and its equipment.[81]

The conclusion of this discussion of neglect of duty and negligence brings to an end the treatment of common court-martial offenses under the naval justice system for the period from 1800 to 1861. As in the other offenses that we have treated in previous chapters, the pattern of a differential standard of treatment for officers and enlisted men emerges clearly. With regard to thefts, for example, it is obvious that officers actually attempted the most ambitious frauds and embezzlements and that the sums they diverted could occasionally amount to thousands of dollars. With the exception of pursers and pursers' stewards, however, none of the peculating officers we have dealt with was ever obliged to leave the service. Five years' suspension from duty with some loss of pay was the most painful penalty assessed, and this did nothing to alter the offender's standing on the navy list or deprive him of the other prerogatives of his rank.

In the matter of assault, differential treatment was also in evidence. Enlisted men were prosecuted for assault whenever they could be identified as the perpetrators of a physical attack regardless of the circumstances. When officers committed assaults, they usually managed to do it in the context of a duel—an affair of honor—and thus escaped any serious penalties. Even in those few cases, such as that of Lieutenant Sands, where no formal duel was indicated, the perpetrator of the assault was not punished once his apology had been accepted. There are a few cases wherein officers assaulted other officers and enlisted men. In these instances, when charges were brought, the offense was called cruelty and oppression rather than assault and belonged in a different category of transgression.

It was only in the matter of neglect of duty that officers were frequently charged and severely punished while enlisted men were seldom prosecuted. Up until the Civil War, however, another kind of discrimination was practiced in that midshipmen and junior lieutenants convicted of neglect of duty were often cashiered, the most severe penalty that could be applied under the circumstances, and the one most commonly imposed on junior officers for other offenses as well. When senior officers—those holding the rank of commander or above—were found guilty of neglect of duty, even to the extent of having lost a vessel under their command, they were *never* cashiered and seldom even suspended. There were even a few instances where an officer was investigated twice for neglect of duty during the course of his career. Before he lost the *Missouri*, for example, Captain Newton had been investigated by a court of inquiry to determine what role, if any, he had played in the chain of events that led to the explosion of an experimental gun on board the steamer *Princeton* which killed or wounded several prominent government officials. Newton had been commanding officer of the *Princeton* at the time of the incident. Despite the grave nature of the accident that had occurred under his command, Newton was exonerated of all blame.

It should be noted that there are other categories of offenses to be found in the judge advocate general's files which have not been covered in the four preceding chapters. These are, however, of negligible importance since very few men were tried for them. The more common offenses that give us the general picture of the workings of the system and of life in the navy are included in this volume.

Finally, the judge advocate general's records, which consist of literally millions of pages of statements, documents, and testimony, constitute a voluminous and extremely comprehensive source of highly detailed historical data on nearly every aspect of the nineteenth century navy. Sea fights, shipwrecks, accidents, disasters, feuds, controversies, administrative problems, famous voyages of exploration, entire tenures of commodores in charge of squadrons, and many other areas of interest to naval historians are exhaustively detailed and described.

Among historians of the American navy, biographical treatment of important personages has always constituted a disproportionate amount of the writing on the Old Navy. Even a casual perusal of the judge advocate general's files shows that they can be a very rich source of personal information about most naval officers of importance. One can find, for instance, occasions where officers of fame and distinction served as presidents of long-since-forgotten naval courts, passed either harsh or lenient judgments on brother officers, prosecuted enemies, or testified on behalf of friends. It is surprising, indeed, to scan the index of cases and discover how often the famous heroes of the Old Navy were themselves court-martialed and forced to defend their actions or answer for transgressions of the rules before a naval court. There are even a few officers, such as Jesse Duncan Elliott or Uriah Phillips Levy, whose appearances before naval courts were so frequent that a goodly amount of their biographies could be written solely on the basis of this source.

Ultimately, however, the greatest value of the judge advocate general's records lies in the incredible wealth of detailed information they contain about every aspect of the social history of the navy. By familiarizing themselves with this source, modern naval historians can gain invaluable insights into every phase of shipboard life, every nuance of interpersonal relationships that existed between naval personnel of all ranks, and administrative practices relative to an immense variety of subjects. At the present time, this is a sadly neglected field in American naval history, and many scholars have called for it to be opened up and developed. This author can think of no better source of raw data and primary manuscript source material than the judge advocate general's court-martial and court of inquiry records and proceedings.

Chapter IX

Naval Discipline in Perspective

A system of law and justice is nearly always a reflection of the society which it serves. Unless it is arbitrarily and forcefully imposed by conquest, it more or less mirrors the attitudes, mores, and ethical values of its host community. Most of the people not intimately connected with the inner workings of a legal system tend to assume that it is absolute in its procedures, consistent in its interpretation of its ordinances, scrupulous in its judgments, and generally fair and unbiased. They expect that it should constitute a useful tool in protecting the innocent and law-abiding majority from the aggression of the more predatory elements which exist in every human culture and subculture. As a rule, in most settled societies an average citizen seldom has occasion to appear in a law court or defend himself in any serious criminal context. Hence, his knowledge of the system of justice under which he lives is likely to be vague, theoretical, and highly oversimplified.

In contrast to these assumptions, the attitudes held by the policemen, judges, prosecutors, counselors, court functionaries, and hard-core repeating offenders—those persons whose lives and professional careers are bound up in the day-to-day operation of courts and legal systems—are often diametrically opposite. These persons have a different perspective and often a different attitude towards the system they serve. They see the human failings, the "politics," the unfair sentences, the "loopholes," the obvious absurdities and the subtle discriminations that all legal systems feature. They are the ones who are most aware of the gaps between public expectations and actual performance, between the ideal and the real world of the law.

Among military justice systems, these same perspectives exist together with a few additional variables. Military men generally tend to view their legal systems as more rigorous, consistent, and arbitrary than those which serve the civilian community. Tight regulation of behavior is considered much more essential to the workings of a military organization than it is to a civil society. Also, within a military service a minority of the personnel—the officers and senior noncommissioned officers—are always assumed to have considerably more interest in the state of discipline and the effectiveness of the justice system than the "privates" who constitute the majority of the military "community" and have little authority and few responsibilities.

Because of the nature of military life, intimate relations between officers and enlisted men are few and highly restricted. Consequently, the state of morale and the receptivity on the part of the "privates" to the ideals and mission of the service is always something of a mystery or unknown quantity. The officers can never know exactly what their men are thinking, exactly how far they can be trusted, or at what point they might suddenly refuse to follow orders, become actively or passively insubordinate, or even dangerous. The enlisted men outnumber the officers dramatically and in a few extreme cases have been known to escape the bonds of military discipline and impose their own will through acts of mass defiance of authority. The mutiny of the German High Seas Fleet in 1918 is but one example that illustrates this potential.

Therefore, among military officers the state of discipline in the service to which they belong is always a matter of concern and speculation. On a less dramatic and more mundane level, they also concern themselves with disciplinary problems simply because much of the pleasure and psychological satisfaction of military life derives from the smartness, willingness, and agreeableness with which orders are issued, acknowledged, and obeyed. Slackness, peevishness, disrespectfulness, and unwilling or resentful compliance with directives take much of the joy out of being an officer or petty officer. In combat situations, poor disciplinary habits can rob an operation of success or result in a defeat. During emergencies, they can be costly in terms of lost lives or property. In the worst cases, officers and other executive personnel can even find their lives threatened by the men they lead. Perhaps nothing is so profoundly destructive to the morale and effectiveness of a fighting force than the overt fear of mutiny or assassination on the part of the leadership.

Another area of concern in the realm of military discipline is trustworthiness among peers. Officers and noncommissioned officers are consciously indoctrinated and encouraged to develop a high degree of self-discipline and loyalty to their service. That every other officer or petty officer shares this high level of rigorous dedication is implicit in the educational process they undergo. Of course, human nature is much more complex and the idealistic neophyte sooner or later learns that among his peers and superiors there exists approximately the same degrees of vanity, ambitiousness, opportunism, dishonesty, and willingness to flout rules and regulations that characterize society at large and mankind in general. This discovery breeds in turn cynicism, factionalism, intragroup conflicts, bitterness, feuds, and a sense of betrayal, all occurrences common to organized human institutions but destructive to the spirit of good discipline and decent human relations. In the Old Navy, these trends gave rise to what were called "heartburnings," which were as common then as serious morale problems are now.

In fact, the heartburnings, opinions, and complaints that the officers and men of the Old Navy committed to pen and ink are perhaps the most useful sources historians possess for discovering what was uppermost in their minds concerning morale and discipline. Two repositories of such information that are particularly valuable are the social and professional writings of navy men, particularly officers, and the various courts-martial and courts of inquiry recorded in the judge advocate general's records which deal with cases of cruelty, oppression, and the inflicting of punishments.

The writings of nineteenth century naval officers are particularly valuable because they were much closer to the workings of the naval justice system than officers in the contemporary service. Regular officers in the Old Navy generally served for a longer period of time on active duty and sat on literally dozens of courts-martial and courts of inquiry boards. Such tribunals were a regular feature of service life in naval squadrons, particularly on foreign stations. Seldom did the ships of a widely dispersed squadron rendezvous without the opportunity being taken to form court-martial boards and dispose of a backlog of cases. At such times, a prudent commodore generally used officers from one ship to try cases involving others, hoping in that way to achieve some impartiality in the dispensation of justice. The more sizeable ships in the squadron usually were selected arbitrarily to serve as the settings for these tribunals, which were held in the captain's or commodore's day cabin between 1000 and 1400. The practical effect of this was that every legal proceeding and controversy was spread throughout the command, principally through the medium of wardroom gossip soon to be repeated in the steerage and ultimately served up in garbled form on the berth deck.

The officers of the Old Navy had prolonged periods of time between tours of sea duty when they resided ashore "awaiting orders." During such intervals, they were often given short-term assignments to sit on various courts-martial or courts of inquiry being held within the territorial United States. For example, Commander Raphael Semmes spent the years from 1849 through 1851 living in his home at Pensacola. During that time he served on six court-martial boards. A typical summons from the Navy Department for such duty was received by Semmes on 17 November 1849:

Sir: A naval general court-martial, of which you are appointed a member, is ordered to convene on board the U. S. Ship *Raritan*, at Pensacola, Fla. on the first day of December 1849—at which time and place you will appear and report yourself to the presiding officer of the court.

[signed] Wm. Ballard Preston[1]

At one point during this period, orders to serve on disciplinary boards were coming in so fast that Semmes was appointed to serve as judge advocate at a court-martial at Pensacola and almost immediately thereafter received orders to proceed to Memphis to act as judge advocate at a court of inquiry in that city. He was obliged to write to Commodore Rousseau, president of the Memphis court, explaining that he would be delayed in reporting for duty there on account of the previous business in Pensacola.[2] It is possible, by scanning the judge advocate general's records of cases and noting the frequency with which the names of officers residing ashore are listed on the boards of consecutive tribunals, to confirm that the experience of Commander Semmes was typical. Under these circumstances, an officer could easily participate in a score or more of naval courts during a long service career. Because of this, they knew the inner workings of the naval justice system much more intimately than modern naval officers do. They were in a much better position to comment knowledgeably on matters of disciplinary practice and to become reformers.

The irony is that so few of them chose to do so. Only three officers ever truly emerged as prominent students of disciplinary theory and practice. Commodores Robert F. Stockton and Uriah P. Levy were reformers and experimenters who gave much thought and effort to the task of trying to liberalize, rationalize, and humanize the naval justice system. Rear Admiral Samuel Francis Du Pont, on the other hand, was a staunch defender of the status quo and a recognized expert in the history and workings of the orthodox philosophy of naval justice and discipline.

Among the reformers, Levy was the first to emerge publicly. Since he was highly unpopular among certain elements within the navy on account of his Jewish ancestry and because of his status as one of the very few "mustang" officers in the service, the role of a disciplinary maverick suited him well. Since he had served before the mast, Levy claimed to have a special understanding of the common seaman's point of view and a particular abhorrence for flogging. In 1841 he received his first major command, the sloop-of-war *Vandalia*, and put into effect on board her a "system" of discipline that he had been working out in theory for some time.

Levy's system consisted of the almost total abandonment of the usual forms of corporal punishment and the substitution of what he called "moral correctives." For drunkards, he suspended a wooden bottle around their necks. Thieves were made to wear a wooden yoke. When two men attempted to desert, he had them fastened together for several days. For miscellaneous punishments, there was sweeping decks, polishing brass, or riding a wooden horse slung outboard from a mizzen stay for a period of from one to three hours. This last punishment was one that could be inflicted by any officer in charge of a watch on his own authority.[3] Levy also compiled and made public on board the *Vandalia* a "black list" or "blackguard list" which included the names of all the men who were known or thought to be chronic trouble-makers.

Levy's disciplinary system outraged his First Luff, Lieutenant George Mason Hooe. Hooe waited until Levy devised what he considered a particularly bizarre and irregular corrective and then brought charges against him for cruelty and oppression and inflicting an illegal punishment. The charges were based on a chastisement that Levy had evolved for Ship's Boy John Thompson, who had been caught slandering another crewman. When confronted by his captain, Thompson had stated that he had merely been repeating what he had heard other men saying. Levy accused Thompson of acting like a "parrot" and promised to make a real parrot of him. He caused the boy

> to be seized to a gun, his trousers to be let down, and a quantity of tar to be applied to his naked skin, such punishment being highly scandalous and unbecoming the dignity of an officer to inflict.[4]

Not mentioned in the specification is that Levy also had several feathers stuck into the tar to represent the tail of a parrot.

In a statement read before the court-martial board, Levy defended his philosophy at length, stating that

> Commencing . . . as a cabin boy, I made the character, temper, and habits of seamen a close and particular study, and in the forecastle and yardarm had ample opportunities of ascertaining the peculiar characteristics of the sailor, and years of practical illustration has served to convince me that strict discipline, obedience to orders, sobriety and a sense of duty; can be secured without the constant, unwavering and unflinching application of the lash for almost every offence. No one will deny, who are familiar with seamen, that an occasional use of the cat to the refractory, cannot be dispensed with, but my own experience has led me to place a high estimate of the value of a mild and moral system, which sinks deep into the heart,

without the necessity of lacerating the body; of using light punishments for subordinate offences; of efforts to create shame and regret by proper examples and salutory reproofs.[5]

Levy claimed that the results of his system were highly gratifying. "No ship in the Navy had a better or more orderly set of men," he stated. Severe punishments were rare, there was little mutinous spirit or sense of disaffection, and orders were cheerfully obeyed.[6]

The court-martial board had little regard for Levy's arguments, however. Captain John B. Nicholson, the president of the court, spoke for all of his colleagues when he wrote:

> If the service is to exist and prosper, this introduction into it of *systems* by officers on their own responsibilities must be put an end to. The officer who introduces them tramples on the rules and regulations of the service and substitutes his own arbitrary will for the recognized provisions of law. If this is not arrested the day is not distant when seamen will avoid our national ships, because sailors know that if an officer be allowed to substitute his will, the law is practically a nullity, and that there is nothing to protect him from the most tyrannical punishment. A safe and wholesome discipline is impossible except in strict obedience to law and the rightful exercise of lawful authority.[7]

Levy was sentenced to five years' suspension from duty; but this punishment was remitted by President Tyler, who pointed out that the commander was actually following an official directive originating from Secretary of the Navy Levi Woodbury instructing all commanding officers to discontinue flogging where practical and substitute badges of disgrace, fines, and other alternate punishments could be substituted.[8]

A much more powerful voice than Levy's advocating the reform of the naval justice system from within was that of Commodore Robert F. Stockton. Stockton's early career as a midshipman and junior lieutenant had been fairly ordinary; and his attitudes towards disciplinary matters had been orthodox until 1817, when he signed, along with several other junior officers, a memorial to Congress protesting the acquittal of Captain John Orde Creighton and Commodore Oliver Hazard Perry of charges of cruelty and oppression that grew out of their treatment of junior officers on the Mediterranean Station. It was the general feeling of Stockton and his friends that the behavior of several officers who had won fame during the War of 1812 was becoming outrageous and insupportable in the matter of tyrannical behavior towards subordinates.[9]

Upon assuming command of the schooner *Alligator* on 3 April 1821, Stockton ceremoniously staged "the burial of the Cat," throwing a cat-o'-nine-tails overboard and informing his crew that he would never use flogging to discipline them. He succeeded in maintaining order and never had recourse to flogging in any of the ships he subsequently commanded, although as a commodore he did not interfere when his flag captain or subordinate captains whipped their men.[10] So far as can be ascertained, the *Alligator* was the first American naval vessel to make a cruise without a flogging since the adoption of the Articles of War of 1800.

One of Commodore Stockton's favorite devices was to inspire his crews to good behavior by making long, florid speeches, a habit which earned him the nickname of "Gassy Bob." Apparently, this method failed on only one occasion, when the enlistments of the crew of the frigate *Savannah* expired right in the middle of negotiations with Mexican authorities over the surrender of California during the campaign of 1847. Unable to restore them to subordination through rhetoric, the commodore discreetly looked the other way while the ship's officers flogged the men back into good order with exceptional severity.[11]

In 1849 Stockton resigned his commission in the navy and ran successfully for the United States Senate. It was as a senator that he struck his most telling blows for naval reform, helping to mastermind the campaign to outlaw flogging and defeating repeated attempts to get the practice reinstated. It was Stockton who helped devise the summary court system and several other major naval administrative reforms that were adopted between 1850 and 1862.[12] Unfortunately, few letters or memoranda written by Commodore Stockton seem to have survived. Consequently, it is impossible to reconstruct his personal theories and philosophy of naval discipline apart from the speeches he made in the superheated atmosphere of the Senate chamber when he was answering his critics and had little time to be reflective.

Although Stockton and Levy are two of the most prominent gadflies of naval disciplinary theory, they naturally represent the view from the top. One of the most engrossing of their contemporary commentators was a man from the lower decks, one Soloman H. Sanborn, master-at-arms from 1837 to 1839 on board the sloop of war *Fairfield*. In a forty-page pamphlet published in New York in 1840, Sanborn explicitly detailed and strongly criticized numerous examples of illegal punishments which he had witnessed during a cruise on the Brazil Station. He cited the first lieutenant of the *Fairfield*, Hugh Y. Purviance, for numerous coltings and illegal floggings with the cats and also accused several other officers, including Commander Charles Boarman, with complicity in that they allowed these punishments to go unrecorded in the ship's logs. He also described in detail the court-martial on trumped-up charges of a seaman named John Smith when his only crime was that he wished to be discharged at the end of his term of enlistment. Captain Boarman, according to Sanborn, wanted Smith to reenlist and used the disciplinary tribunal in order to keep him on board.[13]

After describing similar atrocities in other ships and soliciting his readers to send him additional information and anecdotes, Sanborn concluded his polemic by claiming that

> The cruelties practiced toward the crews of our ships of war far exceed anything I have ever witnessed where slavery exists in its most odious form; and while *some men* on board our ships of war escape with impunity for offences which deserve the severest punishment, others are severely flogged for UNAVOIDABLE ACCIDENTS.
>
> I could fill volumes with the records of outrages like the foregoing; they almost daily and hourly occurred on board the *Fairfield* during the greater part of her cruise, and I am satisfied that the unjust and illegal treatment of our seamen is one of the PRINCIPAL causes why so few Americans enter our service—THEY PREFER THE ENGLISH Service, where they are better treated, and are sure to be advanced to petty officers.[14]

In contrast to the attitudes of Levy, Stockton, and Sanborn, at least two voices were raised to defend the system of naval discipline as it existed. These belonged to Rear Admiral Samuel Francis Du Pont and Chaplain Fitch W. Taylor. These two men were orthodox thinkers and spoke for the vast majority of the officers who served in the Old Navy. Du Pont, in particular, had been a serious student of disciplinary tactics ever since his days as a midshipman. His brother officers recognized him as an expert in this field. In February 1837 his intimate friend, Alexander Slidell McKenzie, wrote him to solicit advice on the eve of reporting for duty on his maiden cruise as first lieutenant of a major warship. Concerning disciplinary practice, Du Pont wrote:

> The discipline of the service has undergone & is still under a process of change—in some ways for the better—in others for the worse—The men are infinitely more subordinate than formerly—the officers less so—You will find it I think an easy matter to establish most thorough good conduct among the former with one twentieth the whipping heretofore used—Consistency—No favoritism—Great firmness & severity at times—enough to convince them that you can use the lash & that most soundly, but would infinitely prefer not being compelled to resort to it—will readily effect all

you may wish—half the punishments I have seen in the Navy were done in such a manner and under such circumstances that the men were led to believe the officers took personal satisfaction in the matter.[15]

Du Pont went on to advocate that to a limited extent watch officers should be allowed to whip the men on their own authority "if for no other reason but to put a stop to the usual cry that the men won't work in their watches." He advised McKenzie to make as much use as possible of stopping grog as a punishment but regretted that many seamen were taking money in lieu of their liquor ration. He asserted that this practice not only deprived the officers of a significant disciplinary restraint but that the proceeds were often used to purchase liquor ashore and smuggle it back on board, a habit which, "with the present negligent race of midshipn. it is almost impossible to arrest. . . ."

Du Pont concluded his brief treatise on disciplinary practice by recommending that the master-at-arms should "dress and behave like a gentleman" and that the decks should be well lighted with a sentry posted at each berth deck hatchway at all times after dark. With regard to the officers, he advocated that McKenzie should

> exact from the lieutenants a strict attention on deck to their divisions; discourage intimacies with the midshipn., the prevailing sin of the day—as to the latter if anyone can get along with them it will be yourself, who unites firmness of character with mildness of manner—make no difference as to the Pass'd Midshipn. exact from them the regular duties belonging to the grade—never let them off from breaking their leave, which is another of the prevalent encroachments—& keep them to their places whilst in the ship. . . .[16]

This letter is a representative sample of the thinking of a thoughtful and rational advocate of the traditional view of naval discipline. Obviously, Du Pont saw flogging as a powerful tool to be used sparingly and deliberately to establish a psychological ascendancy over the crew. He was alive also to the problems involved in disciplining officers and clearly indicates that in his estimation the midshipmen and passed midshipmen were the single most troublesome element in the service. With all his insight, he was, however, capable of reacting in the strongest and most uncompromising terms to any suggestion that the naval justice system should be comprehensively reformed or significantly altered. Upon purchasing and scanning a copy of *White Jacket,* he wrote to his friend, Senator Henry Winter Davis of Maryland, that

> the author an unalloyed villain, has given us through his talents & lies, the worst stab yet—one that we will reel under, if it do not swamp us—. . . you can conceive an educated, gifted, unprincipled man, brought by his vices to

a whaler & a man of war, ascribing his condition to any thing and any body but his own worthless self, with his intellect keen and his sense of depredation complete—a precious fellow this to [word illegible] of a system or to speak for sailors—his lies are plausible difficult often to meet & yet more false, in the inference they produce, than if they were of the most barefaced description—the time was propitious for his making money too.[17]

In later letters, Du Pont moderated his attitude slightly, but he never acknowledged that *White Jacket* contained any elements of truth, and constantly searched it for passages that might open its author up to libel suits. At one point, he speculated that the whole book was actually the work of Senator Stockton, whom he considered a personal as well as institutional enemy.

During the crisis years following the abolition of flogging, Du Pont exercised considerable influence on the two secretaries of the navy, William A. Graham and James C. Dobbin, who shouldered the burden of administering the service while its disciplinary system was in disarray. His correspondence indicates that he may have been at least partly responsible for Secretary Graham's remarks to Congress upon the occasion of making his annual report for 1851. Discussing the abolition of flogging, the secretary maintained that

The consequences of the change have been thus far detrimental to the service and it is apprehended will become more serious unless speedily remedied.

When vessels arrive in port after a cruise, it is found impossible to keep the men on board until a proper muster, exercise at quarters, and inspection have taken place, which are the means adopted to ascertain whether officers have done their duty in keeping the ships and crews in effective condition, and independently of numerous cases of delinquencies overlooked, or disposed of by discharge, honorable or dishonorable, there have been nearly one hundred trials of enlisted men by court-martial since the passage of the law in question.[18]

Graham urged that a new bureau, which he proposed to call the Bureau of Orders and Discipline, be established within the Navy Department, claiming that it was "highly essential to give accuracy, uniformity, and precision to the administration of justice and discipline" because the abolition of flogging had caused so many enlisted men to be tried by naval courts.[19]

Du Pont and Graham were, of course, concerned with the condition and effectiveness of the naval justice system in its entirety and with trying to preserve as much as possible its traditional assumptions and procedures. The Reverend Fitch W. Taylor, chaplain of the steam frigate *Cumberland,* flagship of the Home Squadron during the Mexican War, had a narrower concern. His task was to uphold and justify the system to one of its victims, Seaman Samuel Jackson, whose court-martial and execution for mutiny was a significant event in Taylor's naval career.

In his capacity as senior chaplain in the squadron, Taylor had prolonged and intimate contact with Jackson between the time he was sentenced and actually executed. During this period, the sailor, who was actually a comely young man not without some subtlety of mind, argued the merits of his case and the appropriateness of his death sentence with his clerical confidante. He pointed out that he was being executed even though he had not killed anyone and had, in fact, committed an offense considered relatively minor in civilian law— certainly not one that he should pay for by being hanged "like a murderer." Taylor was obliged to defend the Articles of War, which he did with great conviction. He explained that

> Your death, though a violent one, will not be the same as the *murders on the gallows,* yours is a punishment at the yard arm, according to the usages of the service at sea; and the charges on which your sentence was based, will be known as they are—a high crime indeed, at sea, but not *murder.*[20]

In an effort to demonstrate the humane nature of a naval hanging, Taylor described the execution of Jackson in minute detail, stressing the measures taken to insure that he would feel no pain. According to his account, a whip was rove through the end of the fore yardarm of the sloop-of-war *St. Marys* with a noose in one end and a quantity of round shot secured to the other. The net full of shot was suspended from the main top by a line attached to a belaying pin on deck and stretched taut over the muzzle of a shotted cannon. This gun was situated in close proximity to the small platform upon which Jackson was to stand and aimed in such a way as to kill or stun him with its muzzle blast on discharge. The shot in the cannon served to part the line over the muzzle so that the net full of shot in the main top plunged towards the deck and jerked the prisoner violently off his platform, breaking his neck quickly and cleanly in the process.[21]

The execution, as described by Taylor, went off exactly as planned —a lugubrious occasion during which everybody from the most hardbitten lieutenant to the most callow ship's boy sympathized with the young prisoner but understood and agreed with the need to carry out the sentence. As the chaplain put it after Jackson had been cut down and rowed ashore,

There we interred *the poor sailor boy* who, in a rash hour, sacrificed his life in his early years.

On the Sabbath succeeding the melancholy exhibition before our fleet, in the execution of this unhappy man, I preached again aboard the *Saint Mary's* [sic]. I found the officers grave—the men depressed, perhaps superstitiously disheartened. A solemn lesson by a solemn scene had been read to that ship's company, as well as the whole squadron, which none who witnessed it could ever forget. . . .[22]

Although the letters, books, and pamphlets written by the men of the Old Navy can provide us with at least a partial overview of their theories, attitudes, and controversies regarding the general topic of naval discipline, there is another source which goes far to illuminate specific instances of disciplinary controversy. This is the relatively small number of courts-martial and courts of inquiry which dealt with charges of cruelty, oppression, and illegal punishment which can be found in the judge advocate general's index of cases. These cases are important because, taken together, they help to establish the permissible limits of disciplinary severity and also because they show instances when theories, laws, and practices parted company and how the resulting problems were resolved. We can also discover what remedies were available for officers and even enlisted men who were caught, or believed they were caught, in the toils of gross and unreasonable naval tyranny.

The very first case of cruelty and oppression to be heard under the Articles of War was that of Captain Christopher Perry of the frigate *General Greene*. At the end of a cruise to the Caribbean in 1800, Perry was prosecuted on charges brought by five of his midshipmen—Simon Martin, William Rhodes, Joseph Boss III, and John and Lewis Durgas. The specifications included accusations that Captain Perry had established a pillory on the quarter-deck and humiliated his midshipmen there in violation of naval regulations, that he had found one midshipman drunk and ordered several ship's boys to urinate in his mouth, and that he had put three midshipmen under arrest for no just cause.[23]

As the trial got under way, a much more complicated and disturbing picture began to emerge which involved nearly all of the *General Greene*'s complement of midshipmen. It appears that the ship had acquired a particularly rowdy and ungovernable contingent of young warrant officers. The first inkling of trouble had occurred after the frigate had been commissioned in Boston and sailed down to Newport, Rhode Island, to complete her complement and stores before clearing for the Caribbean. While friends and relatives were visiting the ship, three of the midshipmen—Thomas Wilson, Abyjah Weston, and Simon

Martin—perpetrated a sexual assault on the wife of a seaman named Joseph Paul. Using their authority as officers, they had sent Paul on an errand and dragged his wife, who was far advanced in pregnancy, into a storeroom, where they stripped her and commenced to establish the order in which they would possess her. Thomas Wilson was elected to go first and had just removed his clothes when a group of seamen forced their way into the compartment and put a stop to the business. Captain Perry arrested the trio and publicly disgraced them in the presence of the crew.[24]

As the cruise progressed, the behavior of the midshipmen degenerated into outright defiance. Most of them were actually "bad characters" and "wastrel sons" of good Boston families who had been sent to sea in hopes that a little naval discipline would reform them. They drank excessively, pilfered ship's stores, slept on watch, fought among themselves, cursed the ship, the lieutenants, and the navy in general. In one act of flagrant blasphemy, Midshipman Rhodes actually tore up a copy of the Articles of War in the presence of Captain Perry.[25]

According to the *General Greene*'s lieutenants, most of whom offered testimony at the trial, Perry's response to these provocations was, if anything, too mild. The punishments he imposed, even if they were more severe than those permitted under the Articles of War, were not harsh enough to bring the midshipmen under control. On one occasion, Perry had tried to devise a "therapeutic" corrective. It was described by Thomas Lang, the frigate's first lieutenant:

> *Question.* (by Captain Perry to Lieutenant Lang) Did Capn. Perry order Thomas Wilson, acting midshipman to be brought upon deck and thrown down on the deck and held there for three men to piss in his mouth?
>
> *A.* He [Wilson] was missing in his watch and found drunk below—Capt. Perry ordered him to be brought upon deck to see what the matter was & he was so far gone in liquor it was thought best for three or four small boys to piss in his mouth and make him vomit.
>
> *Q.* Was the urine administered to Wilson as a remedy or as a Punishment?
>
> *A.* As a remedy—I heard Capt. Perry say it would be of service to him.[26]

After hearing and considering all of the testimony, the court decreed that the five complaining midshipmen should be made to resign from the service and censured Perry for having "been very much wanting in not having the proper discipline and good order kept aboard his Ship. . . ."[27] Why the court did not simply cashier the offending warrant officers is something of a mystery. Perhaps its members believed that if more or less voluntary resignations could be extracted, the men's families would suffer less damage to their reputations.

Closely following the Perry case was another involving Lieutenant John Latimer and Midshipman Joshua Giddings of the brig *Scammel*. Giddings was in charge of a small boat engaged in running errands in the roadstead at Port-au-Prince, Haiti.[28] One of his passengers was Lieutenant Latimer, who requested the midshipman to take him to a merchant ship and wait for him. Giddings's boat was heavily laden, so he asked permission to continue on and deliver his cargo to the frigate *John Adams* and come back for the lieutenant later. When he had off-loaded, Lieutenant John Roche of the *Adams* sent him on yet another mission so that he was delayed in returning to pick up Latimer. When he finally returned to the merchantman, the lieutenant flew into a rage and struck him in the presence of the boat crew and later in view of several members of the crew of the *John Adams*.

Giddings protested these blows and requested Latimer "not to abuse me like a dog, but to arrest me by the Laws of the U. States if I had been guilty of any misdemeanor." Latimer persisted in striking him, however, and taunted him saying, "do you suppose a piece of newspaper [meaning Giddings's warrant] makes you a gentleman?" Giddings replied that

> that piece of newspaper was as good to him—as Lieutenant Latimer's was to him—to which Latimer reply'd do you want another thump? Mr. Giddings said no—but that he might use his pleasure—Mr. Latimer said that if he did give him another, he would knock him over the stern. . . .[29]

The court decided that Latimer had committed a breach of Article XXX of the Articles of War, which prohibited physical punishment of officers and reserved the inflicting of punishments for commanding officers only. It was recommended that Latimer be cashiered, and he was duly dismissed by action of President Jefferson on 10 July 1801.[30]

After the Federal Navy had achieved a better state of organization and eliminated many of the unfit and incapable officers who had originally been recruited, there was a pause in the incidence of cruelty and oppression cases. This lasted until after the War of 1812. Starting in 1816, however, several of the captains and commodores who had served with distinction and won military fame and honors developed an exaggerated sense of prestige and a concomitant conviction that they were somehow immune to prosecution for violations of the Articles of War and particularly the provisions of Article XXX. Their conduct resulted in the development of extremely bitter resentment among the ranks of midshipmen and junior lieutenants. This, in turn, led to several courts-martial of senior officers on charges of oppression.

The first of these cases was heard in the fall of 1816 and involved

Captain John Orde Creighton, commanding officer of the ship of the line *Washington* and flag captain for Commodore Isaac Chauncey on the Mediterranean Station. The charge was brought by Midshipman John Martin, Jr., who specified that Creighton had struck him during an unprovoked attack, falsely accused him of uttering a malicious lie, and "threatened to heave me overboard, assuming thereby an authority not granted by the laws of the U. States, nor by the Sacred principles of Justice."[31] The blow had been delivered on 8 July 1816 while the *Washington* was being sailed out of a crowded anchorage at Gibraltar in the face of flukey winds and contrary tidal currents.

Like her sister ships among the earliest ships of the line built for the navy, the *Washington* was a somewhat poor sailer; and Captain Creighton, whose previous experience had been limited to frigates, was laboring under the double anxiety of handling his ship on a lee shore with the critical eyes of his commodore upon him. In his nervousness, he ordered Martin to take a pull at the fore braces, but the midshipman did not seem to respond immediately. In a sudden fit of anger, Creighton struck him and roughly repeated his order.[32]

Martin brooded over the incident for a couple of days and finally wrote a formal letter to Commodore Chauncey protesting Creighton's treatment of him. Chauncey showed the letter to his flag captain, who then summoned Martin to an interview. On this occasion he lost his temper again and after berating the midshipman soundly accused him of having been the author of a "false and mischievous" missive and threatened to throw him overboard. By now Martin considered himself a grievously offended man. Brushing aside Chauncey's efforts to compose the quarrel, he pressed formal charges against his captain. Just prior to the convening of the tribunal, Commodore Chauncey gave Martin a letter from Creighton offering to compose their difficulties privately. Martin rejected the offer.

During the trial, Martin called to the witness stand a seaman who testified that Creighton had struck him deliberately and in anger. This witness was quickly discredited by the court when it was discovered that he had previously been disrated from captain of the foretop to seaman by order of the captain. Then Creighton called Commodore Chauncey to the stand; and he testified that, under great pressure and anxiety for the safety of his ship, Creighton had merely shoved Martin out of his path while he was moving about the quarter-deck seeing to the proper trimming of the sails.[33]

When Chauncey had completed his testimony, the court arbitrarily decided that it had heard enough evidence. Martin's efforts to call additional witnesses, including two of the *Washington*'s lieutenants, was summarily cut off. Reminding the midshipman that he had been "highly favored in consequence of your youth," they accused him of lack of respect for the court and declared that Creighton's overture to settle the affair privately should have been enough to secure proper satisfaction.

> The Court do believe therefrom, that the prosecution was persisted in from malicious motives & they feel it a duty they owe to the service to express their decided disapprobation of such malicious, frivolous & vexatious accusations.[34]

There were strong hints that Martin had been put up to prosecuting Creighton by other officers, and it is interesting to note that the flag captain made no attempt to call any of his subordinates as witnesses.

It is also noteworthy that some fifteen years later, in January of 1831, Captain Creighton was again court-martialed on charges of cruelty and oppression brought by several midshipmen and junior lieutenants at the conclusion of a cruise on the Brazil Station in the frigate *Hudson*, which he commanded between 1828 and 1830. This time the officers complained that he had threatened to put them in irons, hang them from the yardarm, or otherwise do bodily injury to them. He was alleged to have expelled midshipmen from the steerage and forced them to mess with the crew, deprived lieutenants of shore liberty and other "indulgences," and once kept a lieutenant under confinement below decks for several months without benefit of formal court-martial proceedings.[35]

The principal witness against Creighton on this occasion was Lieutenant William Freelon, who had sailed in the *Hudson* as a passenger en route to join another ship in the Brazil Squadron. He had kept a secret log of Creighton's abuses and sent letters detailing his conduct to his brother who was editor of a newspaper. Consequently, the matter became something of a minor national scandal. Unfortunately, when called to testify, Freelon proved to be an unsatisfactory witness. He refused to furnish notes and memoranda which he claimed to possess and even refused to answer certain questions, citing the Fifth Amendment of the Constitution, an unusual tactic to employ in a naval court.[36] Once again, the court threw out all the charges except one that accused Creighton of falsifying some accounts. He was sentenced "to be admonished by the Honorable Secretary of the Navy to be more circumspect in his accounts for the future."[37]

This gave little satisfaction to the junior officers. The court simply chose to ignore an overwhelming preponderance of testimony which made it clear, despite the poor showing of Lieutenant Freelon, that

Creighton had no gift for leadership and was subject to fits of temper during which he indulged in the most unrestrained verbal abuse of his officers and imposed severe penalties on them in an arbitrary and capricious manner. By now, however, he limited his physical abuse to striking marine enlisted men who appeared on deck in dirty uniforms.[38]

The most celebrated case of bullying and oppression that occurred in the years following the War of 1812 was the court-martial of Captain Oliver Hazard Perry for striking Marine Captain John Heath. The trial, which took place at Port Mahon on 10 January 1817, was actually a double tribunal during which Heath was first tried on charges brought by Perry and then Perry was tried on Heath's accusations. The court-martial board that heard the case was identical in membership to the one that had acquitted Creighton except that now Creighton occupied Perry's former place as President of the court.[39]

The controversy between Perry and Heath had arisen while the newly commissioned frigate *Java* was enroute to join the Mediterranean Squadron. The marine contingent in the ship was a particularly unruly and unsoldierly group, and Captain Heath seemed to be making little headway in disciplining them. Perry became increasingly exasperated but held his impatience in check until two privates jumped overboard in Naples harbor with the obvious intention of deserting. Perry ordered the marines mustered to see who the missing men were. Heath never came on deck to give the necessary orders to the sergeants. There was considerable confusion until one of the *Java*'s midshipmen stepped in and organized the muster. Finally, the dilatory Heath made his appearance but consumed so much time calling the roll that Perry asked him with some asperity if he "intended to take all night about it." Heath then made his report, and Perry told him to "go below, I have no further need of your services."[40]

This dismissal was both stark and ambiguous. Was Heath excused for the moment or was he relieved of his command or was he temporarily suspended from duty? He waited a few days and then penned a note to Perry:

> Sir: On the evening of the 16th Inst. I was ordered below by you, from the quarter-deck of this ship with these words, or to this effect "I have no further use of your services on board this ship."
>
> I have waited until this moment to know why I have been thus treated & being ignorant of the Cause request my arrest & charges.[41]

The letter was delivered to Perry at 2300 on 18 December 1816 after he had been ashore at a party, where he had consumed a considerable quantity of liquor. He immediately sent for Heath and began to reprimand him heatedly. The captain made no reply but heard Perry out with "a sardonic grin on his face & a Contemptuous look."[42] Goaded by Heath's bearing, Perry ordered him to remain silent and threatened to put him in irons. Heath replied, "very good, sir," whereupon Perry struck him and ordered the sentries to take him below and iron him. Later he reconsidered and placed Heath in his cabin under guard.

Out of this incident, Heath extracted a charge of oppression, which he lodged against Perry, while the latter taxed Heath with disobedience of orders, writing a disrespectful letter, and contempt for his superior officer.[43] The court found Heath guilty and sentenced him to be reprimanded by Commodore Chauncey. It then considered Perry's actions and found him guilty of using improper language to Heath and striking him. He was sentenced to receive a private reprimand from the commodore, a light penalty assessed mainly as a formality. Perry had offered Heath an apology before the verdict of the court had become known, and in the members' eyes this went a considerable way towards mitigating his offense.[44] Although the Heath-Perry affair was officially closed with the disbanding of the court, the two men subsequently fought a token duel in which, by prearrangement, no one was harmed.[45]

The outcome of the Creighton and Perry cases, coming as they did less than two months apart, made it clear to the junior officers that their superiors could not be easily or satisfactorily prosecuted for violations of Article XXX. Perhaps for this reason, few cruelty and oppression charges were lodged during the 1820s; and when they began to reappear in the 1830s, the accused parties were mostly relatively junior master commandants and lieutenants commanding. For example, on 11 August 1834, Master Commandant Thomas Newell was court-martialed on charges of

> Unofficerlike and ungentlemanly conduct, neglect of duty, Incapacity, Scandalous Conduct & Conduct unbecoming an officer and a gentleman, Oppressive Conduct, unofficerlike conduct & want of proper respect to the Flag of the U. S."[46]

All of these charges, supported by dozens of specifications, were brought against Newell by Surgeon John S. Wiley and Assistant Surgeon Euclid Boland of the sloop of war *St. Louis*. Some of them related to accidental groundings and related attempts to falsify the ship's log, but the oppressive conduct charge was obviously the one that meant the most to the prosecutors. Its specifications appear to have been the best founded and most damaging ones. In fact, this was so much the case that although Newell was found substantially innocent of all the other charges preferred against him in August and given a perfunctory sentence, he was immediately court-martialed again on 6 September 1834 on charges of oppression, disobedience of orders, and neglect of duty.[47]

During the second trial, the two surgeons and other officers of the *St. Louis* successfully demonstrated that Newell had been unduly harsh in his treatment of the midshipmen, had humiliated them by addressing them in "profane language, and words too gross and indecent to be repeated," and had punished them in such ways as to indicate complete "ignorance of the customs and traditions of the sea." Newell's defense consisted of trying to show that the surgeons, and particularly the "wily" Mr. Wiley, had tried to turn the ship's warrant officers and junior lieutenants against him, allegations which were supported by the testimony of the *St. Louis'* senior lieutenants. The court found Newell guilty and sentenced him "to be suspended from all command in the Navy of the United States for the period and term of five years. . . ."[48]

Secretary of the Navy Mahlon Dickerson, who had shown a decided partiality to Newell during the course of his first court-martial, mitigated the sentence to two years' suspension from command. In an unusual and highly successful counteroffensive, Newell employed the period of his suspension to bring charges against each of the officers who had testified against him and succeeded in getting them all found guilty and cashiered.[49] In their turn, these officers, still led by the two surgeons, memorialized the President, seeking to be reinstated, but apparently met with little success.

The year 1841 saw two cases brought to trial in which for the first time an officer was prosecuted for inflicting illegal punishments on enlisted personnel. On 8 June, Commander William H. Latimer was court-martialed on specifications that alleged that he had, while in command of the sloop of war *Cyane*, knocked down, kicked, and stomped Seaman James Cobett after the latter had been reported to him by one of the lieutenants for mutinous conduct. He also

> did cruelly, oppressively, and illegally order Lorenzo D. Pierpont [schoolmaster of the *Cyane*] to keep school for the apprentice boys, he being then on the sick list, reported by the surgeon to be unfit for duty & being in fact unfit for duty.

In addition to these specifications, it was also mentioned that he had struck four other crewmen at various times and inflicted floggings in excess of twelve lashes without benefit of court-martial proceedings.[50]

The Latimer court-martial is an unusually interesting one because the charges were preferred once again by the ship's surgeon, establishing—as does the case of Surgeon Sherman cited in Chapter VII and others—that the medical officers bore the brunt of the effort to curb excessive disciplinary practices after 1830. It is also of interest because Commander Latimer raised some rather unique and revealing arguments in defense of his actions. The weight of eyewitness testimony on the part of both officers and enlisted men was sufficiently conclusive to convince the court that all of the specific acts mentioned in the specifications had indeed taken place. Latimer's officers were so alienated from him that not a single one of them would testify in his defense, and it was evident that they had not supported him on shipboard either.

In his defense summation, Latimer denied that striking or kicking enlisted men constituted an illegal punishment. He pointed out that the Articles of War never mentioned kicks or blows and only forbade the inflicting of a punishment beyond twelve lashes without benefit of a court-martial. In Latimer's opinion, a kick or blow actually constituted a punishment of a lesser or milder degree than a dozen with the cats.[51] He defended his practice of administering twenty-four or thirty-six lashes on his own authority. He explained the system of multiple charges for serious offenses—in effect the same policy Edward Preble had followed during his cruise in the *Constitution* in the days of the Barbary Wars and used by some officers ever since that time. He deplored the cumbersome nature of courts-martial and advocated the institution of a lesser tribunal, which he called a "drum head court-martial." This would allow a commanding officer to punish sailors for crimes that were too serious to be punished with a mere dozen lashes but not worthy of a full-dress court-martial.[52]

The court found Latimer guilty and sentenced him to a reprimand and suspended him from rank and command for three years. The verdict was accompanied by a memorandum which stated that all of the members of the court had known Latimer well and respected his thirty-two years of service in the navy. Therefore, they hoped that the Secretary of the Navy would see fit to remit the part of his sentence that called for his suspension from duty.[53] Secretary George E. Badger opted to impose the full sentence, however, an act which Latimer tried to counter by writing directly to the President, citing the cases of other officers whose sentences for oppression had been reduced, including that of Master Commandant Newell. The letter was accompanied by another written by Commodore Isaac Hull requesting that Latimer be given the benefit of the doubt.[54]

None of it did any good. Latimer's sentence stood, and he went ashore for three years. A decade later, he stood trial again on charges of administering illegal punishment, disobedience of orders, scandalous conduct, neglect of duty, tyrannical and oppressive conduct, and conduct unbecoming an officer and a gentleman. On this occasion, he was again censured but, perhaps in deference to the fact that he was now a captain, he was only placed on furlough for twelve months.[55]

Soon after the Latimer trial, Lieutenant John Rodgers was charged with inflicting illegal punishments on marine enlisted men. Rodgers had been involved in the campaign against the Seminole indians in Florida during 1841 and had commanded in succession the brig *Jefferson* and schooner *Wave*. During his forays into the swamps, he had experienced a considerable amount of drunkenness among his men and particularly the marine detachment, which came into frequent contact with Indian traders and purchased a good deal of illicit liquor. Rodgers chose on one occasion to deal with this problem by imposing severe floggings on four marines who had upset two boats while intoxicated. One of the marines who received approximately forty lashes later died while under the care of a naval surgeon at Indian Key.[56]

When the *Wave* returned to her home port at Norfolk, Marine Lieutenant Robert C. Tansill preferred five charges of cruelty and improper punishment against Rodgers and in one specification indicated that he was responsible for the death of the man who had expired at Indian Key. In a letter to the Navy Department, Rodgers admitted that he had inflicted lashes in excess of the amount permitted by the regulations because

> The men were charged with stealing liquor & the charge can be proved. By the law defining the ration and making it part of the contract with the men we were obliged to carry the whiskey [on a river expedition]. We had no place other than the canoes to carry it in; it was exposed; drunkenness endangered in those small boats not only the lives of the offenders but of those who might attempt to succor them. The men punished had actually capsized two small boats, lost part of their arms, ammunition and provisions, besides putting the lives of several people in jeopardy. The risk was greater because the water was deep and we were far from land with canoes laden down nearly to the water's edge . . . It is notorious in the navy that twelve lashes with the cat will not prevent many sailors from indulging in a vice so dear to their hearts; it was absolutely necessary that the men should be kept sober, we had no place of confinement, we could not dispense with the offender's services, a court-martial was in the circumstances impossible, by promptness and severity only could the crime be repressed.[57]

The surgeon who had attended the dead marine explained in a supplementary letter that he had died of tuberculosis. Secretary of the Navy Abel P. Upshur reviewed the Rodgers controversy; and while he did not agree that conditions in Florida justified Rodgers' disregard for the regulations, he quashed the charges on the grounds that the lieutenant did not properly understand them and was therefore not guilty of a deliberate violation. Undaunted, Tansill tried again, submitting a charge stating that Rodgers "did punish or cause men to be punished in a cruel and illegal manner . . . ," This charge was also dismissed by Upshur on the grounds that it was too vague. Tansill continued his vendetta against Rodgers and other officers who had served in Florida until Upshur's successor, David Henshaw, ordered him dismissed from the Marine Corps. President Tyler intervened, however; and the Rodgers-Tansill dispute died out without noticeable effect on either man's career.[58]

Of course, the best-known instance of cruelty and oppression to be investigated during the period from 1800 to 1862 was the case of Lieutenant Charles Wilkes, who commanded the navy's first major scientific expedition on a voyage that lasted from 1838 to 1842. The Wilkes Expedition was badly organized, poorly equipped, inadequately provisioned, and charged with tasks of almost unreasonable difficulty. Nevertheless, Wilkes managed to keep things together and to carry out most of his assignments; but the methods he was obliged to resort to were so drastic that upon his return he stood court-martial on charges of oppression, cruelty, disobedience of orders, inflicting illegal punishment, illegally detaching men from the service, scandalous conduct tending to the destruction of good morals, scandalous conduct unbecoming an officer, cruelty, and oppression. After a long and tedious proceeding, which actually constitutes a unique history of the entire expedition as seen from its underside, Wilkes was exonerated of all charges except those relating to illegal punishment, for which he was reprimanded. From that time on, however, the reputation of being one of the Old Navy's most fearsome martinets followed him wherever he went.[59]

One of the more unusual cases involving illegal punishment was that of Lieutenant Murray Mason. In this instance, the lieutenant was tried for an act which was technically illegal but sanctioned by tradition and usage, the "mastheading" of a midshipman. Mastheading was a customary punishment for junior warrant officers, a practice which the Old Navy had inherited from the British. It consisted of sending a minor offender to the highest point of the foremast, the peak located above the royals where there were no yardarms, footropes, shrouds, or trestle trees. The offender was obliged to wrap his arms and legs around the bole of the royal mast and support himself in that position until called down again, usually a matter of hours.

One afternoon in July of 1842, Lieutenant Mason, acting in his capacity as First Luff of the sloop-of-war *Cyane*, ordered Midshipman H. G. D. Brown to the fore top masthead as a punishment for disobeying the orders of Acting Master Francis E. Baker. Brown remained there from about one o'clock until dusk. When he had recovered from the ordeal, the midshipman wrote a letter of protest to Commodore Thomas ap Catesby Jones, who promptly brought charges against Mason for the unlawful punishment of an officer.[60]

The resulting tribunal, which convened on 14 July 1842, quickly became a forum for the airing of conflicting theories on the disciplining of junior officers and midshipmen. Lieutenant Mason made his case by calling several lieutenants and asking them if they regarded confinement to quarters, watch and watch, and mastheading as customary correctives for midshipmen. All of them answered in the affirmative. A few of Mason's witnesses were also asked if they had ever heard any midshipman complain about having been sent to the masthead. Again they answered "yes," whereupon Mason then asked if the practice had been continued after the complaints had been made, and the reply was again in the affirmative.[61]

On the basis of this testimony, Lieutenant Mason wrote out a defense summation defending the practice of assigning minor punishments to midshipmen in lieu of the more drastic penalties called for in the Articles of War:

> The high military offence of "disobedience of Orders" which would have justly dismissed an officer of experience from the service, would appear unnecessarily severe when awarded to a midshipman scarcely emerged from boyhood, and who from want of that experience which his limited period of service has precluded, is, in a great measure ignorant of the obligation that he owes to the Service and to his superior officers. For that reason, the Usage and Custom of the service, have sanctioned . . . a resort to other modes of punishment less severe, but not less effectual, such as Quarantine [i.e., confinement to quarters], Watch and Watch, Sending aloft, etc.[62]

The court seemed to half agree with Mason. Although his actions were a clear violation of Article XXX, which prescribed suspension from duty or confinement as the only minor punishments for officers and those only by action of a commanding officer under normal circumstances, Lieutenant Mason was merely sentenced to "be privately reprimanded by the Commander-in-Chief of the squadron."[63] This punishment was a slap on the wrist, and Commodore Jones refused to confirm it. Instead, he sent a blistering letter back to the court ordering them to alter the sentence to a public reprimand and leaving no doubt that he intended to make an example of Mason.

The reason for this was that Jones had some years previously sat on the court-martial board that had tried Captain George C. Reid for mastheading a midshipman, and the experience was still vivid in his memory. After criticizing the court for allowing Mason to develop a defense based on arguments as vague as the customs and usages of the service, he recollected that

> The excitement produced at *home* both in and out of the Navy, and the sympathy which was felt everywhere for [Midshipman] Wilson, must be fresh in the recollection of every member of this court and so far as my knowledge extends, the only fault found anywhere with the sentence of the Court which tried Captain Reid, was that three years suspension was not just measure of retribution for so great an indignity offered to a young officer of the Navy.

Warming to his subject, the Commodore continued by pointing out that since the *Cyane*'s commanding officer was on board at the time Brown was sent to the masthead, Lieutenant Mason had no legal authority to assign any punishments. He elaborated at length on the theory and practice of discipline in the navy, stressing particularly the need to safeguard the honor and dignity of officers of all ranks. This, he maintained, was so that they would not find themselves degraded and insulted without means of redress "other than by their own hand." He concluded with a harsh condemnation of the court that fairly simmered with indignation:

> The accused is declared to be guilty of an open violation of the law, of *publicly* inflicting *unlawful* punishment on an officer of the Navy, whose feelings and rights it would seem the accused entirely disregarded, in as much as he would not allow Midshipman Brown to *speak in his own defence*, yet so tenacious is the Court, and so watchful are its members over the feelings of the offender, as to sentence him to a *private* tete-a-tete with the Commodore of the Squadron, as a punishment for an *open* and *palpable* violation of a *Law!*—Yes, for the identical offence for which another Court-Martial, governed by the same Laws, Rules, and Regulations, sentenced a Captain of the Navy, to three years suspension which sentence he worked out to the uttermost end!![64]

In reading this letter, it is hard to recognize the man who in the fullness of time stood trial himself on charges of oppression and scandalous conduct stemming in part from his treatment of his junior lieutenants and midshipmen during a commission on the Pacific Station between 1848 and 1850.[65]

Of course, not every charge of cruelty and oppression was a straightforward matter of quarter-deck tyranny. In September of 1843, for instance, Lieutenant Raphael Semmes brought charges of cruelty and oppression and using provoking and reproachful words, gestures, and menaces against Commodore Alexander Dallas.[66] These accusations grew out of a feud that had developed between the two men when Semmes had tried to get Dallas to appoint his brother-in-law, Mr. Francis Spencer, to the post of chief clerk of the Pensacola Navy Yard. Dallas, acting in his capacity as commandant of the yard, ignored the request of Semmes, who was serving as one of his lieutenants, and instead appointed the son of one of his friends, a young man named Edwin B. Vanbaun.

Acting in a spirit of vengeance, Semmes wrote to the Navy Department accusing Dallas of making out and signing a false muster, and describing the new chief clerk as being absent from his post too frequently and careless about the discharge of his duties. When Dallas received word of Semmes's actions, a row ensued. The commodore roundly reviled Semmes in the presence of witnesses and suspended him from duty for six weeks, during which time he was to be confined to his quarters. Half an hour later, Dallas was standing in the orderly room when Semmes knocked on the door and handed a letter to Commander George A. Hollins, the executive officer of the yard. This act sent the commodore into a rage. Seeing Dallas stalking towards him, Semmes began to run back to his quarters. The commodore pursued him as far as the veranda, where he stood firing salvo after salvo of threats and curses at the lieutenant's rapidly retreating backside.[67]

A court-martial was convened to try Dallas both for the conduct of his chief clerk and for his treatment of Semmes. The commodore beat down the earlier charges by explaining that although Vanbaun was seldom present at the yard, his duties were discharged by his father, an arrangement which Dallas had known would be followed even before the young man was put on the payroll. He defended his conduct in the orderly room by calling attention to Semmes's boldness in leaving his quarters so soon after being sent there. He was fully exonerated by the court.[68]

Perhaps the most trivial and inconsequential courts-martial ever heard by naval courts involved a few courts-martial for cruelty and oppression relating to the use of profanity. On 14 February 1851, Acting Master's Mate Hamilton Bell was tried on a charge of "Using improper, unbecoming, and unofficerlike language to Samuel Merritt, an ordinary seaman belonging to the U. S. Ship *St. Louis.*" The charge was preferred by Seaman Merritt on the basis of Article III of the Articles of War, which forbade "profane swearing" on the part of "Any officer, or other person in the navy." Witnesses established that Bell had cursed Merritt in profane terms after the latter had made an error which resulted in some damage to the ship's rigging. Bell was sentenced "To be dismissed from the U. S. Ship *St. Louis* and sent home at the public charge; on his arrival in the U. S. to be discharged from the service." This sentence was simply "Disapproved" by the commodore of Bell's squadron and he never even left his ship.[69] Cursing and swearing was simply so common in the Old Navy that any attempt to suppress it through the mechanisms of the naval court system would have been impractical. Apparently, this consideration did not stop an occasional sea lawyer like Merritt from invoking Article III, but this was very rare.

Certainly not every case of cruelty and oppression that occurred in the navy was reported and resulted in a court-martial. It is impossible to establish just how many cases of gross or subtle abuse of subordinates were never recorded and are now forgotten. Yeoman Downey of the *Portsmouth* gives some idea of the degree of abuse that a seaman could suffer at the hands of an officer without official notice being taken. He recorded an incident that he witnessed on a march overland during the campaign to take Los Angeles in 1847.

At one bivouac, a group of drunken sailors were "growling" and grumbling in a tent and making considerable noise. Eventually, one of them stumbled outside and issued a slurred and almost incoherent challenge to his tent mates to come out and fight. At this point, Lieutenant Edward Higgins intervened. He rushed up to the man and struck him over the head with his cutlass. A second blow felled the sailor, who lay on the ground

> stunned and motionless while the officer continued to belabor him, inflicting cuts in two places on his head, and then was only stopped by two officers who were *men*, who jumped in and dragged him off.[70]

Downey infers throughout this account that Higgins was himself a hard drinker and may have been inebriated when he made this attack.

Despite instances such as the one above, this examination of courts-martial and courts of inquiry that heard charges of cruelty, oppression, and the inflicting of illegal punishment shows that naval officers were subject to some restraint in their treatment of subordinates. Although oppression charges were not common except for a brief period in the late 1830s and early 1840s, they were lodged and occasionally resulted in penalties of some seriousness being assessed against particularly obnoxious quarter-deck tyrants. It is interesting to note that a few officers—John Orde Creighton, William Latimer, and Joshua Sands—stood trial more than once on oppression charges.[71] Apparently, one brush with the strictures of Articles III and XXX was not enough to curb their overbearing natures. Another obvious fact is that it was very hard to secure both a conviction and a meaningful sentence against an officer, particularly an officer of great seniority, on the complaint of one or more subordinates.

One final perspective on the state of discipline within the Old Navy is to be gained from the comments and writings of the various secretaries of the navy that served from 1800 to 1865. These men were actually the chief disciplinarians of the service and, in the absence of a regular judge advocate general, the only persons in a position from which the full range and scope of the naval justice system could be surveyed. As the principal reviewers of every case tried in a naval court and as the conduit through which appeals to the president were normally channeled, they were privy to the innermost secrets of the underside of naval administration. They were also "outsiders," civilian politicians for the most part, who had little professional connection with the naval establishment. They had everything to gain by promoting a greater degree of order, fidelity to regulations, and subordination among all ranks.

Of course, not all secretaries of the navy were particularly competent or energetic; and most were not inclined to pay close attention to the state of discipline within the service or even to comment on it at length. Of those who were so inclined, the chief preoccupation, except for the crisis years from 1850 to 1855, was the state of discipline and subordination among the officers. The enlisted men were simply too transient, too insignificant as individuals, and too far removed from the lofty plane upon which the secretaries resided to be of much interest to them. Consequently, most of the remarks and attitudes which they recorded on the subject of discipline involve the state of subordination and the good conduct, or lack of it, of the officers.

The first Secretary of the Navy, Benjamin Stoddert, discovered how difficult the senior captains could be to manage when he offended several of them in establishing the order of precedence on the first navy list. Rivalries, jealousies, and resentments stemming from this issue made it extremely hard for the Navy Department to administer the service. It was particularly difficult to arrange duties and assignments because it was well known that many officers could not or would not work together.[72]

John Adams, the first President to have a navy to administer, also noted the spirit of uncooperativeness and insubordination that characterized the service. He took a harsh attitude towards slackness, as befitted the author of the earliest Articles of War, and once reprimanded the entire officer corps *en masse* for their tendency to write letters to relatives, friends, and newspapers critical of the internal administration of the Navy Department. He directed that all such writings should cease and threatened any officer who violated this order with court-martial proceedings. Adams was also concerned about the behavior of the sailors, particularly while on shore. He believed that the men were too prone to visit prostitutes and consequently returned to duty diseased and inefficient. He instructed captains to remain at sea as much as possible and curtail the granting of liberty to an absolute minimum.[73]

As political appointees, the secretaries were particularly sensitive to the repercussions of controversies involving naval discipline on public opinion. When Commodore David Porter brought charges in 1823 against Lieutenant Beverly Kennon for "Defaming his character," Secretary Samuel Southard wrote him a letter claiming that the court-martial had "excited" the country and expressing the hope that in the future high-ranking officers "would perceive the necessity of avoiding . . . whatever will have a tendency to end in court action." Porter had little sympathy for the secretary's dislike of "court action," which was the general attitude of most of the men who governed the navy from Washington. He wrote back that

> Courts-martial are at all times inconvenient, and occasion more or less "public excitement." Yet they are a necessary evil, are provided for by the Laws of the Government of the Navy, are the only proper appeal of those in the Navy who believe themselves injured, [and] it is made the duty of every officer to prevent a violation of the Laws which regulate them, and this duty I felt myself in the performance of when I arrested and brought to trial Lieut. Kennon.[74]

In other words, courts-martial were a matter of honor and a source of vindication for the officers of the navy, and they would have them whether or not the secretaries found them inexpedient.

This kind of attitude, which regulated each successive secretary to a more-or-less negligible force in matters of naval regulation and discipline—a transient figure with only a brief tenure in office—drove some of them to fury. Secretary James K. Paulding made officer discipline the chief concern of his administration from 1838 to 1841. In March of 1839, he wrote that

the President [Van Buren] stands by me manfully and please God, if I live
and Congress does not counteract me, I will make both high and low,
young and old, know who is their master, before I have done with them.[75]

In spite of his determination, Paulding made little headway. Although
he earned the enmity of many officers, he left the navy pretty much as
he found it.

To some extent, much of the problem that the navy experienced in
establishing a proper spirit of subordination stemmed from the denial
of the rank of admiral to the navy's officers. Instead of having an
orderly chain of command, with a fleet admiral, a few vice-admirals,
and several well-placed rear admirals that he could transmit his orders
through, each secretary was obliged to deal with an unstructured collection of captains and honorary commodores who were determined
not to be subordinate to one another. Also, after twenty or thirty years
in grade with secretaries coming and going, the captains were not inclined to pay much attention to them.

Secretary of the Navy Abel Parker Upshur was particularly sensitive
to the tendency of senior officers to ignore the department because they
were effectively beyond its grasp. In 1842, he complained that

> The belief, hitherto prevailing, that an officer of any standing [in the
> navy] could not be driven out of it . . . has had a strong influence in
> ruining its discipline and corrupting its morals and manners.
> The necessity of some mode of proceeding, by which the Navy may be
> rid of the incompetent as well as the guilty is universally admitted.[76]

As a trained lawyer, Upshur's sense of propriety was outraged by the
lack of status and system in naval law and by the sketchy and inadequate nature of the Articles of War and the *Naval Regulations*. Unfortunately, his effort to draft new regulations, to which he devoted
considerable time and attention, was frustrated by congressional inattention and dilatoriness.

A few secretaries, including Levi Woodbury and George Bancroft,
also addressed themselves to the effort to reform disciplinary practices
for the enlisted men; but for the most part, this was limited to trying
to reduce the incidence of flogging and eliminating some of the irregular practices indulged in with regard to the use of colts and starters.
Apparently, only Secretary William A. Graham, whose tenure in the
Navy Department coincided with the abolition of flogging, seemed to
have any real fear that the navy's enlisted personnel might be seriously
out of control.

One final perspective of naval discipline that existed was that held
by the general public. At this juncture in time, it is hard to reconstruct

a comprehensive picture of how the American public viewed naval disciplinary policy. There were a few major controversies wherein public opinion played a major role, such as the *Somers* affair and the campaign to abolish flogging. In each case, although there were spokesmen on both sides of the issues, the preponderance of public opinion was in favor of a more lenient, reforming approach and against the strict and traditional attitudes held by most naval officers.

In at least one case, the public was able to intervene directly for the purpose of setting aside a decision arrived at by a naval court. This was the situation of Lieutenant Charles G. Hunter, who was court-martialed by Commodore Matthew C. Perry for insubordination in the wake of an unauthorized attack he made on the town of Alvarado during the Mexican War.[77] Acting under the impetus of Perry's desire to crush Hunter, a court made up of officers from the Home Squadron found him guilty, dismissed him from the squadron, and sent him back to the United States in disgrace.

When he arrived in New York, Hunter's cause was taken up by Whig newspapers seeking to embarrass the Democratic administration of President Polk. The lieutenant was hailed as a hero who had stormed a veritable Gibraltar in an "old Boston-Bangor steamboat." He was tendered banquets, presented with ceremonial swords, given an escort of militia for a triumphal procession to his hometown of Trenton, New Jersey, and was generally lionized as a martyred hero. By public acclamation, he received the nickname "Alvarado" Hunter, and popular pressure forced President Polk to quash the court-martial's sentence and restore him to duty.[78]

This review of the contemporary perspectives that were held on the status and problems of the disciplinary system of the Old Navy cannot, within the limits of a single chapter, be totally comprehensive. It does point out, however, that naval justice was a complex and controversial subject and that there were at least three significant points of view.

The officers were overwhelmingly preoccupied with the fine points of technique, methodology, and propriety. Typically, they concerned themselves with the minor issues within the system and, with the notable exception of Commodores Stockton and Levy, left the question of basic principles and major reforms to the civilians. When provoked by attacks upon the system from outside the service, they would staunchly defend the conservative principles of the Articles of War. Left to themselves, however, they tended to engage in hair-splitting over questions of honor, such as those involved in the practice of mast-heading midshipmen.

Among the officers, differences centered around such specific theoretical questions as how best to set examples, secure subordination, safeguard honor, accomplish the objectives of the Articles of War, resolve the contradictions between custom and usage and the letter of the law, and how to handle those commanders who pushed the general atmosphere of severity too far in the direction of cruelty and oppression.

The secretaries and, perhaps by extension, some of the presidents as well, were mostly concerned with the dangerous state of indiscipline and insubordination which they perceived among the senior officers and the turbulent behavior and disorderly character of many of the midshipmen. Occasionally problems relating to the state of discipline among the enlisted men also intruded upon the consciousness of the Navy Department, as was the case during the 1850s.

The public at large probably had little comprehension of the technical and routine functions of the naval justice system. They could, however, be galvanized at various times by cases that seemed to feature undue harshness or slavish adherence to the letter of the law and the pitiless customs of the sea at the expense of some apparently harmless individual. This was particularly the case when the victim of the system appeared to be young or humble and his superiors were suspected of taking an unreasonably narrow approach or an unusually autocratic attitude towards him.

Chapter X

Conclusion

The justice system which evolved within the United States Navy between 1800 and 1861 was, in retrospect, something of an anomaly. From the beginning it was characterized by ideological confusion which to some extent mirrored that of the larger society of which the Old Navy was a part. It was also a component of government that was small and intimate by the standards of our own times; and, therefore, its workings were more vulnerable to political considerations, favoritism, and a truly crippling degree of outside interference, particularly by Congress. It existed during a time of highly conspicuous class differences. Consequently, its treatment of enlisted offenders was remarkably different from its policies towards officers, particularly in the matter of setting aside verdicts and sentences. Finally, it was, as a legal system, poorly developed, a problem which was not seriously rectified until a coherent set of navy regulations was introduced in 1862. Its basic organic law, the Articles of War of 1800, was sketchy and rudimentary; and its body of statutory law resided in a state of confusion bordering on chaos, as repeated attempts to reform the *Naval Regulations* collapsed in the face of congressional indifference prior to 1862.

The ideological problems that characterized naval disciplinary practice were rooted in the peculiar nature of the United States itself and in its unique approach to government and the status of individuals within a society. In 1800, when the Articles of War were framed, America was still a pioneer exponent of constitutional government and the only nation on earth except for revolutionary France to have a written bill of rights as part of its basic system of law. These rights were granted to American citizens of all ranks and stations. They were widely understood to be guarantees of protection against judicial tyranny and were considered to be the very cornerstones of political liberty.

Unfortunately, the granting of such widely dispersed guarantees was not universally applauded, particularly by the more conservative wing of the Federalist Party, which was the most active political sponsor of the early navy. The navy was an element of society that assumed from the beginning that it could never grant to its personnel the same rights and immunities possessed by ordinary citizens and still be able to function. Indeed, it seemed to assume that it had to be even more draconian in some respects than was the usual case in European-style military organizations of that era. This was precisely because its sailors and marines were accustomed to a more liberal civilian political culture. It was taken for granted that the imperatives of naval service made it necessary to suspend constitutional rights and guarantees among its personnel.

Ultimately, the American conscience could never quite accept such a stark cleavage between the practices of civil law and the workings of the naval justice system. Isolated instances of naval tyranny became matters of public scandal. The officers quickly learned to use political connections and leverage to mitigate the rigors of the Articles of War and set aside punishments. Those who were skilled at such maneuvering could purchase for themselves a high degree of immunity from the strictures of legitimate military discipline. Civilian reformers mounted an effective campaign that forced the navy to set aside the lash in spite of the almost unanimous resistance of the entire naval establishment. Stinging literary exposes such as Melville's *White Jacket* pointed out in painstaking detail just how divergent naval justice was from the civilian practice and dramatized how completely the navy ignored the political and libertarian ideals of the larger community.

Under this pressure, the navy gave ground grudgingly in a process that began in the storm of controversy that attended the execution of the *Somers* mutineers, attained its stride with the abolition of flogging in 1850, and culminated in the thorough overhaul of the rules and regulations that took place in 1862. Its ultimate achievement was the scrapping of the Articles of War in 1950 in favor of the Uniform Code of Military Justice.

It is significant that all of these changes have been forced upon the navy from without. Traditional opinion within the service has always held that each successive reform would bring ruin and collapse. Even though the *ideal* of Roman discipline was never attained, the original attitude of John Adams that a military body needs a "Roman and British" disciplinary code in order to remain reliable died hard.

Differential treatment of officers and enlisted men has likewise been a perennial source of contention. A society which held the basic political ideal of egalitarianism produced one of the most restrictive and rigidly structured military organizations of its day. It was, for example, virtually impossible for an enlisted man to win a commission. No enlisted men were allowed to participate in the trying of naval judicial cases except as witnesses until 1855, when they were allowed to serve as recorders in summary courts-martial. Fraternization was strictly forbidden, and informal exchanges between sailors and officers hardly existed. In appealing verdicts and sentences, enlisted men were effectively restricted to petitioning their squadron commodores or the remote and distant secretary of the navy, and this usually in cases involving very severe penalties. Several sailors were actually executed while serving on foreign stations without *any* chance to have their cases reviewed or their sentence mitigated by either the secretary or the president. Likewise, not one single instance has come to light wherein a sentence assessed against an enlisted man was ever mitigated on account of intervention by a congressman or other prominent political personage.

One major cumulative effect of this was that officer discipline was a problem of major proportions in the Old Navy. This existed in complete contrast to the modern fleet, where most disorderly behavior is confined to the enlisted men. Even when the historian discounts the obvious bias of sources which record much more exhaustively and take into account much more seriously the disciplinary transgressions of officers on intrinsic grounds, it remains inescapable that the behavior of the Old Navy's officers was much more turbulent, irregular, and insubordinate than is currently the case. Careful screening of officer candidates, relatively short times in grade, speedy promotions for competent and cooperative individuals, and "up or out" retirement practices have wrought a revolution in officer deportment. Where once a man could weather three or four courts-martial and still arrive at the top of the navy list and command the most prestigious squadron, now it is axiomatic that even the mildest letter of reprimand weighs heavily in determining an officer's future prospects for advancement.

With regard to the enlisted men, the trends and patterns of behavioral evolution are less clear. By the standards of our own times, the landsmen and seamen of the Old Navy labored under disadvantages of appalling magnitude. Many were illiterate, alcoholic, bereft of ties to the shorebound population or even the nation they served. Often profoundly alienated by birth or inclination, they had to be held in virtual penal servitude for the duration of their enlistments. Under these conditions, some proved dangerous and difficult to manage and responded most readily to the drastic and easily comprehended corrective of the lash and sweatbox, applied and repeated with monotonous regularity. Few had any permanent attachment to the navy, and their life spans were frequently short and marked by self-destructive behavior in an age innocent of most of the tools of sociological insight and psychological analysis.

Over the decades, the quality of the navy's enlisted component has improved as a consequence of the general progress that society has made in the fields of education and social betterment. Persons with severe sociopathic problems or prior criminal records can now be eliminated in the recruiting process or admitted only in limited numbers. Men who have good basic skills can be offered technical training and a career that is competitive with opportunities in the civilian job market. Contemporary studies, notably Ronald W. Perry's *Racial Discrimination and Military Justice*, show that highly qualified enlisted men making a career of the navy have relatively little trouble with the modern naval justice system.

Of course, there are disciplinary problems. Those men who most resemble the typical enlisted men of the Old Navy, the poorly educated recruits from deprived and disadvantaged backgrounds who are profoundly alienated from the dominant social culture and who are not "school eligible" in the parlance of the modern fleet, still behave in ways that are remarkably similar to the conduct of the "children of calamity" and the "sons of adversity" who populated the berth decks of the frigates and sloops of war of yesteryear. Drunkenness still flourishes, complicated now by patterns of drug dependency. Smuggling networks exist in the larger ships for the purpose of dealing in narcotics in much the same way that they did in the Old Navy when contraband liquor was brought aboard for distribution. Desertion is still the navy's greatest disciplinary problem on the judicial level. Life at sea has always been rigorous and hard to adjust to by the standards of life on shore.

But if some things have remained the same, others have changed. Although the twenty-two crimes that were punishable by death were still enumerated as late as 1949, the navy had probably refrained from executing anybody at least since the Civil War, a tacit admission that the death penalty is really unwarranted for any crimes less compelling than murder and treason, both of which are exceedingly rare in the sea service. The establishment of regular brigs on shore, where serious offenders can be taken to remove them from the proximity of their mates, has allowed the navy to dispense officially with all forms of corporal punishment and effectively limit correctives to confinement, confinement on a limited diet, extra duty, and loss of liberties or leaves.

The conduct of naval courts-martial and courts of inquiry are now in the hands of legal professionals working out of a regular judge advocate general's department within the navy's administrative structure. Procedures are more regular, sentences more consistent, the appeals process is more uniformly accessible, and the basic organic law of the navy is more in tune with the constitutional principles of American justice. Consequently, navy law is more defensible in the court of public opinion. Political interference, although still felt in a few cases involving a high degree of publicity, has largely disappeared; and most sentences, once levied by a military court, are actually carried out. Cashiered officers, for example, rarely find their way back into the service.

One last speculation remains to be considered. Under the circumstances, could the Old Navy have devised a significantly better system? Given the limited knowledge of that era and the relatively primitive insight into the workings of both individual and group dynamics, could the system have been more just and equitable? Finally, when the personal and moral habits of the largely illiterate, polyglot, and destitute social underclass that furnished the bulk of the crews for warships are taken into account, could any other system but one of drastic and immediate physical punishment have worked, particularly for officers not extraordinarily gifted with the talents of leadership?

Probably not. The naval justice system could have been improved from the administrative point of view. It could have been more uniform in its approach, more consistent, and less capricious. The Articles of War might have been better developed, and the *Naval Regulations* could certainly have been vastly improved. But the basic character of naval justice was actually determined by the social conditions of the times and by the physical limitations of the ships themselves. There were few trained legal experts available to ensure scrupulous proceedings, although there is evidence that a few commodores shipped civilian lawyers as supernumeraries to serve as judge advocates on long cruises. There was virtually no brig space available either at sea or on shore, so prolonged incarceration was automatically ruled out as a punishment in most cases. The need to pack upwards of five hundred men into the limited confines of a frigate's berth deck insured that only the most drastic application of public and physical chastisement would provide the example necessary to deter crimes that threatened the safety or efficiency of the ship. Crimes of a petty nature—such as gambling, theft, or homosexuality—could only be suppressed, never wholly eliminated under those circumstances. The technology of the day created the living conditions of the navy's officers and men, and the naval justice system reflected those conditions more than anything else. Until those conditions improved, naval discipline was obliged to remain essentially summary in character and highly physical in terms of applied correctives.

When steam, refrigeration, electricity, and labor-saving technology improved living conditions and when social and educational progress began to furnish a more trustworthy and tractable class of sailors, the old ways of maintaining discipline could be dispensed with. The lash, the sweatbox, the irons, and eventually the Articles of War themselves all went the way of things that had outlived the conditions that created them. There were, of course, those who mourned their passing and longed to have once again the kind of power and control that summary physical punishment gives over the short haul. But the navy itself, after more or less uncomfortable periods of adjustment, has always been able to reconstitute its disciplinary system and survive the changes. The naval justice system is a creature of evolutionary development. Alterations come when the time for them is ripe, when older methods are no longer needed within the service and therefore become counterproductive.

Appendix A

Deck Layouts
for a Typical Warship

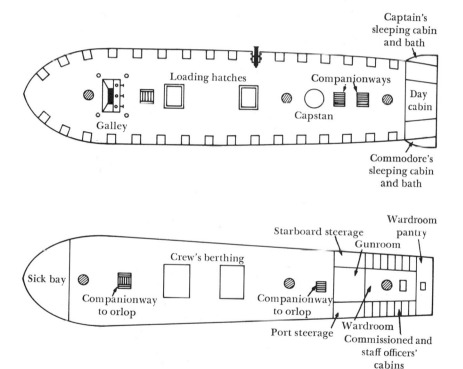

Captain's
sleeping cabin
and bath

Loading hatches

Companionways

Day
cabin

Galley

Capstan

Commodore's
sleeping cabin
and bath

Wardroom
pantry

Starboard steerage

Gunroom

Crew's berthing

Sick bay

Companionway
to orlop

Companionway
to orlop

Wardroom

Port steerage

Commissioned and
staff officers'
cabins

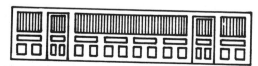

Typical partitions on the berth deck had a wooden grille on top
and a solid bottom. Same design was used for doors to officers'
quarters.

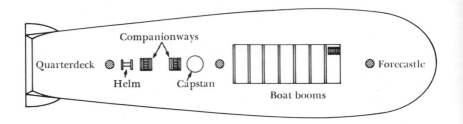

Quarterdeck   Companionways

Helm   Capstan   Boat booms   Forecastle

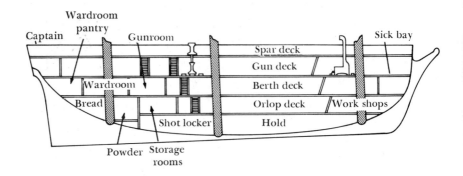

Captain   Wardroom pantry   Gunroom   Sick bay

Spar deck

Gun deck

Wardroom   Berth deck

Bread   Orlop deck   Work shops

Shot locker   Hold

Powder   Storage rooms

Articles of War

[23 April 1800]

Rules and Regulations for the Government of the United States Navy

[SIXTH CONGRESS, SESS. I. 1800.]

April 23, 1800.

Rules and regulations for the government of the navy.

An Act for the better government of the Navy of the United States.

SECTION 1. *Be it enacted by the Senate and House of Representatives of the United States of America in Congress assembled,* That from and after the first day of June next, the following rules and regulations be adopted and put in force, for the government of the navy of the United States.

Exemplary conduct incumbent on commanders.

Art. I. The commanders of all ships and vessels of war belonging to the navy, are strictly enjoined and required to show in themselves a good example of virtue, honour, patriotism and subordination; and be vigilant in inspecting the conduct of all such as are placed under their command; and to guard against, and suppress, all dissolute and immoral practices, and to correct all such as are guilty of them, according to the usage of the sea service.

Divine service and preaching.

Art. II. The commanders of all ships and vessels in the navy, having chaplains on board, shall take care that divine service be performed in a solemn, orderly, and reverent manner twice a day, and a sermon preached on Sunday, unless bad weather, or other extraordinary accidents prevent it; and that they cause all, or as many of the ship's company as can be spared from duty, to attend at every performance of the worship of Almighty God.

Punishment of certain scandalous offences.

Art. III. Any officer, or other person in the navy, who shall be guilty of oppression, cruelty, fraud, profane swearing, drunkenness, or any other scandalous conduct, tending to the destruction of good morals, shall, if an officer, be cashiered, or suffer such other punishment as a court martial shall adjudge; if a private, shall be put in irons, or flogged, at the discretion of the captain, not exceeding twelve lashes; but if the offence require severer punishment, he shall be tried by a court martial, and suffer such punishment as said court shall inflict.

Penalties on the breach of duty in respect of attack and battle.

Art. IV. Every commander or other officer who shall, upon signal for battle, or on the probability of an engagement, neglect to clear his ship for action, or shall not use

285

his utmost exertions to bring his ship to battle, or shall fail to encourage, in his own person, his inferior officers and men to fight courageously, such offender shall suffer death, or such other punishment as a court martial shall adjudge; or any officer neglecting, on sight of any vessel or vessels of an enemy, to clear his ship for action, shall suffer such punishment as a court martial shall adjudge; and if any person in the navy shall treacherously yield, or pusillanimously cry for quarters, he shall suffer death, on conviction thereof, by a general court martial.

Art. V. Every officer or private who shall not properly observe the orders of his commanding officer, or shall not use his utmost exertions to carry them into execution, when ordered to prepare for, join in, or when actually engaged in battle; or shall at such time, basely desert his duty or station, either then, or while in sight of an enemy, or shall induce others to do so, every person so offending shall, on conviction thereof by a general court martial, suffer death or such other punishment as the said court shall adjudge. *Disobedience in time of battle.* *Deserting duty.*

Art. VI. Every officer or private who shall through cowardice, negligence, or disaffection in time of action, withdraw from, or keep out of battle, or shall not do his utmost to take or destroy every vessel which it is his duty to encounter, or shall not do his utmost endeavour to afford relief to ships belonging to the United States, every such offender shall, on conviction thereof by a general court martial, suffer death, or such other punishment as the said court shall adjudge. *Punishment of cowardice, &c. death.*

Art. VII. The commanding officer of every ship or vessel in the navy, who shall capture, or seize upon any vessel as a prize, shall carefully preserve all the papers and writings found on board, and transmit the whole of the originals unmutilated to the judge of the district to which such prize is ordered to proceed, and shall transmit to the navy department, and to the agent appointed to pay the prize money, complete lists of the officers and men entitled to a share of the capture, inserting therein the quality of every person rating, on pain of forfeiting his whole share of the prize money resulting from such capture, and suffering such further punishment as a court martial shall adjudge. *Papers to be transmitted respecting captures to the district judge of the district to which the prize is ordered. List of officers, &c.*

Art. VIII. No person in the navy shall take out of a prize, or vessel seized as prize, any money, plate, goods, or any part of her rigging, unless it be for the better preservation thereof, or absolutely necessary for the use of any of the vessels of the United States, before the same shall be adjudged lawful prize by a competent court; but the whole, without fraud, concealment, or embezzlement, shall be brought in, and judgment passed thereon, upon pain that every person offending herein shall forfeit his share of the capture, and suffer such further punishment as a court martial, or the court of admiralty in which the prize is adjudged, shall impose. *Penalty on pillaging a prize, or maltreating the persons on board the same.*

Art. IX. No person in the navy shall strip of their clothes, or pillage, or in any manner maltreat persons taken on board a prize, on pain of such punishment as a court martial shall adjudge.

Protection of persons taken on board of prizes.

Art. X. No person in the navy shall give, hold, or entertain any intercourse or intelligence to or with any enemy or rebel, without leave from the President of the United States, the Secretary of the Navy, the commander in chief of the fleet, or the commander of a squadron; or in case of a vessel acting singly from his commanding officer, on pain of death, or such other punishment as a court martial shall adjudge.

Intercourse with enemies and rebels, forbidden.

Art. XI. If any letter or message from an enemy or rebel, be conveyed to any officer or private of the navy, and he shall not, within twelve hours, make the same known, having opportunity so to do, to his superior or commanding officer; or if any officer commanding a ship or vessel, being acquainted therewith, shall not, with all convenient speed, reveal the same to the commander in chief of the fleet, commander of a squadron, or other proper officer whose duty it may be to take cognizance thereof, every such offender shall suffer death, or such other punishment as a court martial shall adjudge.

Message from an enemy to be communicated.

Art. XII. Spies, and all persons who shall come or be found in the capacity of spies, or who shall bring or deliver any seducing letter or message from an enemy or rebel, or endeavour to corrupt any person in the navy to betray his trust, shall suffer death, or such other punishment as a court martial shall adjudge.

Mutiny and sedition.

Art. XIII. If any person in the navy shall make or attempt to make any mutinous assembly, he shall on conviction thereof by a court martial, suffer death; and if any person as aforesaid shall utter any seditious or mutinous words, or shall conceal or connive at any mutinous or seditious practices, or shall treat with contempt his superior, being in the execution of his office; or being witness to any mutiny or sedition, shall not do his utmost to suppress it, he shall be punished at the discretion of a court martial.

Attempt at mutiny.

Art. XIV. No officer or private in the navy shall disobey the lawful orders of his superior officer, or strike him, or draw, or offer to draw, or raise any weapon against him, while in the execution of the duties of his office, on pain of death, or such other punishment as a court martial shall inflict.

Disobedience of orders and assault of a superior officer.

Art. XV. No person in the navy shall quarrel with any other person in the navy, nor use provoking or reproachful words, gestures, or menaces, on pain of such punishment as a court martial shall adjudge.

Quarreling.

Art. XVI. If any person in the navy shall desert to an enemy or rebel, he shall suffer death.

Desertion.

Art. XVII. If any person in the navy shall desert, or shall entice others to desert, he shall suffer death, or such other punishment as a court martial shall adjudge;

and if any officer or other person belonging to the navy, shall receive or entertain any deserter from any other vessel of the navy, knowing him to be such, and shall not, with all convenient speed, give notice of such deserter to the commander of the vessel to which he belongs, or to the commander in chief, or to the commander of the squadron, he shall on conviction thereof, be cashiered, or be punished at the discretion of a court martial. All offences committed by persons belonging to the navy while on shore, shall be punished in the same manner as if they had been committed at sea. ^{Offences committed on shore.}

Art. XVIII. If any person in the navy shall knowingly make or sign, or shall aid, abet, direct, or procure the making or signing of any false muster, or shall execute, or attempt, or countenance any fraud against the United States, he shall, on conviction, be cashiered and rendered forever incapable of any future employment in the service of the United States, and shall forfeit all the pay and subsistence due him, and suffer such other punishment as a court martial shall inflict. ^{Frauds against the United States.}

Art. XIX. If any officer, or other person in the navy, shall, through intention, (a) negligence, or any other fault, suffer any vessel of the navy to be stranded, or run upon rocks or shoals, or hazarded, he shall suffer such punishment as a court martial shall adjudge. ^{Improper navigation of vessels.}

Art. XX. If any person in the navy shall sleep upon his watch, or negligently perform the duty assigned him, or leave his station before regularly relieved, he shall suffer death, or such punishment as a court martial shall adjudge; or, if the offender be a private, he may, at the discretion of the captain, be put in irons, or flogged not exceeding twelve lashes. ^{Negligence in the performance of duty, &c.}

Art. XXI. The crime of murder, when committed by any officer, seaman, or marine, belonging to any public ship or vessel of the United States, without the territorial jurisdiction of the same, may be punished with death by the sentence of a court martial. ^{Murder.}

Art. XXII. The officers and privates of every ship or vessel, appointed as convoy to merchant or other vessels, shall diligently and faithfully discharge the duties of their appointment, nor shall they demand or exact any compensation for their services, nor maltreat any of the officers or crews of such merchant or other vessels, on pain of making such reparation as a court of admiralty may award, and of suffering such further punishment as a court martial shall adjudge. ^{Duties in relation to convoy.}

Art. XXIII. If any commander or other officer shall receive or permit to be received, on board his vessel, any goods or merchandise, other than for the sole use of his vessel, except gold, silver, or jewels, and except the goods or merchandise of vessels which may be in distress, or shipwrecked, or in imminent danger of being shipwrecked, in order to preserve them for their owner, without orders ^{Penalty on receiving merchandise on board.}

(a) So in original. Perhaps *inattention* is meant.

from the President of the United States or the navy department, he shall, on conviction thereof, be cashiered, and be incapacitated forever afterwards, for any place or office in the navy.

Waste, embezzlement, &c., of public property.

Art. XXIV. If any person in the navy shall waste, embezzle, or fraudulently buy, sell, or receive any ammuniton, provisions, or other public stores; or if any officer or other person shall, knowingly, permit through design, negligence, or inattention, any such waste, embezzlement, sale or receipt, every such person shall forfeit all the pay and subsistence then due him, and suffer such further punishment as a court martial shall direct.

Burning of public property.

Art. XXV. If any person in the navy shall unlawfully set fire to or burn any kind of public property, not then in the possession of an enemy, pirate, or rebel, he shall suffer death: And if any person shall, in any other manner, destroy such property, or shall not use his best exertions to prevent the destruction thereof by others, he shall be punished at the discretion of a court martial.

Theft.

Art. XXVI. Any theft not exceeding twenty dollars may be punished at the discretion of the captain, and above that sum, as a court martial shall direct.

Offences against people on shore.

Art. XXVII. If any person in the navy shall, when on shore, plunder, abuse, or maltreat any inhabitant, or injure his property in any way, he shall suffer such punishment as a court martial shall adjudge.

Detection and apprehension of offenders.

Art. XXVIII. Every person in the navy shall use his utmost exertions to detect, apprehend, and bring to punishment all offenders, and shall at all times, aid and assist all persons appointed for this purpose, on pain of such punishment as a court martial shall adjudge.

Muster rolls and ship's books.

Art. XXIX. Each commanding officer shall, whenever a seamen enters on board, cause an accurate entry to be made in the ship's books, of his name, time, and term of his service; and before sailing transmit to the Secretary of the Navy, a complete list or muster roll of the officers and men under his command, with the date of their entering, time and terms of their service annexed; and shall cause similar lists to be made out on the first day of every second month, to be transmitted to the Secretary of the Navy, as opportunities shall occur; accounting in such lists or muster rolls, for any casualties which may have taken place since the last list or muster roll. He shall cause to be accurately minuted on the ship's books, the names of, and times at which any death or desertion may occur; and in case of death, shall take care that the purser secure all the property of the deceased for the

Inspection of provisions.

benefit of his legal representative or representatives. He shall cause frequent inspections to be made into the condition of the provisions, and use every precaution for its preservation. He shall, whenever he orders officers

Officers and men detached from the ship to be furnished with certain statements.

and men to take charge of a prize, and proceed to the United States, and whenever officers or men are sent from his ship from whatever cause, take care that each man be furnished with a complete statement of his account, specifying the date of his enlistment, and the period and terms of his service; which account shall be signed by the commanding officer and purser. He shall cause the rules for the government of the navy to be hung up in some public part of the ship, and read once a month to his ship's company. He shall cause a convenient place to be set apart for sick or disabled men, to which he shall have them removed, with their hammocks and bedding, when the surgeon shall so advise, and shall direct that some of the crew attend them and keep the place clean; and if necessary, shall direct that cradles, and buckets with covers, be made for their use: And when his crew is finally paid off, he shall attend in person, or appoint a proper officer, to see that justice be done to the men, and to the United States, in the settlement of the accounts. Any commanding officer, offending herein, shall be punished at the discretion of a court martial. *Rules to be hung up and read.* *Treatment of the sick.* *Paying off.*

Art. XXX. No commanding officer shall, of his own authority, discharge a commissioned or warrant officer, nor strike, nor punish him otherwise than by suspension or confinement, nor shall he, of his own authority, inflict a punishment on any private beyond twelve lashes with a cat-of-nine-tails, nor shall he suffer any wired, or other than a plain cat-of-nine-tails, to be used on board his ship; nor shall any officer who may command by accident, or in the absence of the commanding officer (except such commander be absent for a time by leave) order or inflict any other punishment than confinement, for which he shall account on the return of such absent commanding officer. Nor shall any commanding officer receive on board any petty officers or men turned over from any other vessel to him, unless each of such officers and men produce to him an account signed by the captain and purser of the vessel from which they came, specifying the date of such officer's or man's entry, the period and terms of service, the sums paid and the balance due him, and the quality in which he was rated on board such ship. Nor shall any commanding officer, having received any petty officer or man as aforesaid, rate him in a lower or worse station than that in which he formerly served. Any commanding officer offending herein, shall be punished at the discretion of a court martial. *Treatment of inferior officers and men.*

Art. XXXI. Any master at arms, or other person of whom the duty of master at arms is required, who shall refuse to receive such prisoners as shall be committed to his charge, or having received them, shall suffer them to escape, or dismiss them without orders from proper authority, shall suffer in such prisoners' stead, or be punished otherwise at the discretion of a court martial. *Master at arms.*

Art. XXXII. All crimes committed by persons belonging to the navy, which are not specified in the foregoing articles, shall be punished according to the laws and customs in such cases at sea. *Crimes not specified.*

Art. XXXIII. All officers, not holding commissions or warrants, or who are not entitled to them, except such as are temporarily appointed to the duties of a commissioned or warrant officer, are deemed petty officers.

Art. XXXIV. Any person entitled to wages or prize money, may have the same paid to his assignee, provided the assignment be attested by the captain and purser; and in case of the assignment of wages, the power shall specify the precise time they commence. But the commander of every vessel is required to discourage his crew from selling any part of their wages or prize money, and never to attest any power of attorney, until he is satisfied that the same is not granted in consideration of money given for the purchase of wages or prize money.

Naval General Courts Martial.

Art. XXXV. General courts martial may be convened as often as the President of the United States, the Secretary of the Navy, or the commander in chief of the fleet, or commander of a squadron, while acting out of the United States, shall deem it necessary: *Provided*, that no general court martial shall consist of more than thirteen, nor less than five members, and as many officers shall be summoned on every such court as can be convened without injury to the service, so as not to exceed thirteen, and the senior officer shall always preside, the others ranking agreeably to the date of their commissions; and in no case, where it can be avoided without injury to the service, shall more than one half the members, exclusive of the president, be junior to the officer to be tried.

Art. XXXVI. Each member of the court, before proceeding to trial, shall take the following oath or affirmation, which the judge advocate or person officiating as such, is hereby authorized to administer.

"I, *A. B.* do swear (or affirm) that I will truly try, without prejudice or partiality, the case now depending, according to the evidence which shall come before the court, the rules for the government of the navy, and my own conscience; and that I will not by any means divulge or disclose the sentence of the court, until it shall have been approved by the proper authority, nor will I at any time divulge or disclose the vote or opinion of any particular member of the court, unless required so to do before a court of justice in due course of law."

This oath or affirmation being duly administered, the president is authorized and required to administer the following oath or affirmation to the judge advocate, or person officiating as such.

"I, *A. B.* do swear (or affirm) that I will keep a true record of the evidence given to and the proceedings of this court; nor will I divulge or by any means disclose the sentence of the court until it shall have been approved by the proper authority; nor will I at any time divulge or disclose the vote or opinion of any particular member of the court, unless required so to do before a court of justice in due course of law."

Art. XXXVII. All testimony given to a general court martial shall be on oath or affirmation, which the president of the court is hereby authorized to administer, and if any person shall refuse to give his evidence as aforesaid, or shall prevaricate, or shall behave with contempt to the court, it shall and may be lawful for the court to imprison such offender at their discretion; provided that the imprisonment in no case shall exceed two months: and every person who shall commit wilful perjury on examination on oath or affirmation before such court, or who shall corruptly procure, or suborn any person to commit such wilful perjury, shall and may be prosecuted by indictment or information in any court of justice of the United States, and shall suffer such penalties as are authorized by the laws of the United States in case of perjury or the subornation thereof. And in every prosecution for perjury or the subornation thereof under this act, it shall be sufficient to set forth the offence charged on the defendant, without setting forth the authority by which the court was held, or the particular matters brought or intended to be brought before the said court. *Giving of testimony.*

Art. XXXVIII. All charges, on which an application for a general court martial is founded, shall be exhibited in writing to the proper officer, and the person demanding the court shall take care that the person accused be furnished with a true copy of the charges, with the specifications, at the time he is put under arrest, nor shall any other charge or charges, than those so exhibited, be urged against the person to be tried before the court, unless it appear to the court that intelligence of such charge had not reached the person demanding the court, when the person so to be tried was put under arrest, or that some witness material to the support of such charge, who was at that time absent, can be produced; in which case, reasonable time shall be given to the person to be tried to make his defence against such new charge. Every officer so arrested is to deliver up his sword to his commanding officer, and to confine himself to the limits assigned him, under pain of dismission from service. *Exhibition of charges.* *Treatment of an arrested officer.*

Art. XXXIX. When the proceedings of any general court martial shall have commenced, they shall not be suspended or delayed on account of the absence of any of the members, provided five or more be assembled; but the court is enjoined to sit from day to day, Sundays excepted, until sentence be given: and no member of said court shall, after the proceedings are begun, absent himself therefrom, unless in case of sickness or orders to go on duty from a superior officer, on pain of being cashiered. *Continuance of general courts martial.*

Art. XL. Whenever a court martial shall sentence any officer to be suspended, the court shall have power to suspend his pay and emoluments for the whole, or any part of the time of his suspension.

Art. XLI. All sentences of courts martial, which shall extend to the loss of life, shall require the concurrence of two thirds of the members present; and no such sentence shall be carried into execution, until confirmed by the President of the United States; or if the trial take place out of the United States, until it be confirmed by the commander of the fleet or squadron: all other sentences may be determined by a majority of votes, and carried into execution on confirmation of the commander of the fleet, or officer ordering the court, except such as go to the dismission of a commissioned or warrant officer, which are first to be approved by the President of the United States.

A court martial shall not, for any one offence not capital, inflict a punishment beyond one hundred lashes.

Art. XLII. The President of the United States, or when the trial takes place out of the United States, the commander of the fleet or squadron, shall possess full power to pardon any offence committed against these articles, after conviction, or to mitigate the punishment decreed by a court martial.

Sec. 2. Art. I. *And be it further enacted,* That courts of inquiry may be ordered by the President of the United States, the Secretary of the Navy, or the commander of a fleet or squadron, provided such court shall not consist of more than three members who shall be commissioned officers, and a judge advocate, or person to do duty as such; and such courts shall have power to summon witnesses, administer oaths, and punish contempt in the same manner as courts martial. But such court shall merely state facts, and not give their opinion, unless expressly required so to do in the order for convening; and the party, whose conduct shall be the subject of inquiry, shall have permission to cross examine all the witnesses.

Art. II. The proceedings of courts of inquiry shall be authenticated by the signature of the president of the court and judge advocate, and shall, in all cases not capital, or extending to the dismission of a commissioned or warrant officer, be evidence before a court martial, provided oral testimony cannot be obtained.

Art. III. The judge advocate, or person officiating as such, shall administer to the members the following oath or affirmation:

"You do swear, (or affirm) well and truly to examine and inquire according to the evidence, into the matter now before you, without partiality or prejudice."

After which, the president shall administer to the judge advocate, or person officiating as such, the following oath or affirmation:

"You do swear (or affirm) truly to record the proceedings of this court, and the evidence to be given in the case in hearing."

SEC. 3. *And be it further enacted,* That in all cases, where the crews of the ships or vessels of the United States shall be separated from their vessels, by the latter being wrecked, lost or destroyed, all the command, power, and authority, given to the officers of such ships or vessels, shall remain and be in full force as effectually as if such ship or vessel were not so wrecked, lost, or destroyed, until such ship's company be regularly discharged from, or ordered again into the service, or until a court martial shall be held to inquire into the loss of such ship or vessel; and if by the sentence of such court, or other satisfactory evidence, it shall appear that all or any of the officers and men of such ship's company did their utmost to preserve her, and after the loss thereof behaved themselves agreeably to the discipline of the navy, then the pay and emoluments of such officers and men, or such of them as shall have done their duty as aforesaid, shall go on until their discharge or death; and every officer or private who shall, after the loss of such vessel, act contrary to the discipline of the navy, shall be punished at the discretion of a court martial, in the same manner as if such vessel had not been so lost. *[In case of loss of the vessel, the command of the officers shall remain in force.]*

SEC. 4. *And be it further enacted,* That all the pay and emoluments of such officers and men, of any of the ships or vessels of the United States taken by an enemy, who shall appear by the sentence of a court martial, or otherwise, to have done their utmost to preserve and defend their ship or vessel, and, after the taking thereof, have behaved themselves obediently to their superiors, agreeably to the discipline of the navy, shall go on and be paid them until their death, exchange, or discharge. *[Pay of captives to continue.]*

SEC 5. *And be it further enacted,* That the proceeds of all ships and vessels, and the goods taken on board of them, which shall be adjudged good prize, shall, when of equal or superior force to the vessel or vessels making the capture, be the sole property of the captors; and when of inferior force, shall be divided equally between the United States and the officers and men making the capture. *[To whom the proceeds of prizes shall accrue.]*

SEC. 6. *And be it [further] enacted,* That the prize money, belonging to the officers and men, shall be distributed in the following manner: *[Distribution of prize money.]*

I. To the commanding officers of fleets, squadrons, or single ships, three twentieths, of which the commanding officer of the fleet or squadron shall have one twentieth, if the prize be taken by a ship or vessel acting under his command, and the commander of single ships, two twentieths; but where the prize is taken by a ship acting independently of such superior officer, the three twentieths shall belong to her commander.

II. To sea lieutenants, captains of marines, and sailing masters, two twentieths; but where there is a captain, without a lieutenant of marines, these officers shall be entitled to two twentieths and one third of a twentieth, which third, in such case, shall be deducted from the share of the officers mentioned in article No. III. of this section.

III. To chaplains, lieutenants of marines, surgeons, pursers, boatswains, gunners, carpenters, and master's mates, two twentieths.

IV. To midshipmen, surgeon's mates, captain's clerks, schoolmasters, boatswain's mates, gunner's mates, carpenter's mates, ship's stewards, sail-makers, masters at arms, armorers, cockswains, and coopers, three twentieths and an half.

V. To gunner's yeomen, boatswain's yeomen, quartermasters, quartergunners, sail-maker's mates, sergeants and corporals of marines, drummers, fifers and extra petty officers, two twentieths and an half.

VI. To seamen, ordinary seamen, marines, and all other persons doing duty on board, seven twentieths.

VII. Whenever one or more public ships or vessels are in sight at the time any one or more ships are taking a prize or prizes, they shall all share equally in the prize or prizes, according to the number of men and guns on board each ship in sight.

No commander of a fleet or squadron shall be entitled to receive any share of prizes taken by vessels not under his immediate command; nor of such prizes as may have been taken by ships or vessels intended to be placed under his command, before they have acted under his immediate orders; nor shall a commander of a fleet or squadron, leaving the station where he had the command, have any share in the prizes taken by ships left on such station, after he has gone out of the limits of his said command.

Bounty given in certain cases.

SEC. 7. *And be it further enacted,* That a bounty shall be paid by the United States, of twenty dollars for each person on board any ship of an enemy at the commencement of an engagement, which shall be sunk or destroyed by any ship or vessel belonging to the United States of equal or inferior force, the same to be divided among the officers and crew in the same manner as prize money.

Pensions to persons disabled in the service.

SEC. 8. *And be it further enacted,* That every officer, seaman, or marine, disabled in the line of his duty, shall be entitled to receive for life, or during his disability, a pension from the United States according to the nature and degree of his disability, not exceeding one half his monthly pay.

Appropriation of the part of captured property belonging to the United States.

SEC. 9. *And be it [further] enacted,* That all money accruing, or which has already accrued to the United States from the sale of prizes, shall be and remain forever a fund for the payment of pensions and half pay, should

295

the same be hereafter granted, to the officers and seamen who may be entitled to receive the same; and if the said fund shall be insufficient for the purpose, the public faith is hereby pledged to make up the deficiency; but if it should be more than sufficient, the surplus shall be applied to the making of further provision for the comfort of the disabled officers, seamen, and marines, and for such as, though not disabled, may merit by their bravery, or long and faithful services, the gratitude of their country.

SEC. 10. *And be it further enacted*, That the said fund shall be under the management and direction of the Secretary of the Navy, the Secretary of the Treasury, and the Secretary of War, for the time being, who are hereby authorized to receive any sums to which the United States may be entitled from the sale of prizes, and employ and invest the same, and the interest arising therefrom, in any manner which a majority of them may deem most advantageous. And it shall be the duty of the said commissioners to lay before Congress, annually, in the first week of their session, a minute statement of their proceedings relative to the management of said fund. *Management of the navy fund.*

SEC. 11. *And be it further enacted*, That the act passed the second day of March, in the year one thousand seven hundred and ninety-nine, intituled "An act for the government of the navy of the United States," from and after the first day of June next, shall be, and hereby is repealed. *Repeal of the former act.*

1799, ch. 24.

APPROVED, April 23, 1800.

[U. S. Statute No. II, pp. 45–53.]

Notes

Introduction

1. W. Adolphe Roberts and Lowell Brentano, eds., *The Book of the Navy*.
2. Elmo R. Zumwalt, Jr., *On Watch*, Chapter 5 and pp. 233–34.
3. United States Judge Advocate General's Department. Records of General Courts-Martial and Courts of Inquiry of the Navy Department, 1799–1867, National Archives and Records Service. (Hereinafter cited as JAG Records.)
4. Morris Janowitz, "Changing Patterns of Organizational Authority," pp. 473–76.
5. Eugene S. Ferguson, *Truxtun of the Constellation*, p. 172. *See also* Duane's *Aurora*, Philadelphia, 16 March 1799.
6. Gardner Weld Allen, ed., *The Papers of Isaac Hull*, pp. 151–52.
7. *See* Table II, Chapter IV.
8. Paul L. Savage and Richard A. Gabriel, "Cohesion and Disintegration in the American Army," pp. 340–76.
9. Harold D. Langley, *Social Reform in the United States Navy*, p. 153.
10. *See* Table I, Chapter IV.
11. Herman Melville, *White Jacket*.
12. Charles Oscar Paullin, *Paullin's History of Naval Administration*, pp. 233–34.
13. Record of Proceedings of a Court of Inquiry in the Case of Rear-Admiral Winfield S. Schley, U.S. Navy, 2 Vols.
14. Neil Sheehan, *The Arnheiter Affair*, pp. 261–62.
15. Trevor Armbrister, *A Matter of Accountability, The True Story of the Pueblo Affair*. (New York: Coward McCann, Inc., 1970), p. 387.
16. Sheehan, *Arnheiter Affair*, pp. 269–72.
17. Naval Regulations 1802. Issued by command of the President of the United States of America, 25 January 1802, p. 34.
18. The total officer strength of the Navy never exceeded 1,000 prior to 1862. Total personnel strength never exceeded 12,000 until the Civil War.
19. William T. Generous, Jr., *Swords and Scales*, pp. 11–12. Winthrop served as the Army's JAG during the 1870s. Ansell held the office during World War I.
20. *Ibid.*, note 17, pp. 213–14.
21. *Ibid.*, p. 12.
22. Robert E. Johnson, *Thence Around Cape Horn*, pp. 98–99.

23. Samuel Eliot Morison, *Old Bruin* (Boston: Little Brown and Co., 1967), p. 148.

24. *See* Table II, Chapter IV.

25. *See* Table IV, Chapter VI.

Chapter I

1. George T. Davis, *A Navy Second to None: The Development of Modern American Naval Policy*, pp. 3–11.

2. *Ibid.*, pp. 11–14.

3. Charles Oscar Paullin, *Paullin's History of Naval Administration*, pp. 184–87.

4. *Ibid.*

5. Reuben Elmore Stivers, *Privateers and Volunteers*, p. 161.

6. *Ibid.*, p. 162.

7. Allan R. Bosworth, *My Love Affair with the Navy*, p. 52.

8. John Niven, *Gideon Welles*, p. 213.

9. *Ibid.*, p. 351.

10. *Ibid.*, p. 213.

11. Paullin, *History of Naval Administration*, pp. 188–90.

12. *Ibid.*

13. Francis Leigh Williams, *Matthew Fontaine Maury*, pp. 39–40.

14. Richard S. West, Jr., *The Second Admiral*, pp. 28–29.

15. *Ibid.*, p. 33.

16. Donald W. Griffin, "The American Navy at Work on the Brazil Station," p. 239.

17. Stivers, *Privateers and Volunteers*, p. 166.

18. *Ibid.*

19. Herman Melville, *White Jacket*, pp. 6–8.

20. Peter Karsten, *The Naval Aristocracy*, p. 92.

21. Melville, *White Jacket*, pp. 112–19.

22. Stivers, *Privateers and Volunteers*, p. 165.

23. Bosworth, *Love Affair with the Navy*, p. 52.

24. Melville, *White Jacket*, pp. 119, 127–29.

25. Stivers, *Privateers and Volunteers*, p. 164.

26. John D. Alden, *The American Steel Navy*, p. 265.

27. *Ibid.*, pp. 265–66.

28. *United States Senate Documents*, Annual Report of the Secretary of the Navy; 20th Cong., 2nd Sess., p. 135.

29. Harold D. Langley, *Social Reform in the U. S. Navy*, pp. 89–90.

30. David Hannay, *Naval Courts-Martial*, p. 96.

31. Karsten, *Naval Aristocracy*, p. 80.

32. Langley, *Social Reform in the U. S. Navy*, p. 92.

33. *Ibid.*, pp. 92–93.

34. Karsten, *Naval Aristocracy*, p. 80.

35. Langley, *Social Reform in the U. S. Navy*, pp. 92–93.

36. Karsten, *Naval Aristocracy*, p. 41.

37. *Ibid.*, p. 80.

38. Langley, *Social Reform in the U. S. Navy*, pp. 93-95.

39. *Ibid.*

40. Melville, *White Jacket*, pp. 477–78.

41. Langley, *Social Reform in the U. S. Navy*, pp. 93–95.

42. Benjamin Quarles, *The Negro in the Civil War*, p. 229.

43. JAG Records, cases 12 and 161 are two court-martial proceedings that contain examples of overtly racist testimony on the part of naval officers.

44. Melville, *White Jacket*, pp. 471–72.

45. *See* comparative tables and explanations contained in Ronald W. Perry, *Racial Discrimination and Military Justice*.

46. Anthony M. Brescia, "The American Navy," pp. 217–18.

47. Melville, *White Jacket*, pp. 471–72.

48. Langley, *Social Reform in the U. S. Navy*, pp. 185–86.

49. *Ibid.*, p. viii.

50. This characterization is drawn from Leonard F. Guttridge and Jay D. Smith, *The Commodores*.

51. Williams, *Matthew Fontaine Maury*, pp. 125–42.

52. *Ibid.*

53. John D. Hayes, ed., *Samuel Francis Du Pont*, Vol. I, pp. lxv–lxvi.

54. *Ibid.*, p. lxvi.

55. Letter, Samuel Francis Du Pont to G. J. Pendergrast, Wilmington, 21 January, 1842. From *Ibid.*, p. lxvi.

56. Stivers, *Privateers and Volunteers*, p. 168.

57. *Ibid.*

58. Alden, *American Steel Navy*, p. 252.

59. Kenneth Stampp, *The Peculiar Institution*, p. 143.

60. Williams, *Matthew Fontaine Maury*, pp. 264–70 and Chapter XV.

Chapter II

1. Edward Gibbon, *The Decline and Fall of the Roman Empire*. Vol. I, p. 5.

2. H. M. Holyer, "The Development of Military Law—Your Job and Mine," pp. 31–32.

3. *Ibid.*

4. Sir Matthew Hale, *The History of the Common Law of England*, pp. 26–27.

5. Sir William Blackstone, *Commentaries on the Laws of England*, pp. 323–24.

6. Herman Melville, *White Jacket*, pp. 377–78.

7. *Naval Orientation*, NAVPERS 16138, p. 288.

8. Robert Sherrill, *Military Justice is to Justice as Military Music is to Music*, p. 67.

9. *Ibid.*, pp. 67–68.

10. JAG Records, case 1528.

11. *Ibid.*, see the sentence of the court and the testimony of the several witnesses.

12. JAG Records, cases 1529–1535.

13. JAG Records, case 1531, appended document.

14. JAG Records, case 1528, appended document.

15. *Dynes v. Hoover,* 61 U.S. (28 How.) 65, 1857, pp. 66–71.

16. *Ibid.*

17. *Ibid.*, p. 72.

18. *Ibid.*, p. 79.

19. *Ibid.*, pp. 79–80.

20. *Ibid.*, p. 81.

21. Sherrill, *Military Justice,* p. 68.

22. David Porter, *Constantinople and its Environs,* Vol. II, p. 10.

23. George E. Buker, "Captain's Mast," pp. 139–46.

24. *Ibid.*

25. *Ibid.*

26. Richard A. von Doenhoff, "Biddle, Perry, and Japan," p. 79.

27. Harold D. Langley, *Social Reform in the United States Navy,* p. 131.

28. *Ibid.*, see also David Hannay, *Naval Courts Martial,* introduction.

29. Peter Kemp, ed., *History of the Royal Navy,* pp. 24, 28–30.

30. Hannay, *Naval Courts Martial,* introduction.

31. Kemp, *Royal Navy,* pp. 28–30.

32. Hannay, *Naval Courts Martial,* introduction.

33. Leo F. S. Horan, "Flogging in the United States Navy," pp. 969–70.

34. Sherrill, *Military Justice,* pp. 68–69.

35. Horan, "Flogging in the United States Navy," pp. 969–70, and Langley, *Social Reform in the U. S. Navy,* pp. 137–38.

36. Horan, "Flogging in the United States Navy," pp. 969–70.

37. *Naval Orientation,* p. 278.

38. Langley, *Social Reform in the U. S. Navy,* p. 131.

39. Samuel Eliot Morison, *John Paul Jones,* pp. 123–24, 139–44.

40. Buker, "Captain's Mast," pp. 139–44.

41. *Ibid.*, pp. 133–46.

42. *Naval Orientation,* p. 282.

43. Melville, *White Jacket,* pp. 372–74.

44. Morison, "Old Bruin," pp. 88–98.

45. *Naval Orientation,* p. 279.

46. Charles Oscar Paullin, *Commodore John Rodgers,* pp. 35–36.

47. *Ibid.*

48. Morison, "Old Bruin," pp. 88–98.

49. *Ibid.*

50. Samuel F. Du Pont kept a notebook recording the punishments he awarded to the crew of the frigate *Congress* during a passage from Norfolk to Callao, November 1845 to March 1846. He notes 108 floggings in 131 days

and seems to have used no other correctives at all during this time. The Letters and Papers of Rear Admiral Samuel Francis Du Pont, Document No. 49–18470.

51. Morison, *"Old Bruin,"* pp. 88–98.

52. Christopher McKee, *Edward Preble*, p. 221.

53. *Ibid.*

54. *Ibid.*, pp. 225–26.

55. *Ibid.*

56. *Ibid.*, pp. 222–23.

57. Langley, *Social Reform in the U. S. Navy*, p. 142.

58. JAG Records, index and case no. 462.

59. Melville, *White Jacket*, pp. 178–79.

Chapter III

1. *Naval Orientation*, NAVPERS 16138, pp. 275–76.

2. Charles Oscar Paullin, *History of Naval Administration*, pp. 262–63.

3. These old works are mentioned in the transcripts of various court-martial proceedings. Because they have all but vanished from modern law libraries, complete citations have so far proven impossible to obtain.

4. The courts-martial of Uriah P. Levy are JAG Records, case numbers 243, 324, 330, 389, 404, 454, and 795. For information on Levy's naval career, *see* Mary Cable and Annabelle Praeger, "The Levys of Monticello," pp. 32–35.

5. The courts-martial of George Crutch are JAG Records, case numbers 94, 108, 121, and 462. The first trial was held in 1805, the last in 1811.

6. Paullin, *History of Naval Administration*, pp. 231–34.

7. Reuben E. Stivers, *Privateers and Volunteers*, p. 366.

8. *Ibid.*

9. Harold D. Langley, *Social Reform in the United States Navy*, pp. 21–24.

10. Herman Melville, *White Jacket*, pp. 174–176.

11. Allen, *Papers of Isaac Hull*, p. 259.

12. *Congressional Globe*, 34th Cong., 1st Sess., Appendix, pp. 573–574.

13. Robert E. Johnson, "A Long Chase," pp. 144–46, *Thence Around Cape Horn*, pp. 100–101.

14. Langley, *Social Reform in the U. S. Navy*, p. 131.

15. Norman C. Delaney, *John McIntosh Kell of the Raider Alabama*, pp. 61–62. *See also*, JAG Records, cases 1149 and 1151.

16. Langley, *Social Reform in the U. S. Navy*, p. 131.

17. Melville, *White Jacket*, p. 466.

18. Allen R. Bosworth, *Love Affair with the Navy*, p. 71.

19. *See* Samuel Eliot Morison, *"Old Bruin,"* pp. 106–107 for a typical example.

20. Melville's *White Jacket* is a classic in this genre.

21. The campaign to abolish flogging is described in detail in Langley's *Social Reform in the U. S. Navy, 1798–1862.*

22. David F. Long, *Nothing too Daring*, p. 178.

23. SFDP Papers, "Fragment Relating to Regulations in the Navy," Document No. W9–694, written in 1841.

24. *See Ibid.* and *Naval Orientation*, p. 280.

25. *Ibid.,* (SFDP Papers, Document No. W9–694).

26. Allen, *Papers of Isaac Hull*, p. 266.

27. SFDP Papers, Document No. W9–694.

28. *Ibid.*

29. *Ibid.*

30. SFDP Papers, "Informal Report to the Secretary of the Navy," Document No. W9–1657, written January 1855.

31. Henry A. Du Pont, *Rear Admiral Samuel Francis Du Pont, United States Navy, a Biography*, pp. 63–69.

32. SFDP Papers, See the front flyleaf to a notebook recording the deliberations of the Naval Efficiency Board, Document No. W9–18475, for a text of Secretary Dobbin's instructions to the members of the Board.

33. Paullin, *History of the Naval Administration*, pp. 238–240.

34. *Ibid.*

35. The Henry Francis Du Pont collection of Winterthur Manuscripts. (Hereinafter cited as SFDP Papers) Documents Nos. W9–18475 and W9–18476.

36. *Ibid.* W9–18476.

37. Joseph T. Durkin, *Stephen Mallory, Confederate Navy Chief*, pp. 72–73.

38. Gordon K. Harrington, "The Ringgold Incident: A Matter of Judgment," Clayton R. Barrow, ed., *America Spreads Her Sails.* (United States Naval Institute Press, Annapolis, Md., 1973), pp. 100–111.

39. SFDP Papers, Document W9–18476, pp. 255–256.

40. Quoted in Durkin, *Stephen Mallory*, p. 281.

41. *Congressional Globe*, 34th Cong., 1st Sess., pp. 311–312.

42. Hayes, *Du Pont Letters*, Vol. 1, p. lxiii.

43. Letter, Secretary Dobbin to Matthew F. Maury, Sept. 17, 1855, Quoted in Williams, *Matthew Fontaine Maury*, p. 274.

44. *Ibid.,* pp, 292–294.

45. Du Pont, *Samuel Francis Du Pont*, pp. 83–84. Note that Stivers puts the number at 62 while Hayes claims that "over 100" were restored to active duty.

46. For an example, see the account of the treasonable activities of pro-Confederate officers at the Norfolk Naval Shipyard in 1861 described in Edward William Sloan, III, *Benjamin Franklin Isherwood Naval Engineer; The Years as Engineer-in-Chief, 1861–1869*, pp. 21–26.

47. *Naval Orientation*, p. 280.

48. *See* Paullin, *History of Naval Administration*, p. 253 and Tom Henderson Wells, *The Confederate Navy, A Study in Organization*, p. 43.

49. Paullin, *History of Naval Administration*, p. 253.

50. Wells, *Confederate Navy*, p. 43.

51. Quoted in Paullin, *History of Naval Administration* p. 262.

52. *Ibid.*, p. 263.

Chapter IV

1. Reuben Elmore Stivers, *Privateers and Volunteers, The Men and Women of Our Naval Reserve Forces, 1766 to 1866*, p. 167.

2. Howard I. Chappelle, *The History of American Sailing Ships*, p. 77.

3. Herman Melville, *White Jacket*, p. 473.

4. *Ibid.*, pp. 472–473.

5. *Ibid.*, pp. 232–233, 236.

6. *Ibid.*, p. 102.

7. SFDP Papers, Document No. W9 18470.

8. *Ibid.*

9. *Ibid.*

10. Bosworth, *Love Affair with the Navy*, p. 75.

11. *Ibid.*

12. Leo F. S. Horan, "Flogging in the United States Navy," p. 973.

13. *Ibid. See also* Paullin, *History of Naval Administration*, p. 231.

14. Melville, *White Jacket*, p. 174.

15. *Ibid.*

16. *Ibid.*

17. Charles Oscar Paullin, *History of Naval Administration*, p. 232.

18. *Ibid.*, p. 234.

19. Horan, "Flogging in the United States Navy," p. 973.

20. Samuel Eliot Morison, *"Old Bruin,"* p. 292.

21. *Ibid.*

22. Peter Karsten, *Naval Aristocracy*, pp. 85–86.

23. Morison, *"Old Bruin,"* p. 398.

24. Allan R. Bosworth, *Love Affair with the Navy*, p. 77.

25. George E. Buker, "Captain's Mast," p. 146.

26. Karsten, *Naval Aristocracy*, pp. 85–86.

27. *The United States Nautical Magazine and Naval Journal*, Vol. V, 1857, p. 296.

28. E. Mowbray Tate, "Admiral Bell and the New Asiatic Squadron, 1865–1868," pp. 132–133.

29. Melville, *White Jacket*, p. 472.

30. John D. Milligan, ed., *From the Fresh-Water Navy: 1861–1864 The Letters of Acting Master's Mate Henry R. Browne and Acting Ensign Symmes E. Browne*, Naval Letters Series, Vol. III (United States Naval Institute: Annapolis, Md., 1970), pp. 11, 256, 282.

31. *See* Paullin, *History of Naval Administration*, p. 214, for a complete list of naval shore stations abroad.

32. Gardner W. Allen, *The Papers of Isaac Hull*, pp. 207–220.

33. *Ibid.*, pp. 221–252.

34. Leonard F. Guttridge and Jay D. Smith, *The Commodores*, p. 308.

35. Allen, *Hull Papers*, pp. 207–220.

36. *Ibid.*, pp. 221–252.

37. Paullin, *History of Naval Administration*, p. 215.

38. *Ibid.*

39. Donald W. Griffin, "The American Navy at Work on the Brazil Station," pp. 247–249.

40. Harold D. Langley, *Social Reform in the United States Navy*, p. 24.

41. Bosworth says two-thirds as many. *See Love Affair with the Navy*, p. 79.

42. Charles Lee Lewis, *The Romantic Decatur*, p. 200.

43. Quoted in Edwin H. Simmons, *The United States Marines*, 1775–1975, p. 19.

44. Paullin, *History of Naval Administration*, p. 192.

45. *Ibid.*, pp. 192–93.

46. Marcus Cunliffe, *Soldiers and Civilians, the Martial Spirit in America, 1775–1865*, p. 84.

47. Paullin, *History of Naval Administration*, p. 193.

48. Lewis, *The Romantic Decatur*, p. 200.

49. *Regulations of the Navy*, 1865, p. 30. Quoted in Paullin, *History of Naval Administration*, p. 227.

50. Bosworth, *Love Affair with the Navy*, p. 79.

51. Karsten, *Naval Aristocracy*, p. 37.

52. *Ibid.*

53. *Ibid.*, pp. 37–38.

54. *Ibid.*

55. E. B. Potter, *The Naval Academy Illustrated History of the United States Navy*, pp. 114–15.

56. Karsten, *Naval Aristocracy*, p. 39.

57. *Ibid.*

58. Norman C. Delany, *John McIntosh Kell*, Chapter IV.

59. *Ibid.*

60. E. B. Potter, *History of the Navy*, pp. 114–15.

61. *United States Statutes at Large*, *See* 2, Stat. 729. Quoted in Stivers, *Privateers and Volunteers*, pp. 121–22.

62. Stivers, *Privateers and Volunteers*, pp. 121–22.

63. *Ibid.*

64. See JAG Records index.

65. Stivers, *Privateers and Volunteers*, pp. 122–24.

66. This table was compiled by a random sampling of the *JAG Records* index for the years 1799–1861, which contains 7,333 charges listed for 3,120 courts-martial and courts of inquiry. Some cases involve multiple charges, and the average number of charges per case is 1.7.

67. See Morison, *"Old Bruin,"* 189–190; and James M. Merrill, "Men, Monotony, and Mouldy Beans—Life on Board Civil War Blockaders," pp. 49–50.

68. Niven, *Gideon Welles*, p. 447.

69. Stivers, *Privateers and Volunteers*, pp. 259–61.

70. Milligan, *Browne Letters*, p. 283; and *Ibid.*, p. 251.

71. Merrill, "Men, Monotony, and Mouldy Beans," pp. 49–50; and Karsten, *Naval Aristocracy*, p. 92.

72. James N. J. Henwood, "A Cruise on the U.S.S. Sabine," *American Neptune*, pp. 102–105.

73. Table compiled from JAG Records index and *Historical Statistics of the United States, Colonial Times to 1970*, Part 2, pp. 1142–1143.

Chapter V

1. JAG Records, cases 172 and 178.

2. Samuel Eliot Morison, *"Old Bruin,"* p. 190, and K. Jack Bauer, *Surfboats and Horse Marines, U. S. Naval Operations in the Mexican War, 1846–1848*, p. 42.

3. See Article XLI of the "Act for the Better Government of the Navy of 1800," hereinafter referred to as AGN.

4. Figures compiled from the JAG Records Index for years 1800–1861.

5. JAG Records, case 660.

6. JAG Records, case 192.

7. Frank Donovan, *The Odyssey of the "Essex"*, pp. 185–95.

8. David F. Long, *Nothing too Daring*, p. 139.

9. Joseph T. Downey, *The Cruise of the Portsmouth, 1845–1847; A Sailor's View of the Naval Conquest of California*, Howard Lamar, ed. (Yale University Library, New Haven, Conn., 1958), pp. 163–65.

10. Robert Irwin Johnson, *Thence Around Cape Horn*, p. 99; and Thornton Emons and Homer C. Votaw, "The *Ewing* Mutiny," pp. 65–69.

11. JAG Records, case 1237, see charges and specifications.

12. *Ibid.*, see defense summation.

13. *Ibid.*

14. *Ibid.*

15. Emons and Votaw, "The *Ewing* Mutiny," pp. 65–69.

16. JAG Records, case 1187, see charges and specifications.

17. Morison, *"Old Bruin,"* p. 148.

18. Harrison Hayford, ed., *The Somers Mutiny Affair.* pp. 156–57.

19. Ferguson, *Truxtun*, pp. 144–47.

20. *Ibid.*, p. 146.

21. *Ibid.*, p. 147.

22. U. S. Office of Naval Records and Library, *Naval Documents Related to the Quasi-War between the United States and France*, Vol. V, p. 506, and Library of Congress Manuscript Collection, Letters and Papers of Edward

Preble, Letter, William Ash to Edward Preble, on board frigate *Essex*, 28 August 1800.

23. JAG Records, case 3.

24. *Quasi-War*, Vol. 5, p. 492.

25. *Ibid.*

26. *Ibid.*, Letter Thomas Truxtun to Benjamin Stoddert, Norfolk, Va., 23 April 1800.

27. JAG Records, case 3, appended documents.

28. *Ibid., see* Truxtun's final report to Secretary Stoddert.

29. JAG Records, case 16, see charges and specifications.

30. *Ibid., see* testimony of witnesses.

31. *Ibid., see* Surgeon Marshall's defense statement.

32. *Ibid.*

33. JAG Records, case 24, see Exhibit "A."

34. *Ibid., see* the sentence of the court.

35. U. S. Office of Naval Records and Library, *Naval Documents Related to the United States Wars with the Barbary Powers*, Vol. IV, p. 227.

36. JAG Records, case 29, *see* charges and specifications.

37. *Ibid., see* testimony of Lieutenant Kearny.

38. JAG Records, case 147.

39. *Ibid., see* testimony of witnesses, especially Lowe and Anderson.

40. *Ibid.*

41. *Ibid., see* appended documents.

42. JAG Records, case 1016, *see* testimony of witnesses.

43. Bauer, *Surfboats*, p. 42.

44. JAG Records, case 1016, sentence of the court.

45. Morison, *"Old Bruin,"* p. 190.

46. JAG Records, case 748, *see* testimony of Lieutenant Bushrod Hunter.

47. *Ibid., see* testimony of Lieutenants McBlain and Hunter.

48. *Ibid.*, sentence of the court.

49. JAG Records, case 1148, *see* charges and specifications.

50. *Ibid.*, testimony of Lieutenant Prentiss.

51. *Ibid., see* statement of Captain Smoot.

52. *Ibid., see* statement of Lieutenant Prentiss. Opinion attributed to Mr. Justice Reynolds of the United States District Court, Boston, Massachusetts.

53. Donald W. Griffin, "American Navy on the Brazil Station," p. 246.

54. *Ibid.*

55. *Ibid.*

56. Joseph T. Downey, *Cruise of the Portsmouth*, pp. xv and 83–84.

57. *Ibid.*, pp. 113–19.

58. *Ibid.*, p. 116.

59. Charles Oscar Paullin, *Administrative History of the Navy*, pp. 231–34.

60. JAG Records, case 1399, *see* instructions to the court.

61. *Ibid., see* testimony of Lieutenant Green.

62. *Ibid., see* testimony of Lieutenant Hurst and Surgeon Sharp.

63. *Ibid.*, *see* testimony of Lieutenant Harrison.

64. *Ibid.*, *see* appended document.

65. *Ibid.*, findings of the court of inquiry.

66. JAG Records, case 3111.

67. JAG Records, case 3177.

68. JAG Records, case 3111, *see* findings of the court of inquiry.

69. JAG Records, case 3177, *see* testimony of witnesses.

70. JAG Records, case 27, *see* appended documents.

71. Christopher McKee, *Edward Preble*, p. 174.

72. JAG Records, case 114.

73. JAG Records, case 189, *see* charges and specifications.

74. *Ibid.*, *see* notes of the recording clerk.

75. *Ibid.*, *see* sentence of the court.

76. JAG Records, case 172, *see* charges and specifications.

77. *Ibid.*, *see* appended documents.

78. JAG Records, case 178.

79. See Table III.

80. JAG Records, case 260.

81. JAG Records, case 345, appended documents.

82. JAG Records, case 13.

83. JAG Records, case 173, *see* testimony of witnesses.

84. *Ibid.*

85. JAG Records, case 183.

86. JAG Records, case 467, *see* charges and specifications.

87. *Ibid.*, *see* appended documents.

88. JAG Records, case 921.

89. *Ibid.*, *see* testimony of Purser Murray.

90. *Ibid.*

91. JAG Records, case 1876, *see* the sentence of the court.

92. *Ibid.*, *see* the statement of John Hoover.

93. JAG Records, case 947, *see* the sentence of the court.

94. *Ibid.*, *see* charges and specifications.

95. *Ibid.*, *see* testimony of Lieutenant Pinckney and eyewitnesses.

96. *Ibid.*, *see* the defense summation.

97. JAG Records, *see* case 620.

98. *Ibid.*, *see* charges and specifications.

99. *Ibid.*, *see* the sentence of the court and appended documents.

100. Allan R. Bosworth, *Love Affair with the Navy*, pp. 82–83.

101. JAG Records, case 2, *see* testimony of eyewitnesses.

102. *Ibid.*, *see* the sentence of the court.

103. JAG Records, case 640, *see* testimony of witnesses.

104. *Ibid.*, *see* the defense statement of the prisoner.

105. *Ibid.*, *see* the sentence of the court.

106. JAG Records, case 660, *see* charges and specifications.

107. *Ibid.*, *see* testimony of eyewitnesses.

108. *Ibid., see* cross examination of eyewitnesses by Mr. Lambert.

109. *Ibid., see* defense summation.

110. *Ibid., see* appended documents.

Chapter VI

1. David Le Pere Savageau, "The United States Navy and its 'Half War' Prisoners, 1798–1801," pp. 159–176.

2. JAG Records, case 17, *see* deposition of the French prisoners.

3. JAG Records, case 18, *see* testimony of witnesses.

4. *Ibid., see* the defense summation of Captain Little.

5. *Ibid., see* the verdict of the court.

6. JAG Records, case 25, *see* testimony of witnesses.

7. JAG Records, case 136, *see* statement of Lieutenant Henley.

8. *Ibid., see* testimony of Sailing Master Mooran.

9. JAG Records, case 204, *see* statement of Captain Renshaw.

10. *Ibid., see* the defense summation.

11. *Ibid., see* the opinion of the court.

12. JAG Records, case 203.

13. *See* Jay D. Smith, "Commodore James Barron, Guilty as Charged?"

14. JAG Records, case 158.

15. *Ibid., see* statement of Lieutenant Cox.

16. *Ibid., see* opinion of the court.

17. *Ibid.*

18. Hugh D. Purcell, "Don't Give Up the Ship," p. 83.

19. JAG Records, case 161, *see* charges and specifications.

20. *Ibid., see* testimony of Lieutenant Budd.

21. *Ibid., see* testimony of Midshipman Higginbotham.

22. *Ibid., see* charges and specifications.

23. *Ibid., see* defense summation of Midshipman Cox.

24. *Ibid.*

25. *Ibid.*

26. *Ibid., see* the letter of Captain Decatur to Secretary Smith included in the appended documents.

27. *Ibid., see* the sentence of the court in the case of Midshipman Cox.

28. Arthur Larson, "Scapegoat of the Chesapeake-Shannon Battle," p. 531.

29. JAG Records, case 161, *see* the defense summation of William Brown.

30. *Ibid., see* the verdict of the court in the case of William Brown and the appended document.

31. *Ibid., see* the verdict of the court in the case of Midshipman Forrest.

32. *Ibid., see* the testimony of Midshipman Fleshman.

33. *Ibid., see* the verdict of the court in the case of Midshipman Fleshman.

34. Glenn Tucker, *Dawn Like Thunder, the Barbary Wars and the Birth of the U. S. Navy*, p. 244.

35. *Ibid.*, pp. 256–57.

36. See JAG Records, case 25, testimony of William Godby.

37. JAG Records, case 156, charges and specifications.

38. *Ibid.*, *see* testimony of witnesses.

39. *Ibid.*, *see* cross examination of Lieutenant McCall.

40. *Ibid.*, *see* the defense summation.

41. Leonard F. Guttridge and Jay D. Smith, *The Commodores*, pp. 285–286. A court of inquiry was held, however, and Elliott was exonerated. *See* JAG Records, case 206.

42. JAG Records, case 269, *see* appended documents.

43. JAG Records, case 795, *see* charges and specifications.

44. JAG Records, case 782.

45. SFDP Papers, Fragment of a letter of a SFDP to the editor of an unnamed newspaper, Louvoirs, 1841, Doc. #W9–695.

46. JAG Records, case 1325, *see* instructions to the court.

47. *Ibid.*, *see* testimony of Lieutenants Smith and Tansill.

48. *Ibid.*, *see* testimony of Midshipman Houston.

49. *Ibid.*, *see* testimony of Lieutenant Yard.

50. *Ibid.*, *see* testimony of Surgeon Rubenstien.

51. *Ibid.*, *see* the opinion of the court.

52. John Niven, *Gideon Welles*, pp. 324–325.

53. Quoted in Charles Oscar Paullin, *History of Naval Administration*, pp. 297–298.

54. JAG Records, case 3069, see testimony of Commander Walke.

55. *Ibid.*

56. *Ibid.*, *see* defense summation.

57. *Ibid.*, *see* verdict of the court.

58. JAG Records, case 3071, see charges and specifications.

59. *Ibid.*, *see* testimony of Commodore Armstrong.

60. *Ibid.*

61. *Ibid.*

62. *Ibid.*, *see* the verdict and sentence of the court.

63. Paullin, *History of Naval Administration*, p. 298.

64. Reuben Elmore Stivers, *Privateers and Volunteers*, pp. 359–365.

65. *Ibid.*, p. 365.

66. The JAG Records index contains numerous examples.

67. Langley, *Social Reform in the U. S. Navy*, p. 167.

68. JAG Records, case 462, testimony of Sergeant Mix.

69. *Ibid.*, *see* verdict of the court and appended document.

70. JAG Records, case 632.

71. *Ibid.*, *see* testimony of Andrew Hansen.

72. *Ibid.*

73. *Ibid.*, *see* testimony of John Williams and John Julian.

74. *Ibid.*, *see* testimony of Captain Nicholson.

75. *Ibid.*, *see* testimony of Surgeon Terrill.

76. *Ibid.*, *see* the opinion of the court.

77. *Ibid., see* the letters between the commodore and the court in the appended documents.

78. JAG Records, case 761, *see* charges and specifications.

79. *Ibid., see* cross examination of Phinney by the court.

80. *Ibid., see* the testimony of Flint and Dyer.

81. *Ibid., see* the sentence of the court.

82. JAG Records, case 968, *see* appended documents.

83. *Ibid., see* Commodore Sloat's instructions to the court.

84. *Ibid., see* testimony of Midshipman Griffin.

85. *Ibid., see* the opinion of the court.

86. Joseph T. Downey, *Cruise of the Portsmouth*, p. 143.

87. JAG Records, case 1825, charges and specifications.

88. *Ibid., see* testimony of witnesses.

89. *Ibid., see* Commander Lynch's review of the court's proceedings.

90. Herman Melville, *White Jacket*, pp. 393–94.

91. *Ibid.*, p. 474.

92. Quoted in Allan R. Bosworth, *Love Affair with the Navy*, p. 63.

93. JAG Records, cases 69, 78, 79.

94. JAG Records, case 69, appended document.

95. *Ibid., see* testimony of Sailing Master Fleetwood and others.

96. *Ibid., see* the verdict of the court.

97. *Ibid., see* appended document.

98. JAG Records, case 78, charges and specifications.

99. *Ibid.*

100. *Ibid., see* testimony of Purser's Steward Berryman.

101. *Ibid., see* defense summation of Midshipman Peters.

102. JAG Records, case 79.

103. JAG Records, case 340, charges and specifications.

104. *Ibid., see* testimony of Captain Woolsey.

105. *Ibid., see* the opinion of the court.

106. JAG Records, case 1238, *see* instructions to the court.

107. *Ibid., see* the opinion of the court.

108. JAG Records, case 1120, charges and specifications.

109. *Ibid., see* appended document, defense summation of previous court martial.

110. *Ibid., see* statement of Midshipman Hall.

111. *Ibid.*

112. *Ibid., see* appended document, letter, Commodore Jones to Hall.

113. *Ibid.*, appended document, letter, Commodore Jones to Commander Stribling.

114. *Ibid.*, appended document.

115. SFDP Papers, notebook, Doc. No. W9 18476, p. 246. SFDP's handwritten notes on the deliberations of the Naval Efficiency Board, in two composition notebooks.

116. JAG Records, case 1702, charges and specifications.

117. *Ibid.*, *see* testimony of Commander Ritchie.

118. SFDP Papers, notebook, Doc. No. W9 18476, p. 246.

119. JAG Records, case 1702, *see* the review of the case by Secretary Dobbin in the appended documents.

120. SFDP Papers, Doc. No. W9 1720, Letter, Secretary Dobbin to SFDP, Washington, 15 April 1857.

Chapter VII

1. See Table I, Chapter IV.

2. JAG Records, case 12.

3. *Ibid.*, *see* testimony of Lieutenant Bunbury.

4. *Ibid.*, *see* charges and specifications.

5. *Ibid.*, *see* defense statement of Surgeon Webb.

6. *Ibid.*, *see* the verdict of the court and appended document.

7. JAG Records, case 95.

8. JAG Records, case 103.

9. JAG Records, case 352.

10. *Ibid.*, *see* testimony of Surgeon Dix and other witnesses.

11. *Ibid.*, *see* testimony of defense witness called by Terry.

12. *Ibid.*, *see* verdict and sentence of the court.

13. JAG Records, case 612, *see* charges and specifications.

14. *Ibid.*, *see* testimony of several earlier witnesses.

15. *Ibid.*, *see* testimony of Lieutenant Babbit and cross examination of Babbit by the court.

16. *Ibid.*, *see* testimony of Commodore Elliott and cross examination of Elliott by the court.

17. *Ibid.*, *see* the verdict of the court.

18. Charles Oscar Paullin, *A History of Naval Administration*, p. 185.

19. JAG Records, case 748, testimony of Lieutenant Hunter at Elliott's court-martial in 1840.

20. JAG Records, case 665, testimony of Chaplain Lambert.

21. *Ibid.*, *see* opinion of the court of inquiry.

22. JAG Records, case 544, charges and specifications and testimony of Commander Storer.

23. *Ibid.*, *see* testimony of Lieutenant Jameson.

24. *Ibid.*, *see* the verdict of the court.

25. JAG Records, case 764, charges and specifications.

26. *Ibid.*

27. *Ibid.*, *see* testimony of Quartermaster Thompson.

28. *Ibid.*, *see* charges and specifications.

29. *Ibid.*, *see* testimony of Acting Midshipman Nicholson.

30. *Ibid.*, *see* testimony of Midshipman Dallas.

31. *Ibid.*, *see* the verdict and sentence of the court.

32. JAG Records, case 2366.

33. *Ibid., see* testimony of Surgeon Sherman.

34. *Ibid., see* testimony of Commander McBlair.

35. *Ibid., see* the remarks of the court on passing sentence.

36. *Ibid., see* appended document.

37. JAG Records, case 94.

38. *Ibid., see* testimony of Marine Private Crutch.

39. *Ibid., see* testimony of Marine Corporal McTamnay.

40. *Ibid., see* the sentence of the court.

41. JAG Records, case 326, *see* testimony of Carpenter Parker.

42. *Ibid., see* the sentence of the court.

43. JAG Records, case 744, *see* specification 2.

44. *Ibid., see* specification 3.

45. *Ibid., see* specification 1.

46. JAG Records, case 1327.

47. *Ibid., see* testimony of Lieutenant Bowers.

48. *Ibid., see* testimony of Marine Corporal Mulholland.

49. *Ibid., see* defense statement of Seaman Thompson.

50. *Ibid., see* the sentence of the court.

51. *See* JAG Records, case 1184, court of inquiry into the causes of the loss of the U.S.S. *Yorktown* for details of the wreck.

52. JAG Records, case 1196, testimony of Lieutenant Rootes.

53. *Ibid.,* testimony of Lieutenant Frailey.

54. JAG case 1184, opinion of the court of inquiry.

55. *Ibid.*

56. See JAG Records, cases 1196 through 1204.

57. Allan R. Bosworth, *Love Affair with the Navy*, p. 51.

58. Herman Melville, *White Jacket*, p. 221.

59. Bosworth, *Love Affair with the Navy*, p. 51.

60. Melville, *White Jacket*, pp. 225–229.

61. JAG Records, case 763, testimony of Seaman Frederick Matzinger and Boatswain's Mate Philip Jordan.

62. *Ibid., see* the opinion of the court of inquiry.

63. JAG Records, case 1, *see* testimony of Midshipman Pitts.

64. JAG Records, case 394.

65. JAG Records, case 437, see appended documents.

66. *Ibid.,* sentence of the court.

67. *Ibid., see* appended document.

68. See JAG Records, case 1192.

69. JAG Records, case 1284.

70. *Ibid., see* the appended document.

71. *Ibid., see* testimony of Commodore Ballard.

72. *Ibid., see* testimony of Commander Kearney.

73. *Ibid., see* testimony of Commander Bailey.

74. *Ibid., see* the defense summation.

75. *Ibid., see* the opinion of the court of inquiry.

76. SFDP Papers, notes on the deliberations of the Naval Efficiency Board, Doc. #W9 18475, p. 15 and p. 21.

77. Douglas Kolb and E. K. Eric Gunderson, "Alcoholism in the United States Navy," pp. 183–85.

Chapter VIII

1. See Table I, Chapter IV.
2. Allan R. Bosworth, *Love Affair with the Navy*, p. 69.
3. *Ibid.*
4. JAG Records, case 462, *see* the statement of Midshipman Goodwin.
5. *Ibid., see* the testimony of Seaman Clark.
6. JAG Records, case 629, *see* the statement of Midshipman Le Roy.
7. *Ibid., see* testimony of eyewitnesses and the instructions of the court to Seaman Jones.
8. JAG Records, case 1098, *see* charges and specifications.
9. *Ibid., see* the testimony of Storekeeper Spaulding and Pursers' Clerk Henriques.
10. *Ibid., see* the testimony of Storekeeper Spaulding.
11. *Ibid., see* the testimony of Pursers' Clerk Henriques.
12. *Ibid., see* the defense summation of Seaman McDermot.
13. *Ibid., see* the sentence of the court and appended remarks.
14. *Ibid., see* the appended document.
15. Joseph T. Downey, *Cruise of the Portsmouth*, pp. 228–29.
16. See JAG Records, cases 1489–1493, charges and specifications.
17. *Ibid., see* the sentences of the courts. Note that Seaman Biddle's case is 1490.
18. *See* JAG Records, case 1720.
19. *See* JAG Records, case 1746.
20. JAG Records, case 439, *see* the charges and specifications.
21. *Ibid., see* the testimony of eyewitnesses and the statement of Lieutenant Sands.
22. *Ibid., see* the defense summation of Lieutenant Sands.
23. *Ibid., see* the sentence of the court and appended document.
24. JAG Records, case 1515, *see* charges and specifications.
25. *Ibid., see* the testimony of Commander Buchanan.
26. *Ibid., see* the testimony of Acting Master Lowry.
27. *Ibid., see* the testimony of other eyewitnesses.
28. *Ibid., see* the statement of Lieutenant Randolph.
29. *Ibid., see* the vedict and sentence of the court and appended document.
30. Herman Melville, *White Jacket*, p. 48.
31. *Ibid.*, pp. 47–48.
32. *See* JAG Records, case 1479.
33. JAG Records, case 265, *see* charges and specifications.
34. *Ibid., see* testimony of witnesses and verdict and sentence of the court.

35. JAG Records, case 1095, *see* the charges and specifications and the testimony of Midshipman Laughlin.

36. *Ibid., see* the defense statement of Seaman Brown.

37. *Ibid., see* the sentence of the court and appended documents.

38. *See* JAG Records, case 393.

39. JAG Records, case 748.

40. *Ibid., see* testimony and defense summation of Commodore Elliott.

41. JAG Records, case 1187, *see* the charges and specifications.

42. *Ibid., see* the testimony of Commodore Jones and Purser Wilson.

43. *Ibid., see* the verdict and sentence of the court.

44. JAG Records, case 403, *see* charges and specifications.

45. *Ibid., see* the verdict of the court and appended document.

46. Charles Oscar Paullin, *A History of Naval Administration*, pp. 142–145; and JAG Records, case 399½.

47. Melville, *White Jacket*, p. 256.

48. JAG Records, case 1690, *see* the instructions to the court.

49. *Ibid., see* the testimony of Petty Officer Fowler.

50. *Ibid., see* the testimony of Coxwain Fisher.

51. *Ibid., see* the testimony of Purser Heiskill.

52. *Ibid., see* the testimony of Captain Powell.

53. *Ibid., see* the defense statement of Pursers' Steward Henriques.

54. *Ibid., see* the opinion of the court of inquiry.

55. JAG Records, case 2361, *see* the charges and specifications.

56. *Ibid.*

57. *Ibid., see* the defense statement of Purser Danforth.

58. *Ibid., see* the verdict and sentence of the court and appended document.

59. JAG Records, case 572, charges and specifications.

60. *Ibid., see* the defense summation of Private Brody.

61. JAG Records, case 310, *see* the charges and specifications.

62. *Ibid., see* the sentence of the court and appended documents.

63. JAG Records, case 25, *see* appended documents.

64. *Ibid., see* statement of Lieutenant Maley.

65. *Ibid., see* appended document, letter, Commodore Dale to Secretary Stoddert.

66. Tucker, *Dawn Like Thunder*, pp. 158–159.

67. JAG Records, case 910, *see* the opinion of the court of inquiry.

68. *Ibid., see* the testimony of several engineering officers.

69. *Ibid., see* the opinion of the court of inquiry.

70. JAG Records, 915, *see* the charges and specifications.

71. *Ibid., see* the initial statement of Captain Newton.

72. *Ibid., see* the verdict of the court and appended document.

73. JAG Records, case 1024; this account is drawn from the testimony of several witnesses and from a chart prepared by Commander Pearson and submitted as Exhibit "A."

74. *Ibid., see* the opinion of the court of inquiry.

75. JAG Records, case 1025, *see* the charges and specifications.

76. *Ibid., see* the testimony of Lieutenant Haggarty.

77. *Ibid., see* the verdict and sentence of the court.

78. Quoted in Reuben Elmore Stivers, *Privateers and Volunteers*, pp. 317–318.

79. Welles, *Diary*, Vol. II, p. 163.

80. JAG Records, case 3670.

81. Gideon Welles, *Diary*, Vol. 11, p. 163.

Chapter IX

1. Letterbook of Commander Raphael Semmes, 1848–1858, MSS Collection of the Library of Congress, Washington, D. C., *see* correspondence for the years 1848, 1849, and 1850.

2. *Ibid., see* correspondence for 1849.

3. Papers of Captain Uriah P. Levy, 1842–1857, MSS Collection of the Library of Congress, Washington, D. C., Minutes of the court-martial of 1842. *See* testimony of Midshipman J. N. Maffitt. (JAG Records case number on this proceeding is 795.)

4. JAG Records, case 795, *see* charges and specifications.

5. *Ibid., see* the defense summation of Commander Levy.

6. *Ibid.*

7. *Ibid., see* the opinion and verdict of the court.

8. *Ibid., see* appended document.

9. Alfred Hoyt Bill, *Fighting Bob, The Life and Exploits of Commodore Robert Field Stockton, United States Navy*, unpublished MSS biography, The Stockton Family Papers, Manuscript Collection of the Firestone Library, Princeton University, Princeton, N.J., pp. 44–45.

10. Samuel Francis Du Pont described Stockton's practices in this regard in several letters written to friends and associates in 1850. In particular, *see* his correspondence with Henry Winter Davis, documents numbered W9–1160 and W9–1172. *See also* letter, SFDP to James Stokes Biddle, Annapolis, 27 April 1850.

11. Bill, *Fighting Bob*, pp. 109, 119.

12. *Ibid.*, p. 163.

13. Solomon H. Sanborn, *An Exposition of Official Tyranny in the United States Navy*. (no publisher listed, New York, 1841), pp. 5–15.

14. *Ibid.*, p. 16.

15. SFDP Papers, letter, SFDP to Alexander Slidell McKenzie, Louvoirs, 8 February 1837, document number W9–463.

16. *Ibid.*

17. SFDP Papers, letter, SFDP to Henry Winter Davis, Wilmington, 17 April 1850, document number W9–1160.

18. Annual Report of the Secretary of the Navy for 1851, Doc. 2, p. 12, from *Reports of the Secretaries of the Navy, 1849–1851.*

19. *Ibid.*

20. Rev. Fitch W. Taylor, A.M., U.S.N., *The Broad Pennant or a Cruise in the United States Flag Ship of the Gulf Squadron During the Mexican Difficulties.* (Leavitt, Trow and Co.: New York, 1848), p. 275.

21. *Ibid.*, pp. 282–83.

22. *Ibid.*, p. 283.

23. JAG Records, case 6, charges and specifications.

24. *Ibid., see* testimony of Seaman Joseph Paul.

25. *Ibid., see* testimony of Captain Perry.

26. *Ibid., see* testimony of Lieutenant Lang.

27. *Ibid., see* the verdict of the court.

28. JAG Records, case 13.

29. *Ibid., see* testimony of Seaman Charles Delavoir.

30. *Ibid., see* the opinion of the court and appended document.

31. JAG Records, case 242, *see* charges and specifications.

32. *Ibid., see* the statement of Captain Creighton.

33. *Ibid., see* testimony of Commodore Chauncey.

34. *Ibid., see* the verdict and opinion of the court.

35. JAG Records, case 532, charges and specifications.

36. *Ibid., see* testimony of Lieutenant Freelon.

37. *Ibid., see* the verdict and sentence of the court.

38. *Ibid., see* testimony of several prosecution witnesses.

39. Leonard F. Guttridge and Jay D. Smith, *The Commodores*, p. 285.

40. JAG Records, case 601, charges and specifications.

41. *Ibid., see* appended document.

42. *Ibid., see* the statement of Captain Perry.

43. *Ibid., see* charges and specifications.

44. *Ibid., see* the verdict of the court and the sentences of Marine Captain Heath and Captain Perry.

45. Guttridge and Smith, *The Commodores*, p. 285.

46. JAG Records, case 601, charges and specifications.

47. *Ibid., see* verdict and sentence of the court and JAG Records, case 602.

48. JAG Records, case 602, *see* verdict and sentence of the court.

49. JAG Records, *see* cases 603 through 609.

50. JAG Records, case 769, *see* charges and specifications.

51. Refer to the Articles of War of 1800, Articles III and XXX.

52. JAG Records, case 769, defense summation of Commander Latimer.

53. *Ibid., see* verdict of the court and appended document.

54. *Ibid., see* appended documents.

55. JAG Records, case 1269.

56. Robert E. Johnson, *Rear Admiral John Rodgers, 1812–1882.* p. 61.

57. Quoted in *Ibid.*, pp. 61–62.

58. *Ibid.*, p. 62.

59. Eloise Engle and Arnold S. Lott, *America's Maritime Heritage*, pp. 161–64. *See also,* JAG Records, case 827.

60. JAG Records, case 930, charges and specifications.

61. *Ibid., see* testimony of defense witnesses.

62. *Ibid., see* defense summation of Lieutenant Mason.

63. *Ibid., see* the verdict and sentence of the court.

64. *Ibid., see* the appended document.

65. *See* JAG Records, case 1187.

66. JAG Records, case 833.

67. *Ibid., see* testimony of Commander Hollins.

68. *Ibid., see* statement of Commodore Dallas and verdict of the court.

69. *See* JAG Records, case 1263.

70. Downey, *Cruise of the Portsmouth*, pp. 193–94.

71. *See* JAG Records, cases 572 and 1304.

72. Charles Oscar Paullin, *History of Naval Administration*, p. 189.

73. William G. Anderson, "John Adams, the Navy, and the Quasi-War with France," p. 128.

74. David F. Long, *Nothing too Daring*, p. 223.

75. Paullin, *History of Naval Administration*, p. 191.

76. Donald W. Mitchell, "Abel Upshur, Forgotten Prophet of the Old Navy," United States Naval Institute *Proceedings*, p. 1374.

77. *See* JAG Records, case 1167, for details of Hunter's attack.

78. Samuel Eliot Morison, *"Old Bruin,"* pp. 222–24.

Bibliography

Primary Sources

Manuscripts and Papers

The Henry Francis Du Pont Collection of Winterthur Manuscripts, Group 9, Series A, The Letters and Papers of Rear Admiral Samuel Francis Du Pont. The Hagley Foundation Library, Wilmington, Delaware. (Cited as SFDP Papers.)

The Stockton Family Papers. MSS Collection of the Firestone Library, Princeton University, Princeton, New Jersey.

Letterbook of Commander Raphael Semmes, 1848–1858. The MSS Collection of the Library of Congress, Library of Congress Annex, Washington, D. C.

The Bancroft-Bliss Papers, including the papers of Secretary of the Navy George Bancroft. The MSS Collection of the Library of Congress, Library of Congress Annex, Washington, D. C.

The Papers of Levi Woodbury, Secretary of the Navy. The MSS Collection of the Library of Congress, Library of Congress Annex, Washington, D. C.

The Papers of Captain Uriah P. Levy. The MSS Collection of the Library of Congress, Library of Congress Annex, Washington, D. C.

United States Judge Advocate General's Department. Records of General Courts-Martial and Courts of Inquiry of the Navy Department, 1799–1867, National Archives and Records Service. (Cited as JAG Records.)

Official Records and Documents

U. S. Department of Commerce. *Historical Statistics of the United States, Colonial Times to Present.* 2 parts. Washington: GPO, 1975.

U. S. Office of Naval Records and Library. *Naval Documents Related to the Quasi-War Between the United States and France; Naval Operations from February 1797 to December 1801.* 7 vols. Washington: GPO, 1935–1938.

———. *Naval Documents Related to the United States Wars with the Barbary Powers; Naval Operations Including Diplomatic Background from 1785 through 1807.* 6 vols. Washington: GPO, 1939–1944.

U. S. Navy Department. *Record of Proceedings of a Court of Inquiry in the Case of Rear-Admiral Winfield S. Schley, USN.* 2 vols. Washington: GPO, 1902.

———. Naval Orientation (NAVPERS 16138, revised and restricted). Washington: 1945.

————. *Reports of the Secretaries of the Navy, 1849–1851*. Washington: 1852.
"Annual Report of the Secretary of the Navy for 1828." *Senate Doc.*, 20th Cong., 2nd Sess.
Congressional Globe. 6th Cong., 1st Sess., 1800.
Congressional Globe. 34th Cong., 1st Sess., 1854.

Printed Papers and Letters

Allen, Gardner Weld, ed., *The Papers of Isaac Hull*, Boston: The Boston Athenaeum, 1929.

Hayes, John D., ed. *Samuel Francis Du Pont, A Selection of His Civil War Letters*. 3 vols. Ithaca, N.Y.: Cornell University Press, 1969.

Milligan, John D., ed. *From the Fresh-Water Navy: The Letters of Acting Master's Mate Henry R. Browne and Acting Ensign Symmes E. Browne, 1861–1864*. Naval Letters Series, Vol. III. Annapolis, Md.: The United States Naval Institute, 1970.

Supreme Court Decisions

Frank Dynes, Plaintiff in Error, vs. Jonah D. Hoover. United States Supreme Court, December Term, 1857. 61 U.S. (28 How.) 65, 1857.

Reference Works on the Common Law

Blackstone, Sir William. *Commentaries on the Laws of England*. 2 vols. Philadelphia: J. B. Lippincott and Co., 1859.

Hale, Sir Matthew. *The History of the Common Law of England*, edited and with an introduction by Charles M. Gray. Chicago: The University of Chicago Press, 1971.

Diaries, Journals, and Memoirs

Downey, Joseph T. *The Cruise of the Portsmouth, 1845–1847; A Sailor's View of the Naval Conquest of California*. Howard Lamar, ed. New Haven, Conn.: Yale University Press, 1958.

Marchand, John B. *Charleston Blockade, The Journals of John B. Marchand, U. S. Navy, 1861–1862*. Craig L. Symonds, ed. Newport, R.I.: The Naval War College, 1976.

Porter, David. *Constantinople and its Environs*. 2 vols. New York: n.p., 1835.

Sanborn, Solomon H. *An Exposition of Official Tyranny in the United States Navy*. New York: n.p., 1841.

Taylor, Fitch W. *The Broad Pennant or a Cruise in the United States Flagship of the Gulf Squadron During the Mexican Difficulties*. New York: Leavitt, Trow, and Co., 1848.

Welles, Gideon. *The Diary of Gideon Welles, Secretary of the Navy under Lincoln and Johnson*, Howard K. Beale, ed. New York: W. W. Norton and Co., Inc., 1960.

Secondary Sources

Books

Alden, John D. *The American Steel Navy.* The United States Naval Institute, Annapolis, Md.: 1972.

Armbrister, Trevor. *A Matter of Accountability, The True Story of the Pueblo Affair.* New York: Coward-McCann, Inc., 1970.

Bauer, K. Jack. *Surfboats and Horse Marines, U. S. Naval Operations in the Mexican War, 1846–1848.* Annapolis, Md.: The United States Naval Institute, 1969.

Bearss, Edwin C. *Hardluck Ironclad, The Sinking and Salvage of the "Cairo."* Baton Rouge: Louisiana State University Press, 1966.

Bosworth, Allan R. *My Love Affair with the Navy.* New York: W. W. Norton and Co., Inc., 1969.

Cranwell, John Phillips and William Bower Crane. *Men of Marque: A History of Private Armed Vessels Out of Baltimore During the War of 1812.* New York: W. W. Norton and Co., Inc., 1940.

Cunliffe, Marcus. *Soldiers and Civilians, The Martial Spirit in America, 1775–1865.* Boston: Little, Brown and Co., 1968.

Delany, Norman C. *John McIntosh Kell of the Raider "Alabama."* University, Ala.: The University of Alabama Press, 1973.

Donovan, Frank. *The Odyssey of the "Essex."* New York: David McKay Co., Inc., 1969.

Dugan, James. *The Great Mutiny.* New York: G. P. Putnam's Sons, 1965.

Durkin, Joseph T. *Stephen R. Mallory; Confederate Navy Chief.* Chapel Hill: University of North Carolina Press, 1954.

Engle, Eloise, and Arnold S. Lott. *America's Maritime Heritage.* Annapolis, Md.: The United States Naval Institute, 1975.

Ferguson, Eugene S. *Truxtun of the Constellation: The Life of Commodore Thomas Truxtun, U. S. Navy, 1755–1822.* Baltimore, Md.: The Johns Hopkins University Press, 1956.

Footner, Hulbert. *Sailor of Fortune, The Life and Adventures of Commodore Barney, U.S.N.* New York: Harper and Brothers, 1940.

Generous, William T., Jr. *Swords and Scales: The Development of the Uniform Code of Military Justice.* n.c.: Kennikat Press, 1973.

Gibbon, Edward. *The Decline and Fall of the Roman Empire.* 2 vols. London: J. S. Virtue and Co., Ltd., n.d.

Gibson, E. Lawrence. *Get Off My Ship: Ensign Berg vs. the U. S. Navy.* New York: Avon Books, 1978.

Guttridge, Leonard F., and Jay D. Smith. *The Commodores.* New York: Harper and Row, 1969.

Hannay, David. *Naval Courts-Martial.* London: Cambridge University Press, 1914.

Hayford, Harrison, ed. *The Somers Mutiny Affair.* Englewood Cliffs, N.J.: Prentice Hall, Inc., 1959.

Hicken, Victor. *The American Fighting Man.* New York: The Macmillan Co., 1969.

Hill, Jim Dan. *Sea Dogs of the Sixties.* New York: Perpetua Books, A. S. Barnes and Co., Inc., 1961.

Horn, Daniel. *The German Naval Mutinies of World War I.* New Brunswick, N.J.: Rutgers University Press, 1969.

Johnson, Robert Erwin. *Thence Around Cape Horn; The Story of United States Naval Forces on Pacific Station, 1818–1923.* Annapolis, Md.: The United States Naval Institute, 1967.

————. *Rear Admiral John Rodgers 1812, 1882.* Annapolis, Md.: The United States Naval Institute, 1967.

Karsten, Peter. *The Naval Aristocracy; The Golden Age of Annapolis and the Emergence of Modern American Navalism.* New York: The Free Press, 1972.

Kemp, Peter, ed. *History of the Royal Navy.* New York: G. P. Putnam's Sons, 1969.

Langley, Harold D. *Social Reform in the United States Navy, 1798–1862.* Urbana, Ill.: University of Illinois Press, 1967.

Lewis, Charles Lee. *The Romantic Decatur.* Philadelphia, Penna.: The University of Pennsylvania Press, 1937.

————. *David Glasgow Farragut.* 2 vols. Annapolis, Md.: The United States Naval Institute, 1943.

Long, David F. *Nothing Too Daring; A Biography of Commodore David Porter, 1780–1843.* Annapolis, Md.: The United States Naval Institute, 1970.

McKee, Christopher. *Edward Preble, A Naval Biography, 1761–1807.* Annapolis, Md.: The United States Naval Institute, 1972.

Melville, Herman. *White Jacket or the World in a Man-of-War.* Standard ed. New York: Russell and Russell, Inc., 1963. First published in the United States in 1850.

Morison, Samuel Eliot. *John Paul Jones, A Sailor's Biography.* Boston: Little, Brown and Co., 1967.

————. *"Old Bruin" Commodore Matthew C. Perry, 1794–1858.* Boston: Little, Brown and Co., 1967.

Niven, John. *Gideon Welles; Lincoln's Secretary of the Navy.* New York: Oxford University Press, 1973.

Owsley, Frank L., Jr. *The C.S.S. Florida: Her Building and Operations.* Philadelphia: The University of Pennsylvania Press, 1965.

Paullin, Charles Oscar. *Commodore John Rodgers; A Biography.* Cleveland: Arthur H. Clark, 1910.

————. *Diplomatic Negotiations of American Naval Officers, 1778–1883.* Baltimore: The Johns Hopkins University Press, 1912.

————. *Paullin's History of Naval Administration, 1775–1911.* Annapolis, Md.: The United States Naval Institute, 1968.

Perry, Ronald W. *Racial Discrimination and Military Justice.* New York: Praeger Publishers, 1977.

Pierce, Philip N., and Frank O. Hough. *The Compact History of the United States Marine Corps.* New York: Hawthorn Books, Inc., 1960.

Potter, E. B. *The Naval Academy Illustrated History of the United States Navy.* New York: Galahad Books, 1971.

Quarles, Benjamin. *The Negro in the Civil War.* New York: Russell and Russell Co., 1953, reissued 1968.

Riegel, Robert E. *Young America, 1830–1840.* n.c., The University of Oklahoma Press, 1949.

Sheehan, Neil. *The Arnheiter Affair.* New York: Random House, 1971.

Sherrill, Robert. *Military Justice is to Justice as Military Music is to Music.* New York: Harper and Row, Publishers, 1976.

Simmons, Edwin H. *The United States Marines, 1775–1975.* New York: Viking Press, Inc., 1976.

Sloan, Edward William, III. *Benjamin Franklin Isherwood, Naval Engineer; The Years as Engineer-in-Chief, 1861–1869.* Annapolis, Md.: The United States Naval Institute, 1965.

Stampp, Kenneth. *The Peculiar Institution.* New York: Alfred A. Knopf, 1956.

Stivers, Reuben Elmore. *Privateers and Volunteers, The Men and Women of Our Naval Reserve Forces, 1766 to 1866.* Annapolis, Md.: The United States Naval Institute, 1975.

Tucker, Glenn. *'Dawn Like Thunder,' The Barbary Wars and the Birth of the U. S. Navy.* New York: The Bobbs-Merrill Co., Inc., 1963.

Van De Water, Frederick F. *The Captain Called It Mutiny.* New York: Ives Washburn, Inc., 1954.

Wainwright, Nicholas B. *Commodore James Biddle and His Sketch Book.* Philadelphia: The Historical Society of Pennsylvania, 1966.

Wells, Tom Henderson. *The Confederate Navy—A Study in Organization.* University, Ala.: The University of Alabama Press, 1971.

West, Richard S., Jr. *The Second Admiral, A Life of David Dixon Porter, 1813–1891.* New York: Coward, McCann, Inc., 1937.

———. *Mr. Lincoln's Navy.* New York: Longmans Green and Co., 1957.

Wilcox, L. A. *Mr. Pepys' Navy.* London: G. Bell and Sons, Ltd., 1966.

Williams, Francis Leigh. *Matthew Fontaine Maury; Scientist of the Sea.* New Brunswick, N.J.: Rutgers University Press, 1963.

Zumwalt, Elmo R. *On Watch, A Memoir.* New York: Quadrangle, The New York Times Book Company, 1976.

Periodicals

Anderson, William G. "John Adams, the Navy, and the Quasi-War with France." vol. XXX, *American Neptune*, April 1940, pp. 125–34.

Bauer, K. Jack. "The Sancala Affair: Captain Voorhees Seizes an Argentine Squadron." vol. XXIX, *American Neptune*, July 1969, pp. 174–86.

Brescia, Anthony M. "The American Navy, 1817–1822: Comments of Richard Rush." vol. XXXI, *American Neptune*, July 1971, pp. 217–25.

Buker, George E. "Captain's Mast: Conservatism vs. Liberalism." vol. XXX, *American Neptune*, April 1970, pp. 139–46.

Castro, Luis V. "Conduct Unbecoming an Officer and a Gentleman." *Judge Advocate General's Journal*, NAVEXOS P–523, June 1949, pp. 10–13.

Crawford, Kent S., and Edmund D. Thomas. "Organizational Climate and Disciplinary Rates on Navy Ships." vol. 3 *Armed Forces and Society*, winter 1977, pp. 265–71.

Eckert, Edward K. "Early Reform in the Navy Department." vol. XXXIII, *American Neptune*, October 1973, pp. 231–45.

Emmons, Thornton, and Homer C. Votaw. "The *Ewing* Mutiny." vol. 82, United States Naval Institute *Proceedings*, January 1956, pp. 62–69.

Griffin, Donald W. "The American Navy at Work on the Brazil Station." vol. XIX, *American Neptune*, October 1959, pp. 239–56.

Harrington, Gordon K. "The Ringgold Incident: A Matter of Judgment." From Clayton R. Barrow, Jr., ed., *America Spreads Her Sails; U. S. Seapower in the Nineteenth Century*, Annapolis, Md.: United States Naval Institute, 1973, pp. 100–11.

Helms, Raymond E., Jr. "Shipboard Drug Abuse." vol. 101, United States Naval Institute *Proceedings*, December 1975, pp. 44–51.

Henwood, James N. J. "A Cruise on the U.S.S. *Sabine*." vol. XXIX, *American Neptune*, April 1969, pp. 102–05.

Horan, Leo F. S. "Flogging in the United States Navy—Unfamiliar Facts Regarding its Origins and Abolition." vol. 76, United States Naval Institute *Proceedings*, September 1950, pp. 969–75.

Hoyler, H. M. "The Development of Military Law—Your Job and Mine." vol. 87, United States Naval Institute *Proceedings*, June 1961, pp. 29–32.

Janowitz, Morris. "Changing Patterns of Organizational Authority." *Administrative Science Quarterly*, 3 March 1959, pp. 473–76.

Johnson, Robert Erwin. "A Long Chase." vol. 85. United States Naval Institute *Proceedings*, January 1959, pp. 144–46.

Kolb, Douglas, and E. K. Gunderson, "Alcoholism in the United States Navy." vol. 3, *Armed Forces and Society*, winter 1977, pp. 182–87.

Larson, Arthur. "Scapegoat of the Chesapeake-Shannon Battle." vol. 79, United States Naval Institute *Proceedings*, May 1953, pp. 528–31.

McKee, Christopher. "Fantasies of Mutiny and Murder, A Suggested Psycho-History of the Seamen in the United States Navy, 1798–1815." vol. 4, *Armed Forces and Society*, winter 1978, pp. 293–304.

Merrill, James M. "Men, Monotony, and Mouldy Beans—Life on Board Civil War Blockaders." vol. XVI, *American Neptune*, January 1956, pp. 49–59.

Mitchell, Donald W. "Abel Upshur, Forgotten Prophet of the Old Navy." vol. 75, United States Naval Institute *Proceedings*, December 1949, pp. 1367–75.

Praeger, Annabelle, and Mary Cable. "The Levys of Monticello." vol. 29, *American Heritage*, February-March 1978, pp. 32–35.

Purcell, Hugh D. "Don't Give Up the Ship." vol. 91, United States Naval Institute *Proceedings*, May 1965, pp. 83–94.

Savageau, David Le Pere. "The United States Navy and Its 'Half War' Prisoners, 1798–1801." vol. XXXI, *American Neptune*, July 1971, pp. 159–76.

Savage, Paul L., and Richard A. Gabriel. "Cohesion and Disintegration in the American Army." vol. 2, *Armed Forces and Society*, spring 1976, pp. 340–76.

Smith, Jay D. "Commodore James Barron; Guilty as Charged?" vol. 93, United States Naval Institute *Proceedings*, November 1967, pp. 340–76.

Tate, E. Mowbray. "Admiral Bell and the New Asiatic Squadron, 1865–1868." vol. XXXII, *American Neptune*, April 1972, pp. 123–35.

von Doenhoff, Richard A. "Biddle, Perry, and Japan." vol. 92, United States Naval Institute *Proceedings*, November 1966, pp. 78–87.

II.

Glossary

Andrew Miller: Slang. The seaman's nickname for an American man-of-war. The connotation is one of minute regulation and strictness.

Born under the gun and educated on the bowsprit: Slang. A career enlisted man, particularly one who cannot stay out of trouble while ashore.

Brig: Any place of confinement. In the Old Navy, it was usually improvised. An empty storeroom or a screened-off space between two main battery guns were the areas most frequently used. A marine sentry stood guard whenever there was a prisoner. Permanent brigs or "cells" became common after the abolition of flogging.

Brought up to the mast: To be accused of an offense at captain's mast.

Bull ring: Slang. The area just aft of the mainmast on the spar deck where captain's mast proceedings were usually held.

Cape Horn fever: Slang. An illness feigned by a seaman seeking relief from duty.

Cat-o'-nine-tails: The only instrument legally specified for use in a naval flogging. Its characteristics are described in Article XXX of the Articles of War along with limitations on its use and examples of cats which may not be used, such as wired cats.

Chicken: Slang. The regular partner of an aggressive homosexual.

Colt: A short length of knotted rope used by petty officers to whip seamen for minor infractions or to speed them in the performance of their duties. Its use was not recognized by the Articles of War, and therefore it was technically illegal.

Damage his pepper box: Slang. To attempt to assassinate the master-at-arms by dropping a round shot on his head from aloft or through an open hatchway.

Damn-my-eyes-tar: Slang. An inexperienced seaman who tried to cover his ignorance with blustering or boisterous behavior.

Dance at the gratings: Slang. To be flogged formally with a cat.

Darbies: Slang. Wrist and ankle irons.

Double darbies: Slang. Double irons.

Double the grog tub: To get an extra ration of liquor by rejoining the line filing past the grog tub while liquor was being issued to the crew. The master-at-arms was supposed to be present to prevent this practice whenever liquor was dispensed.

Fancy man: Slang. An informer. Especially a regular source of information or spy for the master-at-arms.

Flogging: A legal whipping administered to a seaman and entered in the ship's log. It was distinct from "colting" or "starting," which was an illegal whipping administered by a petty officer using a rope end or rattan cane. A cat-o'-nine-tails was the only legal instrument for flogging, and by custom each man was entitled to a fresh cat—that is, one not previously used that day.

French leave: Slang. A sailor who absented himself temporarily with the intention of returning to his ship was said to have taken "French Leave."

Frig: Slang. To masturbate another person at his request.

Grog: Liquor mixed with water and served out in a regular ration twice a day. Originally rum was prescribed; but in the American Navy, rye or corn whiskey was most commonly served. Each issue consisted of one-half pint of liquor mixed with one-half pint of water.

Guardo: Slang. A receiving ship, usually a ship of the line in ordinary. These vessels were reputed to be havens of clandestine vice within the Navy.

Guardo moves: Slang. Tricks or stratagems used by berth deck gamblers and clandestine drinkers to avoid detection by the master-at-arms.

Horse marine: Slang. An insulting reference to a marine by the seamen. A great insult when applied to a sailor, it implied that he was unhandy or lubberly.

Hot copper: Slang. An aching head caused by the after effects of a drunken binge ashore.

Irons: Wrist and leg manacles and handcuffs. They were used both as restraints and as instruments of punishment. They could be doubled or weighted by a specified amount and left on for extended periods of time. The use of irons increased greatly after the abolition of flogging.

Jimmy Leggs: Slang. The traditional sailor's nickname for the master-at-arms. Sometimes shortened to "Leggs."

Kiss the wooden lady: Slang. To be forced to stand facing the bole of a mast with arms encircling it and wrists lashed as a minor punishment. Shipmates were encouraged to kick the offender in the buttocks while passing by.

Knock off duty: To engage in a work stoppage aboard a man-of-war.

Old bruin. Slang. A very strict officer. A martinet or severe disciplinarian.

Quarantine: To confine a junior officer to his quarters.

Masthead: To send a midshipman to the peak of the foremast for several hours as punishment for a minor infraction. Technically illegal, this punishment was sanctioned by custom and usage.

Nipcheese: Slang. A purser, particularly one who short-weighted the ship while purchasing provisions.

Pay with a flying fore-topsail: Slang. To depart without paying one's debts, particularly debts contracted ashore.

People: The enlisted personnel of a man-of-war were referred to as the "people."

Purser rigged and parish damned: Slang. A man who entered the navy to escape problems ashore. Also a man who entered the navy in a destitute condition.

Rattan cane: A knotted wooden cane. When worn in a hatband, it served as the badge of office for the master-at-arms.

Red eye: Slang. Contraband liquor, especially brandy.

Rosewater sailor: Slang. An incompetent, foppish, or unseamanlike officer.

Scuttlebutt. Slang. Gossip or rumors.

Sea lawyer: Slang. A berth deck agitator, particularly one who encourages his messmates to protest illegal or irregular actions on the part of the ship's officers.

Ship a quarterdeck face again: Slang. After the relaxation of normal shipboard discipline during skylarking or a theatrical performance, officers customarily signified that all rules and regulations were back in force by resuming their customary formal demeanor towards the crew. This was called "shipping a quarterdeck face again."

Skin: Slang. A tube made out of livestock intestines and worn wrapped around the body, particularly the ankles. Used to smuggle liquor from shore into the ship.

Skylark: To engage in rough horseplay by official sanction. It was usually allowed in the dog watches during passages through the tropics.

Snake: Slang. Another word for a skin.

Suck the monkey: Slang. To draw liquor out of a cask or puncheon with a straw.

Sweatbox: A small compartment used to punish minor offenders. It was commonly located near the ship's galley or boilers. The use of sweatboxes was introduced into the Navy by officers who had served on the Asiatic Station, probably in the 1840s. Its use increased after the abolition of flogging. Sweatboxes were abolished by law in the 1870s.

Sundowner: Slang. A very tough commanding officer. Particularly one who combined the characteristics of a martinet with a marked tendency to personally administer corporal punishments not sanctioned by the Articles of War. Term is said to have originated because those men insisted that all members of their crew must be aboard ship by sundown on the evening prior to the day the ship was scheduled to leave port.

Watch and watch: A punishment assigned to junior officers for minor offenses. It consisted of having them stand watch every four hours. Normal watches for officers in the navy were arranged so that they had twelve hours off watch for each four hours on watch. An officer on "watch and watch" had only four hours off duty at a time. This punishment could be imposed for a few days or for months at a time.

Whipped through the squadron: The American equivalent of flogging 'round the fleet. The offender was rowed in a boat from gangway to gangway among the assembled ships of his squadron. At each ship, an equal portion of his lashes was administered. Anywhere from seventy-five to four hundred lashes could be inflicted in this way. This punishment was usually imposed in lieu of a death sentence.

White Mouse: Slang. A lower deck informer or spy for the master-at-arms.

Index

Newton, John T., Captain, USN (neglect of duty), 237–39, 243
Niagara, brig of war, 156
Nichols, Robert N., Midshipman, USN (keeping a prostitute on board ship), 178–79
Nicholson, John B., Lieutenant, USN (keeping a prostitute on board ship), 177–78
Nicholson, John B., Captain, USN: opinion of Commander Levy's disciplinary system, 250
Nicholson, John Hopper, Congressman, 137
Nicholson, Joseph, Commodore, USN, 121, 168
Nicholson, William R., Midshipman, USN, 137
Nore Mutiny, 110
North Carolina: ship of the line, 45–46; illustrated, 86

Ohio, ship of the line, 25
Ontario, sloop of war, illustrated, 86, 129

Pacific Squadron, 11, 79, 122, 218, 226
Patterson, Daniel, Commodore, USN, 87, 168
Patterson, John S., Acting Midshipman, USN (neglect of duty), 135–36
Paulding, James K., Secretary of the Navy: criticized by S. F. Du Pont, 26; regulates flogging by general order, 56–57; attempts to draft new regulations, 63–64; concerned with indiscipline among officers, 272–73, mentioned, 81
Pearson, G. T., Commander, USN (neglect of duty), 239–40
Pennsylvania, ship of the line, 133
Penobscot Bay Expedition, 42
Perry, Christopher Raymond, Captain, USN (cruelty and oppression), 256–57
Perry, Matthew C., Commodore, USN: serves on Naval Efficiency Board, 68; on recruiting for Japan Expedition, 83; and Bennett case, 221–22; prosecutes Lieutenant Hunter, 274–75; mentioned, 9, 26
Perry, Oliver Hazard, Commodore, USN: and feud with Lieutenant Elliott, 156; captures *Mashuda*, 160;

and Heath affair, 261–62; mentioned, 250
Peters, William, Midshipman, USN (keeping a prostitute on board ship), 177–78
Philadelphia, frigate, 145, 154–55, 160, 161
Pierce, Franklin, 34, 65, 67, 69, 218
Pigot, Hugh, Captain, RN, 111, 113
Pinckney, William, Lieutenant, USN, 134–35
Plymouth, sloop of war, 199
Polk, James K, 274
Porpoise, schooner, 132
Porter, David, Commodore, USN: on naval command, 36–37; as naval commissioner, 62; prosecutes Lieutenant Kennon, 272; mentioned, 14, 105, 177
Porter, David Dixon, Rear Admiral, USN: as passed midshipman, 14; on foreign seamen, 19; almost fights duel, 88; at Naval Academy, 93
Port Mahon: seaman's amature theater at, 16; depravity of, 46; poor relations between sailors and citizens at, 85–87; mentioned, 119, 141, 190, 208, 261
Portsmouth, sloop of war, 105, 121–22, 172, 217, 270
Potomac, frigate, 167–68, 189, 229
Preble, Edward, Commodore, USN: disciplinary philosophy of, 46; in command of frigate *Constitution*, 47–48; awards illegal punishment, 48; finds mutineer on board frigate *Essex*, 111; and desertion, 128, investigates loss of frigate *Philadelphia*, 155; mentioned, 24, 49, 53, 81, 264
Preble, sloop of war, 134–35
Prentiss, George A., Lieutenant, USN, 119–21
President, frigate, 114, 147, 150
Preston, William Ballard, 108
Princeton, war steamer, 243
Pueblo, electronic surveillance ship, 6, 9

Quasi-War with France, 4, 24, 144, 160, 185, 235
Quinn, Robert, Seaman (mutiny), 114–15, 127

Randolph, Victor M., Lieutenant, USN, (disobedience), 191–92
Rankins, James, Private, USMC (desertion), 130